McClellan and Failure

[signature]

Sept. 20, 2007

McClellan and Failure

*A Study of Civil War
Fear, Incompetence and Worse*

Edward H. Bonekemper, II

McFarland & Company, Inc., hers
Jefferson, North Carolina, anon

LIBRARY CONGRESS CATALOGUING-IN-PUBLICATION DATA

Bonekemper, Edward H.
McClan and failure : a study of Civil War fear,
incomplce and worse / Edward H. Bonekemper, III.
p.   cm.
Incls bibliographical references and index.

ISBN-13: 978-0-7864-2894-6
(illustl case binding : 50# alkaline paper) ∞

1. McClellanorge Brinton, 1826–1885—Military leadership.
2. McCle George Brinton, 1826–1885—Psychology.
3. United St--History—Civil War, 1861–1865—Campaigns.
4. Cond of troops—History—19th century.
5.aerals—United States—Biography.
6. UiStates. Army—Biography.   I. Title.
E467.1.M2B66)7   973.7'3092—dc22   2006039755

Britibrary cataloguing data are available

On the cover: *foregroun*rait of Major General George Brinton McClellan,
1861-62 *(National Archi*ckground Battle of Antietam ©2007 Pictures Now

Manufa in the United States of America

McFo& Company, Inc., Publishers
Box &rson, North Carolina 28640
w.mcfarlandpub.com

To the men and women, past and present,
of the United States Coast Guard

Acknowledgments

Special credit for his excellent maps goes to my cartographer, David Deis of Dreamline Cartography of Northridge, California. His professionalism, promptness, and patience are remarkable.

The following readers of my manuscript provided me with critical comments and advice: F. Doré Hunter, Ed Baldrige, Brian Jones, Jim MacDonald, Jim Meade, Elaine Joost, the late Bill Schmidt, Ed Powell, Larry Clowers, Nancy Machado, and Steve Farbman. Thanks to their diligence and knowledge, the book's quality was vastly improved and many errors were avoided. As for those errors that remain in this book, I take full responsibility.

Kudos to the Muhlenberg College Library staff, especially Kelly Cannon. I am also indebted to my wife, Susan, for her usual patience and support, and to John Weidemoyer for his invaluable technical assistance.

Contents

Preface

While writing an earlier book, *How Robert E. Lee Lost the Civil War*, I became impressed with the well-demonstrated incompetence of George Brinton McClellan. His abysmal performances on the Virginia Peninsula and at Antietam provided Lee with an opportunity for success in the war.

Then, when writing my next book, *A Victor, Not a Butcher: Ulysses S. Grant's Overlooked Military Genius*, I discussed what an aggressive Union general, using all the resources he had, could accomplish. The sharp contrast between Grant and McClellan so intrigued me that I decided to explore the performance and motivations of McClellan in depth. This book is the result.

I have examined McClellan's Western Virginia, Peninsula, and Maryland (or Antietam) campaigns. I also have explored General McClellan's activities as a passive General-in-Chief from 1861 to 1862 and his successful attempt to undermine a fellow Union general, John Pope, before and after the Battle of Second Manassas (Bull Run).

After describing McClellan's failures and his disregard of orders while undermining Pope, I have provided a final chapter examining his possible motives. My conclusion is that he was driven by a lust for fame and glory and an even greater fear of failure and blame. These traits caused him not only to avoid the aggressive actions that were necessary for Union success in the war but also to foster Union failure when it served his purposes.

In order to analyze McClellan's motivations, I have studied and included many excerpts from his orders and correspondence. Thus, the reader can see what he was thinking and saying as his campaigns and other actions unfolded. His own words and deeds, in the context of the events swirling about him, present the sad and shocking picture of a senior Union general who failed in all his major missions, probably extended the war by two or three years, and engaged in traitorous conduct for reasons that history must judge.

Introduction:
The General Who Failed

Why write a book focusing on the deficiencies of Union Major General George Brinton McClellan, some of whose failures are well known to Civil War buffs and even those with only a general interest in American history? The reason is that his failures were so complete and so devastating to the Union cause in 1861 and 1862 that he probably single-handedly extended the war by two to three years. In addition, the evidence of his motives for failure, seen particularly in his own contemporaneous actions and words during the war, deserves scrutiny to determine if he was egotistical, timid, paranoid, fearful of defeat, vengeful, close-minded, disloyal, traitorous, or some combination of these qualities. This volume sets forth the evidence and my conclusions.

McClellan was, and remains, one of the most controversial generals of the Civil War, and judgments about him have varied greatly. I suggest that he has not yet received the ignominy that he so richly deserves. For example, a recent poll of six Civil War historians placed McClellan in a tie for the fifth-worst general of the war—of the more than twelve hundred generals on both sides. Although two historians rated him the worst, three did not even place him in the worst ten.[1] So long as three out of six historians do not even place him among the ten worst generals of the war or another recent historian can conclude, "I categorically disagree with those who charge McClellan as the worst, or among the worst, Northern commanders during the war,"[2] this book is necessary. Given his great responsibilities and concomitant great failures, I believe McClellan was the worst Union Civil War general and provide readers with information to justify that position in these pages. As for his motives, I will set forth comprehensive evidence and my opinions, but the reader will have to make his or her own determination.

Among the cast of more than twelve hundred Civil War generals, McClellan probably superseded all of them in his imagined greatness. Given the viable candidates (including Daniel Sickles, John A. McClernand, John Bell Hood, and John C. Fremont), that is quite an accomplishment. The relevance of McClellan's inflated ego is that it caused him to believe he could do no wrong, that anyone (including President Lincoln and Secretary of War Edwin Stanton) who disagreed with him was crazy, stupid, or malicious, and that he was justified in taking whatever actions he deemed appropriate to promote his own ideas and advance his own career—regardless of the consequences for the Union war effort.

The diminutive (5'8" but barrel-chested) McClellan often was called "Little Mac," and perhaps that was part of his problem. In any event, he graduated second in the illustrious West Point Class of 1846, which contributed twenty generals to the Civil War (out of fifty-nine graduates). He performed well as an engineering officer in the Mexican War and received two brevet (temporary) promotions for his actions in that conflict.

McClellan's career and self-image continued to soar after the Mexican War. He served at West Point and translated a French bayonet exercise treatise into English. He then participated in a famous expedition to find the source of the Red River, helped survey for transcontinental railroad routes, and was an American observer of European armies, including their fighting the Crimean War. From the Hungarians, McClellan adapted a saddle, which became known as the "McClellan saddle" and remained standard Army equipment for almost a hundred years.

After serving in the First Cavalry, McClellan resigned from the Army in 1857 to become the Chief Engineer of the Illinois Central Railroad. By 1861, he had advanced to the position of president of the Eastern Division of the Ohio & Mississippi Railroad. From his position of power and wealth, McClellan re-entered the Union Army near the top— as Major General of Ohio Volunteers. Three weeks later, he was appointed a major general in the regular army.

In that position, McClellan organized an invasion of western Virginia and set his sights on higher command—the position of general-in-chief held by 74-year-old Winfield Scott, a hero of the War of 1812 and the Mexican War. Although McClellan's western Virginia efforts in the field were less than impressive, his competent subordinates performed well. McClellan carried along telegraph wires to provide the world (especially Lincoln) with the story of his army's successes.

That western Virginia campaign resulted in continued Union control of the Baltimore & Ohio Railroad—critical for east-west transportation—and of the mountainous portions of western Virginia, critical for control of the Ohio River. This success, for which McClellan claimed credit, led to his being selected to command the major eastern Union Army of the Potomac, which had just suffered an embarrassing defeat at First Manassas (First Bull Run).

Following that promotion, McClellan moved to Washington, where he could pursue his goal of even higher command. As he effectively reorganized and trained the Army of the Potomac, McClellan worked to undermine General-in-Chief Scott. His efforts were so successful that Scott resigned within three months, and the 35-year-old McClellan became General-in-Chief of the Armies of the United States on November 1, 1861.

The young commander assembled an effective fighting force, and his men adored him. He was aided by the fact that, in his mid-thirties, he was trim, had a 45-inch barrel chest, and was imposing when mounted on a horse.[3] Unfortunately, one of the reasons for his troops' adoration of him may have been his reluctance to send them into battle. Because the burden was on the North to win the war and thus end Southern independence, Lincoln wanted action taken. For months, McClellan ignored, insulted, and avoided the president.

Lincoln, however, persisted in demanding action. His commanding general was reluctant to directly assault the Confederate forces assembled in northern Virginia and therefore developed an alternative plan, which he refused to divulge to anyone, including Lincoln. When Lincoln finally ordered a direct assault, McClellan at last revealed a plan calling for a waterborne movement followed by an overland march on Richmond. This plan evolved into the Peninsula Campaign, in which McClellan slowly moved his army up the peninsula between the James and York rivers in an effort to threaten and capture the Confederate capital of Richmond.

That campaign provided an opportunity for McClellan to demonstrate his major weaknesses. First, he took two months to move his troops seventy miles up the peninsula; he spent a whole month besieging weakly defended Yorktown. Second, he allowed the enemy to concentrate its force against him because of his failure to take the initiative.[4] Third, he overestimated the strength of his opponent by making it clear to his intelligence chief that he wanted high estimates of Rebel forces arrayed against him. Fourth, he claimed even higher numbers of the enemy than those estimates, consistently demanded reinforcements that were not readily available, and refused to attack until he received them.[5] Fifth, when the enemy imposed battle on his army, McClellan was nowhere to be found.

As a result of these shortfalls, McClellan's grand thrust at Richmond was a strategic failure. Robert E. Lee was able to drive the Union forces away from Richmond during the Seven Days' Battle by launching aggressive assaults. As soon as Lee began his attacks, McClellan put his army into full retreat. By virtue of Lee's constant and costly assaults, as well as Lee's poor coordination of his troops, Union casualties were only 16,000, compared to Lee's 20,000.

Instead of counter-attacking the disorganized and wounded Rebels, however, McClellan sat on the James River demanding reinforcements from Washington. Meanwhile, Lee slipped away and moved into central and northern Virginia to attack

Major General George B. McClellan strikes a Napoleonic pose. Photograph taken around 1861–62 (National Archives).

the newly formed Union Army of Virginia under John Pope, which consisted of troops previously commanded by McClellan. While Lee was bypassing and befuddling Pope in the Second Manassas Campaign, McClellan's conduct reached a new low.

In response to War Department orders that he provide reinforcements to save Pope's army and protect Washington, McClellan delayed the start of the departure of his troops from the Peninsula for half a month. Later, when his troops reached Alexandria, Virginia, and were desperately needed at nearby Manassas, he held 25,000 of them at Alexandria in direct defiance of six specific orders from Major General Henry Halleck, the new General-in-Chief. McClellan's deliberate disobedience of his orders and failure to support

Pope resulted in Union defeat at Second Manassas (Bull Run), chaotic conditions among
Union troops in northern Virginia, and a serious Confederate threat to Washington itself.
The defeat and chaos were what McClellan
desired and caused.

Ironically, McClellan's conduct resulted in
his restoration to command of all the Union
troops near Washington because Lincoln
believed he had no one else to turn to who was
capable of quickly restoring order and morale.
Union troops cheered his return to command.
Once again, McClellan rebuilt the Army of the
Potomac and briefly revived military and civilian morale in Washington.

Unfortunately for McClellan, he was to
have no respite and would have to fight Lee
again. Shortly after Second Manassas and on
his own initiative, Lee led his Army of Northern Virginia out of the Confederacy and into
Maryland, where he had high, but unfulfilled,
hopes of locals flocking to join his army. Lee,
probably assuming that McClellan would be

Profile of Major General George B.
McClellan, ca. 1861–62 (National Archives).

slow to react, divided his army into five segments. He had three of them surround Union
troops in Harpers Ferry, Virginia, one head toward Pennsylvania, and another one defend
his eastern flank.

McClellan stayed between Lee and Washington by slowly proceeding northwest to
Frederick, Maryland. There McClellan received as great a gift as any general has ever
had when a copy of Lee's troop disposition order fell into his hands. McClellan foolishly
bragged about his good fortune. Thereby, he probably alerted Lee to what had occurred
and also raised false hopes in Washington that McClellan would actually go quickly on
the offensive.

Instead, the Union commander pursued Lee's divided forces with just slightly more
than his usual timidity. By doing so, he gave Lee just enough time to halt the Union
assault at South Mountain (west of Frederick), capture Harpers Ferry and over 10,000
Union troops, and then gradually reassemble his army at the town of Sharpsburg on
Antietam Creek. For two days, McClellan overwhelmingly outnumbered Lee at Antietam
but refused to attack.

Finally, on September 17, 1862, McClellan attacked Lee's army—but only after obvious maneuvering that made his plans transparent to the enemy. The Union assault was
preceded by neither a council of Union generals nor a battle plan issued by the commander.[6] The assault was pitiful. First, three Union corps attacked, one after the other,
on the north end of the battlefield in the early hours of the day. Second, in the mid-
morning, more of McClellan's soldiers attacked the Confederate middle. Third, at
midday, another portion of them attacked the southern sector of the Confederate line.
Finally, McClellan kept a quarter of his troops in reserve all day and never used them.
As a result of McClellan's uncoordinated battle "plan," Lee was able to move his men
from one position to another to repel all the Union assaults. The bloodiest day of the
Civil War could have resulted in the destruction of Lee's army, which was backed up

against the Potomac River, but instead was just another missed opportunity for McClellan.

He then compounded his failure by not attacking Lee's battered—and unentrenched—army the following day when Lee ignored his generals' advice and stayed in his vulnerable position for yet another day. Lee defied McClellan, and the Union commander blinked.

When Lee crossed the Potomac and reluctantly returned to Virginia, McClellan claimed victory. But Lincoln realized that Lee's army had to be destroyed or captured to end the war and that McClellan had missed a golden opportunity to do just that. Within days, Lincoln visited his army commander at Antietam and urged prompt pursuit of the retreating Lee. Once again McClellan defied his commander-in-chief and dawdled while Lee safely retreated to the heart of Virginia and then moved troops between McClellan and Richmond. An exasperated President Lincoln at long last removed McClellan from command on November 5, 1862, and ordered him home to Trenton, New Jersey.

For more than a year, Lincoln had provided McClellan with an opportunity to command the nation's largest army and to make headway against the Confederacy. McClellan, however, had failed miserably. The eastern Union and Rebel armies were in about the same positions before and after McClellan commanded, and the only Union "progress" was the high number of Confederate casualties caused by Lee's aggressiveness. That number would have been higher had McClellan fought well—or even competently.

Unfortunately for the Union cause, McClellan's attitudes and practices permeated his army long after he had departed. As historian Keith Poulter has commented, "Temperamentally unfit to hold a field command, [McClellan] imparted his own super-cautious approach to the officer corps of the Army of the Potomac—to the lasting detriment of that army." Similarly, Stephen Sears succinctly said, "McClellan's final disservice was permanently staining the Potomac army's officer corps with his paranoia."[7] That army's 1861–62 performance (primarily under McClellan's command) was compared most unfavorably to that of its counterparts by the Congressional Joint Committee on the Conduct of the War in its April 1863 report: "Had the success of the army of the Potomac during [1861–62] corresponded with the success of our arms in other parts of the country, there is reason to believe that the termination of the campaign of 1862 would have seen the rebellion well-nigh, if not entirely, overthrown."[8]

The following chapters explore the details of McClellan's failed campaigns and provide insight into his actions and motivations. The main unresolved question posed is whether he was merely grossly negligent or whether, at least before and during Second Bull Run, he deliberately attempted to undercut the Union war effort. McClellan was a reluctant warrior, respected southerners' property rights (including their slave-holdings), disrespected the president and secretary of war, inflated his foes' strength to justify nonaction, fumbled a grand opportunity for success at Antietam, and failed to pursue Lee afterward. His failures are clear, but the issues surrounding his motivations deserve exploration.

1
Rising to Power and Prestige

George McClellan excels as a West Point cadet, performs well in the Mexican War, moves among the nation's elite, revels in "plum" assignments, and assumes powerful positions with railroads—while demonstrating a tendency to challenge and even defy his superiors.

George Brinton McClellan was the precocious son of a prominent Philadelphia physician. At the age of eleven, he entered the University of Pennsylvania's preparatory school. At thirteen, he entered the university itself to study law. Having already completed two years of study there, the under-age youngster received a waiver of the age requirement to pursue his dream of entering West Point and becoming a soldier. Although he entered the Academy at fifteen years and seven months (more than two years under the minimum age), he was brilliant in, and excelled at, languages, the classics, literature, and mathematics.[1]

At West Point, he preferred genteel, patrician southerners to his northern counterparts. He was frustrated whenever he was not the top-ranked cadet and did finish (unfairly, he believed) a disappointing second in his class.[2] Nevertheless, his classmates and the other cadets recognized him as the star of the class. One classmate described him as "the ablest man in the class.... We expected him to make a great record in the army, and if opportunity presented, we predicted real military fame for him."[3]

McClellan's second-place finish in his 1846 class earned him a coveted position in the Corps of Engineers. Because Congress had declared war on Mexico just a month before his class's graduation, most of the new officers were soon off to war. A thrilled McClellan had written home when he learned of the war declaration: "Hip! Hip! Hurrah! War at last sure enough! Aint [*sic*] it glorious!" He was deprived of the glory of war for three months while he and two other officers effectively trained seventy enlisted men as sappers, miners, and pontooners.[4]

During the Mexican War, McClellan, like Robert E. Lee, served under Major General Winfield Scott, the 300-pounder known as "Old Fuss and Feathers." Unlike Ulysses S. Grant, neither McClellan nor Lee served in northern Mexico under the more down-to-earth Major General Zachary ("Old Rough and Ready") Taylor. During Scott's Vera Cruz-to-Mexico City campaign, McClellan was eager for fighting and honors. At Cordova, he had two horses shot out from under him and was knocked down by a piece of canister that had struck the hilt of his sword. At the culminating Battle of Chapultepec outside Mexico City, McClellan and his engineers smashed their way through a series of houses to reach a three-story building from which they unleashed deadly musket fire into the Mexican garrison. At the conclusion of the fighting, a relieved McClellan said, "Here we are—the deed is done—I am glad no one can say 'poor Mac' over me."[5]

According to historian Timothy D. Johnson, McClellan admired Scott's Vera Cruz-to-Mexico City Campaign for its siege of Vera Cruz (in lieu of an assault), its pacific approach to civilians, and its use of turning movements instead of frontal assaults (except at Molino del Rey and Chapultepec). Johnson also quoted an admiring letter from McClellan to his brother; in it, he referred to Scott as "the noble old fellow" and praised the "hold he has upon the respect & affection of every man in the army."[6] That view would change years later when Scott stood in the way of McClellan's advancement.

McClellan's career and self-image continued to soar after the Mexican War, but his ego was the cause of several disputes. He was hand-picked to serve in an independent command at West Point, where he was involved in disputes with the superintendent and the army's chief engineer. For three years, he had continuing arguments about such petty issues as whether he was required to attend mandatory chapel and where a storage shed should be located.[7] Then he was selected to be part of a famous expedition to find the source of the Red River and helped survey for transcontinental railroad routes in the Cascade Mountains of Washington. He performed the surveying duties cautiously and sloppily (by incorrectly concluding that there were no practical railroad routes through the Cascades), and he acted defiantly toward Washington's governor, whose contrary findings embarrassed McClellan.[8] The Red River expedition introduced McClellan to Captain Randolph B. Marcy. Marcy soon decided that McClellan, because of his high social status in Philadelphia, would be the perfect husband for his beautiful daughter, Mary Ellen.

Mary Ellen, however, had other ideas. She rejected McClellan's rather hasty proposal of marriage. McClellan then launched an indirect campaign to persuade Mary Ellen's mother that he would be the perfect son-in-law. That campaign had no effect on Mary Ellen. She instead fell in love with another Army officer, Ambrose P. Hill, and became engaged to him without her parents' permission. Her father cruelly told her that his love for her could turn to hate. Mrs. Marcy threatened to go public with information about the sexual disease Hill had contacted on a New York City fling as a cadet—and apparently she did. This parental onslaught drove Hill away and left Mary Ellen to deal with a bevy of other suitors.[9]

Meanwhile, beginning in 1854, McClellan served as one of three American military observers of the organization and practices of European armies. Secretary of War Jefferson Davis[10] directed Majors Richard Delafield and Alfred Mordecai and Captain McClellan (cumulatively known as the Delafield Commission) to pay particular attention to small arms and artillery developments in Europe. While in Europe, McClellan was able to observe several armies in action in the Crimean War (in which Great Britain, France, Turkey and Sardinia defeated Russia). The successful siege at Sevastopol impressed him. The three-officer commission also inspected Austrian, British, French, Prussian, and Russian military fortifications.[11]

McClellan's correspondence from Europe reflected his disdain for the two senior American officers with whom he traveled. He complained about "these d——d old fogies!! I hope that I may never be tied to two corpses again—it is a hell upon earth…."[12] McClellan submitted his report first (in 1856) and focused on European cavalry and the Russian army's organization and methods. Because Mordecai and Delafield responded to the Commission's mission and focused on the technical aspects of new developments in Europe, especially rifle-muskets and rifled artillery, their later reports had a much greater practical impact than McClellan's.[13]

After serving in the First Cavalry, McClellan resigned from the Army in 1857 to become the Chief Engineer of the Illinois Central Railroad. Randolph Marcy told his daughter, Mary Ellen, he was pleased by McClellan's leaving the army. Within a year, McClellan started corresponding with Mary Ellen, not just her mother. In the fall of 1859, he invited the Marcy family to visit him in his Chicago lakefront home and then, on his private railroad car, proposed again to Mary Ellen (her ninth proposal). She accepted, and the two married on May 22, 1860, in a grand New York City wedding

Major General George B. McClellan and his wife, Mary Ellen, ca. 1861–62. McClellan won Mary Ellen's hand away from later Confederate Lieutenant General A.P. Hill (Library of Congress).

attended by many of the nation's elite, including General Scott.[14] In August 1860, McClellan transferred to a higher position at another railroad and became president of the Eastern Division of the Ohio & Mississippi Railroad.

From his Cincinnati home, McClellan watched the nation move toward war after the November 1860 election of Abraham Lincoln. Late the next month, McClellan wrote to Samuel L. M. Barlow, a New York Democratic friend, that western Republicans were willing to pay compensation for runaway slaves not returned to the South. He added that southerners unfortunately were listening to the Radical Republicans in Washington, and westerners would stand united in "war or peace—but the general opinion is that it will be *war*."[15] Early in February 1861, however, he wrote to his brother-in-law in Alabama in a different vein:

> The feeling among the *people* in this vicinity is strongly in favor of doing justice to the South & leaving out the ultra men in certain limited districts, I think that feeling is prevalent in the North. I do believe that the border states will be satisfied, & that being accomplished, I think the further steps of satisfying all the other slave states save South Carolina will not be difficult.[16]

It is probably significant that McClellan was living in *southern* Ohio, where there was more sympathy for the South than elsewhere in the state.

On the eve of the Civil War, therefore, McClellan moved among the nation's elite. He had been born well, lived well, and assumed high-echelon positions and public respect with an ease that created a sense of entitlement. He had achieved military success and renown in the Mexican War and other endeavors. What he had never encountered, however, were failure and recovery.

2

Winning Through Others in Western Virginia

McClellan assumes command of Ohio Volunteers, sends them off to fight in western Virginia, telegraphs the world of their successes, claims credit for their victories won in his absence or despite his inaction, and is elevated to command of the Union's largest army.

After the Confederates shelled Fort Sumter on April 12, 1861, President Lincoln called for 75,000 volunteers from northern states. McClellan saw an opportunity to re-enter the military near the top.

Because of his superb military record and high-level connections, McClellan was sought after by the governors of the three most populous northern states to command their troops. New York, Pennsylvania, and Ohio's governors all offered him command of their volunteer forces. Desiring the command in his native Pennsylvania more than the Ohio and New York positions, McClellan wrote to Major Fitz John Porter in Washington urging him to ask General Winfield Scott to recommend his appointment to Pennsylvania's Governor Andrew G. Curtin: "Say to the Genl that I am ready as ever to serve under his command; I trust I need not assure him that he can count on my loyalty to him & the dear old flag he has so long upheld."[1]

New York and Pennsylvania's offers to McClellan, however, arrived after he had accepted the position of Major General of Ohio's Volunteers. McClellan's seeking clarification of the rank he would hold in Pennsylvania and a misdirected telegram clarifying that issue caused a fatal delay of the preferred Pennsylvania offer. The formal offer and acceptance of the Ohio command occurred in the interim. McClellan stopped in Columbus, Ohio, to see Governor William Dennison to discuss the Ohio Valley military situation while McClellan was on his way from Cincinnati to Harrisburg to see Governor Curtin about the Pennsylvania position. Within hours of his meeting with McClellan, Dennison rushed a bill through the Ohio legislature naming McClellan a major general of volunteers. As a result of these developments, McClellan's first Civil War command would be in the Midwest rather than the East. Within two weeks, his political sponsor, former Ohio Governor and Senator Salmon P. Chase (Lincoln's Secretary of the Treasury), secured for McClellan a major generalship in the Regular Army.[2]

Even before he had locked up the Ohio command, McClellan wrote to Governor Dennison about defending Ohio—especially Cincinnati on the Ohio River—from Con-

13

federate attack. He urged organizing and arming volunteers to defend that city and planning for its defense, including possible defensive positions on the Kentucky side of the
river. Then, in a single sentence, McClellan expressed a defensive philosophy that would
doom his Civil War efforts: "It may well be that the necessity for all this will not occur,
but *there is only one safe rule in war—i.e., to decide what is the very worst thing that can happen to you, & prepare to meet it.*"[3]

On April 23, McClellan wrote to General Scott, U.S. Army General-in-Chief, to
advise him that he had been appointed major general of all the Ohio volunteers. He
informed Scott that Ohio could provide up to 40,000 more troops than the 10,000 envisioned in Lincoln's call-up. He praised his men with a caveat: "The material is superb,
but has no organization or discipline." McClellan added, "I find myself, general, in the
position of a commander with nothing but men—neither arms nor supplies." Thus, he
asked for at least ten thousand weapons and five million cartridges. This was only the
first of many requests the War Department would receive from him. Finally, the general
asked for the assignment to him of Major Fitz John Porter and other specific staff officers—
a request that was quickly denied because of the shortage of regular army officers caused
by southerners' resignations.[4]

On April 24, McClellan wrote to railroad detective Allan Pinkerton requesting him
to come immediately "to make arrangements ... of an important nature." Secretively, the
communication told Pinkerton, "If you telegraph me, better use your first name alone.
Let no one know that you come to see me, and keep as quiet as possible."[5] Pinkerton was
to become the general's intelligence chief—a relationship that was to reinforce and facilitate McClellan's frequent reticence to engage in combat.

The next day, McClellan issued his General Order No. 1 to the Ohio Volunteer Militia. He asked for their cooperation to establish discipline and efficiency. The heart of his
order proclaimed: "We do not enter upon this war as a pastime, but with the stern determination to repel the insults offered to our flag, and uphold the honor and integrity of
our Union. In the coming struggle, we have not only battles to fight, but hardships and
privations to endure, fatigue to encounter."[6]

Two days after that order, on April 27, McClellan made some grand proposals in a
letter to General Scott. He proposed that an 80,000-man army under his command cross
the Ohio, move up the Kanawha River Valley in western Virginia and sweep on to Richmond. As a alternative, he proposed, if Kentucky seceded, to sweep across Kentucky to
Nashville and then farther into the Deep South. He warned, however:

> To enable us to carry out either of these plans, it is absolutely necessary that the General
> Government should strain every nerve to supply the West with arms, ammunition & equip-
> ments. Even to maintain the defensive we must be largely assisted. I beg to urge upon you
> that we are very badly supplied at present, and that a vast population eager to fight are ren-
> dered powerless by the want of arms, the nation being thus deprived of their aid.

In a May 2 endorsement on the letter, Scott noted that the three-month volunteers' enlistments would have expired before McClellan organized a campaign, the proposed invasion would foment secession in western Virginia, and "The general eschews water
transportation by the Ohio & Mississippi, in favor of long, tedious & *break-down* (of men,
horses & wagons) marches."[7]

Partly on the basis of Scott's (later regretted) recommendation, Lincoln on May 3,
1861, appointed McClellan a major general in the regular army—junior only to Scott himself. The Department of Ohio, of which McClellan was named commander, initially consisted of Ohio, Indiana, and Illinois. It later was expanded to include western Pennsylvania,
western Virginia, and Missouri. By early July, however, McClellan lost the western por-

tion of his command to the new Western Department under John C. Fremont. Thus, Mac focused primarily on Kentucky and western Virginia along the Ohio River.

In a May 7 letter to Scott, McClellan said he agreed with his Anaconda Plan (to blockade the Confederate Coast and move down the Mississippi River) and then added a sentence that reeked of obsequiousness and implied future dissent: "Even if I did not agree with you I have that implicit confidence in the General under whom I first learned the art of war that would free me thereby to carry out his views."[8]

Two days later, amidst a plea for supplies, money, and specific officers, McClellan again so highly praised Scott that the latter must have been suspicious. He wrote:

> Next to maintaining the honor of my country, general, the first aim of my life is to justify the good opinion you have expressed concerning me, and to prove that the great soldier of our country can not only command armies himself, but teach others to do so. I do not expect your mantle to fall on my shoulders, for no man is worthy to wear it; but I hope that it may be said hereafter that I was no unworthy disciple of your school.[9]

Within four days of writing these words, McClellan, on May 13, complained to Governor Dennison that "apathy in Washington is very singular & very discouraging" and added, "I almost regret having entered upon my present duty." A week later, in a telegram to Secretary of War Simon Cameron, he urged occupation of Cumberland in western Maryland and complained, "I have as yet received neither instructions nor authority. My hands tied until I have one or the other." Now aware of McClellan's true loyalty (to himself), Scott responded the next day that he was "surprised at your complaint to the Secretary of War against me that you are without instructions or authority and with your hands tied up." Scott then reviewed his past correspondence with McClellan and asked how the direction could have been clearer.[10]

Scott's scolding probably led to McClellan's sending an astounding telegram to Governor Dennison four days later:

> Genl. Scott is as you are aware eminently sensitive, and does not at all times take suggestions kindly from military subordinates especially when they conflict with his own preconceived notions. In view of this, and of the importance of his hearty cooperation in future military operations in this department, I beg to suggest that you request Gov. Yates [of Illinois] by telegraph in carrying out the objects of his mission at Washington not to use my name in such a way as to disturb the sensitive complexion of the General's mind.[11]

After receiving orders to invade Virginia, McClellan issued a May 26 implementing order to his troops. That order "to rescue our brethren from the grasp of armed traitors" optimistically foresaw his men's return to their homes after they had enabled the loyal men of western Virginia to organize and arm themselves. It also stressed the need for "the strictest discipline" and urged respect for Virginians' rights and property: "I place under the safeguard of your honor the persons and property of the Virginians. I know that you will respect their feelings and all their rights." He wrote, "...remember that your only foes are the armed traitors, and show mercy even to them when they are in your power, for many of them are misguided."[12]

That same day, McClellan issued an open letter to the Union men of western Virginia. He advised them that he was entering their state to oppose the "armed rebels who are preying upon you." He gave them strong assurance that their property rights—including their slaveholdings—would not be in jeopardy:

> Your homes, your families, and your property are safe under our protection. All your rights shall be religiously respected. Notwithstanding all that has been said by the traitors to induce you to believe that our advent among you will be signalized by interference with your slaves,

understand one thing clearly—not only will we abstain from all such interference but we will on the contrary, with an iron hand, crush any attempt at insurrection on their part.[13]

With McClellan back in Cincinnati, troops under his command successfully occupied Grafton, Virginia, in late May. McClellan wrote, "It is a source of very great satisfaction to me that we have occupied Grafton without the sacrifice of a single life."[14]

A few days later, on June 3, other troops under his command routed a Confederate force under Colonel George A. Porterfield at Philippi, Virginia, in a brief battle that gained fame as "the Philippi Races." No one was killed in this first land battle of the war, but McClellan (still 250 miles away in Cincinnati) was receiving kudos for his first victory. As a result of the Rebel rout, Porterfield was relieved of command and replaced by Robert E. Lee's adjutant and newly promoted Brigadier General Robert S. Garnett. The Confederates also sent reinforcements to regain their lost territory in northwestern Virginia. Meanwhile, McClellan did not leave Cincinnati for Virginia until June 20.[15]

On May 30, McClellan wrote an unofficial letter to President Lincoln seeking his retroactive approval for his proclamation to the men of western Virginia. He wrote that his proclamation was having a positive effect in Kentucky—as was the president's policy of providing arms to loyal Unionists in that state. Portions of that letter walked the line between politeness and obsequiousness: "The issue of the arms to Kentuckians is regarded by the staunch men as a masterpiece of policy on your part, & has—if I may be permitted to say so—very much strengthened your position among them." and "Rest assured that I will exert all my energies to carry out what I suppose to be your policy, & that I will be glad to be informed if I have misconstrued your words."[16]

Two days later he violated the chain of command to directly and successfully request the president to appoint his father-in-law, Major Randolph Marcy, as his chief of staff. Marcy assumed those duties—first as a colonel and then as a brigadier general of volunteers.[17]

On the night of June 7–8, McClellan met with Major General Simon B. Buckner, commander of Kentucky's home guard. McClellan reported that Buckner had assured him that if Tennessee troops invaded Kentucky, he (Buckner) would drive them out or request McClellan's assistance to do so.[18] Buckner later went public with a different version of their conversations. Buckner's action caused McClellan to gather evidence from witnesses and assure General Scott that Buckner was misrepresenting what McClellan had said.[19]

After departing Cincinnati by train on June 20 and arriving the next day in Parkersburg, Virginia, on the Ohio River, McClellan could hardly wait to write to his wife about the adulation he had encountered on his journey from Cincinnati. He wrote, " We ... had a continual ovation all along the road. At every station where we stopped, crowds had assembled to see the 'Young General.' ... The trouble will be to fill their expectations, they seem to be so high." He told her that he had eighteen regiments, two batteries, and two companies of cavalry at his disposal: "—enough to thrash anything I find. I think the danger has been greatly exaggerated & anticipate little or no chance of winning laurels."[20]

McClellan wisely sought cavalry to act as scouts in western Virginia, but his requests were rebuffed by Washington officials. It was July before he was authorized to raise even a single company of volunteer cavalry for three years of military service. But he did creatively obtain additional companies of horsemen by appealing directly to the governors in his military department.[21]

Between June 29 and July 2, 1861, McClellan told Mary Ellen from western Virginia that he was having "a telegraph line built to follow us up," that "it is a proud & glorious thing to see a whole people here, simple & unsophisticated, looking up to me as their deliverer from tyranny," and that "I doubt whether the rebels will fight—it is possible they may, but I begin to think that my successes will be due to manoeuvres, & that I shall have no brilliant victories to record. I would be glad to clear them out of West Virginia & liberate the country without bloodshed if possible. The people are rejoiced to see us."[22]

On June 26, McClellan wrote to Secretary of Treasury Chase that reports of a conflict with Governor Dennison were false and that he had "pretty good reason to believe that we have Georgia, So Car, & Tenna troops in front of us." He explained that the Rebel "main force is at the Laurel Mountain between Phillipi & Beverly—I shall move the main column rapidly from Clarksburg on Buckhannon & Beverly to turn that position while the force now at Phillipi slowly advances to distract their attention."[23]

A few days later, however, in a scathing July 3 letter to his subordinate Brigadier General T.A. Morris at Phillipi, McClellan expressed his surprise that Morris was so concerned about defending Phillipi. McClellan told Morris, "You have only to defend a strong position, or at most to follow a retreating enemy." He condescendingly and harshly concluded:

> I propose taking the really difficult and dangerous part of this work on my own hands—I will not ask you to do anything that I would not be willing to do myself. But let us understand each other. I can give you no more re-enforcements. I cannot consent to weaken any further the really active and important column which is to decide the fate of the campaign. If you cannot undertake the defense of Phillipi with the force now under your control, I must find some one who will. I have ordered up Latham's company, all of Key's cavalry that are fit to take the field, and the 6th Ohio.
>
> Do not ask for further reinforcements. If you do, I shall take it as a request to be relieved from your command and to return to Indiana.
>
> I have spoken plainly. I speak officially. The crisis is a grave one, and I must have generals under me who are willing to risk as much as I am, and to be content to risk their lives and reputation with such means as I can give them. Let this be the last of it. Give me full details as to the information you obtained—not mere rumors, but facts—and leave it to my judgment to determine what force you need. I wish action now and determination.[24]

Time would tell whether McClellan himself was a general willing to risk his life and reputation with only such means as would be given to him.

In the meantime, McClellan had to make do with what he deemed to be incompetent brigadier generals. He complained to Mary Ellen, "I have not a Brig Genl worth his salt—Morris is a timid old woman—Rosecranz [William Starke Rosecrans] a silly fussy goose—[Newton] Schleich knows nothing." But he was able to tell her that he had made her father the Inspector General of his army.[25]

According to historian Albert Castel, McClellan's real problem with Rosecrans was that "Rosy" was too competent a subordinate for McClellan's taste: "[McClellan] disliked Rosecrans—disliked him because he distrusted him. What he wanted in subordinates were men who lacked either the desire or the ability, or both, to be other than subordinates and so would be content to remain such while advancing his own aspirations by doing what he ordered them to do—this and nothing more nor less.... McClellan realized that Rosecrans was not that kind of man."[26]

These concerns led McClellan to try to put Rosecrans in his place. As McClellan's troops moved toward Buckhannon, McClellan sent a written reprimand to Rosecrans for camping his brigade beyond the point that had been specified and thus exposing the army's movement to enemy detection. Rosecrans responded that there had been inadequate space at the specified place and that he had ascertained that the enemy was not at Buckhannon, which he was about to occupy. He added, "None under your command are more loyally, cheerfully ready to conform to the duties of a subordinate position, and I even flatter myself I understand the position as well as most of your brigadiers. Review, if you please, that letter which you have put on record, and say whether, after you receive this, both private feelings and public interest are likely to be the better for it." McClellan's bluff had been called, and his original reprimand is not in the *Official Records*.[27]

Meanwhile, Garnett, with about 5,300 Rebel troops, had posted most of them on Laurel Hill and a mere thousand to the south on Rich Mountain. These two mountains were strong defensive positions that blocked McClellan's movement to the east. McClellan decided to hold Garnett in place on Laurel Hill with one brigade while he moved on Rich Mountain with his other three brigades. He intended to seize that mountain and the town of Beverly to the east, outflank Garnett, and compel him to retreat. When McClellan finally arrived at a position near the enemy, he decided that his opponents totaled 10,000 troops, with 2,000 facing him at Rich Mountain. These numbers were more than he originally had estimated and almost double the enemy's true strength.[28]

McClellan was still at Buckhannon when he wrote to Colonel E.D. Townsend, Scott's adjutant, on July 6. As for not moving on the enemy, he wrote, "Say to the General, too, that I am trying to follow a lesson long ago learned from him, *i.e.* not to move until I know that everything is ready, and then to move with the utmost rapidity and energy." Again, time would tell whether McClellan had learned both of those precepts—or only the first one. He told Townsend that he expected to maneuver around the enemy, thereby repeating Scott's Cerro Gordo victory in Mexico, and asked him to assure the general of his "intention of gaining success by maneuvering rather than by fighting."[29]

McClellan's plan to avoid a difficult battle appeared to evaporate when on July 9 he discovered that Rich Mountain was steep, brush covered, and well defended by Confederate infantry and artillery. In his July 14 official report, McClellan claimed credit for sending Rosecrans on a successful flanking movement that resulted in a Union victory and Rebel retreat from Rich Mountain. McClellan, however, failed to provide details about what really happened.[30]

Several years later, in an 1883 newspaper account of the preliminaries to the Battle of Rich Mountain, Rosecrans told how he had found a local man who knew of a path around the strong Confederate lines on Rich Mountain. According to Rosecrans, McClellan had reluctantly approved Rosecrans' plan to get behind the Rebels after his father-in-law gave his assent, and McClellan was to commence the main attack from below when he heard the firing created by Rosecrans' four-regiment flanking maneuver.[31]

Not only did Rosecrans devise and execute the plan for a flanking march, he won the battle without McClellan's promised support. Beginning at 4 A.M. on July 11, 1861, Rosecrans marched his 1,200 or more men around the southern (left) Confederate flank on a difficult cattle path in order to launch what he hoped would be a surprise attack on the Rebel rear. Conditions, which included rain, were so difficult that Rosecrans did not see any purpose in complying with McClellan's order to report the progress of his march every hour. "Old Rosy" could not even see the top of the mountain until 11 A.M. and required three more hours to complete the climb and reach the Hart farm two miles behind the Rebel line.[32]

To Rosecrans' shock and dismay, three hundred Confederates, commanded by Colonel Julius A. de Lagnel, and a cannon in strong positions awaited his arrival at the farm. Their presence was the result of an over-anxious McClellan sending a courier around the north flank to determine what was happening, the courier foolishly being captured by the Rebels, and the Confederates thereby learning of Rosecrans' movement.[33]

Rosecrans' force attacked three times over three hours late in the day and finally over-

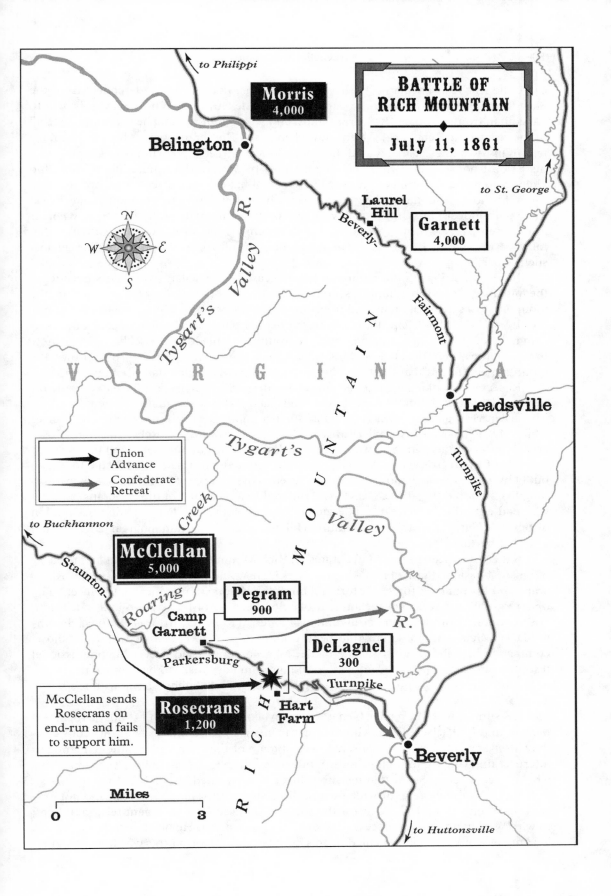

to Philippi

Morris
4,000

Belington

BATTLE OF
RICH MOUNTAIN

July 11, 1861

to St. George

Laurel
Hill

Beverly-

Garnett
4,000

N
W   E
S

Tygart's Valley R.

Fairmont

VIRGINIA

Leadsville

Tygart's

Turnpike

Union
Advance

Confederate
Retreat

Creek

MOUNTAIN

Valley

to Buckhannon

McClellan
5,000

Roaring

Staunton-

Pegram
900

Camp
Garnett

R.

Parkersburg

DeLagnel
300

Turnpike

McClellan sends
Rosecrans on
end-run and fails
to support him.

Rosecrans
1,200

Hart
Farm

RICH

Beverly

Miles

0   3

to Huttonsville

came the stiff resistance as "Old Rosy" led a charge that drove the defenders from the Hart farm. He did so without assistance from McClellan, who, in his own words, was to "assault in front as soon as Rosecrans' musketry would indicate that he was immediately" in the rear of the Rebel line. When McClellan heard Rosecrans' battle, he rode from his tent to his own lines, listened, and did not order the agreed-upon supporting attack with his 5,000 troops against the Rebel line manned by a mere six to nine hundred.[34] Ohio Colonel John Beatty observed him: "The General halted a few paces from our line and sat on his horse listening to the guns, apparently in doubt as to what to do; and as he sat there with indecision stamped on every line of his countenance, the battle grew fiercer in the enemy rear." Beatty pondered, "If the enemy is too strong for us to attack, what must be the fate of Rosecrans' four regiments, cut off from us and struggling against such odds?"[35]

When the firing up the mountain finally ceased, McClellan (who had surrendered the initiative to the Rebels and Rosecrans) went so far as to withdraw his troops from the mountain to a safe position behind Roaring Creek. Rosecrans was on his own until morning. Even then, McClellan did not come to his aid but instead engaged in a time-consuming effort to place guns on nearby high ground to enfilade the Rebel line. Fortunately for Rosecrans, he did not need McClellan's help. Rosecrans sent his troops down the mountain and found that the Rebel lines across from McClellan had been abandoned.[36]

Rosecrans' flanking assault had succeeded despite McClellan's failure to execute his own battleplan and simultaneously—or even later—attack the main Confederate line. McClellan was satisfied to let Rosecrans' smaller contingent fight the enemy themselves while McClellan had his artillery throw some shells toward the Rebel position. Rosecrans' droll comment in 1883 was: "We heard no noise from our front, and had no time to think of the reason why." Most of the 1,200 Confederates fled from Rich Mountain, but between sixty-three and one hundred seventy-five were captured. The following evening five hundred fifty-three Rebels surrendered to a detachment of Rosecrans' soldiers who had cut off their retreat.[37] The victory at Rich Mountain led to Union occupation of Beverly, Garnett's retreat from Laurel Hill, and Garnett's death in a rear-guard action covering his army's retreat.

If there had been more Confederates on Rich Mountain, McClellan's failure to carry out his self-assigned task of attacking the Rebel line would have spelled disaster for Rosecrans and his flanking force. Historian Timothy Johnson summed up that failure: "The operation did not go as McClellan had planned because of his caution and indecision. His intentions, however, were clear, and his model [Winfield Scott] was obvious. He simply lacked Scott's moral courage to bend events to his will. He glossed over the shortcomings in his official report of the battle...."[38] Rosecrans said it best in congressional testimony in 1865: "[McClellan] was bound, as a military man, to have made the attack in his front, for the purpose of preventing the enemy from falling on me with too heavy a force."[39]

His subordinate, Brigadier General (later Major General) Jacob D. Cox, wrote after the war that McClellan's Rich Mountain performance previewed his later timorous conduct elsewhere: "There was the same overestimate of the enemy, the same tendency to interpret unfavorably the sights and sounds in front, the same hesitancy to throw in his whole force when he knew that his subordinate was engaged."[40]

McClellan's failure to provide the promised support for his subordinate did not prevent him from taking full credit for the victory. He used his convenient telegraph line[41] to wire Washington of his success ("all that I could desire"). He blustered, "Our success is complete and secession is killed in this country." He went on to say, "I may say that we have driven out some ten thousand troops strongly entrenched with the loss of eleven killed & thirty five wounded. Provision returns found here show Garnett's force to have been ten thousand men."[42] Historian Stephen Sears reported that those numbers included four reinforcing regiments that never arrived; thus, the actual Confederate number was about 5,300.[43]

After Rich Mountain, the General wrote to his beloved Mary Ellen of the beauty of the valley in which he was located: "Beverly is a quiet, old fashioned town in a lovely valley; a beautiful stream running by it. A perfectly pastoral scene such as the old painters dreamed of, but never realized. I half think I should be King of it."[44] His ego was further swelled by a telegram from General Scott that, in part, read, "The General in Chief, & what is more the Cabinet, including the Presdt, are charmed with your activity, valour, & consequent success."[45]

McClellan's men pursued the fleeing Confederates, routed them at Carrick's Ford on the Cheat River, and killed Brigadier General Garnett (the first general killed in Civil War combat). McClellan's comment to Mary Ellen was, "Such is the fate of traitors— one of their comdrs a prisoner, the other killed! Their armies annihilated—their cause crushed in this region.... You ask what my plans are—why, you little witch, don't you know that my movements depend much on those of Mons. L'ennemi? I expect to hear in a few hours of the final extermination of the remnants of Garnett's army. Then I am almost hourly awaiting news of [Cox's] success in the Kanawha. Should Coxe [*sic*] not be prompt enough I will go down there myself & bring the matter to a close."[46] Biographer Peter Michie criticized McClellan for allowing the bulk of Garnett's forces to escape what should have been a deadly trap.[47]

Very quickly thereafter McClellan was blaming his subordinates for failures. Having heard nothing from the Kanawha River Valley, he told his wife on July 15 that he feared Cox was slow and added, "If my generals had obeyed my orders I should before this have captured every rebel in this region but unfortunately I have not a single Brig[adier general] who is worth his salt." The next day he wired Brigadier General Charles W. Hill to halt his pursuit of the Rebels farther into Virginia—"movement which seems likely to become too extended and is not in the spirit of your instructions which were to cut off the enemy's retreat, not to go into the heart of Virginia unless you are directly on the enemy's track and you are sure to cut him off at once." Hill had occupied the position McClellan had ordered, but the Rebels escaped by another route.[48]

McClellan's complaints about and to his subordinates continued. On July 19, he wired Townsend that Cox had been checked on the Kanawha and that he (McClellan) would go to his rescue. He complained, "In Heaven's name give me some general officers who understand their profession. I give orders and find some who cannot execute then unless I stand by them. Unless I command every picket and lead every column I cannot be sure of success. Give me such men as Marcy, Stevenson, Sackett, Lander &c., and I will answer for it with my life that I meet with no disaster. Had my orders been executed from beginning, our success would have been brief and final."[49]

To Cox himself, McClellan sent an insulting July 19 telegram, which began with a hostile note and went downhill from there:

> I am entirely disappointed with the result of your operations. You have in front of you but twenty five hundred men badly armed, disciplined and commanded and disaffected to their cause. You should have advanced to the Gauley Bridge without a check. Your Army is nearly as numerous as that which has achieved brilliant results on this line. I see that your army is demoralized. Encourage your men by telling them that I myself will move upon the enemy's rear and accomplish what ought to have been done without my personal presence.

In the mean time hold your own and at least save me the disgrace of a detachment of my
Army being routed.

Without McClellan's help, Cox outflanked General Henry A. Wise's Confederate army
and captured both Gauley Bridge and Charleston.[50]

After passage of a congressional resolution praising his western Virginia victories,
McClellan issued an open letter thanking his troops. He told them, "I am more than
satisfied with you. You have annihilated two armies, commanded by educated and experienced soldiers, intrenched in mountain fastnesses fortified at their leisure…. You have
proved that Union men, fighting for the preservation of our Government, are more than
a match for our misguided and erring brethren; more than this, you have shown mercy
to the vanquished…. I am proud to say that you have gained the highest reward that American troops can receive—the thanks of Congress, and the applause of your fellow-
citizens."[51] He apparently printed this letter on a portable press he had brought along
and distributed copies to his troops.[52]

He also took the opportunity to send General Scott an obsequious letter thanking
him for his commendation. McClellan told his superior, "…I value the commendation,
you have been kind enough to bestow upon me, more highly than any reward I can receive
from any other source. All that I know of war I have learned from you, & in all that I
have done I have endeavored to conform to your manner of conducting a campaign, as
I understand the history of your achievements. It is my ambition to merit your praise &
never to deserve your censure."[53] McClellan would be singing a different tune in a few
months.

Following the initial victories of his troops, McClellan advised Scott, through his
father-in-law, that he would move into the Staunton area in the Shenandoah Valley after
he bailed out Cox in the Kanawha Valley. Beyond that, McClellan grandiosely pronounced
that "a movement through Kentucky, Western Tennessee and Northern Alabama would
be decisive of the war." As he planned to move south, the general told his wife, "Cox lost
more men in getting a detachment thrashed than I did in routing two armies. The consequence is I shall move down with a heavy column to take Mr. Wise in rear & hope
either to drive him out without a battle or to catch him with his whole force. It is absolutely
necessary for me to go in person. I have no one to whom I can entrust the operation."[54]

Meanwhile, McClellan had continued to set up telegraph lines in his wake. This new
method of military communication allowed him to send messages not only to his troops
but also to Washington and the press. His self-promotional wires praised his successes,
understated Rosecrans' role in the victories, and implied that McClellan himself had
devised the flanking movement at Rich Mountain. In the absence of conflicting information, he was hailed as a hero in the North and respected as a great commander in the
South.[55] McClellan's campaign soon bore fruit.

The first sign of change occurred when McClellan learned of Union forces' disastrous defeat at First Bull Run near Manassas, Virginia. On July 21, Scott wired him,
"[Irvin] McDowell has been checked. Come down to the Shenandoah Valley with such
troops as can be spared from Western Virginia, and make head against the enemy in that
quarter…."[56] McClellan proposed a movement into the northern end of the Shenandoah
with 15,000 of his troops—a movement that he said would take six or seven days after he
received orders to do so.[57]

The next day, July 22, brought a bigger change. Officials in Washington, desperate
for a winning general, mistakenly thought that McClellan's pompous proclamations and
the battlefield successes of his subordinates against inferior forces indicated that he

deserved promotion.[58] Scott, through his Adjutant General, wired McClellan, "Circumstances make your presence here necessary. Charge Rosecrans or some other general with your present department and come hither without delay." McClellan responded, "Your dispatch of this date has been received. I will make the necessary arrangements for the security of W. Va. & proceed without delay to Washington & report in person at the War Dept. I will take with me three or four Western Regiments." General Scott, however, made it clear that the orders were personal by telling McClellan not to bring any troops with him.[59]

After a parting shot to Cox ("...Genl Rosecrantz [*sic*] ... is about to repair to the Kanawha to retrieve your want of success.... It is not too late for you to justify my first impression of you."[60]), McClellan left Grafton, Virginia, by train on July 24. The dearth of Union victories elsewhere and McClellan's successful claim of credit for the victories at Philippi, Rich Mountain, and Corrick's Ford catapulted him to senior command in the East. The weak underpinning of his credentials was explained by historian John C. Waugh:

> There was irony in these three little mountain victories. The new savior of the Republic had won three engagements, but had not been present at any of them. He hadn't been in the same state for the first—the races at Philippi. He had only heard the thunder of the second, two miles away on Rich Mountain, and had misread it. And he was twenty-six miles from the third and final skirmish at Corricks Ford. Yet on the strength of these mud-spattered encounters, none of which he had personally commanded, he was being called out of the West to save the Union. Closely scrutinized, the credentials were somewhat suspect. But who else had done as much?[61]

Whether deserving or not, McClellan was off to Washington and an opportunity for greatness.

3

Maneuvering in Washington

As commander of the Army of the Potomac, McClellan creates a powerful fighting force; declines to use it because of his exaggerations of enemy strength; sets in motion and then disclaims responsibility for a Union disaster at Ball's Bluff; and undermines his mentor, General Winfield Scott, so that he can become general-in-chief of all union armies.

After arriving in Washington, McClellan was appointed commander of the Division of the Potomac, in which he commanded departments headed by generals Irvin McDowell and Joseph K.F. Mansfield ("neither of whom like it much," he told his wife). His situation in Washington quickly went to his head, and on July 27 he wrote to Mary Ellen a frighteningly self-centered portrait of his position:

> I find myself in a new & strange position here—Presdt, cabinet, Genl Scott & all deferring to me—by some strange operation of magic I seem to have become *the* power of the land. I almost think that were I to win some small success now I could become Dictator or anything else that might please me—but nothing of that kind would please me—*therefore I won't* be Dictator. Admirable self-denial! I see already the main causes of our recent failure—I am *sure* that I can remedy these & am confident that I can lead these armies of men to victory once more.[1]

Historian Timothy Johnson pointed to this letter as "mark[ing] a dramatic change in McClellan's thinking. Until then he had considered himself to be a student of Scott's, but now he behaved as if his teacher were a nuisance." Johnson concluded that his promotion was to blame: "McClellan's tone changed. Elevation to such prominent command brought out the worst of his character flaws. McClellan became arrogant ... and began to snipe at his superiors."[2]

On July 30, McClellan reported to Mary Ellen the continuing deluge of adulation he was experiencing: "I went to the Senate.... They give me my way in everything, full swing & unbounded confidence. All tell me that I am held responsible for the fate of the Nation & that all its resources shall be placed at my disposal.... Who would have thought when we were married, that I should so soon be called upon to save my country? I learn that before I came on they said in Richmond, that there was only one man they feared & that was McClellan."[3]

Also on July 30, McClellan sent for his old friend, Allan Pinkerton (alias Major E.J. Allen), and later he appointed him chief of intelligence for the Army of the Potomac.[4]

The combination of McClellan and Pinkerton proved to be debilitating for that army. Military intelligence historian Edwin C. Fishel described them as a "neurotic general and a sycophantic intelligence officer—... surely a dangerous combination." McClellan would look to Pinkerton for inflated estimates of enemy strength to support his own belief that his army was always outnumbered.[5]

By August 2, McClellan was so sure of himself that he wrote President Lincoln a letter ("submitted at his request," said McClellan in his general report on his campaigns) setting forth his nationwide views on how to win the war. He envisioned a movement down the Mississippi, expulsion of the Rebels from Missouri, seizure of the railroads running east from Memphis, movements from Kansas and Nebraska all the way to western Texas, and an advance from California through New Mexico in alliance with Mexico. Having superseded General Scott's role as general-in-chief, McClellan proceeded to outline a grandiose plan to assemble a force of "overwhelming strength" to crush the Confederates in Virginia. He urged creation of an army of two hundred eighty-three infantry, artillery, cavalry and engineer regiments totaling 273,000 men—almost twice as many men as would ever constitute a single Civil War army.[6] McClellan reiterated this strategic plan in a February 1862 letter to Stanton.

Although some have praised McClellan's plan for a decisive, compelling victory as consistent with accepted principles of war and politics,[7] the plan called for an unrealistic number of military resources that would have stripped all other theaters of their minimal needs. Ironically, progress was made elsewhere during the next six months while McClellan failed to effectively use those resources that were available to him. Major General Ambrose E. Burnside on the North Carolina coast and Brigadier General Ulysses S. Grant at Forts Henry and Donelson achieved success with minimal resources and with little direction from McClellan.[8]

On August 2, McClellan also advised his wife of his declining confidence in General Scott, the same general he had idolized only days before. He wrote, "Genl Scott ... is fast becoming very slow & very old. He cannot long retain command I think—when he retires I am sure to succeed him, unless in the mean time I lose a battle—which I do not expect to do...."[9] As events unfolded, not losing a battle continued to be a consistent McClellan goal. Two days later, McClellan told Mary Ellen of a White House dinner, said that "Mrs. Lincoln doesn't shine particularly as a hostess," and spoke more certainly of succeeding Scott: "It made me feel a little strangely last evening when I went in to the Presdt's with the old General leaning on me—the old veteran (Scott) & his young successor; I could see that many marked the contrast."[10]

In his comprehensive early August 1861 Instructions to General Officers, McClellan demonstrated his organizational abilities. He ordered a top-down system of establishing schools of instruction to ensure the "instruction, discipline & efficiency of the troops." After providing guidance concerning sentinels and marches, McClellan discussed battles. He made it clear that individual initiative was discouraged:

> In regard to *battles & affairs* the Genl Officers will receive such specific instructions as the particular circumstances may require, the Comdg Genl now desires only to call attention to some general principles which must always be observed.
>
> The orders must be strictly conformed to; no excuse can be received for bringing on an action against or without his instructions, & every Genl Officer, of whatever rank, will be held accountable that the directions given to him are carried out in both the spirit & letter. The Genl Officers must understand that success can only be obtained by carefully observing the orders they receive, & will in no case allow their impulses or individual judgment to induce them to depart from their instructions.

He directed that artillery should almost always have a clear space of at least 500 or 600 yards in its front and that cavalry "in no case should ... be required to act in woods, or along a road skirted by timber."[11] He was establishing himself as a micro-manager who expected his generals to strictly obey his orders—and do nothing on their own initiative. Time would reveal, however, that strict adherence to orders was a one-way, downward-looking standard for McClellan.

McClellan did effectively organize and train his army. Regiments were formally organized into brigades, and brigade-wide exercises were carried out. Continual training and drills occurred. Officers no longer fraternized with their men.[12] There was, however, an ominous sign of McClellan's egotism. According to Bruce Catton, his troops were "almost ritually drilled to have and to express a high admiration for him; when he made an inspection, staff officers used to ride ahead to tell the troops that he was coming and to warn them that they were expected to give him a warm reception."[13] Some, like Brigadier General William T. Sherman, were not impressed that, instead of camping with his army in Virginia, "he took a house in Washington, and only came over from time to time to have a review or inspection."[14]

It was not long before McClellan saw the potential everywhere for enemy attacks. On August 4 and 6, he notified all of his brigade commanders that he was informed that the enemy might attack within forty-eight hours. He directed his subordinates to telegraph him at least four times daily.[15] By August 8, he was raising false alarms to General Scott:

> Information from various sources ... through spies, letters and telegrams confirm [sic] my impressions derived from previous advices, that the enemy intend attacking our positions on the other side of the [Potomac] river, as well as to cross the Potomac north of us. I have also to-day received a telegram from a reliable agent just from Knoxville Tenn. that large reinforcements are still passing through there to Richmond. I am induced to believe that the enemy has at least 100,000 men in our front. Were I in Beauregard's place, with that force at my disposal, I would attack the positions on the other side of the Potomac and at the same time cross the river above the city in force.

McClellan went on to cite the alleged insufficiency of infantry, artillery, and cavalry. He urged that troops from all rear garrisons be forwarded to Washington, new regiments of volunteers be sent "without one hour's delay," and eight or ten Ohio and Indiana regiments be sent from western Virginia to bring his strength in Washington up to 100,000. For emphasis, he added, "The vital importance of rendering Washington perfectly secure, and its *imminent danger*, impel me to urge these requests with the utmost earnestness, and that not an hour be lost in carrying them to execution." He concluded by stating that his sense of duty compelled him to recommend the merging of the commands of northeastern Virginia, Washington, the Shenandoah, Pennsylvania, Baltimore, and southeastern Virginia under the command of a single general.[16] It is not difficult to conclude whom he had in mind.

The imminent danger McClellan saw "was very disturbing; especially so since the danger actually existed almost exclusively in the mind of the commanding general"—so said Bruce Catton. He said reality was that Joseph Johnston and P.G.T. Beauregard had only 30,000 troops near Manassas, "and their troubles in respect to organization, discipline, and leadership were quite as pressing as those of the Federals, if not a little more so, the Southern private being a rugged individualist not readily amenable to military rule."[17] Military intelligence expert Edwin Fishel agreed that there were only 30,000 Rebels opposing McClellan at that time and added, "Although McClellan claimed 'spies, letters and telegrams' as his immediate sources, the ultimate sources were guesswork and rumor, or some tall storytelling by Confederate officers.... McClellan was now committed to six-figure estimates of an army that in four years of war would never reach that point." Significantly, he arrived at his estimate with no input from Pinkerton, who was just getting organized at the time.[18]

Perhaps to demonstrate the strength of his convictions or bypass his more calm and collected commander, McClellan went outside the chain of command and had a copy of his August 8 letter to General Scott hand-carried to President Lincoln.[19] Thus, both Lincoln and Scott were aware of McClellan's inflated 100,000 estimate of Rebel strength in his front. Because Allan Pinkerton had not yet set up his intelligence operation, McClellan had tripled enemy strength all on his own. Once he was locked into this estimate, McClellan had nowhere to go but up. By mid–September, he would claim the enemy had 170,000 troops, and by the following spring the total would be 200,000.[20]

In the first week of August, McClellan denounced Scott's policies to Secretary of State William Seward. McClellan complained to Mary Ellen:

> How does he [Seward] think that I can save this country when stopped by Genl Scott—I do not know whether he is a *dotard* or a *traitor*! I can't tell which. He *cannot* or *will* not comprehend the condition in which we are placed & is entirely unequal to the emergency. If he cannot be taken out of my path I will not retain my position, but will resign & let the admin take care of itself. I have hardly slept one moment for the last three nights, knowing well that the enemy intend some movement & fully recognizing our own weakness. If Beauregard does not attack tonight I shall look upon it as a dispensation of Providence— he *ought* to do it. Every day strengthens me—and I am leaving nothing undone to increase our force—but that confounded old Genl always comes in the way—he is a perfect imbecile. He understands nothing, appreciates nothing & is ever in my way.[21]

On August 9, McClellan again called Scott an "obstacle ... either a traitor or an incompetent," speculated that he (McClellan) would be given an independent command, and concluded, "... I have no choice—the people call upon me to save the country—I *must* save it & cannot respect anything that is in the way." He did allow, however, that "I will never accept the Presidency...."[22] The same day Scott commented to Secretary of War Cameron on McClellan's alarmist letter, "I am confident in the opposite opinion; ... I have not the slightest apprehension for the safety of the Government here." At the same time, however, the old and infirm general-in-chief reacted to McClellan's impudence and asked to be retired.[23] Lincoln tried to dissuade Scott from retiring by successfully requesting McClellan to approve the withdrawal of his August 8 "imminent danger" letter to Scott and by showing the withdrawal approval letter to Scott.

Citing the disrespect and neglect of his "ambitious junior," as well as McClellan's direct communications with Cabinet members, Scott declined to cancel his resignation. He may have been influenced by McClellan's reiteration, in his requested "withdrawal approval" letter to Lincoln, of his "imminent peril" threat and his statements that, "Every moment's reflection and every fact transpiring convinced me of the urgent necessity of the measures there indicated, and I felt it my duty to [Scott] and to the country to communicate them frankly. It is therefore with great pain that I have learned from you this morning that my views do not meet with the approbation of the Lieutenant-General, and that my letter is unfavorably regarded by him." Scott probably doubted McClellan's assurances to Lincoln that, "... I would abstain from any conduct or act that could give offense to General Scott or embarrass the President or any Department of the Government."[24]

On August 12, McClellan expanded his alarms to the Navy. He told Secretary of the Navy Gideon Welles that information indicated the enemy would invade Maryland south of Washington by launching an attack from Aquia Creek on Virginia side of the Potomac.

He even told the Secretary what vessels could be moved where to better defend Washington.[25] A couple of days later, he was still in fear of his real enemy ("... looking out sharply for Beauregard, who I think has some notion of making a dash in this direction.") and his imagined foe ("Genl Scott is the most dangerous antagonist I have—either he or I must leave here...").[26]

Matters, in his mind, were no better on August 16, when he wrote, "... I am here in a terrible place—the enemy have from 3 to 4 times my force—the Presdt is an idiot, the old General in his dotage—they cannot or will not see the true state of affairs. Most of my troops are demoralized by the defeat at Bull Run ... I have, I believe, made the best possible disposition of the few men under my command—will quietly await events & if the enemy attacks will try to make my movements as rapid & desperate as may be.... I have no ambition in the present affairs—only wish to save my country—& find the incapables around me will not permit it."[27] Clearly, Lincoln had joined Scott in the group that McClellan regarded as incompetent or worse.

McClellan continued spreading his apprehensions when he wrote to Brigadier General Charles P. Stone, who was headquartered at Poolesville, Maryland, and commanded a brigade on the Potomac above Washington. He told Stone of the likelihood of Confederate crossings in his area as a prelude to attacking Washington or Baltimore and of indications of a Confederate crossing south of Washington. He set a defensive tone by urging Stone, as well as General Nathaniel P. Banks to the south, to "continually bear in mind the necessity of securing your retreat ... should you be unable to prevent the passage of the enemy."[28]

McClellan seemed not to understand that the North had the burden of winning of the war; his strategy was purely defensive. McClellan's expanding numerical delusions were reflected in his August 19 letter to his wife: "... Beauregard probably has 150,000 men—I cannot count on more than 55,000!"[29] In less than two weeks, he had boosted enemy strength in his front from 100,000 to 150,000, and they were soon to grow in his mind to 170,000. In reality, Johnston by then had no more than 45,000 to 50,000 Rebel troops in the Manassas area. McClellan chose to ignore accurate reports from his own generals. Stephen Sears later marveled: "McClellan himself, an experienced army administrator and engineer, might have wondered at Richmond's ability to maintain such a vast army as Pinkerton described at the end of a single railroad line more than a hundred miles from its home base, particularly since just then he was detailing the trials of supplying and arming his own forces that had yet to venture beyond sight of their depots."[30]

Despite, or perhaps because of, his hostility to Scott, McClellan was elevated to command of the newly-created Army of the Potomac on August 17. He formally assumed command and issued his first army general order on August 20.[31] In that order, McClellan announced his staff, which continued to include his father-in-law, Colonel Marcy, as his inspector general. That same day he forwarded to the president a dispatch, from Marcy in New York, stating that a draft was necessary because men were not volunteering for military service. McClellan recommended that the Secretary of War ascertain the enlistment situation and, if necessary, institute a draft because "We must have men without delay."[32]

On September 6, McClellan made a thoughtful, offensively oriented recommendation to the Secretary of War. He proposed formation of an amphibious military force that would work with the Navy to conduct operations in inlets of the Chesapeake Bay and the Potomac River. The unit, to be part of the Army of the Potomac, would enable troops to be landed along the coast to follow up the army's movements over land. Although the proposal eventually led to a successful waterborne operation in North Carolina in February 1862, McClellan's own onshore movements were non-existent for many months after he made this proposal.[33] This lack of activity was consistent with his September 7 letter to his wife stating, "… Do not expect Beauregard to attack—will not be ready to advance (ourselves) before November…."[34]

An early September exchange of correspondence between Secretary Cameron and McClellan sheds additional light on McClellan's view of the military situation and the importance of his own army. On September 7, Cameron wrote to him, "It is evident that we are on the eve of a great battle—one that may decide the fate of the country. Its success must depend on you, and the means that may be placed at your disposal. Impressed with this belief, and anxious to aid you with all the powers of my Department, I will be glad if you inform me how I can do so."[35] McClellan eagerly responded the next day. He asserted that he had 85,000 troops in the Washington area and would only be able to respond with 60,000 to 70,000 of them to an expected Confederate upstream crossing of the Potomac and movement on Baltimore to cut northern communications with Washington. McClellan, therefore, recommended that his army be reinforced "at once by all the disposable troops that the East and West and North can furnish" and that virtually "the whole of the Regular Army, old and new, be at once ordered to report here."[36]

In a draft of the letter, he had been more specific: "In view of these facts I respectfully urge that all the available troops in Ohio, Indiana, Michigan, Wisconsin and at least ten thousand Illinois troops (there being fifteen thousand there unarmed) and all those of the Eastern and Northern states be at once directed to report to me for duty. I beg leave to repeat the opinion I have heretofore expressed that the Army of the Potomac should number not less than three hundred thousand men in order to insure complete success and an early termination of the war."[37] Very early in the war, therefore, McClellan was so focused on his own perceived needs that he proposed that his army be almost twice the size of any army that either side would ever assemble during the war—and demonstrated that impacts on other Union armies were of little or no concern to him.

Just to be certain that the Secretary of War understood the importance of McClellan and his army, the general also told him:

> In organizing the Army of the Potomac I have selected general and staff officers with distinct reference to their fitness for the important duties that may devolve upon them. Any change or disposition of such officers without consulting the Commanding General may fatally impair the efficiency of this army and the success of its operations. I therefore earnestly request that in future every general officer appointed upon my recommendation shall be assigned to this army; that I shall have full control of the officers and troops in this department, and that no orders shall be given respecting my command without my being first consulted. It is evident that I cannot otherwise be responsible for the success of our arms.[38]

Within weeks of arriving in Washington, therefore, McClellan had established his position that he could not be held accountable for any defeat unless he had a 300,000-man army and unfettered authority with regard to personnel and orders affecting his army. The audacity of this position certainly made him unique among all Civil War generals.

In mid–September, 1861, McClellan oversaw the arrest of secession-minded members of the Maryland Legislature who were meeting secretly in Frederick (instead of the capital of Annapolis) to pass a secession ordinance and perhaps invite a Confederate invasion.[39] He pointed to the legislators' arrests as the reason his dire predictions of a Confederate attack had not been fulfilled: "… The enemy keeps· very quiet & do not seem disposed to move just now—the arrest of the Maryland Legislature has no doubt taken them by surprise & defeated their calculations…."[40]

Meanwhile, the general had continued to sound the alarms of enemy movements and to lobby for enhancement of his own army's strength. On September 13, he wrote to Cameron that all his intelligence indicated the enemy was about to advance or already was doing so. He added that it was more than probable that the enemy was concentrating all its forces—including troops from Missouri and the Mississippi Valley—in front of McClellan and that "it is therefore clear that we must follow the enemy's example and reinforce the Army of the Potomac by all available troops."[41]

To address this perceived crisis, McClellan had suggestions and a warning:

> I am told that Genl Fremont has some fifty thousand troops in the vicinity of St Louis; if this is the case the safety of the nation requires that twenty five thousand of them be sent here without one day's delay; and that the orders already given for other troops to be sent from the West and the East to this Army should be repeated and steps taken to insure immediate compliance with them. Unless the force of the enemy is greatly overrated and all the information I have received concerning it be erroneous it will be found when we meet in the field, that their Active Army outnumbers ours by nearly two to one.

He enclosed calculations showing that he only had 60,000 to 80,000 troops (out of his 122,000) to actively oppose a Confederate incursion and added, "The enemy probably have 170,000!"[42] By mid–September 1861, therefore, McClellan had established a firm and consistent pattern of overestimating enemy strength and urging massive reinforcement of his own army. According to historian Jeffry Wert, "Pinkerton deliberately overstated the number of Rebels, and McClellan knew it. On October 4, when the agent reported Johnston's strength as 98,400, far less than the 170,000 that McClellan had stated earlier, the general did not forward this estimate to the War Department."[43] Pinkerton's exaggerated numbers were insufficient for McClellan.

McClellan's relationship with Scott continued to deteriorate. His perspective on the matter came through clearly in his September 27 letter to Mary Ellen:

> He (the Presdt) sent a carriage for me to meet him & the Cabinet at Genl Scott's office. Before we got through the General "raised a row with me." I kept cool, looked him square in the face, & *rather* I think I got the advantage of him. In the course of the conversation he very strongly intimated that we were no longer friends. I said nothing, merely looked at him, & bowed assent. He tried to avoid me when we left, but I walked square up to him, looked him fully in the eye, extended my hand & said "Good morning, General Scott." He had to take my hand, & so we parted. As he threw down the glove & took it up, I presume war is declared—so be it. I do not fear him. I have one strong point; that I do not care one iota for my present position.[44]

In his diary, Gideon Welles called the meeting an "unpleasant interview," in which Scott complained to Lincoln that he could get no information on the numbers and condition of McClellan's army and implied that McClellan instead was communicating directly with Secretary Seward, who did possess and reveal that information at the meeting. Afterward, Welles reported, Scott rebuked McClellan, "You were called here by my advice. The times require vigilance and activity. I am not active and never shall be again. When I proposed that you should come here to aid, not supersede, me, you had my friendship and confidence. You still have my confidence."[45]

McClellan's written tirades continued on October 2 ("I am becoming daily more disgusted with this administration—perfectly sick of it.")[46] and October 6 ("Genl Scott did try to send some of my troops to Kentucky, but did not succeed—he has become my inveterate enemy!").[47] They reached something of a climax with his explosion of October 11:

I can't tell you how disgusted I am becoming with these wretched politicians—they are a most despicable set of men & I think Seward is the meanest of them all—a meddling, officious, incompetent little puppy—he has done more than any other one man to bring all this misery upon the country & is one of the least competent to get us out of the scrape. The Presdt is nothing more than a well meaning baboon. Welles is weaker than the most garrulous old woman you were ever annoyed by. [Attorney General Edward] Bates is a good inoffensive old man—so it goes—only keep these complimentary opinions to yourself, or you may get me into premature trouble.[48]

McClellan was not, however, losing his focus on Scott and Scott's position. He wrote to Mary Ellen on October 13 that, "I am firmly determined to force the issue with Genl Scott—a very few days will determine whether his policy or mine is to prevail—*he* is for inaction & the defensive, he endeavors to cripple me in every way—yet I see that the newspapers begin to accuse me of want of energy."[49] His wish was granted when the Cabinet, at an October 18 meeting, decided to accept Scott's previously proffered resignation. The next day, McClellan passed the good news on to his wife: "It seems to be pretty well settled that I will be Comdr in Chf within a week. Genl Scott proposes to retire in favor of Halleck. The Presdt & Cabinet have determined to accept his retirement, but *not* in favor of Halleck. The old————-'s antiquity is wonderful and lasting...."[50] Scott, however, remained in command and sought to have someone other than McClellan succeed him; Lincoln would have the final word.

After telling Cameron on September 30 that he was sending 4,000 men to deal with a threatened Confederate blockade on the lower Potomac River and then not sending either them or a later scheduled expedition,[51] McClellan finally did launch an offensive elsewhere—with disastrous results. That disaster was the Battle of Ball's Bluff, which was fought along the upper Potomac River near Leesburg, Virginia. McClellan first encouraged, and then directed, Brigadier General Stone to take Leesburg. He also told Stone that Brigadier General George A. McCall's Union division had occupied nearby Dranesville, Virginia, thereby encouraging Stone to believe that he had support on the Virginia side of the river. But he then failed to advise Stone that he had ordered McCall's troops back to Maryland.[52]

When it appeared that Stone was in trouble after crossing the Potomac, McClellan, on the night of October 21, told him to hold his position "on the Virginia side of the Potomac at all hazards" and "under no circumstances [to] abandon the Virginia shore." He also urged General Banks to push forward to relieve Stone.[53] By then, he was too late. Stone's troops had been routed at Ball's Bluff, and many of them drowned in the Potomac attempting to flee the battlefield. This small-scale disaster resulted in nine hundred twenty Union casualties to a mere one hundred fifty for the Confederates. Just as significantly, it convinced McClellan that his army was unready for battle.[54]

After advising Lincoln of the "serious disaster," McClellan briefly investigated what had occurred and began covering his tracks to escape blame for it. On October 24, he advised his division commanders that the blame lay with the dead Colonel Edward D. Baker (who also was a U.S. Senator from Oregon): "The disaster was caused by errors committed by the immediate commander, not General Stone. I have withdrawn all the troops from the other side, since they went there without my orders and nothing was to be gained by retaining them there."[55] To his wife, he claimed total non-involvement: "That affair at Leesburg ... took place some 40 miles from here without my orders or knowledge—it was entirely unauthorized by me & I am in no manner responsible for it.... During the night I withdrew everything & everybody to this side of the river—which in truth they should never have left."[56]

By continuing his western Virginia policy of avoiding actual battlefields, McClellan hoped to take credit for any victories and avoid responsibility for any defeats. However, it is unclear how McClellan expected Stone to use his troops in Maryland to carry out McClellan's October 21 order to "Take Leesburg," a couple of miles into Virginia from the Potomac, without crossing the river. In fact, McClellan had ordered Stone to cross to, and stay on, the Virginia shore.

A little over three months later, McClellan would issue an arrest order for General Stone as directed by Secretary Stanton. The Joint Committee on the Conduct of the War had heard testimony questioning the loyalty of Stone. The committee was upset that the moderate Stone previously had ordered Massachusetts troops to return runaway slaves and informally decided that he had somehow been indirectly responsible for the death of Republican Senator Baker. McClellan played his apparently reluctant role in mandating the incarceration of Stone at Fort Lafayette in New York Harbor and barring him from communicating with anyone. In one of the injustices of the war, Stone was imprisoned for one hundred eighty-nine days and never formally charged with anything.[57]

Late in 1862, McClellan wrote to Stone that Secretary Stanton had compelled Stone's arrest and thereafter resisted McClellan's pleas for a prompt trial. In a crossed-out portion of a draft of his letter, McClellan wrote that he had intervened with the Joint Committee on Stone's behalf. In reality, McClellan had provided Stanton with a Pinkerton report damning Stone and ensuring that the Joint Committee would hold Stone accountable and not pursue McClellan on the issue.[58]

McClellan soon returned to the major task at hand: superseding Scott as general-in-chief. On the 26th of October, he told Mary Ellen of a three-hour meeting that day with moderate Republican Postmaster General Montgomery Blair and radical Republican Senators Benjamin Wade, Lyman Trumbull, and Zachariah Chandler about "war matters." He reported, "… they will make a desperate effort tomorrow to have Genl Scott retired at once. Until that is accomplished I can effect but little good—he is ever in my way & I am sure does not desire effective action—I want to get thro' with the war as quickly as possible…."[59] The sincerity of that desire would be tested over the course of the next year.

By October 30, McClellan believed the end of Scott's tenure at last was near. He wrote to Mary Ellen, "You may have heard from the papers etc of the small row that is going on just now between Genl Scott & myself—in which the vox populi is coming out strongly on my side…. I presume the Scott war will culminate this week—& as it is now very clear that the people will not permit me to be passed over it seems easy to predict the result." Despite all of his maneuvering to secure the top command, McClellan assured his wife, "I do not feel that I am an instrument worthy of the great task, but I *do* feel that I did not seek it—it was thrust upon me."[60]

McClellan's maneuvers to replace Scott at last resulted in the old soldier's "final" resignation on November 1, 1861. Historian Timothy Johnson concluded, "The aged general's resignation on November 1 signified McClellan's victory. The master of maneuver had been outmaneuvered."[61]

On the last day of October, McClellan told his wife he was "'concealed' at [Edwin M.] Stanton's to dodge all enemies in shape of 'browsing' Presdt etc…." in order to write a long letter to the Secretary of War about future military operations. The paper was, he said, "intended to place on record the fact that I have left nothing undone to make this army what it ought to be & that the necessity for delay has not been my fault." Again he revealed to his wife the extent of his loyalty to the President and his administration:

Cover sheet to "McClellan's Grand March" (1861) reflected high hopes for McClellan's performance (Rare Book, Manuscript, and Special Collections Library, Duke University).

I have a set of scamps to deal with—unscrupulous & false—if possible they will throw whatever blame there is on my shoulders, & I do not intend to be sacrificed by such people. It is
perfectly sickening to have to work with such people & to see the fate of the nation in such
hands. I still trust that the all wise creator does not intend our destruction, & that in his own
good time he will free the nation from imbeciles who curse it & will restore us to his favor. I
know that as a nation we have grievously sinned, but I trust that there is a limit to his wrath
& that ere long we will begin to experience his mercy. But it is terrible to stand by & see the
cowardice of the Presdt, the vileness of Seward, & the rascality of Cameron—Welles is an old
woman—Bates an old fool. The only man of courage & sense in the Cabinet is Blair [who
had conferred with McClellan about dumping Scott], & I do not altogether fancy him![62]

McClellan's final act before becoming general-in-chief (while remaining commander
of the Army of the Potomac) was submission of a misleading October 31 report to the
secretary of war. The report was co-authored by Edwin Stanton, who himself soon would
become the secretary of war. He told the Secretary that there were two options: go into
winter quarters or assume the offensive with fewer troops than required. He outlined a
plan for strengthening the Army of the Potomac, which he deemed necessary because
the enemy allegedly had on the Potomac a force "not less than 150,000 strong, well drilled
and equipped, ably commanded & strongly intrenched." To combat that number, based
on estimates from Pinkerton and subordinate Brigadier General Winfield Scott Hancock,
McClellan contended he needed a force of 240,000 troops, about 72,000 more than cur-
rently in his army. He recommended that all new men and weapons, as well as "surplus
troops" from elsewhere be sent to the Army of the Potomac and that no offensives be
initiated anywhere else.[63]

McClellan was basing his recommendations on inflated estimates of Confederate
strength. Who was responsible for them—McClellan or Pinkerton? An authoritative analysis by Edwin Fishel concluded that McClellan was primarily responsible and Pinkerton
helped. Prior to McClellan's October 31 estimate of 150,000 Rebels, Pinkerton had provided him with an October 4 estimate of 98,400, "a figure 42 percent less than McClellan had estimated to Cameron, but about 70 percent above [the Rebels'] true strength."
In a November 15 letter to McClellan, Pinkerton said that the October 4 estimate "was
made large, as intimated to you at the time, so as to be sure and cover the entire number
of the Enemy...." About this, Fishel concluded, "Here is unmistakable evidence not only
that Pinkerton was padding the troop totals, but also that McClellan was aware of the
padding."[64] Pinkerton's October 4 report and November 15 attempt to rationalize it in
light of lower numbers reported later by his best operative were riddled with self-evident
mathematical and logical errors; these problems may have been one reason that McClellan never forwarded Pinkerton's documents to Cameron or Lincoln.[65] Another reason
may be that McClellan was not satisfied with the padded 98,400 figure and added more
than fifty percent to it when he advised his superiors that the enemy numbered 150,000.[66]

Although Stanton ultimately changed his language, McClellan's draft closing of his
memo to Secretary Cameron provided good insight into his thinking as he assumed command of all Union armies: "But I wish to have again on record the fact that I have neither underestimated the force of the enemy [never a problem for him] nor failed to
perceive the means by which that force may be broken. I urge as the only means of salvation the energetic course which has ever been my choice. No time is to be lost—we
have lost too much already—every consideration requires us to prepare at once, but not
to move until we are ready."[67] The latter refrain would become more and more familiar
in the following months as McClellan dithered while other Union armies achieved
offensive successes.

4

Evading Battle as General-in-Chief

As general-in-chief of all Union armies and commander of the Army of the Potomac, McClellan sat motionless on the banks of the Potomac (while Union armies swept over the Confederates on several other fronts), continued to inflate the enemy's imaginary numbers in Virginia, defied and denigrated the president, lost the confidence of Lincoln, and was removed as general-in-chief on the threshold of the first significant campaign he had been compelled to undertake.

From November 1, 1861, to March 11, 1862, McClellan held the two most powerful positions in the Union military structure: general-in-chief and commander of the Army of the Potomac. Because his wife lived with him in Washington during most of this time, there were fewer of his frank and revealing letters to her. Nevertheless, there is much evidence of the president's desire for action and the general's disinclination to fulfill that desire.

On the night before his ascension to Scott's position, McClellan told his wife of the likelihood of that occurrence and, in his self-deluded fashion, wrote, "I feel a sense of relief at the prospect of having my own way untrammeled, but I cannot discover in my own heart one symptom of gratified vanity or ambition."[1] Although Lincoln would defer to him for some time, the general would soon learn that he was accountable to the president, the secretary of war, and Congress and thus would not have his "own way untrammeled."

Upon assuming command, McClellan issued a flowery general order lavishly praising General Scott's service to his country.[2] A few days later, McClellan commented about the order to Mary Ellen: "I am glad to learn that my order (the military obituary) changed Genl Scott's feelings entirely, & that he now says I am the best man & the best General that ever existed! Such is human nature—the order *was* a little rhetorical—but I wrote it *at* him—for a particular market! It seems to have accomplished the object."[3]

One of the General-in-chief's first duties was to escort General Scott to Union Station for his early morning departure from Washington on November 2. McClellan appears to have had mixed feelings about the event:

> I have already been up once this morning—that was at 4 o'clock to escort Genl Scott to the depot—it was pitch dark & pouring rain—but with most of the staff & a squadron of

35

cavalry I saw the old man off. He was very polite to me.... The old man said that his sensations were very peculiar in leaving Washn & active life—I can easily understand them— & it may be that at some distant day I too shall totter away from Washn—a worn out soldier, with naught to do but make my peace with God. The sight of this morning was a lesson to me which I hope not soon to forget. I saw the end of a long, active & ambitious life—the end of the career of the first soldier of his nation—& it was a feeble old man scarce able to walk—hardly anyone there to see him off but his successor. Should I ever become vainglorious & ambitious remind me of that spectacle.[4]

It was too late for the requested warning.

Time would quickly tell whether McClellan was capable of performing dual duties as general-in-chief with national oversight and commander of the Army of the Potomac in the eastern theater. When the president expressed concern about the vast labor involved in both positions, the general responded confidently, "I can do it all."[5] In reality, he eventually proved that he could do neither effectively.

In a November 7 set of instructions to Major General Don Carlos Buell, Commander of the Department of Ohio, McClellan directed him to move from Bowling Green, Kentucky, against Knoxville, Tennessee, in order to support the loyal Unionists there and to disrupt railroad communication between Virginia and the Mississippi (and presumably any reinforcements to the army facing McClellan in Virginia). He also provided directions not to interfere with slavery in Kentucky (without ever mentioning the word "slavery"): "The inhabitants of Kentucky may rely upon it that their domestic institutions will in no manner be interfered with, and that they will receive at our hands every constitutional protection. I have only to repeat that you will in all respects carefully regard the local institutions of the region in which you command, allowing nothing but the dictates of military necessity to cause you to depart from the spirit of these instructions."[6] A day later, in a letter to a friend and business associate, McClellan left no doubt about his views on this subject: "Help me to dodge the nigger—we want nothing to do with him. *I* am fighting to preserve the integrity of the Union & the power of the Govt—on no other issue. To gain that end we cannot afford to raise up the negro question—it must be incidental & subsidiary."[7]

In that same letter, McClellan explained his reluctance to advance at that time: "I feel however that the issue of this struggle is to be decided by the next great battle, & that I owe it to my country & myself not to advance until I have reasonable chances in my favor." He was sensitive about political and newspaper criticism of his inactivity: "As far as you can, keep the papers & the politicians from running over me—that speech that some rascal made the other day that I did *not dare* to advance, & had said so, was a lie— I have always said, when it was necessary to say anything, that I was not yet strong enough—but, did the public service require it, I would *dare* to advance with 10,000 men & throw my life in the balance."[8] Even in a November 15 letter to Secretary Cameron, McClellan felt compelled to address the inactivity issue: "So long as I retain my present position I must claim to be the best judge of the time to strike—I repeat, what you already know, that no one is more anxious to terminate speedily this fratricidal war than I am."[9]

McClellan's inactivity that pleasant autumn brought his honeymoon in Washington to a sour end. Historian James M. McPherson later wrote of this period, "McClellan's failings began to manifest themselves. He was a perfectionist in a profession where nothing could ever be perfect. His army was perpetually *almost* ready to move, but could not do so until the last horse was shoed and the last soldier fully equipped. McClellan was afraid to risk failure, so he risked nothing."[10]

In mid-November, McClellan reinforced his views on the limited purpose of the war.

On November 11, he wrote to Halleck, the new commander of the Department of Missouri, that, "In regard to the political conduct of affairs, you will please labor to impress upon the inhabitants of Missouri and the adjacent States that we are fighting solely for the integrity of the Union, to uphold the power of our National Government, and to restore to the nation the blessings of peace and good order."[11] The next day he wrote similar words to General Buell and reiterated his concerns about people's rights: "In regard to political matters, bear in mind that we are fighting only to preserve the integrity of the Union and to uphold the power of the General Government. As far as military necessity will permit religiously respect the constitutional rights of all." He then went on to warn against arbitrary arrests.[12]

After bemoaning Negro slaves' susceptibility to mistreatment, he assured Mary Ellen that he was not an abolitionist: "... when the day of adjustment comes I will, if successful, throw my sword into the scale to force an improvement in the condition of those poor blacks. I will never be an abolitionist, but I do think that some of the rights of humanity ought to be secured to the negroes—there should be no power to separate families & the right of marriage ought to be secured to them.... I will not fight for the abolitionists...."[13] In fact, McClellan and his key appointees were "soft" on slavery and the South; they did not want to engage in a war to destroy slavery.[14] This softness led Postmaster-General Blair to write of McClellan, "Lincoln himself begins to think he smells a rat."[15]

The elevation in power and passage of time did not reduce McClellan's disrespect for President Lincoln. On November 17, he wrote to Mary Ellen, "I went to the White House shortly after tea where I found 'the *original gorilla*' about as intelligent as ever. What a specimen to be at the head of our affairs now! ... After I left the Prince's I went to Seward's, where I found the 'Gorilla' again, & was of course much edified by his anecdotes—ever apropos, & ever unworthy of one holding his high position.... It is a terrible dispensation of providence that so weak & cowardly a thing as [Seward] should now control our foreign relations—unhappily the Presdt is not much better, except that he is honest & means well. I suppose our country has richly merited some great punishment, else we should not now have such wretched triflers at the head of affairs...."[16] He may have acquired the "gorilla" terminology about Lincoln from Stanton, who had been President James Buchanan's attorney general and was briefly an ally of McClellan in late 1861.[17]

All too soon, McClellan began openly showing disrespect for the president. When Lincoln arranged a conference with Governor Dennison of Ohio, a Union general, and McClellan, the commanding general chose not to appear. Although the president's other invitees were angered by this action, a resigned Lincoln said, "Never mind. I will hold McClellan's horse if he will only bring us success."[18]

That event was followed in mid–November by an even more blatant snub of the president. On the evening of November 13, the president, Seward and John Hay came to McClellan's home to confer with him. After they had waited an hour because McClellan was out, the general returned, went straight upstairs to his room and ignored their presence. When, a half hour later, the three visitors asked the servant to tell him they were waiting, the servant responded that the general had gone to bed. Although Hay denounced this "unparalleled insolence of epaulettes," Lincoln seemed unperturbed. However, Lincoln rarely again called on McClellan at his quarters but instead summoned him to meetings.[19]

In three early December letters, McClellan encouraged and urged Buell to move troops from eastern Kentucky to eastern Tennessee to support the many Union loyalists there. In addition, he encouraged him to move with the bulk of his troops on the Tennessee capital of Nashville and agreed with Buell's recommendation to send flotilla

SONGS FOR THE UNION.

HOW McCLELLAN TOOK MANASSAS.

BY OLD NAPOLEON.

HEARD ye how the bold McClellan—
He, the wether with the bell on ;
He, the head of all the asses—
Heard ye how he took Manassas ?

When the Anaconda plucky
Flopped its tail in old Kentucky ;
When up stream the gunboats paddled,
And the thieving Floyd skedaddled,
Then the chief of all the asses
Heard the word : Go, take Manassas !

Forty brigades wait around him,
Forty blatant trumpets sound him,
As the pink of all the heroes
Since the time of fiddling Neros :
"Now's the time," cry out the masses,
"Show your pluck and take Manassas ! "

Contrabands come flocking to him :
" Lo ! the enemy flies—pursue him ! "
"No," says George, "don't start a trigger
On the word of any nigger ;
Let no more of the rascals pass us,
I know all about Manassas."

When at last a prowling Yankee—
No doubt long, and lean, and lanky—
Looking out for new devises,
Took the wooden guns as prizes,
Says he : " I sweow, ere daylight passes,
I'll take a peep at famed Manassas." -

Printed for the Union Congressional Committee by John A. Gray & Green, New-York.

Above and opposite: An 1862 song sheet, "How McClellan Took Manassas," mocked McClellan's occupation of Manassas after a peaceful Confederate withdrawal (Library of Congress).

2 SONGS FOR THE UNION.

Then up the trenches boldly
Marched he—they received him coldly;
Nary reb was there to stop him,
Nary Minié-ball to drop him;
Gathering courage, in he passes:
"Jerusalem! I've took Manassas."

Bold McClellan heard the story:
"Onward, men, to fields of glory;
Let us show the rebel foemen,
When we're READY we're not slow, men;
Wait no more for springing grasses—
Onward! onward! to Manassas!"

Baggage-trains are left behind him,
In his eagerness to find them;
Upward the balloons ascended,
To see which way the rebels tended;
Thirty miles away his glasses
Swept the horizon round Manassas.

Out of sight, the foe, retreating,
Answered back no hostile greeting;
None could tell, as off he paddled,
Whitherward he had skedaddled.
Then the chief of all the asses
Cried: "Hurrah! I've got Manassas."

Future days will tell the wonder,
How the mighty Anaconda
Lay supine along the border,
With the mighty Mac to lord her;
Tell on shaft and storied brasses
How he took the famed Manassas.

columns up the Tennessee and Cumberland rivers. At one point, McClellan suggested that Buell's movements might be launched simultaneously with his own in the East.[20] Nothing significant resulted from these suggestions from one slow-moving general to another.

As November turned into December, Lincoln and other civilian leaders in Washington were growing impatient. On November 20, they and 30,000 other spectators had seen 65,000 of McClellan's soldiers march in a grand review; they began to wonder when they would fight instead of parade. As historian Joseph Waugh explained, "Many ... began to ask angrily when this great army planned to attack Richmond. Five months now had passed since the young Napoleon had come out of the West on the wings of such hope and expectation. The only thing to show for it was organization, dress reviews, drills, one unfruitful reconnaissance, and a minor Union disaster at Ball's Bluff near Leesburg." The Rebels in northern Virginia, outnumbered two-to-one, were puzzled that they had not been attacked during the Indian summer, which dried the roads and made an offensive attractive.[21]

McClellan talked about his planned movements but did not actually move forward with his assembled force. Commented historians Robert Pois and Philip Langer: "Not without cause, Lincoln decided it was time to use that army to fight the Confederates. Unfortunately, this was a concept McClellan never enthusiastically embraced. The process of procrastination began immediately. He dragged his heels every time the Government tried to prod him into action."[22]

During the fall and winter of 1861–62, estimating enemy strength by McClellan's generals was hampered by a headquarters order prohibiting their examination of persons coming through the lines and by restrictions on the movement of scouts. Thus, they had little idea of enemy strength, and the estimates ranged from 70,000 to 210,000. The Joint Committee acidly commented, "Those who formed the highest estimate based their opinion on information received at headquarters. As to the strength of the enemy's position, the general impression seemed to be, founded on information obtained from the same source, that it was exceedingly formidable. Subsequent events have proved that the force of the enemy was below even the lowest of these estimates, and the strength of their fortifications very greatly overestimated."[23]

At that same time, McClellan was resisting the first of Lincoln's specific recommendations that he initiate hostilities. On about December 1, Lincoln recommended that he advance south from Alexandria to the area of the Occoquan River to interrupt rail transportation of supplies to the Rebels at Manassas. On December 10, the General responded, "Information received recently leads me to believe that the enemy could meet us in front with equal forces nearly, and I have now my mind actively turned toward another plan of campaign that I do not think at all anticipated by the enemy nor by many of our own people."[24]

Simultaneously, McClellan corresponded with Halleck about the possibility of Mississippi Valley advances. He asked, "Can you yet form any idea of the time necessary to prepare an expedition against Columbus [in Kentucky on the Mississippi River] or one up the Cumberland and Tennessee rivers, in connection with Buell's movements?"[25]

During December, McClellan's lack of aggressiveness and failure to cooperate led Secretary of the Navy Welles to discuss McClellan with Salmon P. Chase, whom Welles and others regarded as his sponsor. Looking back the following September, Welles recalled, "McClellan's hesitating course last fall, his indifference and neglect of my many applications to cooperate with the Navy, his failure in many instances to fulfill his promises, when the Rebels were erecting batteries on the west bank of the Potomac, that they might close the navigation of the river, had shaken my confidence in his efficiency and reliability, for he was not deficient in sagacity or intelligence. But at that time McClellan was a general favorite, and neither he (Chase) nor any one heeded my doubts and apprehensions."[26]

Welles complained to the president and cabinet of McClellan's lack of cooperation that had led to the Rebels' blocking Potomac transportation:

> ... I had been put off by General McClellan with broken promises and frivolous and unsatisfactory answers.... To me it seemed he had no plan or policy of his own, or any realizing sense of the true state of affairs.... He was occupied with reviews, and dress-parades, perhaps with drills and discipline, but was regardless of the necessities of the case,—the political aspect of the question, the effect of the closing of the only avenue from the National Capital to the ocean, and the embarrassment which would follow to the Government itself were the river blockaded.[27]

The Joint Committee later obtained and cited Assistant Secretary of the Navy Gustavus V. Fox's testimony that McClellan during this period had declined to furnish 4,000 troops to destroy the batteries even though he had agreed to do so and the navy was prepared to transport them.[28]

Although he was stricken with typhoid fever on December 23, 1861, McClellan, on January 3, 1862, directed Halleck to send an expedition up the Cumberland River to protect Buell's flank, to support his gunboats with one or two of his best infantry divisions, to make a feint up the Tennessee River, and to demonstrate against or capture Columbus, Kentucky.[29] Again, nothing came of this interaction between two of the Union's least aggressive generals.

In a letter to Buell three days later, McClellan made it clear that the Mississippi Valley movements were secondary only and that his primary concern was a movement by Buell into eastern Tennessee:

> My own general plans for the prosecution of the war make the speedy occupation of East Tennessee and its lines of railway matters of absolute necessity. Bowling Green and Nashville are in that connection of very secondary importance at the present moment. My own advance cannot, according to my present views, be made until your troops are solidly established in the eastern portion of Tennessee. If that is not possible, a complete and prejudicial change in my own plans at once becomes necessary.[30]

It appears that McClellan saw the primary mission of the western troops as ensuring that Confederate reinforcements would be blocked from coming eastward to oppose McClellan.

McClellan confirmed this intent in a letter to Buell the following week. He said, "the pressure brought to bear here upon the Government for a forward movement ... is so strong that it seems absolutely necessary to make the advance on Eastern Tennessee at once. I incline to this as a first step for many reasons. Your possession of the railroad there will surely prevent the main army in my front from being re-enforced and may force [Confederate Western commander Albert Sydney] Johnston to detach. Its political effect will be very great."[31] Thus, Halleck was to protect Buell, and Buell was to protect McClellan.

One offensive movement was initiated—one that had been in the planning and organizational stages before McClellan became general-in-chief. On January 7, he gave the green light for Burnside to launch his joint army/navy campaign against Roanoke Island on the North Carolina coast. The ambitious plans called for Burnside to move inland to capture Newbern (New Bern) and Goldsboro to interrupt rail transportation—and also to seize the port at Fort Macon. The seizure of the major port of Wilmington also was authorized. Once again, McClellan addressed the issue of slavery:

I would urge great caution in regard to proclamation. In no case would I go beyond a moderate joint proclamation with the naval commander, which should say as little as possible about politics or the Negro. Merely state that the true issue for which we are fighting is the preservation of the Union and upholding the laws of the General Government, and stating that all who conduct themselves properly will as far as possible be protected in their persons and property.[32]

Meanwhile, McClellan was throwing a damper on suggestions that forces in his own army take the offensive closer to Washington. In a January 7 telegram to Banks, McClellan chastised Brigadier General Frederick W. Lander as "too suggestive and critical" for recommending and demanding orders to cross the upper Potomac and attack the raiding forces of Major General Thomas J. "Stonewall" Jackson. Lander had defended the town of Hancock, Maryland, against a January 5 attack by Jackson's troops.[33]

Around December 31, McClellan's typhoid fever worsened, and he was unable to carry out his normal duties during the first two weeks of 1862. His illness led to speculation about his replacement and to growing frustration over the inaction of the Army of the Potomac. Attorney General Bates wrote in his diary, "It seems as if all military operations were to stop, just because Genl McClellan is sick! The Sec. Of War and the President himself are kept in ignorance of the actual condition of the army and the intended movements of the General."[34]

At the urging of his cabinet, Lincoln began taking steps to fill the military leadership vacuum. He exchanged telegrams with Generals Halleck in St. Louis and Buell in Louisville. The president unsuccessfully urged them to take offensive action. When, on January 10, the president went to McClellan's home for advice, he was told that the general was too ill to see him. In desperation, Lincoln then consulted his friend, Quartermaster General Montgomery C. Meigs, who urged him to talk to some of the generals in the Army of the Potomac.[35]

That very evening Lincoln met at the White House with Brigadier Generals Irvin McDowell and William B. Franklin. McDowell was not a supporter of McClellan, but Franklin was a friend and supporter of his. Seeking the generals' advice, Lincoln said if McClellan did not want to use the Army of the Potomac, he would like to "borrow it." McDowell recommended that the army be organized into four corps and that they be used to assault Joseph Johnston's Rebel troops at Centreville, near Manassas. Franklin instead favored a water-borne movement to the York River followed by a movement on Richmond. Franklin thereby provided Lincoln with his first insight into McClellan's previously undisclosed plans for what would become the Peninsula Campaign.[36]

Lincoln directed the two generals to explore both options. In the course of deciding whether to alert McClellan to their deliberations, they consulted Treasury Secretary Chase. He advised them they need not alert McClellan and then amazed them by revealing that the commanding general had discussed with him a plan to take his army by water to Urbana on the Rappahannock and then on to Richmond.[37] It became clear, therefore, that McClellan was discussing his future plans, which he would not share with the president, with at least one cabinet member.

At a January 12 meeting with Lincoln, Blair, Seward, and Chase, Franklin and McDowell recommended that an early movement be made by land to Centreville rather than by water to somewhere else. Lincoln told them to discuss water transportation with Meigs and return later that day. Meigs advised the generals that it would take four to six weeks to assemble sufficient transportation for a movement of the army by water.[38]

While they conferred with Meigs, an angry McClellan suddenly showed up at the Executive Mansion. Chase had confided in soon-to-be-War Secretary Stanton, who in turn told McClellan what was going on. He told him, "They are counting on your death and already dividing among themselves your military goods and chattels." After McClellan provided Lincoln with a vague idea of his plans, Lincoln told him he was glad to see him up from his sickbed and invited him to a meeting the next day. That afternoon Lincoln held only a brief meeting with McDowell, Franklin and others; he invited them all to the meeting with McClellan the next day.[39]

At the Executive Mansion conference on January 13, McClellan refused to divulge his plans for the Army of the Potomac. His disrespect for Lincoln and refusal to share his plans became clear in a dialogue he had with Meigs during the meeting. Meigs whispered to him, "The president evidently expects you to speak; can you not promise some movement towards Manassas? You are strong." McClellan insisted to Meigs that the enemy had at least 175,000 with which to contest his army. After McClellan continued, "I cannot move on them with as great a force as they have," Meigs insisted, "The president expects something from you." McClellan blurted, "If I tell him my plans, they will be in the *New York Herald* tomorrow morning. He can't keep a secret; he will tell them to [his son] Tad." Meigs had the final word: "That is a pity, but he is the President—the Commander-in-Chief. He has a right to know; it is not respectful to sit mute when he so clearly requires you to speak."[40] (Ironically, two days later, McClellan himself would give a three-hour briefing on the military situation and his strategy to a *Herald* correspondent.)[41]

McClellan finally began to talk at the conference, but he merely rambled. After Chase pushed him for specifics, McClellan responded that he would not be interrogated by the treasury secretary and only needed to answer to the president or secretary of war—if ordered to do so. Finally, he did, however, agree to press Buell forward with an advance in Kentucky and assured Lincoln he had a plan for using the Army of the Potomac. The president pointedly declined to order him to disclose it and then adjourned the meeting.[42]

Two days later, however, McClellan called Halleck "premature" for ordering a demonstration toward Columbus, Kentucky, to divert attention away from Buell's supposed advance in central and eastern Kentucky. McClellan told Lincoln that "Buell will check [Halleck's] feint until the proper time arrives."[43]

Meanwhile, Welles and the Navy were dissatisfied with McClellan's failure to cooperate with them on undertaking a New Orleans Campaign and on eliminating the Confederate batteries that blocked the Potomac River. Thus, he and Secretary of War Stanton both requested the president to issue an order demanding an offensive.[44] On January 27, an equally frustrated Lincoln responded by issuing his General Orders No. 1 directing a February 22 general movement against the enemy by Union land and naval forces.

Although this order ultimately encouraged Halleck to authorize Grant to move against Fort Henry on the Tennessee River,[45] its impact on McClellan was negligible. McClellan could not make up his mind about what to do. On January 26, he told Stanton about his interest in a massive transfer of troops from the East to Kentucky. Three days later he agreed with Halleck's recommendation of a movement up the Cumberland and Tennessee rivers in lieu of a movement down the Mississippi. That same day he wired Halleck and Buell that a deserter had reported that Beauregard was about to leave for Kentucky with fifteen Rebel regiments. This erroneous information led Halleck to finally approve Ulysses Grant's recommendation for a movement up the Tennessee River against Fort Henry before Beauregard arrived with reinforcements.[46]

Back in the East, Lincoln finally, on January 31, compelled McClellan to reveal his campaign plan (the Urbana Plan). The president did so by issuing Special War Orders

No. 1 directing execution of the president's own Occoquan Plan. Because McClellan opposed Lincoln's plan for a movement, via a crossing of the Occoquan River, against the Confederate forces at Manassas, he quickly sought permission to submit his own plan—at long last. He worked all weekend and, on Monday, February 3, in a letter to Stanton, McClellan outlined his past actions and plans, described problems with Lincoln's plan, and proposed a waterborne movement of the Army of the Potomac to a position closer to Richmond. He said that he had hoped to gain possession of the eastern Tennessee railroads and then move immediately on Richmond and Nashville but that he had been thwarted by the lack of readiness of the western armies. He opposed Lincoln's plan to move against the Rebels at Manassas as difficult to carry out and unlikely to achieve significant results. After achieving mere possession of the battlefield and Confederate evacuation of the upper Potomac line, he contended, the Union troops would still have a long overland route to Richmond and would have forced the enemy into an undesirable concentration of its forces.[47]

Instead, McClellan urged Stanton (and thus Lincoln), the Army of the Potomac should go to the lower Chesapeake Bay and move on Richmond via a shorter and better route available there. He predicted the Rebels would then have to abandon Manassas to defend Richmond. He foresaw great, and even grandiose, results: "This movement, if successful, gives us the capital, the communications, the supplies of the rebels. Norfolk would fall, all the waters of the Chesapeake would be ours, all Virginia would be in our power, and the enemy forced to abandon Tennessee and North Carolina." But that was not all: "After a successful battle our position would be: Burnside forming our left, Norfolk held securely; our center connecting Burnside with Buell, both by Raleigh and Lynchburg; Buell in Eastern Tennessee and North Alabama; Halleck at Nashville and Memphis."[48]

To carry out his plan, McClellan recommended a landing at Urbana on the lower Rappahannock River—a three-day march from Richmond. His alternatives were "Mob Jack Bay; or, the worst coming to the worst, we can take Fort Monroe as a base, and operate with complete security, although with less celerity and brilliancy of results, up the Peninsula." Aware of Lincoln's concern for the safety of the capital, he assured that, "This movement, if adopted, will not at all expose the city of Washington to danger." McClellan requested immediate authorization for the movement via Urbana, stated that it could be done simultaneously with the final advance of Buell and Halleck, and concluded, "I will stake my life, my reputation on the result—more than that, I will stake upon it the success of our cause."[49]

In the western theater, meanwhile, there was actual offensive movement by Union troops. On February 4, Grant had moved from Paducah up the Tennessee River toward Confederate Fort Henry. On February 6, McClellan belatedly wrote Grant's superior, Henry Halleck: "The roads being impassable between Buell and his opponents, it now becomes a question whether we cannot throw all our available force by the two rivers upon Nashville. Can we move there now in that manner?" After Halleck responded that Rebel reinforcements at Fort Henry might be too strong for Grant and the accompanying navy vessels, McClellan wired Buell: "Halleck telegraphs that Fort Henry largely reenforced from Columbus and Bowling Green. If road so bad in your front, had we not better throw all available force on Forts Henry and Donelson [on the Cumberland River near Fort Henry]? What think you of making that the main line of operations? Answer quick." Buell concurred but warned the operation would be hazardous.[50]

Despite the hesitancy of McClellan, Halleck, and Buell, Grant and Flag Officer Andrew H. Foote moved quickly up the Tennessee River and captured Fort Henry after a mere two-hour artillery duel. The same day, February 7, McClellan received telegrams from Halleck advising him of the capture of Fort Henry and requesting transfer of troops from Buell to him. McClellan responded with a congratulatory wire telling him to forget Columbus and to gather "a sufficient force near Forts Henry and Donelson to make success sure." He gave further instructions: "Either Buell or yourself should soon go to the scene of operations. Why not have Buell take the line of Tennessee and operate on Nashville, while your troops turn Columbus? Those two points gained, a combined movement on Memphis will be next in order." He also sent his thanks to Grant, Foote, and their commands.[51]

On February 12, McClellan wrote to Burnside, who had captured Roanoke Island. He urged Burnside to proceed inland to Goldsboro, told him of the Fort Henry victory, and concluded, "Everything goes well with us but your success seems to be the most brilliant yet. I expect still more from you."[52] Two days later McClellan told Brigadier General Thomas W. Sherman, commanding at Port Royal, South Carolina, to bombard and capture Fort Pulaski near Savannah, Georgia; to take Savannah only if he could do so without a time-consuming siege, and to begin planning for an assault on Charleston, South Carolina. He cautioned, "Fleets are *en route* and armies in motion which have certain preliminary objects to accomplish before we are ready to take Charleston in hand...." He concluded optimistically, "Success attends us everywhere at present."[53]

As Grant was winning battlefield successes, Halleck tried to capitalize on them. He never bothered to acknowledge Grant's aggressiveness or his successes but instead took the opportunity to advance his own interests. On February 8, Halleck recommended to McClellan that the western forces be reorganized into a single Western Division and that Halleck be in command with Buell, Ethan Allen Hitchcock, and David Hunter as his lieutenants. In responding on February 14, McClellan pointed out that Hunter was senior to Halleck and sought more details about the western troops on the Cumberland and Tennessee rivers. He also said that if Halleck was not going to those river sites, he (McClellan) would probably have Buell move up the Tennessee as far as Nashville.[54] The next day McClellan inquired directly of Grant, "Telegraph in full the state of affairs with you." But Grant did not receive this telegram in the field until March 3.[55]

Instead of achieving sole control in the West, Halleck was seeing his own territory being opened to incursion by Buell from central Kentucky. Halleck argued against McClellan's suggestion that Buell move on Nashville and recommended that Buell instead assist Grant at Fort Donelson and then move into Alabama.[56] But McClellan responded that an advance on Nashville by Buell would cut off and force the retreat of the Confederates at Donelson. Thus, McClellan directed Buell to move from Bowling Green to Nashville and then provide assistance to Grant if Confederates remained at Fort Donelson.[57] He then advised Stanton that "We have a brilliant chance to bag Nashville," and that he had "taken such steps as will make Grant safe & I think force the evacuation of Donelson or its surrender."[58]

Grant accepted the surrender of Fort Donelson and an army of 14,000 troops before Buell had come close to Nashville or Donelson. Grant's only problems were to his rear, where Buell slowly moved toward Nashville and sought reinforcements while Halleck sought reinforcements from Buell to move on Columbus, Kentucky (which, unknown to him, the Rebels would soon abandon).[59] After Grant's double victory, Halleck haughtily demanded of McClellan, "I must have command of the armies in the West. Hesitation and delay are losing us the golden opportunity. Lay this before the President and Secretary of War. May I assume the command? Answer quickly." McClellan replied that he would not act before he had heard from Buell.[60]

While Grant won victories and Halleck and Buell squabbled about command and reinforcements, McClellan stood still in Washington. He did draft (but not issue) an order to the Army of the Potomac announcing the "glorious victories" at "Mill Spring[s] [in eastern Kentucky], Roanoke, Fort Henry & Fort Donelson," and pronouncing that, "The time has well nigh arrived when your mission is to be accomplished," and "You have battles to win, fatigues to endure, sufferings to encounter, but remember that they will conduct you to a goal from which you will return, covered with glory, to your homes, & that each one of you will bear through life the proud honor of being one of the men who crushed the most wicked rebellion that ever threatened free institutions & a beneficent government."[61] Perhaps McClellan withheld the order for fear of reminding his troops that Union soldiers elsewhere were actually attacking Confederates.

In denying reinforcements to Buell, McClellan held on to his own Army of the Potomac troops: "At present no troops will move from East. Ample occupation for them here. Rebels hold firm at Manassas Junction."[62] In a delaying letter to Lincoln, McClellan appeared to take credit for the recent victories that had occurred without his meaningful involvement: "I am pushing to prompt completion the measures of which we have spoken, & I beg that you will not allow military affairs to give you one moment's trouble [Lincoln's son, Willie, had just died]—but that you will rest assured that nothing shall be left undone to follow up the successes that have been such an auspicious commencement of our new campaign."[63] Meanwhile, the General told Buell of his grand plans in the East: "If the force in West can take Nashville or even hold its own for the present, I hope to have Richmond and Norfolk in from three to four weeks."[64]

McClellan remained willing to impose herculean tasks on others—even tasks that he had declined. In late January, he had recommended suspension of an army-navy operation against New Orleans, the South's major port—an operation he told Secretary Stanton would require 30,000 to 50,000 troops and which he expected to command. By February 23, however, he was ordering Major General Benjamin F. Butler to take command of such a force with a mere 15,255 troops, possibly augmented by almost 3,000 troops that might be borrowed from Union commands in Florida. Not only was Butler's expedition to capture and hold New Orleans; it also was expected to move on to Baton Rouge, Jackson (Mississippi), Mobile, Pensacola, and Galveston—possibly with reinforcements being provided.[65]

McClellan had similarly grandiose plans for the western troops. On February 24, he wired Halleck that he should cooperate with Buell to secure Nashville and seize Decatur, Alabama, and that Buell would be ordered to occupy and hold Chattanooga in southeastern Tennessee. McClellan also wanted Halleck to move on Memphis, Tennessee, or Columbus, Kentucky, on the Mississippi River and to occupy Corinth in northwestern Mississippi.[66]

Although McClellan expected his western generals to move against positions hundreds of miles distant, he could not even move his own troops the fifty or so miles from Harpers Ferry to Winchester, Virginia. In late February, the general-in-chief involved himself in the minutiae of an attempted movement from Harpers Ferry against Confederates in Virginia upstream from Washington. In addition to rebuilding the crucial east/west Baltimore & Ohio Railroad bridge at Harpers Ferry, McClellan intended to cross the Potomac and move on Winchester. On February 26, McClellan's Union troops threw a temporary bridge across the Potomac near Harpers Ferry and had crossed 8,500 infantry troops, at least twelve guns, and two cavalry squadrons into Virginia by that night. Then McClellan wired Stanton of his success and his plans to build the next day a permanent bridge consisting of canal boats.[67]

Early that next day, McClellan wrote to Mary Ellen of the "magnificent spectacle—

one of the grandest I ever saw" that occurred when his men and guns crossed the river.[68] That afternoon, however, he had bad news for Stanton: "The lift-lock is too small to permit the canal-boats to enter the river, so that it is impossible to construct the permanent bridge, as I intended. I shall probably be obliged to fall back upon the safe and slow plan of merely covering the reconstruction of the railroad.... I cannot, as things now are, be sure of my supplies for the force necessary to seize Winchester, which is probably re-enforced from Manassas. The wiser plan is to rebuild the railroad bridge as rapidly as possible, and then act according to the state of affairs."[69]

Because the canal boats that were to be used to construct a permanent bridge were a few inches too wide to fit through the canal locks, McClellan had to abandon the bridge project. However, he panicked and cancelled his entire operation. The next day he wired Lincoln that supply problems kept him from advancing to Winchester and added hopefully, "I know that I have acted wisely, and that you will cheerfully agree with me when I explain."[70] In fact, Lincoln and Stanton were infuriated at McClellan's failure and lack of offensive progress.

McClellan's self-serving explanation of the fiasco written a couple of days later did nothing to assuage their concerns. In fact, the following note on that document by McClellan shows that he was becoming aware of presidential concerns about his performance but convinced himself that the trouble would pass: "While up the river I learned that the President was dissatisfied with the state of affairs, but on my return here understood from the Secretary of War that upon learning the whole state of the case the President was fully satisfied."[71] Within days, McClellan would learn that the president was not fully satisfied with the state of affairs. In fact, Lincoln (with McClellan away from Washington) summoned Marcy to his office for a dressing down about the canal fiasco. He concluded with the words, "I am almost despairing at these results," and dismissed Marcy before he could say anything.[72]

One of the issues bothering the president and Stanton was that nothing had been done about the Confederate batteries on the Virginia side of the lower Potomac River that effectively blocked navigation on the waterway from Washington to the Chesapeake Bay. While upriver, McClellan had revoked General Joseph Hooker's authority to attack those batteries by crossing from Maryland.[73] By March 1, however, he was calling for a meeting with five of his generals to discuss an overkill plan for eliminating those batteries by advancing 118,000 Army of the Potomac troops in conjunction with a naval flotilla that would include the new ironclad *Monitor*.[74] Such an attack was exactly what Lincoln had recommended months before as the first step in a movement toward Richmond—a recommendation McClellan had rejected.

In a March 3 letter to Halleck, the general-in-chief connected his proposed opening of the Potomac with his plans to move by water closer to Richmond and rejected any thoughts of his remaining inactive:

> I hope to open the Potomac this week, provided the weather permits. It will require a movement of the whole army in order to keep Manassas off my back. I cannot count upon any effective co-operation on the part of the Navy. As soon as I have cleared the Potomac I shall bring here the water transportation now ready (at least it will be in four or five days), and then move by detachments of about 55,000 men for the region of sandy roads and short land transportation. When you have asked for 50,000 men from here, my dear fellow, you have made one of two mistakes—either you have much overrated my force or you have thought that I intended to remain inactive here.[75]

In the following weeks, McClellan's dreams of "sandy roads & short transportation" to Richmond would be shattered.

On March 3, McClellan sent another communication to Halleck—one that could have had disastrous effects on Union fortunes. The night before, Halleck had wired McClellan that he had not heard from Grant in over a week, that Grant had gone to Nashville without his permission, and that Grant "richly deserves" censure for "this neglect and inefficiency."[76] Halleck, jealous of Grant's initiative and success at Forts Henry and Donelson, was launching a vendetta against him. McClellan went for the bait and responded, "The future success of our cause demands that proceedings such as Grant's should at once be checked. Generals must observe discipline as well as private soldiers. Do not hesitate to arrest him at once if the good of the service requires it, and place C.F. Smith in command. You are at liberty to regard this as a positive order if it will smooth your way."[77] Halleck used this authority to arrest Grant. However, when Lincoln and Stanton learned of Halleck's efforts, they put a stop to them. Grant would continue his western successes despite the lack of support from Halleck and McClellan.[78]

Meanwhile, Union successes elsewhere were resulting in criticism of McClellan. Chase, his former supporter, wrote, "We heard the echoes of victory from the West, but all was quiet on the Potomac." Newspapers questioned his loyalty.[79] Finally, Lincoln grew tired of McClellan's inaction and forced a showdown meeting. On March 7, McClellan presented his Urbana Plan to a council of senior generals. That plan called for a landing of the Union army at Urbana on the Rappahannock River and a swift movement directly on Richmond. Its major advantage was that it would bypass the Confederate lines of Johnston in northern Virginia.

One outgrowth of that meeting was Lincoln's March 8 issuance of General War Orders No. 2 ordering the Army of the Potomac to be organized into five corps and naming the specific corps commanders. Of the five commanders, McDowell, Edwin V. Sumner, Samuel P. Heintzelman, Erasmus D. Keys, and Banks, a majority had opposed McClellan's waterborne movement and supported Lincoln's original overland proposal for moving on Richmond. The president told his staff he had picked "fighting generals."[80]

Also on Saturday, March 8, General Johnston destroyed McClellan's plans for an easy end-run around his forces by withdrawing from Manassas southward to positions behind the Rappahannock and Rapidan Rivers. His withdrawal had been ordered by President Davis on February 20 but was delayed by road conditions and the need to retrieve as many supplies and guns as possible. The Rebel movement meant that McClellan no longer could land his army at Urbana on the Rappahannock and march unimpeded on Richmond. Upon learning of the Rebel movement out of the area, McClellan at long last left Washington and headed into the heart of northern Virginia. On that same busy Sunday, March 9, he excitedly telegraphed Lincoln and Stanton, "We have Sangster's Station & Fairfax Court House"—as though that were some type of accomplishment. He also told them, "I am arranging to move forward to push the retreat of rebels as far as possible."[81] That was another empty and unfulfilled promise. The Rebels had a full-day head-start, had burned huge quantities of immovable supplies, and had settled into new positions that McClellan would not challenge. Most embarrassing to him were the published photographs of "Quaker cannons," logs resembling guns that the Confederates had left behind on their old Manassas lines.

Examination of the Rebel encampment near Manassas also revealed that Johnston's force there consisted of about 60,000 troops—not the 150,000 to 200,000 or so that McClellan had been claiming—or even the 98,400 estimated by Pinkerton. Like many other historians, Pois and Langer concluded that it should have been clear at that point that Pinkerton "was simply out of his league in the military intelligence domain. He was

"Quaker guns" (dummy log cannons) at Manassas, Virginia, after a peaceful Confederate withdrawal in 1862. The withdrawal and discovery of the Quaker guns led to public criticism of McClellan, who for months had declined to attack the supposedly overwhelming Confederate forces near Manassas (Library of Congress).

supplying McClellan with vastly overinflated Confederate numbers."[82] However, Fishel assembled a convincing case that McClellan probably had directed or implied to his old friend Pinkerton that he wanted such estimates and had then further inflated them himself.[83]

By March 8, however, Pinkerton was becoming more of a team player. He provided a new estimate of Confederate strength in Virginia. He changed his methodology to create higher numbers and then added an inflated "summary of general estimates." His calculated "medium estimate" was 115,500—double the actual 56,400 Rebel force—and his overall "summary of general estimates" (a concoction of rumors) was a McClellan-pleasing 150,000. Fishel concluded that Pinkerton either was trying to keep up with the numbers McClellan had been using or had been criticized for his previous "low" estimates.[84]

On Sunday, March 9, in Hampton Roads, Virginia, the Confederate ironclad *Merrimack* (also known as the CSS *Virginia*) ventured out of Norfolk and wreaked havoc on the Union fleet. It sank the *Cumberland*, grounded *Minnesota* and *St. Lawrence*, and

Lincoln poses with Allan Pinkerton (left), McClellan's unsuccessful intelligence chief, and Major General John McClernand (right), an old Lincoln associate from Illinois (October 1862). Understanding what McClellan wanted, Pinkerton provided him with grossly inflated estimates of enemy strength—which McClellan then used to justify his consistent inaction (Library of Congress).

compelled the surrender of the *Congress*. This attack caused fear and near-panic in Washington—especially on the part of Stanton. McClellan responded by stopping transport traffic in the Chesapeake & Delaware Canal, authorizing the evacuation of Newport News (but not adjoining Fort Monroe), and taking steps to block the lower Potomac with sunken scows if the *Merrimack* threatened Washington.[85] In addition, the general noted the possible impact on his own major campaign plans: "The performances of the *Merrimack* place a new aspect upon everything, and may very probably change my old plan of campaign, just on the eve of execution."[86] Even later that day, as the threat abated, McClellan characteristically told Stanton, "… we must take if for granted that the worst will happen."[87]

Lincoln's order mandating the formation of five corps, Johnston's withdrawal from Manassas, and the emergence of the *Merrimack* in Hampton Roads truly made March 8 and 9 McClellan's weekend from hell. Those events threw his Urbana Plan into disarray.

Not overly anxious to carry out the president's five-corps order, McClellan sought to delay its execution. On March 9, from Virginia, he requested its suspension until he had made his movement toward Manassas. Denying the suspension request, Stanton replied that "it is the duty of every officer to obey the President's orders."[88] At 1 A.M. on the tenth, McClellan wired Stanton that he could not immediately comply with the president's order except by delaying his army's march on Manassas in order to form them into corps. McClellan promised that he would not unreasonably delay the formation of corps if allowed to proceed without doing so immediately.[89] Stanton replied, "move just as you think best now, and let the other matter stand until it can be done without impeding movements."[90]

After the watershed weekend, Lincoln convened a March 11 cabinet meeting to discuss McClellan's future. Reflecting the cabinet's loss of confidence in McClellan, Attorney General Bates wrote that the general "has no plans but is fumbling and plunging in confusion and darkness." Unimpressed that "all was quiet on the Potomac" while Union generals were succeeding elsewhere, Lincoln decided that, supposedly because McClellan would now be busy campaigning in the field, it was time to relieve him as general-in-chief. He issued an order to that effect and designated former Governor Dennison to gently break the news to McClellan.[91]

By the evening of March 11, McClellan had forgotten his promise "to push the retreat of rebels as far as possible." From Fairfax Court House, he told Stanton that he had ridden more than forty miles and that, "Except the turnpike, the roads are horrible. The country entirely stripped of forage and provisions." He said that he would occupy Manassas with some of Banks' troops and "at once throw[] all the forces I can concentrate upon the line agreed last week"—the line that would be reached by water transport. Because the Union *Monitor* had stalemated the *Merrimack* in a March 10 follow-up confrontation in Hampton Roads, use of the Potomac appeared safe and McClellan had directed that troop transports be brought to Alexandria instead of Annapolis.[92]

Although McClellan told Stanton that "Circumstances may keep me out here some little time longer,"[93] he told a slightly different story a half-hour later to his father-in-law, now Brigadier General Marcy: "It is impossible for me to come in to-night. I am completely tired out. Besides I think the less I see of Washington the better."[94] McClellan was ignoring a request from his old ally, Governor Dennison, to meet with him before he saw anyone else. Dennison had been delegated the unpleasant task of telling McClellan that he had been relieved as general-in-chief and that Lincoln still had confidence in him but wanted him to fully concentrate on his duties as commander of the Army of the

Potomac while it was on campaign.[95] McClellan probably suspected that good news was not awaiting him when he returned to the capital.

Evidence of that suspicion is found is his letter of that evening (March 11) to Mary Ellen:

> I regret that the rascals are after me again. I had been foolish enough to hope that when I went into the field they would give me some rest, but it seems otherwise—perhaps I should have expected it. If I can get out of this scrape you will never catch me in the power of such a set again—the idea of persecuting a man behind his back. I suppose they are now relieved from the pressure of their fears by the retreat of the enemy & that they will increase in virulence.

He also told her, "From the great number of camps scattered about it is evident that they [the Rebels] had a very large force here."[96] Thus, he was continuing to delude himself about the number of enemy troops he had declined to attack with his large army.

His fears were confirmed the next morning when his father-in-law wired him that the *National Intelligencer* had published the order relieving him as general-in-chief.[97] That day McClellan had his discussion with Governor Dennison. Shortly thereafter, he wrote to the president, "... I thank you most sincerely for the official confidence & kind personal feelings you entertain for me ... I shall work just as cheerfully as ever before [not a very high standard!], & that no consideration of self will in any manner interfere with the discharge of my public duties."[98]

Thus ended McClellan's brief reign as Union general-in-chief. It was a failure. He had stood by and watched while Grant took Forts Henry and Donelson and moved up the Tennessee and Cumberland rivers; Buell won at Mill Springs, Kentucky, and advanced on Nashville; and Burnside captured Roanoke Island. His own Army of the Potomac had stood motionless outside the national capital while McClellan was mesmerized by his delusion that the Confederates in Northern Virginia numbered between 100,000 and 200,000—instead of their actual number of no more than 60,000.[99] His "slows" and his inflation of enemy strength would continue to mark his performance as an army commander.

5

Crawling up the Virginia Peninsula

McClellan slowly moves his army up the Virginia Peninsula toward Richmond, stalls for a month at Yorktown, avoids the battlefield at Williamsburg, dangerously divides his army on two sides of the Chickahominy River, and exposes it to a Confederate attack at Seven Pines—all the while making a mockery of what was supposed to be an aggressive offensive campaign.

During the next two and a half months, McClellan would transport a huge army to the Virginia Peninsula (between the James and York rivers), take two months to move his army seventy miles to the vicinity of Richmond, and squander numerous opportunities to attack and defeat inferior Confederate forces. Historian Timothy Johnson concluded that McClellan was trying to emulate the coast-to-enemy capital, Vera Cruz-to-Mexico City campaign of his mentor, Winfield Scott.[1]

As he looked toward Hampton Roads as the likely new destination for his maritime movement, McClellan was concerned about the threat posed by the *Merrimack*. Thus, on March 12, he asked Assistant Secretary of the Navy Fox whether the *Monitor* could keep the *Merrimack* in check so that he could move to Fort Monroe. Fox replied the next day that he hoped so but there was no certainty.[2] McClellan also asked Fox whether it was possible to bottle up the *Merrimack* in port at Norfolk by sinking hulks filled with stone. General John E. Wool, commanding at Fort Monroe, responded to Stanton that the only way to implement McClellan's proposal was to put the *Monitor* at risk by shelling Confederate shore batteries and that the *Monitor* could not be risked because it was the only hope against the *Merrimack*.[3]

On March 13, McClellan held a council of war with his corps commanders, who agreed on a movement against Richmond via the Virginia Peninsula. General McDowell carried the plan to Stanton, who sought clarification from McClellan. McClellan assured him that the council had unanimously approved the plan and that "if the plan meets your approval the movement can commence early tomorrow morning." Stanton then wired back that the president approved the movement so long as Washington and Manassas Junction were strongly garrisoned and the movement was made "at once."[4] Lincoln must have been relieved that McClellan at long last would initiate any kind of offensive campaign.

That night McClellan reached out for support of his movement. He wired Adjutant General Lorenzo Thomas requesting that Burnside wrap up his coastal Carolina operations and be prepared to cooperate with McClellan.[5] Also, he wired Stanton suggesting that the Navy be requested to send to Fort Monroe all vessels that could be spared from the Atlantic Coast blockade.[6] Finally, he wrote to Gustavus Fox reiterating his request for Atlantic blockade vessels for reducing the Confederate fortifications at Gloucester and Yorktown, which were blocking his access to the York River on the north side of the Peninsula.[7]

McClellan gave his first assurances about protecting Washington in a March 14 letter to Stanton. He said he was sending General George Stoneman with ten squadrons of cavalry to reconnoiter the Rappahannock River and intended to leave General Banks' corps in the Manassas-Centreville area west of Washington.[8] In March 16 orders to Banks, McClellan directed that he place entrenched forces at Manassas and Strasburg (in the Shenandoah Valley), build block-houses at railroad bridges, constantly employ cavalry well to the front, establish guards at Warrenton and toward the Rappahannock, obtain early and full information on the enemy, and generally cover the line of the Potomac and Washington.[9] Assigning such a large territory and great responsibility to Banks would prove inadequate to assure Lincoln and Stanton of the security of the capital.

Looking backward in his March 14 letter to Stanton, McClellan took credit for the Confederate withdrawal from northern Virginia: "I am well assured of the fact that the true reasons for their evacuation of their works were twofold—1st My advance from Harpers Ferry—2nd The intimation that I intended to turn their right flank. Most accounts substantially agree in this, & my information is very full." In a letter to his friend Samuel Barlow, McClellan made the same claims about his having caused the Confederate withdrawal. He also invited Stanton to tour the Confederate works at Manassas and Centreville so that he could see "that it would have been a desperate affair to have attacked Centreville." Why he expected an attack near Richmond to be any easier is difficult to discern.[10]

On the eve of his Peninsula Campaign, McClellan issued a grandiose pronouncement to the soldiers of his army. Some of the highlights follow:

> I have held you back that you might give the death-blow to the rebellion that has distracted our once happy country. The patience you have shown, and your confidence in your General, are worth a dozen victories.... The moment for action has arrived, and I know that I can trust in you to save our country.... It is my business to place you [on the decisive battlefield]. I am to watch over you as a parent over his children; and you know that your General loves you from the depths of his heart.... God smiles upon us, victory attends us, yet I would not have you think that our aim is to be attained without a manly struggle. I will not disguise it from you: you have brave foes to encounter, foemen well worthy of the steel that you will use so well. *I shall demand of you great, heroic exertions, rapid and long marches, desperate combats, privations, perhaps.* We shall share all these together; and when this sad war is over we will return to our homes, and feel that we can ask no higher honor than the proud consciousness that we belonged to the ARMY OF THE POTOMAC.[11]

In fact, McClellan never did demand heroic exertions, rapid and long marches, and desperate combats from his troops. Therein lay his failure.

McClellan's letters of mid–March reflect his concerns about personal attacks on him. In his March 16 letter to Barlow, he said, "Do not mind the abolitionists—all I ask of the papers is that they should defend me from the most malicious attacks—tho' to speak frankly I do not care to pay much attention to my enemies." He added hopefully, "*The President is all right*—he is my strongest friend."[12] The next day he thanked Edmund C. Stedman for writing to a newspaper in support of McClellan. In that letter, he revealed

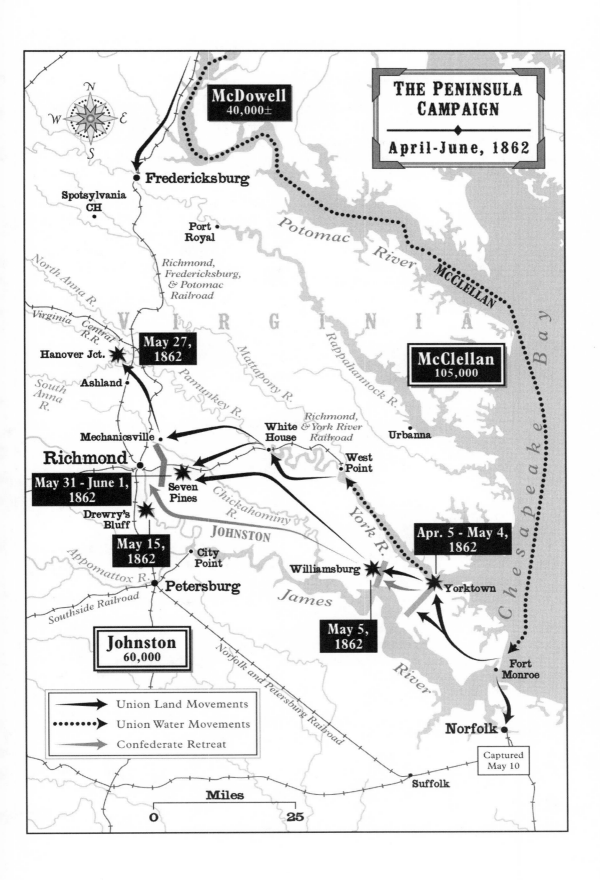

THE PENINSULA
CAMPAIGN
◆
April–June, 1862

McDowell
40,000±

Fredericksburg

Spotsylvania
CH

Port
Royal

Richmond,
Fredericksburg,
& Potomac
Railroad

Potomac River

MCCLELLAN

McClellan
105,000

VIRGINIA

North Anna R.

Virginia Central R.R.

Hanover Jct.

May 27,
1862

Ashland

South
Anna
R.

Mechanicsville

Richmond

May 31 – June 1,
1862

Drewry's
Bluff

May 15,
1862

Appomattox R.

City
Point

Petersburg

Southside Railroad

Johnston
60,000

Pamunkey R.

Mattapony R.

Rappahannock R.

White
House

Richmond
& York River
Railroad

Urbanna

West
Point

Seven
Pines

Chickahominy R.

JOHNSTON

Williamsburg

James River

May 5,
1862

York R.

Apr. 5 – May 4,
1862

Yorktown

Chesapeake Bay

Fort
Monroe

Norfolk

Captured
May 10

Norfolk and Petersburg Railroad

Suffolk

Union Land Movements
Union Water Movements
Confederate Retreat

Miles

0   25

his relief at being left in command of his army and implied some concern about retaining that command: "I believe that we are now on the eve of the success for which we have been so long preparing—yet I have felt for several days that there was a strong probability that I should be denied the satisfaction of leading the Army of the Potomac to victory & of sharing the fruit of the work of many months. I now begin to hope for better things. If permitted to retain command of this Army I feel assured of the result, & trust that end will justify the great confidence that you & so many other friends have placed in me."[13]

Looking forward to the time when he would be able to ascend the York River to West Point (where the Mattapony and Pamunkey rivers form the York), McClellan asked Stanton to have the Director of Military Railroads, Daniel C. McCallum, provide locomotives and railcars sufficient to transport supplies, including 20,000 horses, for an army of 130,000 men. They were to be used on the twenty-eight-mile-long West Point and Richmond Railway, which connected those two points.[14]

The first of McClellan's troops left Alexandria for Fort Monroe on March 17. As early as March 19, however, McClellan was laying the groundwork for possible future delays. He wrote to Stanton of the necessity for naval support against the Rebel guns at Yorktown: "It may be summed up in few words, that for the prompt success of this campaign it is absolutely necessary that the Navy should at once throw its whole available force, its most powerful vessels, against Yorktown." He saw the alternative as reduction of "Yorktown and Gloucester [across the York River from Yorktown] by a siege, in all probability involving a delay of weeks, perhaps."[15] These words became a self-fulfilling prophecy. He also had warned that lack of full Navy cooperation could prolong his operations for many weeks and force his army to "carry in front several strong positions which by their aid could be turned without serious loss of either time or men."[16] In fact, McClellan would discourage and refuse to pursue land-based opportunities to turn or break the Yorktown line.

By the 22nd of March, McClellan realized that "we cannot count upon the Navy to reduce Yorktown by their independent efforts, [and] we must therefore be prepared to do it by our own means." Therefore, he told General Marcy that he would need forty 8" and 10" mortars, twenty siege howitzers, twenty 4–1/2" siege guns, forty 20-pounder Parrott guns, and some number of 24-pounder siege guns. He said that he expected to face forty to fifty heavy Confederate guns at Yorktown and fourteen Columbiad guns across the river at Gloucester. Marcy responded that eighteen siege guns were on board vessels and another fifty-six had been ordered.[17]

In the Shenandoah, meanwhile, Jackson was stirring. On March 24, McClellan received word that Jackson had been repulsed at Kernstown.[18] That was Jackson's only defeat in the famous Shenandoah Valley Campaign he was just beginning.

At the end of March, McClellan declined to release any engineer officers because of the possible need for them for sieges at Yorktown, Richmond, and Norfolk. He wrote, "I do not expect to go through *all* the regular operations of a siege against all these places, but *do* expect to be obliged to establish batteries & perhaps open some trenches...."[19]

On March 27, Union troops moved out from Fort Monroe but were repulsed at Big Bethel, a few miles up the Peninsula from Fort Monroe. The next day McClellan wired Brigadier General Heintzelman, commander of his Third Corps, his concern about Heintzelman's reconnaissance of the prior day: "I hope the movement on Big Bethel was well considered, in view of my wish not to prematurely develop our plans to the enemy."[20]

On March 31, Lincoln advised McClellan that he was ordering Brigadier General Louis Blenker's division transferred from McClellan to Fremont in western Virginia.

Lincoln said he knew McClellan wished to have that division, he made the move "with great pain," and "If you could know the full pressure of the case, I am confident you would justify it—even beyond a mere acknowledgment that the Commander-in-chief may order what he pleases."[21] McClellan's obsequious response included the following:

> I fully appreciate, however, the circumstances of the case, & hasten to assure you that I cheerfully acquiesce in your decision without any mental reservation.
>
> Recognizing as I ever do the plenitude of your power as Commander in Chief, I cannot but regard the tone of your note as in the highest degree complimentary to me, & as adding one more to the many proofs of personal regard you have so often honored me with.
>
> I shall do my best to use all the more activity to make up for the loss of this Division, & beg again to assure you that I will ever do my very best to carry out your views & support your interests in the same frank spirit you have always shown towards me.[22]

McClellan's tone would soon change.

On April 1, McClellan hurriedly departed Alexandria, Virginia, for Hampton Roads. Assistant Secretary of War John Tucker had chartered 389 steamers, schooners, barges, and other vessels to transport McClellan's army, including almost 15,000 animals.[23]

Before leaving Alexandria, McClellan had tried to cleverly deal with the issue of keeping Washington secure in the absence of the bulk of his army—a condition Lincoln and Stanton had imposed on him. First, he communicated with Banks about the "change in affairs in the valley of the Shenandoah." He told Banks that he assumed he had sufficient troops "to drive Jackson before you, provided he is not re-enforced largely," and added, "I doubt whether Johnston will now re-enforce Jackson with a view of offensive operations. The time is probably past when he could have gained anything by doing so." McClellan could not have been more wrong about that. He described some reinforcements he was sending to Banks—including Blenker's division, which he had just accurately described as having been detached for transfer to Fremont! His key direction to Banks was: "… the most important thing at present is to throw Jackson well back, and then to assume such a position as to enable you to prevent his return."[24]

That same day, McClellan wrote to Adjutant General Thomas to provide information on the forces he was leaving "near and in the rear on the Potomac." He summarized the expected troop dispositions as 7,780 at Warrenton, 10,859 at Manassas, 35,467 in the Shenandoah, 1,350 on the lower Potomac, and 18,000 in front of Washington.[25] The general's total of 73,000, however, included Blenker's supposedly transferred division of 10,000 and troops that had not arrived yet from various state capitals. Further, half the troops he described were going to be in the Shenandoah Valley, not in the vicinity of Washington. McClellan must have had doubts that these forces would satisfy Lincoln and Stanton's concern about the capital's security. The facts were that he had left about 28,000 troops—not the agreed-upon 40,000—in and near Washington and that about half of them were untrained new recruits. The general's sleight-of-hand would not go unnoticed for long.[26]

In fact, by the very next day, Thomas and Major General Ethan Allen Hitchcock advised Stanton that McClellan had failed to comply with the president's order to "entirely secure" the safety of Washington.[27] When Stanton investigated the issue, he discovered that there was no fit-for-duty field battery in the city, all the heavy artillery gunners had been taken to the Peninsula, and most cavalrymen in the city had no horses.[28]

In a late afternoon note to his wife, McClellan described his hasty April 1 departure from Alexandria on board the *Commodore*: "… I did not feel safe until I could fairly see Alexandria behind us…. I feared that if I remained at Alexandria I would be annoyed very much & perhaps be sent for from Washn. Officially speaking, I feel very glad to get away from that sink of iniquity...."[29] The next day he wired her of his arrival at Fort Monroe and told her, "The grass will not grow under my feet."[30]

On April 3, he wrote to her of his plans to quickly move up the Peninsula and take Yorktown. He said that the next day three divisions would head straight for Yorktown along the north side of the Peninsula while two others would head more directly toward Richmond on the James River Road along the peninsula's south side. He was optimistic: "I hope to get possession of Yorktown day after tomorrow. Shall then arrange to make the York River my line of supplies.... The great battle will be (I think) near Richmond as I have always hoped & thought. I see my way very clearly—& with my trains once ready will move rapidly...."[31] As things turned out, McClellan would neither move rapidly nor take Yorktown within the month.

Stymied at Yorktown

In an April 3 letter to Flag Officer Louis M. Goldsborough, McClellan asked for naval assistance by April 5 to take Yorktown and said that, with such assistance, "I think we can make short work of it."[32] Because of concerns about the *Merrimack*, Rebel ship-building in Norfolk, and the strength of Confederate batteries at Yorktown and Gloucester, naval officers denied McClellan support in attacking Yorktown or Gloucester or in running past their guns to land troops upstream from Yorktown.[33]

Less optimistically, he wired Stanton that same day, "I expect to move from here tomorrow morning on Yorktown, where a force of some 15,000 of the rebels are in intrenched position, and I think it quite possible they will attempt to resist us."[34] The next day he complained to General McDowell, commanding his First Corps, "You know that we are substantially weakened to the extent of two divisions; first, by the loss of Blenker; next, by the rescinding of the order placing this fort and its dependencies under my command." He eagerly anticipated the arrival of McDowell's corps—an arrival that never occurred.[35]

McClellan and his army left Fort Monroe and started up the Virginia Peninsula on April 4. He quickly learned that his best-laid plans did not match reality. The Navy could provide no support, his maps were grossly inaccurate and inadequate, and the hoped-for sandy roads were impassable morasses of mud.[36] At the same time, McClellan's gamesmanship related to the defense of Washington came back to haunt him. Lincoln and Stanton were furious about the small number of troops McClellan planned to leave in the Washington area. The result was an April 4 decision that rocked McClellan. He learned of it in a telegram from Adjutant Thomas. A contemporaneous letter from Thomas explained, "The President, deeming the force to be left in front of Washington insufficient to insure its safety, has directed that McDowell's army corps should be detached from the forces operating under your immediate direction."[37] Some of the sources of Lincoln's concern were allegations by radical senators Ben Wade and Zachariah Chandler that McClellan's whole campaign reflected a treasonable intent to leave Washington open to attack.[38]

For several days, beginning April 5, Major General John B. ("Prince John") Magruder successfully bluffed McClellan with a force less than one-fifth the size of his.[39] Under orders from Richmond to delay the enemy, Magruder had hastily constructed fortifications at Yorktown on the York River and extended his defensive line from there along the Warwick River all the way to the James River on the opposite side of the Peninsula. Magruder painted trees as "Quaker cannons" to enhance the threatening nature of his lines, and he had his regiments rigorously march back and forth in full view of the Union troops.

McClellan's chief engineer, Brigadier General John G. Bernard, explored the ground along the Warwick River and found a vulnerable seam in the Confederate line. The area could be covered by Union artillery during an infantry assault and was only moderately susceptible to fire from Rebel guns at Yorktown. As early as April 6 or 7, therefore, McClellan could have attacked the Rebel line and turned the defenders out of Yorktown. He declined to take the risk. In fact, as historian William J. Miller pointed out, McClellan made up his mind not to attack even before the crucial reconnaissance had been completed.[40] At 10:30 P.M. on April 5, he wrote, "I cannot turn Yorktown without a battle, in which I must use heavy artillery & go through the preliminary operations of a siege. The reconnaissances of tomorrow will enable me to form a pretty correct judgment of what I have to meet & the best way of overcoming the difficulties before me."[41]

Despite McClellan's subordinates' willingness and apparent ability to break through the Rebel line, McClellan gave orders not to do so. With 100,000 men under his command, McClellan stalled his campaign for a month because of a Confederate force that

Union artillery park at Yorktown, Virginia, during the 1862 Peninsula Campaign. McClellan delayed his campaign one month to besiege Rebel positions at Yorktown, which was abandoned before he ever attacked (Library of Congress).

started at about 15,000 and never exceeded 35,000 until Johnston arrived weeks later. Magruder was surprised that McClellan did not attack, and Joseph E. Johnston, the Rebel commander on the peninsula, commented that McClellan "seems not to value time especially." Celerity was not McClellan's strength.[42]

By the night of April 5, McClellan saw himself as stymied by the Confederates and pleaded to Lincoln for attachment of the First Corps to his Peninsula force. He claimed the enemy was "in large force," that their line of works (many formidable) extended across the entire Peninsula from Yorktown and along the Warwick River, and that deserters reported daily reinforcements from Richmond and Norfolk. He then pleaded:

> Under these circumstances I beg that you will reconsider the order detaching the First Corps from my Command. In my deliberate judgment the success of our cause will be imperiled [by so greatly reducing my force] when it is actually under the fire of the enemy, and active operations have commenced.... I am now of the opinion that I shall have to fight all of the available force of the rebels not far from here. Do not force me to do so with diminished numbers. But whatever your decision may be, I will leave nothing undone to obtain success. If you cannot leave me the whole of the first Corps, I urgently ask that I may not lose Franklin and his division."[43]

That same night McClellan wrote to Flag Officer Goldsborough about his situation. He described the Confederate "strong position," "strongly entrenched" Yorktown, the seven-foot-deep and "almost impassable" Warwick River with its marshy banks, and the "infamous" roads making movement difficult. He concluded, "I cannot turn Yorktown without a *battle*, in which I must use heavy artillery & go through the preliminary operations of a siege." He bemoaned the loss of McDowell's 35,000-man corps and requested naval vessels to join in his eventual bombardment of Yorktown. The next day, Goldsborough responded that he would not be able to assist at Yorktown and Gloucester until the guns at Gloucester Point had been turned by a movement up the more northerly Severn River—a movement for which McClellan had counted on McDowell.[44]

At 1 A.M. the next morning (April 6), McClellan complained to Mary Ellen about the situation in which he had been placed by the loss of McDowell's corps: ".... I find the enemy in strong force & in a very strong position but will drive him out.... While listening this pm. to the sound of the guns, I received the order detaching McDowell's Corps from my command—it is the most infamous thing that history has recorded. I have made such representations as will probably induce a revocation of the order—or at least save Franklin to me. The idea of depriving a General of 35,000 troops when actually under fire...!"[45]

The fact was that McClellan had determined upon a siege, instead of an attack, at Yorktown, even before he learned that McDowell's Corps would be withheld from him.[46] As stated by historian Michael Adams, "Even before a full reconnaissance of the enemy position had been made, McClellan decided that the works were strong enough to necessitate a siege. In fact, the enemy position was a weak one. Not only were the rebels vastly outnumbered but their fortifications were not completed."[47]

Perhaps an aggressive assault on Yorktown and prompt movement on Richmond would have produced a different decision in Washington about the best use of McDowell's Corps. Instead, McClellan's continuous pleas for reinforcements generated nothing but exasperation. Stanton, counting the 100,000 troops McClellan already had, exclaimed, "If he had a million men, he would swear the enemy had two millions, and then he would sit down in the mud and yell for three."[48]

That same morning McClellan urged Lincoln not to allow rigid enforcement of an April 4th order depriving him of wagons, trains, ammunition and a brigade of engineers.

He was concerned about the effects of the order creating a Department of the Rappahannock under McDowell and a Department of the Shenandoah under Banks—an order effectively depriving McClellan of control over those forces. Lincoln responded that afternoon to assure McClellan that the transportation, ammunition and engineers were still coming to him.[49]

McClellan urged General Franklin, in an April 6 telegram, to do all that he could to have his division (in McDowell's corps) restored to McClellan's command. Franklin responded that he had been surprised by McClellan's loss of McDowell's corps and that, "… McDowell told me that it was intended as a blow at you. That Stanton had said that you intended to work by strategy, and not by fighting, that all of the opponents of the policy of the administration centred around you—in other words that you had political aspirations."[50] McClellan's demonstrated reluctance to fight and his political maneuvers in Washington had finally undermined what little confidence Lincoln and Stanton may have had in him.

That same day Stanton had explained to McClellan the reason for McDowell's detachment from him. He wrote that the "force under Banks and Wadsworth was deemed … much less than had been fixed by your corps commanders as necessary to secure Washington."[51] Consistent with his involvement of them in the decision to proceed with a waterborne movement, Lincoln was relying on the corps commanders' judgment as to the number of troops needed to defend the capital.

On April 7, some of Joseph Johnston's reinforcements reached Magruder. That night McClellan appealed to both Stanton and Lincoln for more troops. To Stanton he described the strong Confederate line and batteries, reported that prisoners stated that Johnston had arrived with strong Confederate reinforcements, and asserted that the enemy numbered more than 100,000. Against them, he said, he would have only 85,000 troops because his army had been stripped of 50,000 men by the loss of Blenker's division and the First Corps. He concluded:

> Under the circumstances that have been developed since we arrived here I feel fully impressed with the conviction that here is to be fought the great battle that is to decide the existing contest. I shall of course commence the attack as soon as I can get up my siege train and shall do all in my power to carry the enemy's works; but to do this with a reasonable degree of certainty requires, in my judgment, that I should, if possible, have at least the whole of the First Corps to land upon the Severn River and attack Gloucester in the rear. My present strength will not admit of a detachment sufficient for this purpose without materially impairing the efficiency of this column.[52]

McClellan, however, was not intending to make full military use of his cavalry. He told Stanton, "When my present command all join I shall have about 85,000 men for duty, from which a large force must be taken for guards, scouts, &c."[53] Pointing to that statement, historian Robert F. O'Neill delivered this analysis of McClellan's under-utilization of his cavalry on the Peninsula: "The concept of providing officers with guards and escorts persisted throughout the war and was utilized by both sides, but McClellan and his corps commanders drew from the mounted regiments to an unprecedented degree. The demand for large, flashy mounted escorts during the [Peninsula] campaign practically destroyed the battlefield potential of the Union's mounted arm."[54]

Later that night of April 7, McClellan responded to a strong April 6 telegram from Lincoln that should have made him fully aware that he was expected to attack—and to do so quickly. Lincoln had written, "You now have over one hundred thousand troops, with you independent of Gen. Wool's command. I think you better break the enemies' line from York-town to Warwick River, at once. They will probably use *time*, as advantageously as you can."[55] McClellan responded that he had "… the honor to state that my entire force for duty amounts to only about 85,000 men." He attached his letter to Stanton with calculations showing that his March 31 manpower of 171,602 had been reduced by deletions totaling 87,792. These deletions included the First Corps (32,119), Blenker's division (8,616), Banks' corps (21,759), and Wadsworth's Washington area troops (19,308). McClellan told the president that he had only 53,000 actually with him and that others were coming up as rapidly as his transportation allowed.[56]

On April 9, Lincoln sent McClellan a crushing rejoinder. He opened with, "Your despatches complaining that you are not properly sustained, while they do not offend me, do pain me very much." He pointed out that McClellan had acquiesced in the withdrawal of Blenker's division. Then he explained that McClellan had left a mere 20,000 "unorganized" men, "without a single field battery," for the defense of Washington and Manassas. He added, "This presented, (or would present, when McDowell and Sumner should be gone) a great temptation to the enemy to turn back from the Rappahannock, and sack Washington. My explicit order that Washington should, by the judgment of *all* the commanders of the Army corps, be left entirely secure, has been neglected. It was precisely this that drove me to detain McDowell." And then he queried the general: "And now allow me to ask 'Do you really think I should permit the line from Richmond, *via* Mannassas [sic] Junction, to this city to be entirely open, except what resistance could be presented by less than twenty thousand unorganized troops?' This is a question which the country will not allow me to evade."[57]

Lincoln went on to question McClellan's calculations of his own troop numbers. He referred to a statement from Stanton that McClellan's own returns showed a total of 108,000 men with him or on the way and asked how the discrepancy of 23,000 could be explained. The president then delivered a severe warning:

> I suppose the whole force which has gone forward for you, is with you by this time; and if so, I think it is the precise time for you to strike a blow. By delay the enemy will relatively gain upon you—that is, he will gain faster, by *fortifications* and *re-inforcements*, than you can by re-inforcements alone.
>
> And once more let me tell you, it is indispensable to *you* that you strike a blow. *I* am powerless to help this. You will do me the justice to remember I always insisted, that going down the Bay in search of a field, instead of fighting at or near Mannassas [sic], was only shifting, and not surmounting, a difficulty–that we would find the same enemy, and the same, or equal, intrenchments, at either place. The country will not fail to note—is now noting—that the present hesitation to move upon an intrenched enemy, is but the story of Manassas repeated.
>
> I beg to assure you that I have never written you, or spoken to you, in greater kindness of feeling than now, nor with a fuller purpose to sustain you, so far as in my most anxious judgment, I consistently can. *But you must act.*[58]

McClellan never responded to Lincoln's letter. He did, however, complain to his wife about Lincoln pressing him for action. He haughtily told her, "I have raised an awful row about McDowell's Corps—& have I think rather scared the authorities that be. The Presdt very coolly telegraphed me yesterday that he thought I had better break the enemy's lines at once! I was much tempted to reply that he had better come & do it himself."[59] Little did he know that Lincoln would soon visit Hampton Roads and take an active role in military operations.

On April 11, McClellan pleaded to Stanton for Franklin and McCall's divisions, at least Franklin's, from McDowell's corps. He warned that he wanted it "distinctly understood" that both divisions would be necessary to invest and attack Gloucester Point but stated that he was willing to do that with just Franklin's division.[60] Simultaneously, he was venting to Mary Ellen: "Don't worry about the wretches—they have done nearly their worst & can't do much more. I am sure that I will win in the end, in spite of all their rascality. History will present a sad record of these traitors who are willing to sacrifice the country & its army for personal spite & personal aims. The people will soon understand the whole matter & then woe betide the guilty ones."[61]

The other person to whom McClellan mildly bemoaned his fate was—ironically— retired General Winfield Scott, whom he had pushed out of Washington only months before. After advising Scott on April 11 that his headquarters near Yorktown was named Camp Winfield Scott, McClellan complained of the misleading maps, atrocious roads, strong enemy entrenchments, and the weakening of his army by detachments of almost 50,000 men. He did admit that he had just learned that Franklin's 11,000-man division had been restored to him.[62] Stanton had rapidly responded to his plea and wired him that Franklin's division was coming and that McCall's division would be sent if the safety of Washington permitted.[63]

Before Franklin left Alexandria, Lincoln had him come to the Executive Mansion for a discussion. Lincoln told Franklin his reasons for retaining McDowell's corps near Washington and asked Franklin to relay that information to McClellan. After Franklin told McClellan what the president had said, McClellan wired the president, "I now understand the matter, which I did not before."[64] What he apparently understood, however, was that he had been deprived of troops for personal or political reasons. Thus, after talking to Franklin, McClellan wrote to Mary Ellen, "… I believe I now know who instigated the attack upon me & the country…." He may have been referring to Stanton, McDowell, or both of them.[65]

On April 16, at the Battle of Dam Number 1 (or Lee's Mill), in the center of the peninsula on the Warwick River line between Yorktown and the James River, an attempted Union advance by Brigadier General William "Baldy" Smith was repulsed after gaining a lodgement in the Rebel lines. Neither McClellan nor his subordinates knew how close the attack had come to succeeding.[66] McClellan absolved himself of responsibility for most of the resulting casualties and blamed them on an overly aggressive Smith. He wrote, "In Smith's affair … we lost I fear nearly 200 killed & wounded. The object I proposed [obviously a modest one] had been fully accomplished with the loss of about 20—when after I left the ground a movement was made in direct violation of my orders, by which the remainder of the loss was uselessly incurred."[67]

But Smith reported that, in accordance with McClellan's "warning instructions," he had made a mere reconnaissance against an enemy "one-gun battery" and that "no attempt to mass the troops of the division was made for an assault upon the [Rebel] works."[68] Thus, despite indications that the Rebel lines were vulnerable to assault, McClellan was irrevocably committed to the "safe" option of a siege. McClellan had as much as a four-to-one manpower advantage, and the weakly held enemy line along the Warwick could have been breached by attacking several points at once. But it is clear that he was making no effort to break the Rebel line and thereby outflank and compel the abandonment of Yorktown.

McClellan was comfortable establishing siege lines at Yorktown. He had first seen them used successfully when he accompanied General Scott at Vera Cruz in the Mexican War. Then he had observed their use at Sevastopol in 1855 as an observer in the Crimean War.[69] His observations there had impressed him with the bloody costs of frontal assaults and the ability of a besieging army to impose high casualties on defenders with artillery fire.[70] Although McClellan later cited General John G. Barnard's post–Yorktown report as the basis for concluding that the Rebel line was unassailable, Barnard responded that he was describing the Rebel line after McClellan's one-month delay—not when Union troops first arrived.[71]

Having been promised Franklin's division, McClellan made another effort to get McCall's. On April 18, he wired Lincoln requesting McCall's division for an attack on West Point to turn the enemy's position—"[i]f compatible with your impressions as to the security of the capital and not interfering with operations of which I am ignorant...." He went on to request that McDowell himself not again be assigned for duty with him because of "all that I have heard of things which have occurred since I left Washington and before...."[72]

Meanwhile, McClellan ignored Lincoln's earlier warnings and Blair's advice by continuing to develop his siege lines and taking no offensive action. He rationalized his delay to Mary Ellen in an April 19 letter:

> Don't be at all discouraged—all is going well—the more there are in Yorktown the more decisive will the results be. I know exactly what I am about & am quite confident that with God's blessing I shall utterly defeat them. I can't go "*with a rush*" over strong posts. I must use heavy guns & silence their fire—all that takes much time & I have not been longer than the usual time for such things—much less than the usual in truth....
>
> I can't tell you when Yorktown is to be attacked, for it depends on circumstances that I cannot control. It shall be attacked the first moment I can do so successfully—but *I don't intend to hurry it—I cannot afford to fail.* [This, of course, had become his mantra by this time.] I have a little over 100,000 effective men including Franklin's Division....
>
> I may have the opportunity of carrying the place next week—or may be delayed a couple of weeks—much of course depends on the rapidity with which the heavy guns & ammunition arrive. Never mind what such people as [Senator Benjamin F.] Wade say—they are beneath contempt.... [73]

Since McClellan was going to take his own sweet time in doing anything with his 100,000-man army, it is not surprising that Washington politicians were upset. Continuing success elsewhere, such as the capture of New Orleans on April 25, only made McClellan look worse by comparison. At the same time, his Academy classmate, "Stonewall" Jackson, dismissed McClellan's tedious movement up the peninsula with the perceptive observation, "He lacks nerve."[74]

Confederate President Davis had brought Robert E. Lee to Richmond as his chief of staff on March 13. On April 20, McClellan passed on to Lincoln incorrect information that Lee, not Johnston, commanded in his front. Then he gave Lincoln his laughable analysis of Lee: "I prefer Lee to Johnston—the former is *too* cautious & weak under grave responsibility—personally brave & energetic to a fault, he yet is wanting in moral firmness when pressed by heavy responsibility & is likely to be timid & irresolute in action."[75] Not only had McClellan inaccurately described Lee, but he had provided a perfect description of himself (cautious, weak, timid, and irresolute). Confirmation of this analysis came in McClellan's next letter to Lincoln when he wrote, "... I still hope that we will not be seriously interfered with until I can open an overwhelming fire & give the assault from a reasonable distance under its cover. My course must necessarily depend to a great extent upon that of the enemy—but I see the way clear to success & hope to make it brilliant, although with but little loss of life."[76]

Once again looking to develop a record to protect himself and pleading for more troops, McClellan wrote to Stanton on April 27. He went over all the old ground; he related how he had intended to have 150,000 troops for his operation and been deprived of 50,000 of them without any reason being given. He had conveniently forgotten his earlier correspondence with the president. He also asserted that the Confederates' destruction of the Rappahannock bridges protected Washington and again requested that McCall's division be sent to him.[77]

That same night he warned Mary Ellen: "Be careful not to say one word about Stanton, McDowell or any other of my enemies, let us present a contrast with those people & show by no word or act that we care what they say or do."[78] Three days later he told her that he would not begin his general bombardment of Yorktown for another four days and again bemoaned his circumstances:

> I am tired of public life—& even now when doing the best I can for my country in the field I know that my enemies are pursuing me more remorselessly than ever, & "kind *friends*" are constantly making themselves agreeable by informing me of the pleasant predicament in which I am—the rebels on one side, & the abolitionists & other scoundrels on the other— I believe in my heart & conscience, however, that I am walking on the ridge between the two gulfs, & that all I have to do is try to keep the path of honor & truth that God will bring me safely through—at all events I am willing to leave the matter in his hands & will be content with the decision of the Almighty."[79]

With McClellan willing to leave events to be determined by the enemy and the Almighty, he clearly was not going to demonstrate the "moral firmness" he had found so lacking in Lee. He and his 100,000-man army continued to build siege lines (fortifications and trenches from which to bombard Yorktown).

A frustrated Lincoln wired McClellan on May 1, "Your call for Parrott guns from Washington alarms me—chiefly because it argues indefinite procrastination. Is anything to be done?"[80] McClellan, who had requested the guns on April 28th, missed Lincoln's main point, responded that he was merely trying to hasten the guns along, and weakly assured the president, "My object was to hasten not procrastinate. All is being done that human labor can accomplish."[81]

By May 2, at least some of McClellan's soldiers and officers had become frustrated by his failure to attack what they believed to be an inferior force. That day Private Robert Knox Sneden, a Third Corps staff topographer privy to high-level developments, wrote in his diary,

> We have … fit for duty 103,378 soldiers, while the enemy have not more than 50,000 if he has that! The Fabian [defensive] policy of McClellan has lost him much popularity and 'Little Napoleon' stock is at a very low ebb among dashing leaders as [Brigadier General Philip] Kearny, Hooker, Sumner or [William F.] Smith. These generals, including [John] Sedgwick and Heintzelman, never go to McClellan's headquarters to consult about the military situation. And many generals don't 'pull together' at all, but pull in opposite directions. [That is] mostly caused by McClellan's 'masterly' inactivity with siege operations on the brain, when we all know that we could have walked right over the Rebels when we came here first on April 4. Since then hundreds are sick in hospital while lots have been killed at Lee's Mill and on the picket line, good officers too, who cannot be replaced.[82]

On May 2, McClellan again asked Goldsborough for vessels to join in the bombardment of Yorktown beginning on Monday, May 5.[83] On Saturday, May 3, McClellan described a "perfect quietness" on the field that indicated either an enemy sortie against his troops or an evacuation. He said he hoped it was not an evacuation because he did "not want these rascals to get away from me without a sound drubbing." He reported that all was quiet and "nothing unusual has occurred."[84]

Something had occurred. The Rebels, in fact, had evacuated both Yorktown and Gloucester Point. Early on Sunday, May 4, McClellan's infantry discovered nothing but empty trenches and about eighty abandoned guns at Yorktown. The massive collection of guns it had taken McClellan a month to collect and position fired but one symbolic shot at the abandoned town. It should have been with a heavy heart that he wired Stanton simply that "Yorktown is in our possession."[85] A Massachusetts soldier discovered the lesson of Yorktown—one that McClellan never learned—when he found Rebel graffiti reading "he that fights and runs away, will live to fight another day."[86]

At 9 o'clock that same morning, McClellan assured Stanton that, "I have thrown all my cavalry and horse artillery in pursuit, supported by infantry. I move Franklin and as much more as I can transport by water up to West Point to-day. No time shall be lost ... I shall push the enemy to the wall."[87] Despite the early morning discovery and McClellan's 9 A.M. wire to Stanton, visiting Rhode Island Governor William Sprague reported that McClellan did not actually launch a pursuit by Stoneman's cavalry until several of his generals urged him to do so and that he did so two hours after his "no time shall be lost" promise to Stanton.[88] Union pursuit was delayed by torpedoes (mines) planted by the retreating Rebels, and several of the pursuers were killed or badly injured. McClellan complained of the Confederates' "murderous and barbarous conduct" and compelled Rebel prisoners to remove the devices.[89]

McClellan should have been embarrassed by the successful Confederate withdrawal but probably was not. Evidence of that is his telegram that evening to Mary Ellen; in it he gloated, "Results glorious—eighty two heavy guns and large amounts of stores taken.... All well & in splendid spirits. The enemy's works of very great strength. He must have been badly scared to have abandoned them in such a hurry."[90] McClellan obviously was greatly disappointed by her reaction to the "capture" of Yorktown. Of her letters responding to his assessment, he wrote to her, "... I do not think you overmuch rejoiced at the results I gained. I really thought that you would appreciate a great result gained by pure skill & at little cost more highly than you seem to. It would have been easy for me to have sacrificed 10,000 lives in taking Yorktown, & I presume the world would have thought it more brilliant—I am content with what I have done, & history will give me credit for it. I am sorry that you do not exactly sympathize with me in the matter."[91]

Many of McClellan's officers and soldiers shared the disappointment of Mary Ellen. On the day the Rebels evacuated, Private Sneden wrote,

> The whole army were much chagrined that the enemy had so cleverly 'skipped out' after giving us all the hard work to construct fourteen batteries, corduroy numerous miles of road, etc. [It was] a whole month's work for nothing, and without the opportunity to see the grand 'feu de enfer' [fires of hell] which McClellan had set his heart upon. All the fine guns stood up in the different batteries with ammunition piled in them for a forty-eight hours' continuous bombardment as monuments of McClellan's imbecility and 'fortification on the brain. '... The 'Little Napoleon stock' fell very low among officers who knew anything....[92]

Additional evidence of McClellan's pride in his Yorktown "victory" is that he wired General Scott promptly on May 4 of the abandonment of Yorktown. Although he told his deposed mentor that deserters reported the enemy was "greatly demoralized," he ominously added that "Their numbers are stated to be from 100,000 to 120,000, with large light artillery force."[93] Those numbers, reflecting a May 3 Pinkerton "medium estimate,"[94] would soon increase—at least in McClellan's mind. Historians Pois and Langer commented that, "It can be argued that while McClellan may have devoutly accepted Allan Pinkerton's estimates of overwhelming numbers of Confederates, playing the numbers game with his own administration was an act of incredible arrogance, duplicity, or both."[95]

Williamsburg and on to the Chickahominy

Later on the morning of May 4, McClellan oversaw the embarkation of Franklin's 11,300-man division for their trip up the York River to West Point. That pursuit was delayed by the fact that only the day before he had disembarked those troops to join in the planned attack against the "superior" Confederate force at Yorktown.[96] When McClellan promised Stanton that, "No time shall be lost.... I shall push the enemy to the wall,"[97] it is doubtful that either Stanton or Lincoln believed him. Similarly, they were probably skeptical of his assurances in a telegram sent that evening: "The success is brilliant, and you may rest assured that its effects will be of the greatest importance. There shall be no delay in following up the rebels."[98]

In fact, within twenty-seven hours, McClellan would be backing off from aggressive pursuit and preparing to go on the defensive against the phantom superior forces of the enemy. On May 4, Union and Confederate cavalry clashed near Fort Magruder, just south of Williamsburg. Union cavalrymen charged bravely but were repelled by Confederates with superior numbers and position. Then, on May 5, the Confederate rear-guard engaged McClellan's pursuing troops in the Battle of Williamsburg. Hooker's Union soldiers, followed by those of W.F. Smith and then Edwin Sumner's, fought a disorganized battle against those of James Longstreet. There were sounds of fighting coming from Williamsburg at 9 A.M. and continuing all day. But McClellan stayed away until late in the day when he was specifically called to the battlefield by a corps commander.[99] Shelby Foote described McClellan's talent for avoiding fighting and yet reaping the benefits of the minor victory: "Arriving just at the close of the battle, mud-stained from hard riding, his staff strung out behind him trying desperately to keep up, he went from regiment to regiment, congratulating his men for their victory and acknowledging their cheers."[100]

Later statements by McClellan indicate that he did not desire or expect the battle at Williamsburg. He told the Joint Committee, "The most of their army, I think, did not intend halting at Williamsburg. We overtook them there.... I think if our cavalry had been a few hours later, probably no fight would have occurred there. That action was brought on, I think, by the fact that our cavalry caught their rear-guard, and forced them to bring back their troops." Still later he said the battle was "an accident, brought about by the rapid pursuit of our troops." Historian Robert O'Neill raised the possibility that McClellan intended to rely solely on Franklin's flanking movement, rather than pursuit and battle, to clear the Peninsula.[101]

By the time McClellan arrived at Williamsburg, all the significant fighting was over. However, he quickly convinced himself that his arrival on scene had been the decisive event of the day. He told Mary Ellen that Sumner was "a greater fool than I had supposed," that Hooker and Hancock had fought all day without support, that McClellan had saved the day by sending reinforcements to the right places, and that his dispositions had caused the enemy to flee that night. He concluded, "Had I been on the field five hours earlier I think we would have taken 20,000 prisoners—but the utter stupidity & worthlessness of the Corps Comdrs came near making it a defeat." McClellan's excuse for not being at the battle was that he was "obliged to remain to get Franklin & Sedgwick started up the [York] River for West Point."[102] A Massachusetts soldier-historian commented, "Curiously enough, there was almost always something for McClellan to do more important than to fight his own battles."[103]

His purported selection of priorities was strange at best. He apparently believed it was more important to supervise troops embarking on ships to bypass the enemy than to command troops engaged in an ongoing battle. That decision appears even more peculiar in light of his detaining Franklin and his troops at Yorktown until he was certain the Rebels could be driven from Williamsburg. Late on May 5th, McClellan ordered gunboats into Queen's Creek near Williamsburg and directed Franklin to move up the York and Pamunkey rivers the following morning. On the morning of May 6th, the gunboats entered the creek, Longstreet withdrew from Williamsburg because of them, and Franklin at last moved upstream.[104] McClellan had held Franklin's division at Yorktown for two days after he had told Stanton he was moving it "today." By delaying Franklin until he was sure the Rebels had been driven from Williamsburg, McClellan ensured the failure of Franklin's flanking maneuver to get behind the Confederates.

At 10 P.M. the night of the Williamsburg battle, the apparently shell-shocked (at a distance) McClellan sent another of his classic telegrams to Stanton from Williamsburg. He said,

> … I find Joe Johnston in front of me in strong force, probably greater a good deal than my own, and very strongly intrenched…. I learn from prisoners that they intend disputing every step to Richmond. I shall run the risk of at least holding them in check here while I resume the original plan. My entire force is undoubtedly considerably inferior to that of the rebels, who still fight well, but I will do all I can with the force at my disposal.[105]

Contrary to McClellan's assertions, the enemy was outnumbered by his force, was not entrenched, and allowed him to move within eight miles of Richmond without dispute. Although he described the Battle of Williamsburg as "a brilliant victory" to his wife,[106] McClellan, in its aftermath, seemed to be a shaken man who once again was extremely reluctant to move forward. He was going to "run the risk" of holding his foe in check while "resum[ing] the original plan"—apparently a reference to his 150,000-man army dream.

On May 6, Franklin's division and accompanying cavalry landed at Eltham's Landing on the Pamunkey River after a journey up the York and Pamunkey rivers. Their mission was to intercept Johnston's retreating army. In the May 7 Battle of Eltham's Landing, however, the Confederates successfully bottled up the Union troops and bought time for their retreat toward Richmond. With that success and the earlier delay of McClellan's left wing at Williamsburg, the Rebels had bought enough time to retreat across the Chickahominy and form a defensive line a few miles from Richmond.[107]

Meanwhile Lincoln had come to Fort Monroe to observe and consult. While there he took an active role in compelling the Confederates to abandon Norfolk and destroy the *Merrimack*. According to Foote, "Amazed to find that McClellan had made no provision for the capture of Norfolk, outflanked by the [Union] drive up the opposite bank of the James, the president decided to undertake the operation himself, employing the fortress garrison under [78-year-old] Major General John E. Wool."[108] Lincoln requested McClellan to join him for consultations, but the general declined in a May 7 wire to Stanton: "I dare not leave my command in the present state of affairs, so that it is really impossible for me to go to the rear to meet the President and yourself."[109]

In that same telegram, McClellan requested that gunboats be sent up the James River because the Rebel battery at Jamestown (on the James about ten miles from Williamsburg) had been abandoned.[110] That same day Lincoln ordered Goldsborough to proceed up the James with an ironclad and two gunboats if he could safely do so.[111] Four days later, McClellan congratulated Stanton on the destruction of the *Merrimack* and urged that gunboats and ironclads "be sent as far as possible up the James River without delay" in order to enable him to make his movements "much more decisive."[112]

On May 8, McClellan told Stanton of his own supposed heroics at Williamsburg: "… Had I been one half-hour later on the field on the 5th we would have been routed and would have lost everything. Notwithstanding my positive orders I was informed of nothing that had occurred, and I went to the field of battle myself upon unofficial information that my presence was needed to avoid defeat. I found there the utmost confusion and incompetency, the utmost discouragement on the part of the men. At least a thousand lives were really sacrificed by the organization into corps." These statements, an attack on Lincoln's corps-formation mandate, were made as part of a plea for authority to reorganize the corps of his army and relieve any incompetent corps or division commanders.[113] In a separate wire, he told Stanton of his plans to move ahead and merge with Franklin, and he recommended use of all Union troops on the Rappahannock and in the Shenandoah to join him in opposing Johnston in front of Richmond.[114]

On May 9, from Fort Monroe, Lincoln responded to McClellan's May 8 wires to Stanton. In a telegram, the president refused to allow the breaking up of the corps organization but, in light of the "expected great battle," allowed temporary suspension of that organization and gave McClellan a free hand "until further orders."[115] In a separate letter that same day, the president once again tried to give some practical political advice to the general:

> … I ordered the Army Corps organization not only on the unanimous opinion of the twelve Generals whom you had selected and assigned as Generals of Division, but also on the unanimous opinion of every *military man* I could get an opinion from, and every modern military book, yourself only excepted. Of course, I did not, on my own judgment, pretend to understand the subject. I now think it indispensable for you to know how your struggle against it is received in quarters which we cannot entirely disregard. It is looked upon as merely an effort to pamper one or two of your pets, and to persecute and degrade their supposed rivals. I have had no word from Sumner, Heintzelman, or Keyes. The commanders of these Corps are of course the three highest officers with you, but I am constantly told that you have no consultation or communication with them; that you consult and communicate with nobody but General Fitz John Porter, and perhaps General Franklin. I do not say these complaints are true or just; but at all events it is proper you should know of their existence. Do the Commanders of Corps disobey your orders in any thing?
>
> But, to return, are you strong enough—are you strong enough, even with my help—to set your foot upon the necks of Sumner, Heintzelman, and Keyes all at once? This is a practical and very serious question for you.[116]

Just as McClellan had not responded to Lincoln's major advisory letter of April 9, there is no indication that McClellan ever responded to the president's advice and questions in this May 9 letter. Perhaps his silence was due to the accuracy of Lincoln's information on McClellan's disjointed relationship with his generals and his inability to justify it. Instead, beginning the next day, McClellan resumed his campaign for more troops and painted a bleak picture of his allegedly horrid predicament. At 5 A.M. on May 10, he wired Stanton:

> From the information reaching me from every source I regard it as certain that the enemy will meet us with all his force on or near the Chickahominy. They can concentrate many more men than I have, and are collecting troops from all quarters, especially well disciplined troops from the South. Casualties, sickness, garrisons, and guards have much reduced our numbers, and will continue to do so. I shall fight the rebel army with whatever force I may have, but duty requires me to urge that every effort be made to re-enforce me without delay with all the disposable troops in Eastern Virginia, and that we concentrate all our forces as far as possible to fight the great battle now impending and to make it decisive.
>
> If I am not re-enforced, it is probable that I will be obliged to fight nearly double my numbers, strongly entrenched. I do not think it will be at all possible for me to bring more than 70,000 men upon the field of battle.[117]

In a telegram later that same day, McClellan told Stanton that if the *Merrimack* was destroyed and Norfolk taken, "I can change my line to the James River and dispense with the [Richmond & West Point] railroad." He also asked for two or three of the cavalry regiments he had left on the Potomac.[118]

Thus, as soon as he had merged his left wing with Franklin's right wing on the Pamunkey River, McClellan announced his intention to move his base from the York/Pamunkey rivers south to the James River. He would not complete this change of base until early July after his strategic defeat in the Seven Days' Battle.[119]

In a letter to Mary Ellen written over three days (May 10–12), McClellan claimed the abandonment of Norfolk as his victory, reiterated his belief in bloodless successes, and complained of the lack of Government backing: "... Norfolk is in our possession, the result of my movements.... Are you satisfied now with my bloodless victories? Even the abolitionists seem to be coming around—judging at least from the very handsome Resolution offered by Mr. Lovejoy in the House.[120] ... [T]o have it recognized that I have saved the lives of my men & won success by my own efforts is to me the height of glory.... [The enemy] are concentrating everything for the last death struggle—my government, alas, is not giving me any aid...!"[121] A few days later, however, the general somewhat quirkily told her, "... nor do I understand why [the rebels] abandoned & destroyed Norfolk & the Merrimack unless they also intended to abandon all of Virginia!"[122]

On May 14, General Johnston had no more than 62,500 troops to oppose McClellan, who had more than 100,000 himself.[123] That mismatch did not prevent McClellan on that very date from again pleading to Lincoln for more troops because he was outnumbered. He wired the president:

> ... All my information from every source accessible to me establishes the fixed purpose of the rebels to defend Richmond against this Army by offering us battle with all the troops they can collect from east, west, and south, and my own opinion is confirmed by that of all my commanders whom I have been able to consult.
>
> Casualties, sickness, garrisons, and guards have much weakened my force and will continue to do so. I cannot bring into actual battle against the enemy more than eighty thousand men at the utmost, and with them I must attack in position, probably intrenched, a much larger force, perhaps double my numbers.... I most respectfully and earnestly urge upon Your Excellency that the opportunity has come for striking a fatal blow at the enemies of the Constitution, and I beg that you will cause this army to be re-enforced without delay by all the disposable troops of the Government. I ask for every man that the War Department can send me by water...."[124]

Lincoln responded the next day, "...Have done, and shall do, all I could and can to sustain you—hoped that the opening of James River, and putting Wool and Burnside in communication, with an open road to Richmond, or to you, had effected something in that direction...."[125]

A related problem was, in Sears' words, McClellan's "[s]lack organization. There were any number of able-bodied soldiers in this army who were customarily detailed to duty as orderlies and servants and guards and a score of other noncombatant guards; the equivalent of two regiments did nothing more than serve as escort for the general commanding."[126]

Lincoln explored the situation further to see if more reinforcements were available. On May 16, he asked McDowell how many troops he had with him at Fredericksburg, and McDowell responded that day that he had almost 32,500.[127] After consulting with Quartermaster General Meigs, Lincoln decided to send McDowell overland toward Richmond to assist McClellan. Lincoln's May 17 orders to McDowell cautioned, "While seeking to establish as soon as possible a communication between your left wing and the right wing of General McClellan, you will hold yourself always in such position as to cover the capital of the nation against a sudden dash of any large body of the rebel forces." Lincoln instructed McDowell that McDowell, not McClellan, would decide what was necessary to protect the capital. Stanton told McClellan the same thing.[128]

An early indication that McClellan was not fully satisfied by the president's action appeared in his May 18 letter to Mary Ellen: "Those hounds in Washington are after me again. Stanton is without exception the vilest man I ever knew or heard of."[129] Three days later he wrote to the president to again warn "[a]ll accounts report [enemy] numbers as greatly exceeding our own," to seek clarification and expansion of his authority over McDowell, and to assert that it was a delay-causing mistake to send McDowell by land instead of water.[130] The next day Lincoln sent a succinct rejoinder:

> Your long dispatch of yesterday just received. You will have just such control of Gen. McDowell and his force as you therein indicate. McDowell can reach you by land sooner than he could get aboard of boats if the boats were ready at Fredericks'burg,—unless his march shall be resisted, in which case, the force resisting him, will certainly not be confronting you at Richmond. By land he can reach you in five days after starting, whereas by water he would not reach you in two weeks, judging by past experience. Franklin's single Division did not reach you in ten days after I ordered it.[131]

Meanwhile, McClellan put into effect the plan he had devised before learning that McDowell would come by land instead of water. As Allan Nevins indicated, McClellan's establishment of his headquarters at White House Landing on the Pamunkey created some problems because it was too small to be protected by the navy and its location required a splitting of Union forces to approach Richmond by crossing the swampy and flood-prone Chickahominy River.[132] From White House Landing, McClellan ordered the two corps of Keyes and Heintzelman across the Chickahominy while retaining the three corps of Sumner, Porter, and Franklin north of that river. The crossings took place between May 20 and 25. This divided Union army was a target that even the defensive-minded Joseph Johnston could not resist.[133]

Historians Pois and Langer contended that McClellan's partial move south of the Chickahominy was the first step toward executing a plan to shift his base from the Pamunkey to the James River and avoid an aggressive pursuit of Johnston north of the Chickahominy.[134] McClellan had indeed indicated that such a base shift was his intention in his May 10 telegram to Stanton.

While he was dividing his army, McClellan's disappointment over the McDowell arrangements would soon turn to full-blown disillusionment. On the morning of May 23, Stonewall Jackson's troops surprised and routed Banks' men at Front Royal in the lower Shenandoah Valley and pursued them haphazardly to Winchester. There they fought a short-lived battle that resulted in Banks' farther retreat to and across the Potomac.

These events caused concerns for the safety of Banks' army and perhaps of Washington. Therefore, Lincoln directed a pincers movement intended to trap Jackson. Fremont was to close on Harrisonburg from western Virginia, McDowell (with 20,000 of his 32,000 troops) on Front Royal from the east, and Banks on Jackson's rear from the north.[135] Prompt execution of these orders would have resulted in Jackson being surrounded by three Union armies. However, Jackson and his men swiftly marched south back up the Valley and through Harrisonburg before McDowell and Banks arrived and closed the Valley Pike.

Most significantly, Jackson had successfully diverted much of McDowell's command to the Valley and all of it away from Richmond. McClellan, amazed that the enemy had allowed him to cross the Chickahominy to the Richmond side and hoping that he would not have to witness the sacking of Richmond, planned to move on Richmond by May 24.[136] Late on the 24th, however, he received bad news from Lincoln: "In consequence of Gen. Banks' critical position I have been compelled to suspend Gen. McDowell's movement to join you. The enemy are making a desperate push upon Harpers Ferry, and we are trying to throw Fremont's force & part of McDowell's in their rear."[137] McClellan responded, "I will make my calculations accordingly."[138]

Lincoln soon tested those calculations. On May 25, he telegraphed the general, "The enemy is moving North in sufficient force to drive Banks before him in precisely what force we can not tell.... I think the movement is a general and concerted one, such as could not be if he was acting upon the purpose of a very desperate defence of Richmond. I think the time is near when you must either attack Richmond or give up the job and come to the defence of Washington. Let me hear from you instantly."[139] Lincoln was growing increasingly tired of McClellan's dawdling. The general was in the midst of writing to his wife when Lincoln's wire arrived. He told her, "I have this moment received a dispatch from the Presdt who is terribly scared about Washington—& talks about the necessity of my returning in order to save it! Heaven save a country governed by such counsels! I must reply to his telegram & finish this by & by!"[140]

So McClellan turned to replying to Lincoln. Somewhat defiantly, he said, "Telegram received. Independently of it, the time is very near when I shall attack Richmond. The object of the [enemy's] movement is probably to prevent re-enforcements being sent to me. All the information obtained from balloons, deserters, prisoners, and contrabands [former slaves] agrees in the statement that the mass of rebel troops are still in immediate vicinity of Richmond, ready to defend it."[141] Then he returned to the letter to Mary Ellen and wrote, "Have just finished my reply to his Excellency! It is perfectly sickening to deal with such people & you may rest assured that I will lose as little time as possible in breaking off all connection with them—I get more sick of them every day—for every day brings with it only additional proofs of their hypocrisy, knavery & folly—well, well, I ought not to write in this way, for they may be right & I entirely wrong, so I will drop the subject...." At 10 P.M. that night he added another observation, "It seems from some later dispatches I have received that Banks has been soundly thrashed & that they are terribly alarmed in Washn. A scare will do them good, & may bring them to their senses...."[142]

McClellan was commenting on an 8:30 P.M. wire from Lincoln that told of Banks' multiple defeats and his retreat, described the McDowell and Fremont movements he had ordered, said that without McDowell's force "we would be utterly helpless," and concluded, "Apprehension of something like this, and no unwillingness to sustain you, has always been my reason for withholding McDowell's force from you. Please understand this, and do the best you can with the force you have."[143] To Mary Ellen, McClellan described the president's dispatches as "amazing in the extreme" and added, "I feared last night that I would be ordered back for the defense of Washington! You can imagine the course I had determined to pursue in such a contingency."[144]

On the morning of May 27, at least partly in response to a telegram from Lincoln, McClellan ordered Porter to move west toward Hanover Court House to disperse the enemy and to destroy railroad bridges on the Virginia Central and Richmond, Fredericksburg & Potomac railroads. The next day McClellan reported to Stanton that Porter had won "a glorious victory," the "rout of the rebels was complete," he would try but probably would not be able to cut off Jackson's arrival (which was almost a month away!), and his troops had "cut all but the Fredericksburg and Richmond Railroad." He included the usual, "There is no doubt that the enemy are concentrating everything on Richmond," and defiantly declared, "It is the policy and duty of the Government to send me by water all the well-drilled troops available. I am confident that Washington is in no danger."[145]

A skeptical Lincoln challenged McClellan's assertions: "I am very glad of Gen. F. J. Porter's victory. Still, if it was a total rout of the enemy, I am puzzled to know why the Richmond and Fredericksburg Railroad was not seized. Again, as you say you have *all* the Railroads but the Richmond and Fredericksburg, I am puzzled to see how, lacking that, you can have any, except the scrap from Richmond to West-Point. The scrap of the Virginia Central from Richmond to Hanover Junction, without more, is simply nothing. That the whole force of the enemy is concentrating in Richmond, I think can not be certainly known to you or me.... I shall aid you all I can consistently with my view of due regard to all points."[146]

Bolstering his case for reinforcements, McClellan reported in a late May 30 wire to Stanton that a "contraband" had reported the arrival in Richmond from the West of Beauregard with troops. Unaware of how soon he would need them, he also asked for more ambulances.[147] Just three days before, he had told the Secretary, "Richmond papers urge Johnston to attack.... I think he is too able for that.... Every day is making our result more sure and I am wasting no time."[148] In fact, McClellan had frittered away the months of April and May as he slowly proceeded up the Peninsula to the environs of Richmond. Although he had continuously pleaded that he needed more troops, in the words of historian Stephen Sears, "[W]hen he was finally ready to make his final advance on Richmond, the government had put more troops at his disposal than his plans had called for."[149]

In two months, McClellan had assembled a massive army and slowly moved it up the peninsula toward Richmond. He had squandered opportunities for quick advances and decisive victories. All he had to show for his efforts were a few minor, almost meaningless, successes. Finally, in the vicinity of Richmond, he divided his army and forfeited the initiative to the Confederates.

The Battle of Seven Pines

Ironically, the first major battle in the Richmond area—as would be the case with all subsequent battles there over the next month—was brought on by the Confederate "defenders" and not by the general who was supposedly on the strategic offensive. On May 31 and June 1, at Seven Pines (Fair Oaks), Confederates attacked McClellan's troops along the River Road and elsewhere on his left (southern) flank. To initiate the battle, Johnston's troops attacked two Union corps, those of Keys and Heintzelman, south of the Chickahominy.

Johnston, under pressure from Davis and Lee, had launched an assault with his entire force against the Union troops closest to Richmond—a mere six miles away. McClellan was in his sickbed north of the Chickahominy during the May 31 fighting and arrived on the battlefield after the second day of fighting had ended on June 1. Thus, he continued his near-perfect record of absence from his armies' battlefields.

Meanwhile McClellan's fate was ordained when the defense-oriented Johnston was severely injured on the first day of this battle and was replaced late the next day by the offensive-minded Robert E. Lee. Seven Pines demonstrated again McClellan's timidity, his ceding the initiative to the enemy, and his propensity for absence from the battlefield.

As indicated earlier, Johnston attacked the isolated Union left wing, which was sep-

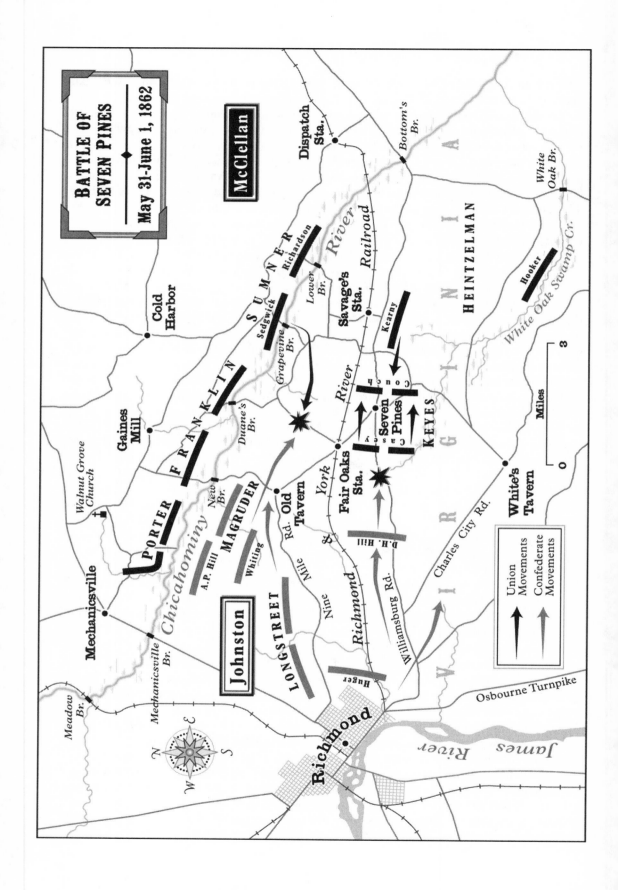

arated from the bulk of McClellan's army by the Chickahominy and which posed the greatest threat to Richmond. Fortuitously for Johnston, an extremely heavy rain the night before the battle, supplementing heavy rains earlier that week, made it even more difficult for any Union reinforcements to cross that river. His battle plan called for a massive attack by 52,000 soldiers of James Longstreet, Daniel Harvey Hill, William H.C. Whiting, and Benjamin Huger against Heintzelman and Keyes' corps, consisting of 31,500 troops.

Johnston planned to crush those two corps with overwhelming force. His battle plan, however, proved to be too complex for generals who had never commanded such large bodies of troops. Greatest reliance was placed on Longstreet, who clearly fell short of what was expected. He had his division take the wrong road and, in doing so, blocked Huger's troops, who were to attack even earlier than his on another road. Taking advantage of verbal orders issued by Johnston, Longstreet appears to have sought greater glory than the orders contemplated—although it is possible Longstreet misunderstood his orders.[150]

In late morning on May 31, the Rebel troops ferociously struck Keyes' corps and began driving them back on Heintzelman's troops. Only after two hours of fighting did McClellan order reinforcements from north of the Chickahominy.[151] By late afternoon, these two Union corps were in serious trouble. Marcy ordered Sumner and his 20,000-man corps to cross the Chickahominy and march to their support. Sumner's corps saved them and the day for the Union army by crossing the river on a flood-swept bridge that survived only long enough for their crossing. Historian Alan Nevins described the scene: "Only one half-wrecked bridge was available. The log approaches were afloat, held by their fastenings to tree stumps, and the bridge itself was precariously kept in place by ropes. Many officers had doubted the feasibility of passage. As the solid infantry column came forward the structure swayed to and fro in the angry flood, settling down safely only when filled with men; and after they had crossed it quickly became worthless."[152]

McClellan's first written communique that day came at 5 P.M. and merely told Heintzelman, commanding the left wing, to hang on and keep him informed.[153] At 9:20 that night, he urged Chief of Staff Marcy to hasten the construction of bridges across the Chickahominy.[154] The near-loss of two of his five corps at Seven Pines had awakened the commander to the serious danger of dividing his army by placing it on both banks of the Chickahominy.

McClellan finally sent word of the battle to Washington at midnight of its second day. He told Stanton of the "desperate battle … against greatly superior numbers." He reported that Brigadier General Silas Casey's division had fallen back "unaccountably & discreditably," Heintzelman and Kearney had gallantly checked the enemy's assault, and Sumner had brought two divisions across the river.[155]

McClellan's treatment of Casey, his front-line commander at Seven Pines, appears to have been cruel and unfair—perhaps intended to deflect attention from McClellan's own failures. Because of Casey's expertise in infantry tactics, he had trained perhaps three quarters of McClellan's army. His reward was to have assigned to his division the "green" officers and troops he happened to be training when the Peninsula Campaign began. In the first fifty-two days of the campaign, he had lost almost 3,600 (forty percent) of his command to sickness and desertion. Three times McClellan advanced this weakest of his divisions to the most forward and exposed position south of the Chickahominy while keeping sixty percent of his army north of that river more than six miles from the single bridge across it. When the Confederates attacked Casey's position in force, some of his inexperienced, overwhelmed, and sick troops fled to the rear. However, the bulk of his troops vigorously resisted the assault by Rebels twice their number.[156]

Above and opposite: **Primitive bridges across the Chickahominy River near Richmond, Virginia, demonstrated the difficulties both armies had crossing that river before and during the battles of Seven Pines and the Seven Days in 1862 (Library of Congress).**

Two hours after the battle began, the Third Corps commander and *de facto* wing commander, Major General Heintzelman, arrived and was told by Fourth Corps commander Erasmus D. Keyes that Casey had been driven back. Heintzelman reported to McClellan that Casey's men had been routed, and McClellan repeated the slanderous hearsay and reported to Stanton that Casey's Division "gave way unaccountably and discreditably." He compounded the injustice by consenting to newspaper publication of his report. Even though an inspector general's report, Casey's high killed and wounded numbers, and other first-hand evidence confirmed that Casey's division had fought well and repelled the enemy for two hours, McClellan relieved Casey of his command and never cleared his name. Historian William J. Miller concluded, "By pointing at Casey and his men, and later at Casey alone, McClellan was able to deflect criticism, evade scrutiny, and escape judgment as the author of the Army of the Potomac's brush with destruction on May 31, 1862. The disaster of Casey should more properly be seen as the disgrace of McClellan."[157]

At Seven Pines, the attacking Confederates suffered over 6,000 casualties, about a thousand more than McClellan's troops. Both sides were appalled by the number of casualties, but, in Alan Nevins' words, "… worst shaken of all was McClellan's reputation as a strategist. He had committed a terrible error in throwing his army astraddle a danger-ous river and leaving Keyes' corps standing isolated for several days within reach of a crushing blow from Johnston. Indeed he was lucky to escape so easily. Johnston always believed that a vigorous renewal of the battle on June 1 would have destroyed Keyes and crippled McClellan."[158]

McClellan, a purported expert on European cavalry, had segregated his regular army cavalrymen from his volunteers, kept three squadrons of regulars as his personal escort, assigned the Second Cavalry to provost marshal duties, and dispersed his volunteer cav-alry to duty with the infantry. His infantry units used the cavalrymen as headquarters guards and couriers (as did McClellan himself). His opponent, Joseph Johnston, consol-idated his cavalry into an effective single entity under Brigadier General J.E.B. ("Jeb") Stuart. On their contrasting use and misuse of cavalry, historian Robert O'Neill con-cluded, "By concentrating his regiments into one brigade, Stuart had a force that could have real impact on a battle or campaign. In contrast, McClellan created a command heavy in brass and braid, but lacking the strength necessary to dominate on the battlefield."[159]

On June 2, again to Stanton, McClellan took credit for ordering Sumner across the river, praised Sumner's performance, and concluded, "The result is that our left is now within 4 miles of Richmond. I only wait for the [Chickahominy] river to fall to cross with the rest of the force and make a general attack." He immediately conditioned that remark by stating he might have to wait for reinforcements from Fort Monroe.[160] In fact, he would dally for more than three additional weeks and end up never making a general attack on Richmond.

McClellan had taken two months to move his army a mere seventy miles from Fort Monroe to the Richmond area, wasted a month establishing siege lines at Yorktown, allowed the enemy time to concentrate its forces, and placed his army in jeopardy by divid-ing it on both sides of the almost impassable Chickahominy River. In summary, his pur-portedly offensive campaign was becoming a disaster waiting to happen.

6

Retreating at a Distance During the Seven Days' Battle

While supposedly on the offensive against Richmond, McClellan dithered until his still-divided army was attacked by Lee's army in a week-long battle that featured daily Union retreats, McClellan's frequent absence from the battlefield, his constant pleas for reinforcements, and a final retreat when victory was in his grasp.

The climax of McClellan's Peninsula Campaign would come at the end of June when Lee launched his week-long series of attacks against the Army of the Potomac in the Seven Days' Battle. Between the time of Seven Pines and the Seven Days', McClellan continued to vacillate. He wasted another three weeks without assaulting the Confederate capital or its defending troops. During that time, the initiative and momentum clearly shifted to Lee—although it is a stretch to say that McClellan ever really had either.

On June 2, McClellan took the time to issue another of his bombastic proclamations to his troops. After praising them for their past successful battles, he asked them for "one last crowning effort" in which they would "meet and crush [the enemy] here in the very center of the rebellion." Then he bravely promised and declared, "Soldiers, I will be with you in this battle, and share its dangers with you. Our confidence in each other is now founded upon the past. Let us strike the blow which is to restore peace and union to this distracted land."[1] Although most of his troops still had confidence in McClellan, before the month was out he would clearly not be with them in battle and would not share the dangers of battle with them.

Also on June 2, in a wire to Mary Ellen, McClellan put a rosy perspective on things: "… success complete. One more & we will have Richmond & I shall be there with Gods blessing this week." He even allowed himself to dream one of his favorite dreams: "It is possible that yesterday's victory will open Richmond to us without further fighting."[2] He still was chasing the chimera of a war-winning bloodless victory. In a letter to her that same day, McClellan indicated that he abhorred the bloodshed that battle inevitably brought: "But I am tired of the sickening sight of the battlefield, with its mangled corpses & poor suffering wounded! Victory has no charms for me when purchased at such a cost."[3]

On June 4, he complained of the flooded Chickahominy, bad bridges, and the loss of 5,000 men in the recent battle. He advised Lincoln, "You must make your calculations on the supposition that I have been correct from the beginning in asserting that the serious opposition was to be made here."[4] The next day he urged Lincoln to see that Chattanooga, Tennessee, and Dalton, Georgia, were occupied. For someone who himself moved at a snail's pace, he had the temerity to advise, "The evacuation of Corinth [Mississippi] would appear to render this very easy. The importance of the move in force cannot be exaggerated."[5] Chattanooga and Dalton were hundreds of miles from Corinth. The importance of occupying them, in McClellan's mind, apparently was prevention of Rebel reinforcements from moving through those points to Richmond. On June 7, the president forwarded a wire from Halleck indicating that his troops were moving eastward from Corinth toward Chattanooga.[6]

Reinforcements on the way from Fort Monroe provided McClellan with another excuse for delay. On the night of June 6, he told Mary Ellen, "If I hear tomorrow that they will surely be here in three or four days I will wait for them, as it would make the result certain & less bloody. I can't afford to have any more men killed than can be avoided...."[7] It appears not to have occurred to him the enemy might also receive additional reinforcements during the extra days—a puzzling oversight by someone so concerned about Rebel reinforcements.

On June 7, Stanton advised McClellan that McCall's division and seven additional regiments would be sent to McClellan from McDowell and then tried to pin him down: "Please state whether you will feel sufficiently strong for your final movement when McCall reaches you."[8] After complaining about flooded conditions, the General responded that day to Stanton, "... I am glad to learn that you are pressing forward reinforcements so vigorously. I shall be in perfect readiness to move forward and take Richmond the moment McCall reaches here and the ground will admit the passage of artillery...."[9] Although the insertion of another condition was typical of McClellan, Stanton must have been astounded that he had not asked for additional reinforcements.

Having received June 8 orders to protect Washington and then proceed to join McClellan with the "residue" of his force, McDowell wired McClellan that he was pleased that he would be arriving with his main body of troops to reinforce McClellan.[10] McClellan did not respond in kind. Instead he told Mary Ellen: "I have not replied to [McDowell], nor shall I—the animal probably sees that the tide is changing & that I am not entirely without friends in the world. The Secy & Presdt are also becoming quite amiable of late—I am afraid that I am a little cross to them & that I do not quite appreciate their sincerity & good feeling—'Time Danaus [sic] et dona ferentes [I fear the Greeks even when they bring gifts].' How glad I will be to get rid of the whole lot...."[11] Interestingly, in this letter, as well as his June 6 letter to her, McClellan expressed his erroneous belief that G.W. Smith, rather than Lee, commanded the opposing army.[12] Smith had been in command for less than a day between Johnston and Lee.

On June 10, McClellan bemoaned the swollen Chickahominy, the muddy ground, and his consequently useless artillery. However, he laid the groundwork for later rationalizing any defeat by explaining, "I regret all this extremely—but take comfort from the thought that God will not leave so great a struggle as this to mere chance—if he ever interferes with the destinies of men & nations this would seem to be a fit occasion for it."[13]

That same day McClellan reported to Stanton that his favorite bogeyman might have arrived. Once again, he said he had information that Beauregard had arrived from Mississippi and that some of his troops would follow. Then he admitted, "No great reliance—perhaps none whatever—can be attached to this; but it is possible, and ought to be their policy." Unsurprisingly, he proceeded to explain that the weather would delay his attack and suggested that reinforcements be sent to him from Halleck in the West. He concluded with his usual hedged assurance: "I will attack with whatever force I may have, although a larger force would enable me to gain much more decisive results."[14] Although he included in that letter another plea for McCall's troops to come by water, the next day he reported that some of McCall's troops had arrived at White House Landing the previous night.[15]

On June 11, Stanton graciously assured McClellan of his confidence in him: "... Be assured, general, that there never has been a moment when my desire has been otherwise than to aid you with my whole heart, mind, and strength since the hour we first met; and whatever others may say for their own purposes, you have never had, and never can have, any one more truly your friend, or more anxious to support you...."[16] Stanton's assurances, however, probably were just as sincere as those given by McClellan to him and Lincoln.

On June 12, McClellan broke camp and moved from the north to the south side of the Chickahominy. He left Porter and Franklin behind in an isolated position on his right (north) flank and thereby presented Lee with a target for attack. They were, however, augmented by the waterborne arrival of McCall's division of Pennsylvania Reserves on June 12 and 13.

Meanwhile, on June 11, Lee had ordered Jeb Stuart to determine what the strength and location of McClellan's right flank were and whether that flank extended far enough north to cover his rail supply line from White House Landing. To find out, Stuart and 1,200 cavalry, from June 12 to 15, rode a hundred miles completely around McClellan's army, skirmished with Union cavalry commanded by Brigadier General Philip St. George Cooke (Stuart's father-in-law), destroyed two small Union supply depots, took one hundred sixty-four prisoners, and returned virtually unscathed (one killed, several wounded) to Richmond. This Chickahominy Raid made McClellan look foolish. The general first reported Stuart's movement in a June 14 midday wire to Stanton.[17]

McClellan had facilitated Stuart's reconnaissance-in-force by disabling his own cavalry. In his August 20, 1861 General Orders No. 1, he had appointed Brigadier General George Stoneman chief of cavalry. However, his March 24, 1862 Special Orders No. 90 dispersed his cavalry regiments among his infantry corps and thus destroyed any coordinating effect the prior order may have intended. As discussed above, this dilution of authority was worsened by further corps dispersal of cavalry among divisions and brigades, where the troopers were used as couriers, bodyguards, escorts, and orderlies. As a result of McClellan's scattering of his horsemen, "the cavalry as a body was practically neutralized," according to a Union cavalry brigade commander.[18]

At midnight on June 14, McClellan sent one of his typical telegrams to Stanton. He said he would advance "as soon as the bridges are completed and the ground fit for artillery to move." Obligatorily, he added that he would be glad for any reinforcements that could be sent. The bulk of his wire, however, was an explosion over a request from McDowell that McClellan place McCall's troops where McDowell's others could join them when they arrived. McClellan interpreted this simple request as a threat to his command and control. He requested that all McDowell's troops be put under his full control and pouted, "... If I cannot fully control all his troops I want none of them, but would prefer to fight the battle with what I have, and let others be responsible for the results." His laughable conclusion read, "The stake at issue is too great to allow personal considerations to be entertained. You know that I have none."[19]

The following evening, McClellan told Stanton the bridges across the Chickahominy were "progressing rapidly and we shall very soon be ready to strike the final blow." He reported that prisoners said four Rebel regiments had arrived within days from North Carolina and therefore urged that transportation be hurried to Burnside so he could move from North Carolina to McClellan's aid.[20] McClellan's plan as of June 15, so he told Mary Ellen, was to advance on June 17 or 18 and seize a point called Old Tavern south of the Chickahominy on the road to Richmond from the New Bridge across the Chickahominy.[21]

In fact, by the 18th an attack had not occurred and McClellan told Lincoln that "[a] general engagement may take place any hour." He failed to add that he was unlikely to be the one initiating it. That reality, however, was probably revealed to Lincoln by the general's conditional assurances: "Our army is well over the Chickahominy, except the very considerable forces necessary to protect our flanks and communications.... After to-morrow we shall fight the rebel army as soon as Providence will permit. We shall await only a favorable condition of the earth and sky and the completion of some necessary preliminaries."[22] Once again, McClellan placed at least partial responsibility on Providence.

Reinforcements continued to be an issue. In a June 15 communication, Lincoln pointed out to McClellan that the addition of the Fort Monroe troops, McCall's division, and other regiments had increased McClellan's strength by 20,000 since Fair Oaks.[23] Three days later McClellan told the president that a considerable portion of Longstreet's division had left Richmond to reinforce Jackson.[24] The president responded that a Frenchman had reported 10,000 to 15,000 Rebel troops moving west through Gordonsville toward the Shenandoah Valley and added, "If this is true, it is as good as a reinforcement to you of an equal force."[25]

In his wire to Lincoln that same day, McClellan rejoined, "If 10,000 or 15,000 men have left Richmond to re-enforce Jackson it illustrates their strength and confidence."[26] Lincoln did not let the matter lie there. The next day he responded that the reported movement meant either that the enemy was very strong at Richmond or did not intend to defend it desperately. He added that, upon reflection, he doubted the reports and concluded, "It induces a doubt whether the Frenchman & your deserters have not all been sent to deceive."[27] Lincoln was reading Lee's intent better than McClellan. Lincoln's skepticism again was reflected in his June 20 wire about a report from General Sigel in the Shenandoah that Jackson had been reinforced from Richmond. His conclusion was: "This may be reality, and yet may only be contrivance for deception; and to determine which, is perplexing."[28]

McClellan, who was simultaneously asking Burnside how quickly he could move from New Bern, North Carolina, either by water to White House Landing or Fort Monroe or inland to Goldsboro,[29] told Lincoln with certainty, " I have no doubt that Jackson has been re-enforced from here." In that June 20 telegram, McClellan, the supposed aggressor, then ominously told the president of his defenses and inquired about the disposition of all Union troops not already his: "By to-morrow night the defensive works covering our position on this side of the Chickahominy should be completed. I am forced to this by my inferiority in numbers so that I may bring the greatest possible numbers into action and secure the army against the consequences of unforeseen disaster.... I would be pleased to learn the disposition as to numbers and position of the troops not under my command in Virginia and elsewhere."[30] The next day the president declined to put those numbers into a telegram or letter for security reasons[31]—in sharp contrast to McClellan's revealing his military plans in his correspondence with his wife.

As of June 20, McClellan had been significantly reinforced. Lincoln had sent him a total of 20,000 more troops from Washington, Fort Monroe, and Fredericksburg. On

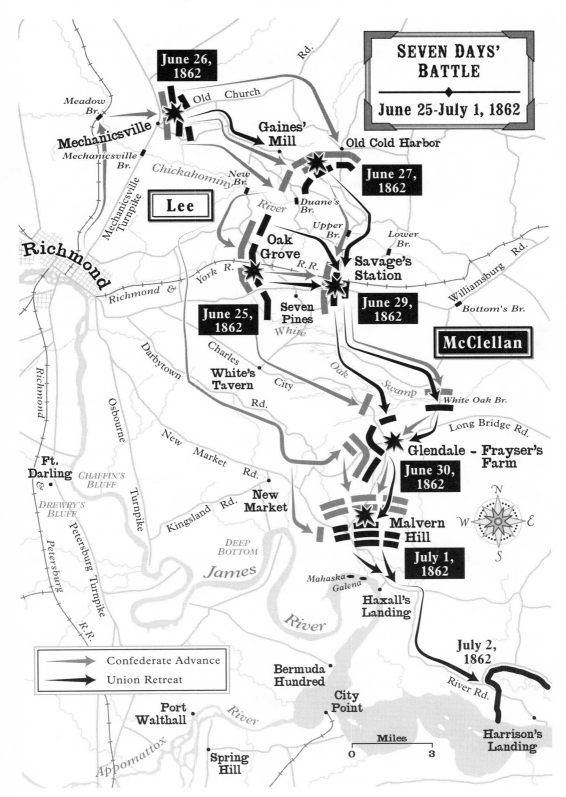

SEVEN DAYS' BATTLE

June 25–July 1, 1862

June 26, 1862

Meadow Br.

Old Church Rd.

Gaines' Mill

Old Cold Harbor

Mechanicsville

Mechanicsville Br.

Mechanicsville Turnpike

Chickahominy New Br.

Duane's Br.

June 27, 1862

Lee

Oak Grove

Upper Br.

Lower Br.

Richmond

York R. R.R.

Savage's Station

Williamsburg Rd.

Richmond &

River

Bottom's Br.

June 25, 1862

Seven Pines

June 29, 1862

McClellan

Darbytown

Charles

White

White's Tavern

City

Oak

White Oak Br.

Swamp

Richmond

Osbourne

New Market Rd.

Long Bridge Rd.

Glendale – Frayser's Farm

Ft. Darling

CHAFFIN'S BLUFF

Turnpike

Kingsland Rd.

New Market

June 30, 1862

DREWRY'S BLUFF

N

W E

S

Petersburg

DEEP BOTTOM

Malvern Hill

Petersburg Turnpike

James

July 1, 1862

R.R.

Mahaska

Galena

River

Haxall's Landing

July 2, 1862

Confederate Advance

Union Retreat

Bermuda Hundred

City Point

River Rd.

Port Walthall

River

Harrison's Landing

Appomattox

Spring Hill

Miles

0 3

that date, McClellan's own reports showed that his army totaled 156,838, including between 115,000 and 127,000 present for duty. At the beginning of the campaign, he had asked Stanton for rail transport sufficient to support 130,000 troops. He had more than that but did not effectively use them. Alan Nevins pointed out that between June 18 and 25 McClellan missed a "golden opportunity" to attack because Jackson was still in the Valley, Richmond remained weak, and Lee had not been reinforced from elsewhere.[32]

Apparently lacking confidence in McClellan's judgment, Lincoln left Washington on June 23 for an unannounced trip to West Point in New York for a strategic conference with retired General Winfield Scott. The president outlined the current situation and asked for Scott's advice. Scott memorialized his advice in a memorandum. He advised that McDowell's remaining force at Fredericksburg was not necessary for the defense of Washington, that it was out of position to support McClellan by land, and that it should be moved by water to reinforce McClellan.[33] McClellan would have been glad to know of this support from the man he had deposed.

Meanwhile McClellan was busy keeping up with political developments in Washington. On June 22, he told Mary Ellen that Allan Pinkerton had learned that Stanton and Chase were warring with each other and "… that Honest A[be Lincoln] has again fallen into the hands of my enemies & is no longer a cordial friend of mine!" He then went on to repeat some familiar themes:

> Alas poor country that should have such rulers. I tremble for my country when I think of these things, but still can trust that God in his infinite wisdom will not punish us as we deserve, but will in his own good time bring order out of chaos & restore peace to this unhappy country. His will be done—whatever it may be. I am as anxious as any human being can be to finish this war, yet when I see such insane folly behind me I feel that the final salvation of the country demands the utmost prudence on my part & that I must not run the slightest risk of disaster, for if anything happened to this army our cause would be lost. I feel too that I must not unnecessarily risk my life—for the fate of my army depends upon me & they all know it....[34]

Here was McClellan using his lead spy to track events in Washington, trusting in God to determine the outcome of the war, protecting his army instead of using it to carry the North's burden of winning the war, and over-estimating his own value. On the eve of the Seven Days' Battle, therefore, McClellan demonstrated that his chief concerns were avoiding disaster and saving his army and himself. He would save his army and himself but certainly not avoid disaster.

Perhaps a better use of Pinkerton would have been to adequately scout the enemy. On the eve of major conflict, McClellan was unsure whether Rebel reinforcements had been sent from the Richmond area to the Shenandoah Valley, could not seem to get reliable information on the whereabouts of Jackson, and continued to delude himself into believing that Beauregard had arrived from the Mississippi Valley. On June 24, he wired Stanton about a deserter who reported fifteen of Jackson's brigades at Gordonsville on their way to attack McClellan's rear on June 28 and requested any information on Jackson's position and movements.[35]

The next day, after advancing his left flank pickets along the James River in the minor Battle of Oak Grove (the first in the Seven Days' Battle), McClellan reported that escaped slaves had reported Jackson's advance to Hanover Court House and Beauregard's arrival (again) in Richmond with strong reinforcements. These reports caused McClellan to bleakly speculate about what was likely to happen next: "I incline to think that Jackson will attack my right & rear. The rebel force is stated at (200,000) two hundred thousand including Jackson & Beauregard. I shall have to contend against vastly superior odds if these reports be true. But this Army will do all in the power of men to hold their position & repulse any attack." Then he launched into an intemperate and self-absolving rant[36]:

> I regret my great inferiority in numbers but feel that I am in no way responsible for it as I have not failed to represent repeatedly the necessity of reinforcements; that this was the decisive point, and that all the available means of the Government should be concentrated here. I will do all that a general can do with the splendid army I have the honor to command, and if it is destroyed by overwhelming numbers can at least die with it and share its fate. But if the result of the action, which will probably occur tomorrow or within a short time, is a disaster, the responsibility cannot be thrown on my shoulders; it must rest where it belongs. I feel that there is no use in again asking for re-enforcements.[37]

The next day Lincoln responded directly and succinctly: "... The [dispatch] suggesting the probability of your being overwhelmed by 200,000, and talking of where the responsibility will belong, pains me very much. I give you all I can, and act on the presumption that you will do the best you can with what you have, while you continue, ungenerously, I think, to assume that I could give you more if I would. I have omitted and shall omit no opportunity to send you reinforcements whenever I possibly can."[38]

On the eve of Lee's initiation of his series of attacks in the Seven Days' Battle,[39] he had assembled 85,000 troops, the largest army he would ever command. However, this number was far less than one-half of the 200,000 Confederates that McClellan claimed he faced.[40] The day after McClellan gave that estimate, Pinkerton delivered to him his own estimate of 180,000. Fishel asserted that Pinkerton's report was "only an average of rumors and other 'sources' of the same quality." Demonstrating Pinkerton's grasp of his function (escalate the numbers), he wrote that 180,000 "is probably considerably short of the real strength of their army," which Fishel described as "an equivocation that would have authorized McClellan to pick a higher number if he had not already done so."[41]

McClellan's numerical delusions undoubtedly were a major cause of his reticence to engage the enemy in combat. After initiating the foray at Oak Grove on June 25, McClellan went strictly on the defensive, forgot all about attacking Richmond, and allowed the initiative to pass over to Lee. That very night, he wired Stanton that he expected to be attacked the next day and added, "If I had another good division I could laugh at Jackson."[42]

McClellan had left his right flank vulnerable to attack. He had retained his largest corps, under the command of Porter, alone north of the Chickahominy. It was connected only by a series of bridges across the Chickahominy River and surrounding swamps to the other four Union corps, those of Franklin, Keyes, Heintzelman, and Sumner. Believing correctly that McClellan, with 75,000 troops in position to do so, would not attack Lee's troops defending Richmond along the James River south and west of the Chickahominy, Lee left a "skeleton" defense of 35,000 troops there and shifted the bulk of his army northward to join with the incoming forces of Jackson and attack Porter's isolated corps of 30,000 with his own 50,000.[43]

A major problem faced by McClellan was that Lee knew him too well. Nevins deftly summarized Lee's analysis of McClellan:

> [Lee] now understood [McClellan] particularly well, for they had served on the same staff in the Mexican War. He had hardly been astonished by McClellan's strange winter inaction, his month-long pause before Yorktown, and his slow creep to White House Landing, for he knew that McClellan's taste was for a war of position. Invariably, in McClellan's strategy, boldness in conception was fettered by an appalling slowness in execution. Though

Lee respected McClellan's abilities, he knew that his operations were always half defensive; that he never caught at a military opportunity without saying to himself, "Suppose the enemy has hidden reserves?" And Lee realized that the timidities of his opponent opened the way for operations impossible in the face of a more resolute foe.[44]

Lee's accurate perception of McClellan's vulnerability would serve him well in the coming months.

The Battle of Mechanicsville

Fortunately for McClellan, however, Lee's plans for offensives on June 26 and subsequent days proved to be too complex, too demanding, and too suicidal for the good of his Army of Northern Virginia. With about two-thirds of his 85,000 troops, Lee was assaulting 30,000 well-positioned and entrenched Union troops north of the Chickahominy, and that assault would prove quite costly.

Lee's major problem was over-estimating the physical and mental condition of Stonewall Jackson and his exhausted troops. Their arrival was to be the starting gun for an all-out assault on McClellan's right flank at Mechanicsville. In a preview of what was to happen repeatedly that week, Jackson's troops arrived late and never reached the Mechanicsville battlefield during Lee's assault of June 26.

Despite Jackson's "no-show," an impatient A.P. Hill[45] started an ill-advised frontal assault against strongly entrenched troops commanded by Porter. Seeing the difficulty A.P. Hill's troops were encountering, Lee authorized Longstreet and D.H. Hill to throw their men into the battle. The Confederates were bloodily repelled all along the line. Casualties that first day were 1,350 for the attacking Rebels and only 360 for the Union defenders.

During the Battle of Mechanicsville, McClellan remained safely at his headquarters south of the Chickahominy until the fighting ceased. That day, in a telegram mainly discussing who was guilty of insulting whom, McClellan requested Goldsborough to have provision transports available on the James River—"a matter of vital importance [that] may involve the existence of this Army."[46] Thus, even before the first day of fighting north of the Chickahominy was over, McClellan again was thinking of the possible retrograde movement of his army to the James River.

At mid-afternoon, McClellan told Porter to hold his position until dark, promised reinforcements if needed, and pessimistically concluded, "Be prepared to throw everything over the Chickahominy if possible—better send your heavy baggage over as soon as possible."[47] From Porter's headquarters that evening, McClellan sent three telegrams to Stanton about the ongoing battle. He praised the men of McCall and Major General George W. Morrell but gave a warning: "My men are behaving superbly, but you must not expect them to contest too long against great odds." Shortly before the intended withdrawal of that night, he told Stanton, "The enemy have not gained a foot...." He thanked Stanton for 5,000 reinforcements that Stanton had promised that day. In his final wire of that night, McClellan concluded, "Victory of to-day complete and against great odds. I almost begin to think we are invincible."[48] But the fighting had only begun.

Moreover, McClellan seemed more interested in uniting his army south of the Chickahominy than in providing Porter with adequate means to continue imposing heavy casualties on Lee or even to save his wing of the army against an all-out Rebel assault. In fact, McClellan moved most of Porter's wagons and heavy guns south of the Chickahominy after the first day's fighting—a clear indication that McClellan was no longer on the offensive.

In addition, McClellan was forfeiting a grand opportunity presented to him by Lee, who was using sixty percent of his army north of the Chickahominy and leaving Richmond vulnerable to attack. However, McClellan gave no indication of any desire to move forward against a mere 35,000 Rebels with the 75,000 troops he had south of the Chickahominy. Another episode of play-acting by Magruder, who marched his Rebel troops back and forth in a display of apparent military might, provided additional insurance against the unlikely possibility that McClellan would attempt an advance.

Fortunately for Porter, Jackson's troops had bivouacked in mid-afternoon about three miles north of the fighting in a location that made it difficult to establish contact with Lee's left (north) flank. Therefore, not only were Jackson's soldiers uninvolved in the Mechanicsville fighting, but their isolated location at the end of the day made it difficult for Jackson to carry out his assigned mission the next day.

The Battle of Gaines' Mill

On June 27, the third day of the Seven Days' Battle, Lee tried to outflank Porter's Mechanicsville position by bringing troops around Porter's right (north) flank and having Jackson bring his troops around to Porter's rear from the north or northeast. By these maneuvers, Lee hoped to trap the isolated Porter north of the Chickahominy. The result was the Battle of Gaines' Mill.

Once again, however, Jackson was a "no-show" on the Confederate left flank, and Lee's troops spent most of another day frontally assaulting Porter's troops. Furthermore, Porter had expected Lee's flanking movement and conducted an overnight three-mile strategic retreat from Mechanicsville to new fortified lines in an area that included Gaines' Mill. McClellan again stayed south of the river away from the fighting. According to historian Sears, "McClellan remained at headquarters throughout the day, judging for himself none of the fighting on Porter's front and none of the bluffing on Magruder's."[49]

Although Porter expected McClellan to attack Richmond while he held off the bulk of Lee's force north of the river, McClellan failed to do so. Also, McClellan at first failed to reinforce the threatened Porter. Because of his unfounded fear—aided by Magruder's continuing theatrical performance—of enemy numbers south of the Chickahominy, the Union commander hesitated to reinforce Porter north of the river and apparently never considered attacking Lee's inferior force by a movement toward Richmond south of the river. McClellan finally did manage to get some critical reinforcements from Sumner northward across the Chickahominy to Porter in order to keep Porter from being overrun. Franklin was unable to follow McClellan's suggestion to do likewise and re-cross the Chickahominy on the advancing Confederates' right flank just north of that river because he had burned a bridge behind him.[50]

Meanwhile, Jackson had managed to march his men down the wrong road and delay their arrival on the Confederate lines until late in the day. His troops were inserted somewhat haphazardly and did not fight as a unified force. The outnumbered Lee, however, finally achieved his desired concentration of force, obtained clear numerical superiority over Porter north of the Chickahominy, and came close to destroying his mammoth corps. McClellan failed to realize the predicament in which he had placed Porter. That morning he had told Stanton, "The troops on the other side are now well in hand, and the whole army so concentrated that it can take advantage of the first mistake made by the enemy."[51]

The Confederates attacked all afternoon and evening. In the early evening, the Rebels used overwhelming numbers and suicidal charges to destroy or capture several Federal batteries and drive Porter back to the river. If Jackson had arrived in a timely manner, Porter's situation would have been desperate. As it was, he barely managed to withdraw his survivors across the river under cover of night. He was compelled to leave his dead and severely wounded behind—a not uncommon occurrence for McClellan's beloved soldiers during this week of battles. The attack had won Lee the field and ended any possibility that his opponent would think of attacking Richmond—but at a tremendous cost: 8,500 casualties to the Union's 6,800.

McClellan stayed south of the river away from the fighting and provided Porter with meager reinforcements as he awaited his collapse. Sears concluded that "Porter had lost a battle he might have won with more timely support." According to Pois and Langer,

> Throughout that time, McClellan did nothing but wait for Porter to collapse. However, with Porter finally defeated, McClellan could continue with his plans. Continuing the fight along the Chickahominy might have provided someone else with a more reasonable alternative to the high-risk operation McClellan was contemplating. Not 'Mac,' though; all that mattered to him was avoiding the responsibility for a defeat not of his own contriving. The James River thus became the Promised Land.... It all could have ended differently, but as Porter finally retreated across the river, McClellan prepared to play the role of victim.[52]

Historian John T. Hubbell concluded, "The army was not beaten, but the general was, most completely." Supporting evidence is found in telegrams McClellan sent to Stanton the night after Gaines' Mill. Defeatism and blame avoidance reared their ugly heads in McClellan's messages. At 8 P.M., he wrote, "Have had a terrible contest. Attacked by greatly superior numbers in all directions. On this side we still hold our own, though a very heavy fire is still kept up. On the left bank of the Chickahominy the odds have been immense. We hold our own very nearly. I may be forced to give up my position during the night, but will not if it is possible to avoid it. Had I 20,000 fresh and good troops we would be sure of a splendid victory to-morrow."[53]

The truth was that the bulk of McClellan's troops south of the Chickahominy had seen no action the first two days of Lee's massive assaults and greatly outnumbered the troops they faced close to the James River. McClellan had fresh troops, and the road to Richmond was lightly protected. In fact, the Union division commanders on that front, Phil Kearny and Joe Hooker, had seen through Magruder's latest theatrics, realized the southern/right Rebel flank was thin, and argued strenuously for permission to break through to Richmond and at least free the 14,000 Union prisoners there. McClellan declined and restated his order to retreat. Kearny then denounced McClellan so vigorously ("I say to you all, such an order can only be prompted by cowardice or treason") that a court-martial or relief from command was expected by observers. Even McClellan's good friend Porter believed that an assault from Malvern Hill (near the James) would have driven Lee back through Richmond.[54]

Just after midnight, McClellan had worked himself into a tizzy and exploded against Stanton and the president in an intemperate wire to Stanton:

> I now know the full history of the day. On this side of the river (the right bank) we repulsed several strong attacks. On the left bank our men did all that men could do, all that soldiers could accomplish, but they were overwhelmed by vastly superior numbers even after I brought my last reserves into action.... Had I 20,000 or even 10,000 fresh troops to use to-

morrow I could take Richmond, but I have not a man in reserve, and shall be glad to cover my retreat and save the material and personnel of the Army.

If we have lost the day we have yet preserved our honor, and no one need blush for the Army of the Potomac. I have lost this battle because my force was too small.

I again repeat that I am not responsible for this, and I say it with the earnestness of a general who feels in his heart the loss of every brave man who has been needlessly sacrificed to-day. I still hope to retrieve our fortunes, but to do this the Government must view the matter in the same earnest light that I do. You must send me very large re-enforcements and send them at once....

In addition to what I have already said, I only wish to say to the President that I think he is wrong in regarding me as ungenerous when I said that my force was too weak. I merely reiterated a truth which to-day has been too plainly proved. If, at this instant, I could dispose of 10,000 fresh men, I could gain a victory to-morrow. I know that a few thousand more men would have changed this battle from a defeat to a victory. As it is, the Government must not and cannot hold me responsible for the result.

I feel too earnestly to-night. I have seen too many dead and wounded comrades to feel otherwise than that the Government has not sustained this army. If you do not do so now the game is lost.

If I save this Army now, I tell you plainly that I owe no thanks to you or to any other persons in Washington. You have done your best to sacrifice this army.[55]

Unfortunately for the Union cause, the head of the War Department's telegraphic office was so shocked by the last two sentences that he deleted them before forwarding the telegram to Stanton. That action was a great disservice to both Stanton and Lincoln because it deprived them of knowledge of McClellan's accusation against them.[56] The fact that McClellan did not know his final words had been deleted may have encouraged his future disrespect for Lincoln and Stanton[57] As demonstrated by this amazing telegram, McClellan had lost sight of his offensive strategic goal, was focused solely on saving his army and himself, was prepared to take any credit for doing so, and had absolved himself of any responsibility for ultimate defeat on the Peninsula.

Lincoln's response to the censored telegram was temperate and concerned:

Save your army at all events. Will send re-inforcements as fast as we can. Of course they can not reach you to-day, to-morrow, or next day. I have not said you were ungenerous for saying you needed re-inforcement. I thought you were ungenerous in assuming that I did not send them as fast as I could. I feel any misfortune to you and your Army quite as keenly as you feel it yourself. If you have had a drawn battle, or a repulse, it is the price we pay for the enemy not being in Washington.... Less than a week ago you notified us that re-inforcements were leaving Richmond to come in front of us.... It is the nature of the case, and neither you or the government that is to blame....[58]

Following through on reinforcements, Lincoln had Stanton wire Halleck and direct him to move 25,000 troops from the West to Richmond.[59] When, however, Halleck replied that such a loss of troops would cause him to call off his movement from Corinth, Mississippi, to Chattanooga, Tennessee, Lincoln cancelled the order. The president regarded the success of that western theater movement "fully as important as the taking and holding of Richmond."[60]

The Battle of Savage's Station

Back on the Peninsula on June 29, the fourth day of the Seven Days' Battle, McClellan ordered—at least by default—an all-out retreat to the James. There is no evidence of any order from him to his corps commanders. They either learned orally or by watching McClellan's own rearward movements that they were expected to retreat toward the James River. Therefore, they retreated south even though Lee's army was primarily north of the Chickahominy and his vulnerable smaller segment of Rebel troops and Richmond lay to the west. Stanton was under the impression that McClellan was concentrating on Richmond and was likely to enter it within two days.[61] Pois and Langer observed that Lee lost a day "trying to find a McClellan who was actually retreating in a direction quite different from that which a sane general might take."[62]

Lee desperately sought to destroy the Army of the Potomac while it was on the move. The first encounter south of the Chickahominy occurred on June 29 at Savage's Station. Confederates kept pressing forward, and McClellan's troops alternately opposed them and retreated. Once again, Jackson failed to provide the hammer on the Union right flank to the anvil consisting of the rest of Lee's army.

To his friend, Major General John A. Dix at Fort Monroe, McClellan wrote on the afternoon of the 29th to plead for reinforcements, authorize the abandonment of Williamsburg, and complain: "May God forgive the men who have caused the loss this army has experienced. It is now clear beyond a doubt that 20,000 more men would have given us a glorious victory. I for one can never forget nor forgive the selfish men who have caused the lives of so many gallant men to be sacrificed."[63]

Private Sneden wrote of the chaotic Union retreat from Savage's Station while the Confederates kept pressuring them. He recorded the destruction of massive quantities of supplies and even the firing and crashing of an entire ammunition train—to keep the supplies and ammunition from falling into Rebel hands. He was most disturbed by the fate of his wounded comrades: "There are 2,500 sick and wounded here now.... Many [were] able to travel off last night with the retreating army, but General Heintzelman says 'all who cannot get off by walking must be left behind to the enemy.' Although there are as many as 500 ambulances, these, by General McClellan's orders must go empty! Probably he reserves these ambulances for officers only.... Not more than 300 wounded managed to get away, leaving 2,300 to fall into the enemy's hands."[64]

The Battle of Glendale (Frayser's Farm)

Never did McClellan "lead" his men as forcefully as he did in the grand Seven Days' retreat; he took the lead and led them directly away from the enemy. By late morning on June 30, he already was at one Haxall's house on Turkey Island in the James River beyond Malvern Hill—several miles south of his troops and any prospect of actual battle. Private Sneden observed that day, "By 9:30 A.M., General McClellan had posted the troops to his satisfaction and about 10 o'clock he left with his staff and escort for Malvern Hill. Why he left was an enigma. He generally places the troops on the eve of battle, then goes off to the rear some miles away, leaving his generals to fight it out as best they can without his further assistance. In the event of victory he alone gets the credit. He would place the troops in position in the morning, then leave the field to seek a position for the next day...."[65]

From his safe location, McClellan told General Marcy to bring his headquarters there. He told him of a probable movement of the army downstream to Harrison's Landing and inquired how things were going back near the enemy: "Send back to Smith and ascertain how much more of the train is yet to move. Also ascertain what roads exist leading from our present position e.g. from White Oak Bridge to Long Bridge & Jones Bridge."[66] As he arranged for additional retreating, McClellan spent that day on the island and on the gunboat *Galena* on the James River—far from the desperate fighting. Perhaps even worse than abandoning his army, McClellan put no one in overall command as imminent battle loomed and thus left his commanders to fend for themselves.[67]

McClellan's absence from the battlefield during the Seven Days' Battle, and particularly at Glendale (Frayser's Farm), was described to the Joint Committee by Heintzelman. He testified that McClellan was too remote from the battlefield and that this remoteness made it difficult to communicate with him. As a consequence, he said that major battlefield decisions were made without input from McClellan. As an example, Heintzelman cited his own decision to fall back at Glendale after Franklin's corps had changed its position and left his corps vulnerable to being cut off. Had Lee's intended three-pronged attack been properly implemented at Frayser's Farm, the Union army would have been in desperate need of decisions from its absent commander. Sears concluded, "Whatever his reason, or combination of reasons, never in his military career was he so derelict of his duty."[68]

Glendale on June 30 presented Lee with his best opportunity to seriously damage the Union army.[69] That army was spread out and vulnerable to attack from the north and west. The Confederate attack, however, was disjointed, and Jackson once again failed to pursue vigorously on the Union right flank and rear. According to Private Sneden, the fighting at Glendale was "desperate and deadly in the extreme."[70] The Union corps commanders and their troops—with no direction, management or leadership from their army commander—fought desperately and bravely against the Rebel attacks. As a result, McClellan's army survived to fight another day. According to Pois and Langer, "The battle demonstrated that from the very beginning of the Seven Days it was McClellan and not his army that was whipped. In spite of (or because of) the fact that McClellan was not even on the field, the Union forces held."[71]

After the desperate defensive action fought by McClellan's corps and their commanders at Glendale, McClellan himself (having returned to his army at 8:30 P.M. after a fine dinner on the *Galena*) sent a panicky plea to Stanton:

> Another day of desperate fighting. We are hard pressed by superior numbers. I fear I shall be forced to abandon my material to save my men under cover of the gunboats. You must send us very large re-enforcements by way of Fort Monroe and they must come very promptly. My army has behaved superbly, and have done all that men could do. If none of us escape, we shall at least have done honor to the country. I shall do my best to save the Army. Send more gunboats.[72]

Much later that night—in fact, at 2:30 the next morning—the virtually sleepless McClellan sent a suddenly inflated troop request to Adjutant General Thomas: "... If it is the intention of the Government to re-enforce me largely, it should be done promptly and in mass. I need 50,000 more men, and with them I will retrieve our fortunes. More would be well, but that number sent at once will, I think, enable me to assume the offensive. I cannot too strongly urge the necessity of prompt action in this matter...."[73]

Lincoln responded to both of McClellan's urgent requests for reinforcements with some notes of realism. On July 1, he wrote, "It is impossible to re-inforce you for your present emergency. If we had a million of men we could not get them to you in time. We have not the men to send. If you are not strong enough to face the enemy you must find a place of security, and wait, rest, and repair. Maintain your ground if you can; but save the Army at all events, even if you fall back to Fortress-Monroe. We still have enough strength in the country, and will bring it out." The next day, the president answered the second plea: "... When you ask for fifty thousand men to be promptly sent you, you surely labor under some gross mistake of fact." He then explained that McClellan's own plan had called for 75,000 troops to remain for the defense of Washington and that only perhaps 60,000 troops remained near Washington or in the Shenandoah Valley. He concluded, "... Thus, the idea of sending you fifty thousand, or any other considerable force promptly, is simply absurd...."[74]

McClellan's continuing protestations about lack of adequate manpower likely were one cause of Lincoln's late June efforts to obtain more Union recruits. On June 28, he sent Secretary of State Seward to New York to discuss the manpower situation with northern governors. At their prompted request, Lincoln issued a July 1 call for 300,000 additional volunteers. A June 30 draft of a call for troops demonstrated that Secretary of State Seward may have bought into much of McClellan's overstated position about western reinforcements reaching Richmond: "The capture of New Orleans, Norfolk, and Corinth by the national forces has enabled the insurgents to concentrate a large force at and about Richmond, which place we must take with the least possible delay; in fact, there will soon be no formidable insurgent force except at Richmond."[75] In reality, Braxton Bragg had succeeded Beauregard in command of a large Rebel army in Mississippi while Kirby Smith commanded a significant force in the Appalachians. Neither Beauregard, Kirby Smith, nor any western troops had come to Richmond.

The Battle of Malvern Hill

After Glendale and before the final battle on the Peninsula, McClellan expressed his fear of further combat in a wire to Adjutant Thomas: "... My men are completely exhausted, and I dread the result if we are attacked to-day by fresh troops...." He then went on to spin the same stories he had been telling: "... Permit me to urge that not an hour should be lost in sending me fresh troops. More gunboats are much needed. I doubt whether more severe battles have ever been fought. We have failed to win only because overpowered by superior numbers."[76] At the same time, he wrote to General Dix at Fort Monroe; he urged him to rush reinforcements and repeated his concern about another attack: "... I pray that the enemy may not be in condition to disturb us today...."[77] McClellan failed to realize that his corps commanders and his troops were well prepared for a Rebel assault—and probably hoped for one.

That assault, or series of assaults, constituted the final of the Seven Days' battles, which occurred at Malvern Hill near the James River. McClellan's corps commanders had assembled a huge array of artillery and numerous regiments of rifles on a ridge that was ideal for defense. Although Lee was present, the Army of Northern Virginia, with his input, went out of control. Its commanders launched an uncoordinated series of attacks that resulted in massive Confederate casualties. As he had done during the Battle of Glendale, McClellan spent most of the day on a Union gunboat safely out of artillery range. He was determining the adequacy of the down-river Harrison's Landing for farther retreat and later sought shelter on a back corner of the battlefield near the James. Except for one brief mid-afternoon inspection of the lines, he did not come onto the battlefield until after dark.[78]

McClellan's absence did not go unnoticed. Private Sneden noted,

General McClellan was not on the ground (as usual) until the battle was over. He was off with Commodore [John] Rodgers, who commanded the gunboats ten miles down [the] James River, selecting a *new* and safer position for the army for the morrow! When the enemy attacked us yesterday he was safe on board the *Galena*! Today he is safe enough where there is no enemy, thus depriving all his corps and division commanders of his abilities and counsel.... McClellan had first placed the troops in position this morning before leaving.... And as there was no headquarters staff, every general did as he pleased in changing battle lines during the day. But the Army of the Potomac has fought so many battles without General McClellan's supervision or assistance, that he is not missed when the fighting commences! His cautionary measures are so well known that the corps commanders win battles, and move troops to ensure the enemy's defeat, and are not hampered with McClellan's orders or presence, though McClellan gets all the credit. The fighting generals, such as Heintzelman, Sumner, Kearny, Hooker, Sedgwick, [Israel B.] Richardson, and others, have a profound contempt for General McClellan's fighting qualities, and several officers high in command denounce him without stint.... The army was saved in spite of General McClellan's ignorance of the situation in the front of battle.[79]

Lee personally directed the uncoordinated Confederate attack on Malvern Hill. First, he exposed his artillery to piecemeal annihilation. Second, two Union batteries slaughtered Rebel attackers with canister shot while not receiving any return fire from Confederate guns.[80] Third, and worst, Lee failed to cancel his previously issued attack orders that resulted in ill-advised and suicidal attacks by one brigade after another from right to left in accordance with the Lee-issued battle plan. The Rebel piecemeal, frontal assaults were the result of poor staff work and lack of command control.[81] Artillery and rifle fire from the Union army's strong and high position decimated the Confederate ranks through the afternoon and resulted in 5,500 Rebel casualties. McClellan's army was ready to fight—even if he was not.

Malvern Hill ended the Seven Days' Battle. A pattern of non-involvement by the commanding general was as apparent to the Joint Committee as it had been to Private Sneden. The committee summarized its observations on this point:

> It would appear ... that the battles were fought, the troops handled, new dispositions made and old ones changed, entirely by the corps commanders, without directions from the commanding general. He would place the troops in the morning, then leave the field and seek the position for the next day, giving no directions until the close of the day's fighting, when the troops would be ordered to fall back during the night to the new position selected by him.[82]

Aftermath

After the slaughter of July 1 at Malvern Hill, Lee's army was on the verge of achieving long-term strategic success (by driving the invaders away from Richmond for an indefinite period) but was in a disorganized and decimated condition. Lee's army had incurred 20,000 casualties—almost all killed and wounded—compared to the Northerners' 16,000. Lee's ultimate campaign victory depended upon McClellan's army's actions on July 2. Some of McClellan's corps commanders, including Porter and Hooker, sensed the vulnerability of the Army of Northern Virginia and thus the Confederate capital. They urged McClellan to attack.[83]

But McClellan instead did what he had done for the past week: retreat to save his army. In the words of historian John Hubbell, "McClellan ordered a retreat from a victorious battlefield."[84] As Pois and Langer concluded, "There was no continuance of the campaign, although the opportunity certainly was there. McClellan, the general, if not his army, was a beaten man."[85]

McClellan had long since forgotten about an offensive campaign, and he ordered a retrograde movement to Harrison's Landing, farther southeast from Malvern Hill and a total of twenty-five miles from Richmond. On June 25, his army had been only four to six miles from the Confederate capital. That final retreat clinched Lee's strategic victory and deferred Union victory in the East for almost three more years. Lee's week-long series of disjointed attacks had resulted in terrible casualties for his army. Malvern Hill, with McClellan absent, was the only time during the week-long struggle that either army in its entirety acted in a coordinated manner.[86] However, McClellan, driven by fear of losing a battle or losing his army, squandered the opportunity to smash Lee's army and take Richmond. Ironically, his failure to take Richmond or defeat Lee's army opened the door to more aggressive warfare and Union action against the institution of slavery—developments that McClellan strongly opposed.

7

Undercutting Pope

McClellan reached a new low in his military career by opposing and then reluctantly complying with orders to move his army from the Peninsula to the aid of Union General Pope in northern Virginia, defying and disobeying six direct orders from the new general-in-chief to move troops toward an expected and then ongoing battle at Manassas, and thereby causing the major Union defeat at Second Bull Run—all for the sake of once again obtaining command of all Union troops in the East.

Having delayed a major Union offensive in the East for half a year, taken two months to move up the Virginia Peninsula, and then squandered an opportunity for a decisive victory at the Seven Days' Battle, McClellan next moved into a period when he would openly defy his commanding general. After the Battle of Malvern Hill, he remained on the Peninsula for seven weeks, including many weeks when his troops were desperately needed elsewhere.

McClellan continued to demonstrate an insatiable appetite for reinforcements and refused to go on the offensive without them. Even worse, when he was ordered to immediately reinforce another Union army, he disobeyed those orders and thereby played a major role in causing a significant Union defeat at Second Manassas (Bull Run).

McClellan's army reached Harrison's Landing (or Harrison's Bar) on the James after a July 2 retreat from Malvern Hill. McClellan failed to secure the high ground overlooking his encampment at Harrison's Landing. Rebel artillery could have wreaked havoc among the Union troops, but Jeb Stuart's horse artillery revealed the Union vulnerability by firing before the Rebels arrived in sufficient strength to hold the high ground.[1] Late on July 2, McClellan advised Lincoln that he had "succeeded" in getting his army there, his men were exhausted from a week of fighting, his men would be ready to repulse the enemy if not attacked that day, and his losses were heavy. He concluded, "I have not yielded an inch of ground unnecessarily but have retired to prevent the superior force of the enemy from cutting me off and to take a different base of operations."[2]

Because of his unrealistic manpower demands and Lincoln and Stanton's loss of confidence in his offensive capabilities, McClellan would not be initiating any operations from his new base. Lincoln, nevertheless, remained reasonably supportive, graciously thanked McClellan on July 3 for his efforts ("I am satisfied that yourself, officers, and men have done the best you could. All accounts say better fighting was never done. Ten thousand thanks for it"), and advised him that Burnside's troops from North Carolina and Hunter's from Port Royal, South Carolina, were on the way.[3]

That same day, McClellan painted a bleak picture for Stanton: "… The Army is thoroughly worn-out, and requires rest and very heavy re-enforcements…. It is of course impossible to estimate as yet our losses, but I doubt whether there are to-day more than 50,000 men with their colors." His proposed solution was the usual one—although a bit magnified: "To accomplish the great task of capturing Richmond and putting an end to this rebellion re-enforcements should be sent to me rather much over than much less than 100,000 men."[4] The next day Lincoln responded that it would be "impossible" to reinforce him for such an offensive within even six weeks and advised him, "Save the Army—first, where you are, if you *can*; and secondly, by removal, if you must." Somewhat wistfully, Lincoln added a postscript saying, "If, at any time, you feel able to take the offensive, you are not restrained from doing so."[5]

Meanwhile, General Marcy's visit to Washington shocked Stanton and Lincoln. It also provided possible insight into McClellan's thinking—greatly to his detriment. A July 3 report from Marcy to Stanton contained his and McClellan's views and provided a gloomy analysis of the army's condition in an effort to generate reinforcements. Then Marcy erred by telling Stanton that he would not be astonished if the army had to capitulate. When an angry Stanton reported those words to Lincoln, the president immediately summoned Marcy to a July 4 meeting. The president told him, "General, I understand you have used the word 'capitulate'; that is a word not to be used in connection with our army." As Nevins commented, "Capitulation would be precisely the treason of which many radicals suspected McClellan!"[6]

That same Independence Day McClellan was churning out extensive correspondence. To Marcy, he wrote, "… Had a long telegram from the Presdt which quite discourages me as it shows a fatal want of appreciation of the glorious achievements of this Army, & of the circumstances of the case, as well as of the causes which led to it. I will save this Army & lead it to victory in spite of all enemies in all directions." To both Marcy and his own wife, McClellan described how he had saved the day by repositioning his army to prevent a successful Rebel attack at Harrison's Landing. He failed to mention who had spent days away from his army planning the initial and apparently erroneous positioning of his army. To General Dix, he provided a summary of the Seven Days' Battle, in which he interestingly noted that after Gaines' Mill he "had to take Richmond or find another base on the James River" and that the lack of success in that battle made changing his base "the only course."[7] Many of his own generals would have disagreed with that rationale.

Also that day he sent two telegrams to Lincoln. In one at noon, he described how he had safely reached Harrison's Landing and concluded, "When all the circumstances of the case are known it will be acknowledged by all competent judges that the movement just completed by this army is unparalleled in the annals of war. Under the most difficult circumstances we have preserved our trains, our guns, our material, and, above all, our honor." Certainly in the annals of war, one would be hard pressed to find a case where so many had retreated in the face of so few and thereby totally failed to accomplish their offensive mission. In a 1 P.M. wire, he assured the president that "[i]f the capital be threatened, I will move this army, at whatever hazard, in such direction as will best divert the enemy."[8]

McClellan capped his July 4 activities with another of his bombastic proclamations to his army. He praised them for changing their base of operations[9] by a flank movement, "always regarded as the most hazardous of military expedients." He told them, "Your conduct ranks you among the celebrated armies of history. No one will now question that each of you may always say with pride, 'I belonged to the Army of the Potomac!'" Among his concluding boasts was, "… we declare to our foes … that this army shall enter the capital of their so-called Confederacy…."[10] That event was three years and three commanding generals in the future. Meanwhile, in the Union ranks that day, diarist Private Elisha Hunt Rhodes wrote, "Well, the war must end some time, and the Union will be restored. I wonder what our next move will be. I hope it will be more successful than our last."[11]

Very early on July 6, McClellan told Mary Ellen he was expecting an attack "by greatly superior numbers" that very day, which "will probably determine the fate of the country…." Just as he had when sitting idle at Washington the prior fall and winter, he kept imagining attacks on his army by superior enemy forces. They were not superior, and they did not plan to attack him. The next morning he was apparently feeling somewhat sheepish about the prior week's happenings and assured her, "You need not be ashamed of your husband or his army—we have accomplished one of the grandest operations of Military History…." Demonstrating his friendship for Porter, McClellan that same day recommended to Stanton that Porter receive brevet promotions for his activities at Hanover Court House, Gaines' Mill, and Malvern Hill.[12] Unlike McClellan, Porter had been on the field during those three battles.

As the result of action taken by Lincoln as the Seven Days' Battle was beginning, McClellan faced a new situation in Virginia. His was not the only major Union army there. Just two days after Lincoln visited General Scott at West Point, he issued a June 26 order creating the Army of Virginia. It consisted of the troops formerly commanded by Fremont, Banks, and McDowell, who became its corps commanders. Jacob Cox's division (primarily consisting of Ohians) also was attached to it. Its commander was Major General John Pope, who had won fame for the capture of Island No. 10, just north of Memphis in the Mississippi River, along with 4,000 Rebel troops. Looking for offense from somewhere, Lincoln ordered Pope's army to defend Washington and western Virginia and to "in the speediest manner attack and overcome the rebel forces under Jackson and Richard S. Ewell, threaten the enemy in the direction of Charlottesville, and render the most effective aid to relieve General McClellan and capture Richmond."[13] The egotistic Fremont, insulted by being placed under the command of a junior officer (Pope), resigned and was replaced by a German-American, Major General Franz Sigel.

On July 7, McClellan began his communications with Pope. Responding to an offer of cooperation from Pope, he assured him of his mutual support: "… I shall carefully watch for any fault committed by the enemy and take advantage of it. As soon as Burnside arrives I will feel the force of the enemy and ascertain his exact position. If I learn that he has moved upon you I will move upon Richmond, do my best to take it, and endeavor to cut off his retreat." Partially conditioned on his receiving reinforcements, McClellan also assured Pope that he would attack the enemy in his front: "Although to insure success it is absolutely necessary that we promptly receive heavy re-enforcements, the spirit of this Army is such that I feel unable to restrain it from speedily resuming the offensive, unless reconnaissances should develop so overwhelming a force of the enemy in front as to render it out of the question. Even in that event we will endeavor to find some weak point in the enemy's lines which we will attack in order to break it."[14] Instead, McClellan would somehow find the strength to restrain his army from attacking and thus violate his assurances to Pope.

On July 8, McClellan personally delivered his infamous July 7 "Harrison's Landing Letter" to Lincoln, who was visiting him at his James River camp. In that letter, McClellan crossed the line from military to political strategy and jeopardized whatever relationship he had with the president by, said Allan Nevins, "expressing all his innate arrogance."[15] Bruce Catton marvelously put that letter in context:

> Here he was, barely a week after the battle of Malvern Hill, with the whole future of the war depending on the speed and energy with which the army could be repaired and thrown into a new campaign, with all of the involved problems growing out of that fact resting chiefly on himself for solution, with his own career, the fate of the army, and the safety of the country itself depending on what might come out of his talks with the President: and to the President he gave, not a plan for renewing the fighting, but a long letter telling him how he should shape the high policy of the war.[16]

Particularly unsolicited were his conservative views on the issue of slavery. Highlights of that letter include the following:

> The time has come when the Government must determine upon a civil and military policy covering the whole ground of our national trouble. The responsibility of determining, declaring, and supporting such civil and military policy, and of directing the whole course of national affairs in regard to the rebellion, must now be assumed and exercised by you, or our cause will be lost. The Constitution gives you power sufficient even for the present exigency.
>
> This rebellion has assumed the character of a war. As such it should be regarded, and it should be conducted upon the highest principles known to Christian Civilization. It should not be a war looking to the subjugation of the people of any State, in any event. It should not be at all a war upon population, but against armed forces and political organizations. Neither confiscation of property, political executions of persons, territorial organization of States, or forcible abolition of slavery should be contemplated for a moment.
>
> Military power should not be allowed to interfere with the relations of servitude, either by supporting or impairing the authority of the master, except for repressing disorder as in other cases. Slaves, contraband under the act of Congress, seeking military protection, should receive it. The right of the Government to appropriate permanently to its own service claims to slave labor should be asserted and the right of the owner to compensation therefor should be recognized.... A declaration of radical views, especially upon slavery, will rapidly disintegrate our present armies.

In closing, McClellan recommended the appointment of a "Commander-in-Chief of the Army," but he stated, "I do not ask that place for myself."[17]

When McClellan handed that letter to Lincoln, the president read the letter in McClellan's presence and, to the latter's consternation, made no comment on it. The general's plea for a limited war and his *laissez-faire* attitude toward slavery were out of tune with Lincoln's thinking at that time. Over the prior several months, the president had become convinced that he had to play the slavery card to indicate to the South that continuation of the war would mean the end of its primary social institution.[18]

Although McClellan's position came as no surprise to Lincoln, the president and his entourage were shocked by the near-treasonous opinions being expressed among some of McClellan's generals. In the words of historian Allen C. Guelzo, "For months there had been whispers about McClellan's 'putting the sword across the government's policy,' 'his sympathies with the South,' and his 'incapacity and want of loyalty.' Quartermaster General Montgomery Meigs, who accompanied Lincoln on the visit, was appalled to hear 'officers of rank' in the camp at Harrison's Landing speak easily about 'a march on Washington' to 'clear out those fellows.'"[19]

McClellan himself was under similar scrutiny. The aggressive Phil Kearny had written a northern friend that "McClellan is a dirty, sneaking traitor" and that behind his strategy "there is either positive treason or at least McClellan or the few with him are devising a game of politics rather than war."[20] In a similar vein, Kearny wrote to his wife on July 1: "McClellan's treasons or mismanagement has thrown on us a great many partial Battles, of much severity, which he should have spared us." On July 10, he complained, "McClellan's want of Generalship, or treason, has gotten us into a place, where we are completely boxed up."[21]

The commanding general continued to dig himself into a deeper hole. After giving Lincoln his political advice, McClellan met in camp with New York's Democratic Copperhead leader, Fernando Wood, who told the general he was presidential timber. The ego-swollen general then drafted a letter to Wood along the lines of the Harrison's Landing Letter but took the cautious step of showing the draft to his friend, "Baldy" Smith. Smith, shocked by the letter, told McClellan that "it looked like treason" and would ruin him and those close to him. McClellan destroyed the letter.[22]

If McClellan hoped to force the president away from emancipation by his blustering, he was to be sorely disappointed. Just two days after returning to Washington, Lincoln told two members of his Cabinet that they could expect some changes in his emancipation policies.[23] On July 12, Lincoln made a final, but unsuccessful, plea to border state representatives for gradual and compensated emancipation.[24] Only two weeks later, on July 22, Lincoln told his Cabinet that he intended to issue an Emancipation Proclamation freeing all slaves in Rebel-controlled areas.[25]

During his July 8 and 9 visit to McClellan's army, Lincoln interviewed McClellan and his corps commanders. Lincoln kept notes of many of their answers to his questions. Based on their answers, the president calculated that they had suffered 10,420 casualties during the recent fighting and that the army still totaled 75,000 to 80,000 troops. While McClellan thought the enemy army was four to five miles away and Porter said they were near Richmond, Sumner, Heintzelman, Keyes and Franklin opined that Lee's army was no longer in force in the vicinity of Harrison's Landing. In fact, Keyes said Lee was preparing to go to Washington.[26]

Thinking ahead, Lincoln asked the commanding general and his corps commanders whether, if it were desired to move the Army of the Potomac away from its present position, that movement could safely be done. McClellan said it would be a delicate and difficult matter, Porter said it was impossible and would ruin the country, Sumner and Heintzelman said it was possible but would be ruinous to the Union, Keyes said it could be accomplished if done quickly, and Franklin said it could and should be done by a movement to the Rappahannock line.[27] In summary, although Sumner and Heintzelman feared the impact on northern morale of such a move, only McClellan sensed the continuing presence of Lee, and only he and Porter thought it would be difficult to move the army elsewhere.[28]

Unimpressed by the president's visit, the commanding general wrote to his wife, "... I do not know to what extent he has profited by his visit—not much I fear, for he really seems quite incapable of rising to the height of the merits of the question & the magnitude of the crisis...."[29] While Lincoln was visiting him, McClellan penned a July 8 letter to Stanton in which he referred to his "policy" letter to Lincoln of the day before. He told the secretary of war, "The nation will support no other policy. None other will call forth its energies in time to save our cause, for none other will our Armies continue to fight." Stanton could not have been pleased by McClellan's summation of their relationship up to that time:

> ... from the time you took office, your official conduct towards me as commander in chief of the Army of the U.S. and afterwards as commander of the Army of the Potomac was marked by repeated acts done in such manner as to be deeply offensive to my feelings and calculated to affect me injuriously in public estimation. After commencing the present campaign your concurrence in the withholding of a large portion of my force, so essential to the success of my plans, led me to believe that your mind was warped by a bitter personal prejudice against me. Your letter compels me to believe that I have been mistaken in regard to your real feelings and opinions and that your conduct so unaccountable to my own fallible judgment, must have proceeded from views and motives which I did not understand.

In the end, McClellan grudgingly accepted Stanton's July 5 offer of cooperation between them.[30]

Beginning on July 10, McClellan's letters took an astounding and virtually treasonous tone. That day he wrote to Mary Ellen that he did not know "what paltry trick the administration will play next" and then observed, "I did not like the Presdt's manner— it seemed that of a man about to do something of which he was much ashamed." After asserting that he had proven that he was a general and that all but the congressional radicals knew why he had not succeeded, McClellan crossed the line by writing, "If I had succeeded in taking Richmond now the fanatics of the North might have been too powerful & reunion impossible. However that may be I am sure that it is all for the best."[31] The Army commander found cause to be glad that he had not captured Richmond! The very next day he wrote his wife, "... I have commenced receiving letters from the North urging me to march on Washington & assume the Govt...!"[32] That language was remarkably similar to that heard by Lincoln and Stanton during their recent visit to McClellan's camp.

In this same spirit of independence, McClellan wrote a July 11 letter to Hill Carter, member of the famed Carter family of Virginia and owner of nearby Shirley Plantation. In response to complaints about property loss, the general told Carter he regretted any losses or inconveniences suffered, inquired how they could be prevented or indemnified, and assured the plantation owner of his own "limited war" policies:

> Permit me here to state that it ever has been, and ever shall be, my constant effort to confine the effects of this contest to the armed masses and political organization directly concerned in carrying it on. I have done my best to secure protection to private property, but I confess that circumstances beyond my control have often defeated my purposes. I have not come here to wage war upon the domestic institutions of the land. I and the Army I command are fighting to secure the Union & to maintain its Constitution & laws—for no other purpose.[33]

McClellan started a new series of correspondence with Lincoln by asserting in a July 11 telegram, "Prisoners all state that I had 200,000 enemy to fight. A good deal more than two to one, and they knowing the ground."[34] The number was ludicrous, and Jackson certainly had not known the ground. The next day he wrote the President, "... I am more and more convinced that this army ought not to be withdrawn from here, but promptly re-enforced and thrown again upon Richmond. If we have a little more than half a chance we can take it. I dread the effects of any retreat upon the morale of the men."[35] The recently retreating general, probably sensing Lincoln's lack of confidence in him and desire to move the army elsewhere, resumed playing the reinforcement card.

Lincoln was not buying. His first response, the next day, inquired about the whereabouts of 45,000 men unaccounted for out of the 160,000 men who had been assigned to McClellan's army. About them, Lincoln said, "I believe half, or two thirds of them are fit for duty to-day. Have you any more perfect knowledge of this than I have? If I am right, and you had these men with you, you could go into Richmond in the next three days. How can they be got to you? And how can they be prevented from getting away in such numbers for the future?"[36]

In his response to Lincoln, McClellan admitted that 144,407 men were assigned to his army and 88,665 were present for duty, but he implied that 16,619 sick and 38,250 absent with and without leave reduced his effective total to perhaps 72,000.[37] Even McClellan's numbers did not add up. He used them, however, to explain to Mary Ellen why, although he "hoped to get to Richmond this summer—unless the Govt commits some *extraordinarily* idiotic act," he could not be expected to attack from 150,000 to 170,000 brave and entrenched Confederates with his mere 70,000 to 75,000 men fit for duty.[38]

A half hour later, a probably exasperated McClellan responded to his father-in-law's July 13 advice from Washington that "it is very generally thought that an advance on Richmond at an early period would be received with more enthusiasm now than at any time since the war commenced. The people seem to demand it…." McClellan's reply was that "Your proposition is easily enunciated but not so readily carried out," and he was "on the spot" and getting "neither men nor a policy."[39]

McClellan may have suspected that Lincoln and Stanton were developing a policy that he would not like. On July 13, he provided his wife with his view of Stanton: "… I think that he is the most unmitigated scoundrel I ever knew, heard or read of; I think that (& I do not wish to be irreverent) had he lived in the time of the Saviour, Judas Iscariot would have remained a respected member of the fraternity of the Apostles, & that the magnificent treachery & rascality of E. M. Stanton would have caused Judas to have raised his arms in holy horror and unaffected wonder—he would certainly have claimed & exercised the right to have been the Betrayer of his Lord & Master, by virtue of the same merit that raised Satan to his 'bad eminence.'"[40] Two days later he complained to his Democratic friend Barlow of "the stupidity & wickedness at Washington which have done their best to sacrifice" his noble army and then exclaimed, "I have lost all regard & respect for the majority of the Administration, & doubt the propriety of my brave men's blood being spilled to further the designs of such a set of heartless villains."[41] The general seemed intent on deciding the purposes for which his soldiers should be used.

In that spirit, he appeared to be dictating policy to the president in a July 17 telegram:

> It appears manifestly to be our policy to concentrate here everything we can possibly spare from less important points to make sure of crushing the enemy at Richmond, which seems clearly to be the most important point in rebeldom. Nothing should be left to chance here. I would recommend that General Burnside, with all his troops, be ordered to this army, to enable it to assume the offensive as soon as possible.

Burnside had written to McClellan two days before that "… The President has ordered me to remain here for the present…. I don't know what it means; but I do know my dear Mac that you have lots of enemies…."[42]

Ever since McClellan had been relieved as general-in-chief, Lincoln and Stanton had operated without one. Perhaps as a result of discussions with both Scott and McClellan, Lincoln, on July 11, summoned Henry Halleck from the West and appointed him his new general-in-chief.[43] Lincoln would learn soon that Halleck was not the dynamic leader or creative offensive planner he needed. Halleck, however, was somewhat useful to Lincoln in dealing with McClellan in the short run.[44]

By July 17, McClellan, unaware of Halleck's appointment, was speculating that some other general might be named to head the whole U.S. Army. By the 18th and 19th, he wrote that he had reason to believe that Halleck would be made "Comdr in Chief of the Army" and that other changes, including his own relief, might be in the works. On the 20th, he wrote to Mary Ellen that he had learned from papers and Washington sources that Halleck was the new commanding general and that he (McClellan) would have to replace his brevet (temporary) three stars with a mere two stars. His reaction to his new status was reflected at the end of that letter: "It is grating to have to serve under the orders of a man whom I know by experience to be my inferior—but so let it be—God's will be done…."[45]

Bitterness Becomes Treason

During these mid–July days, McClellan became increasingly bitter about his political bosses in Washington. On July 17, he wrote to Mary Ellen that he was "… a little disgusted at the stupidity of people in Washington…" and then discussed Lincoln: "I agree with you that a certain eminent individual is 'an old stick'—& of pretty poor timber at that. I confess that I do not at all appreciate his style of friendship." After mentioning how correct it had been to send his Harrison's Landing Letter to the president, he wrote, "You do not feel one bit more bitterly towards those people than I do; I do not say much about it—but I fear they have done all that cowardice, folly & rascality can do to ruin our poor country—& the blind people do not see it…. I feel that my day of usefulness to the country is past—at least under this administ—I have no respect for any member of it…."[46]

The next day he continued in a similar vein as he wrote her: "… *I owe no gratitude to any but my own soldiers here—none to the Govt or to the country.* I have done my best for my country—I expect nothing in return—they are my debtors, not I theirs…." On the 20th, he complained and threatened: "… I cannot remain permanently in the army after this slight [Halleck's appointment]. I must of course stick to this army so long as I am necessary to it, or until the Govt adopts a policy in regard to the war that I cannot conscientiously affirm…."[47] All these words reflect a disloyalty to the administration and his country, as well as a determination to fight only for those policies he approved.

During most of July, McClellan tried to convince Lincoln to provide him with Burnside's troops, who had moved from North Carolina to Fort Monroe and awaited assignment. Over time, McClellan's position vacillated between demanding reinforcements as a prerequisite to his taking the offensive and fearing that he would not be reinforced and then would be relieved of duty for not advancing. He resumed his old habit of reporting Beauregard's western army in the vicinity—specifically 20,000 to 25,000 troops in Petersburg as of July 18. On the 19th, McClellan told his father-in-law that it would be "stupid insanity" for him to advance without Burnside's troops and the "tools to work with." On the 20th, the general told Lincoln he could use a portion of Burnside's troops on the south shore of the James, but he undercut his case for them by reporting the movement of Jackson's troops to Gordonsville or Fredericksburg and recommending "concentration of the masses of troops in front of Washington, and the sending of cavalry far to the front."[48]

Meanwhile, General Pope was heading for disaster with his new 40,000-man Army of Virginia. He had gotten off on the wrong foot in the East by announcing to his troops, on July 14, that "I have come to you from the West, where we have always seen the backs of our enemies … I desire you to dismiss from your minds certain phrases, which I am sorry to find so much in vogue amongst you. I hear constantly of 'taking strong positions and holding them,' of 'line of retreat,' and 'bases of supplies.' Let us discard such ideas…. Let us look before us, and not behind…."[49]

Although there was some truth in this critique aimed at McClellan, Pope was foolish to make it so publicly and to do so in a manner that insulted all of the troops under both his and McClellan's commands. In fact, only eight days later, McClellan seemed to gloat about Pope's impending clash with Jackson—a conflict that would make Pope eat his words: "I see that the Pope bubble is likely to be suddenly collapsed—Stonewall Jackson is after him, & the paltry young man who wanted to teach me the art of war will in less than a week either be in full retreat or badly whipped. He will begin to learn the value of '*entrenchments, lines of communication & of retreat,* bases of supply etc'—they will learn bye & bye."[50]

On July 18, Pope also angered McClellan, Lee, Presidents Davis and Lincoln, and just about everyone else by issuing a series of Stanton-inspired general orders threatening to wreak havoc upon disloyal civilians in Virginia. He authorized his soldiers to requisition supplies from Virginia civilians, demanded oaths of allegiance from male civilians within Union lines, and decreed that civilians would be held accountable for guerilla activities. Porter called Pope "an ass," and Lee condemned him as a "miscreant."[51]

Pope had moved his army across the Rapidan River to threaten Gordonsville and the critical Virginia Central Railroad, which connected Richmond with its primary breadbasket, the Shenandoah Valley. His movement threatened Lee's army with the possibility of being caught between the forces of Pope and McClellan. For Lee, the best defense was a good offense, and he sent Jackson and then, on July 27, A.P. Hill away from Richmond and McClellan and toward Pope. Lee became less and less concerned with McClellan at his rear as time passed. Jackson's movement with 24,000 troops put Pope in a potential trap between the Rapidan and the Rappahannock rivers.

In July 22 and 23 correspondence to his wife and Barlow, McClellan warned that Stanton was reading all his private telegrams, observed that Halleck was being acclaimed as a rising star, and stated that he expected to be relieved of command of his army. He also complained about the lack of reinforcements and reiterated his numerical embellishments about Seven Days': "Stanton's statement that I outnumbered the rebels is simply false—they had more than two to one against me. I could *not* have gone into Richmond with my left."[52]

After his July 23 assumption of the new position, even the dull Halleck was effective enough to be able to determine how unrealistic, demanding, uncooperative, and defiant McClellan could be. Halleck was concerned by the presence of Lee's army between McClellan's on the Peninsula and Pope's in central Virginia and the possibility that Lee (with 200,000 troops, according to McClellan) could defeat either in detail and then turn on the other. Therefore, Halleck traveled to Harrison's Landing to confer with McClellan about what next steps should be taken. Two days before "Old Brains" Halleck's arrival, McClellan had written, "I presume I shall hear something today from that council of military pundits who have been about in Washn—there is not a handful of brains among them all & a nice mess they will make of it."[53]

During their July 26 conference, McClellan initially pushed Halleck for 30,000 reinforcements but then agreed that with 20,000 reinforcements he would be able to resume the offensive against Lee's "200,000" troops.[54] Halleck returned to Washington possibly willing to reinforce McClellan. The last straw for Halleck, however, came when, upon his return, he found a communication from McClellan changing the number of necessary reinforcements to between 50,000 and 55,000.[55] First, McClellan reported that "... reinforcements are pouring into Richmond from the South..." and "... the Southern States are being drained of their garrisons to reinforce the Army in my front." Second, he listed some of the allegedly arriving Rebel units, which he claimed reportedly included—once again—the troops of Beauregard's old army, who actually remained in Mississippi. Third, he urged that all 35,000 troops of Burnside and Hunter and between 15,000 and 20,000 troops from the West be assigned to him for an offensive against Richmond.[56]

Upon reading that document, Halleck must have thrown up his hands in frustration. At that point, he decided that McClellan would never be sufficiently satisfied with the strength of his army to use it against Richmond and that merger of McClellan and Pope's armies was imperative. Therefore, on July 30 Halleck ordered McClellan to evacuate his sick and wounded from the Peninsula, and on August 3 he ordered him to immediately

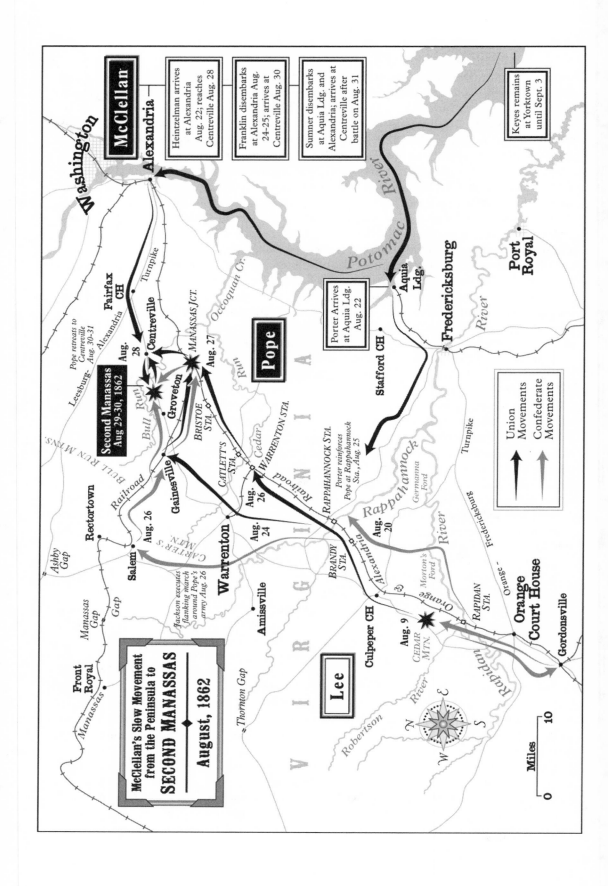

McClellan

Alexandria

Heintzelman arrives at Alexandria Aug. 22; reaches Centreville Aug. 28

Franklin disembarks at Alexandria Aug. 24-25; arrives at Centreville Aug. 30

Sumner disembarks at Aquia Ldg. and Alexandria; arrives at Centreville after battle on Aug. 31

Keyes remains at Yorktown until Sept. 3

Washington

Potomac River

Port Royal

Fredericksburg

Aquia Ldg.

River

Porter Arrives at Aquia Ldg. Aug. 22

Stafford CH

Fairfax CH

Centreville

Turnpike

Alexandria Turnpike

Aug. 28

Pope retreats to Centreville Aug. 30-31

Leesburg-

MANASSAS JCT.

Aug. 27

Second Manassas Aug 29-30, 1862

Groveton

Pope

Bull Run

Occoquan Cr.

BULL RUN MTNS.

Run

BRISTOE STA.

CATLETT'S STA.

Railroad

Gainesville

Aug. 26

Cedar

WARRENTON STA.

RAPPAHANNOCK STA.

Porter reinforces Pope at Rappahannock Sta., Aug. 25

Rappahannock

Germanna Ford

River

Turnpike

Fredericksburg

Railroad

Aug. 26

Rectortown

Ashby Gap

CARTER'S MTN.

Warrenton

Aug. 24

Jackson executes flanking march around Pope's army Aug. 26

Salem

Aug. 26

BRANDY STA.

Alexandria

Aug. 20

Morton's Ford

Orange-Fredericksburg

Manassas Gap

Gap

Amissville

V I R G I N I A

Culpeper CH

Aug. 9

CEDAR MTN.

Rapidan

RAPIDAN STA.

Orange-Alexandria

Orange Court House

Gordonsville

Front Royal

Manassas

Thornton Gap

Lee

Robertson River

River

N E W S

Union Movements

Confederate Movements

McClellan's Slow Movement from the Peninsula to
SECOND MANASSAS
August, 1862

Miles

0   10

move his troops from the Peninsula to support Pope on the Rappahannock Line. McClellan's defiance of those orders over the next several weeks constituted insubordination and was perhaps treasonous.[57]

While awaiting Halleck's decision on his various reinforcement requests, McClellan played the same old tunes—and some disloyal new ones. On July 27, he wrote to Mary Ellen that only Lincoln's "cowardice" kept the president from relieving him and that he regarded Lincoln with "thorough contempt—for his mind, heart & morality." On the 28th, he wrote to Halleck confirming Rebel reinforcements, urging his own reinforcement "by all available troops," and concluding, "Retreat would be disastrous to the Army & the cause—I am confident of that."[58] Two days later, he repeated his plea, said that Jackson probably was alone with 30,000 to 35,000 troops near Gordonsville, and added, "Should it be determined to withdraw [this Army] I shall look upon our cause as lost, & the demoralization of this Army certain...." That same day he repeated the last thought to his friend Barlow and provided this description of the "rascals" in Washington: "I do not believe there is one honest man among them—& I know what I say—I fear none of them wish to save the Union—they prefer ruling a separate Northern Confederacy—God will yet foil their abominable designs & mete out to them the terrible punishment they deserve."[59]

In the same July 30 letter in which he told his wife that Burnside had been offered and declined command of his army, McClellan became even more defiant: "The adm[inistration] have proclaimed a policy that I will not carry out. As soon as I receive the official copy of the Presdt's Proclamation I shall issue orders directly opposite to Pope's—then there will be a furious row."[60] He was upset about Lincoln's July 25 issuance of a proclamation simply implementing the recently passed Second Confiscation Act, which called for forfeiture and seizure of property owned by persons aiding and abetting rebellion.[61] McClellan carried out his threat and issued an order inconsistent with Lincoln's and Pope's pro-confiscation policies. On August 9, he issued General Orders No. 154 stating, "The general commanding takes this occasion to remind the officers and soldiers of this army ... that we are not engaged in a war of rapine, revenge, or subjugation; that this is not a contest against populations, but against armed forces and political organizations; that it ... should be conducted by us upon the highest principles known to Christian civilization."[62]

Even before he had received the order to transfer his army to another front, McClellan had decided not to obey it immediately. Thus, on July 31, he told Mary Ellen, "... if they send me the order I dread [that of withdrawing this army] I will make one last desperate appeal before obeying it & then let matters take their course...."[63] He followed that up two days later with a summary of his differences with virtually the whole Government: "When you contrast the policy I urge in my [Harrison's Landing] letter to the Presdt with that of Congress & Mr. Pope you can readily agree with me that *there can be little mutual confidence between the Govt & myself—we are the antipodes of each other...*"[64]

Although Burnside had been ordered on August 1 to proceed to the Rappahannock line, McClellan was unaware of that development and on that same day made another plea to Halleck for reinforcement, not withdrawal from the Peninsula, of his army. First, he berated the recent acts of Congress and Pope's orders. Second, he spelled out his opposition to emancipation and said, "The people of the South should understand that we are not making war upon the institution of slavery, but that if they submit to the Constitution and Laws of the Union they will be protected in their constitutional rights of every nature." Third, he pleaded for more men. Fourth, he concluded: "It is unnecessary for me to repeat my objections to the idea of withdrawing this Army from its present position. Every day's reflection but serves to strengthen my conviction that the true policy is to re-enforce this army at the earliest possible moment by every available man and to allow it to resume the offensive with the least possible delay."[65]

Two other statements in that letter bode ill for McClellan. He stated, "... I regard the civil or political questions as inseparable from the military in this contest."—which would prove a problem because he and Lincoln were moving in opposite directions on the issue of slavery. McClellan also said to Halleck, "I know that our ideas as to the concentration of forces agree perfectly."[66] Although both generals agreed on the need to concentrate Union troops, McClellan soon would learn that Halleck (as well as Lincoln and Stanton) wanted that concentration elsewhere than the Peninsula.

Lincoln, meanwhile, had to deal with the fallout from the disastrous Peninsula Campaign and the well-known dispute about it between McClellan and Stanton. On August 4, the president wrote, "The moral effect was the worst of the affair before Richmond; and that has run its course downward...." In that same letter, he did not contest an allegation that Union armies were constantly facing numerically superior foes; instead he attributed that "fact" to the enemy's ability to operate on internal lines and the fighting's location among the helpful enemy population.[67] Two days later, Lincoln addressed a pro–Union meeting in Washington. There he said that the friends of McClellan and Stanton were to blame for the public dispute about whether adequate troops had been provided to McClellan and blamed the dispute on the difference between men on the rolls and men fit for duty. The president added that McClellan was blameless for asking for what he wanted and needed, Stanton had provided all the troops he could, and he (Lincoln) took responsibility for Stanton's decisions.[68]

An early indication of Lincoln's final choice between the James River and central Virginia theaters came on August 1, when Halleck ordered Burnside at Newport News to join Pope on the Rappahannock.[69] Burnside promptly complied. The next day he reported to Halleck that his troops were rapidly embarking, would sail at midnight, and would arrive at Aquia Creek the next day. Burnside reminded Halleck that his artillery and cavalry remained in North Carolina.[70] Halleck would find McClellan far less responsive to similar orders. On August 3, Halleck telegraphed orders to McClellan: "It is determined to withdraw your army from the Peninsula to Aquia Creek. You will take *immediate measures* to effect this, covering the movement the best you can."[71]

Setting the stage for his defiant and reluctant compliance, an apoplectic McClellan responded, "Your telegram of last evening is received. I must confess that it has caused me the greatest pain I ever experienced, for I am convinced that the order to withdraw this Army to Aquia Creek will prove disastrous in the extreme to our cause. I fear it will be a fatal blow." He explained that he would have to march seventy miles to Fort Monroe to be transported to a position seventy-five miles from Richmond and argued that the fate of the Union should be decided on the banks of the James. During the "several days" that would be necessary to prepare for the retrograde movement, McClellan requested that the order be rescinded and he be reinforced by every available man from elsewhere in the country. Ominously, he added, "If my counsel does not prevail I will with a sad heart obey your orders to the utmost of my power, directing to the movement, which I clearly foresee will be one of the utmost delicacy and difficulty, whatever skill I may possess."[72]

The next day, Halleck promptly wired back that the order was not going to be rescinded. On the 6th, Halleck told McClellan, "I have no re-enforcements to send you." In a letter that same day, the general-in-chief explained his concerns more fully: "You, general, certainly could not have been more pained at receiving my order than I was at the necessity of issuing it." He then explained the ramifications of McClellan's own strength estimates; with 200,000 troops between McClellan's 90,000 and Pope's 40,000, Lee posed a serious risk. Halleck reasoned, "You are 30 miles from Richmond and General Pope 80 or 90, with the enemy directly between you, ready to fall with his superior numbers upon one or the other, as he may elect. Neither can re-enforce the other in case of such an attack.... If you or any one else had presented a better [plan] I certainly should have adopted it, but all of your plans require re-enforcements, which it is impossible to give you."[73]

Thus, McClellan's own inflated estimates of Confederate strength had come back to haunt him. If Lee had 200,000 troops (including the oft-arrived Beauregard troops), it was hard to argue with Halleck's concern about the safety of both Union armies in Virginia. McClellan had made good on his promise to his wife about challenging the withdrawal order, but his own inflation of Rebel strength made it necessary to unite the two Union armies. Halleck's rebuttal, in Catton's words, "was unanswerable, and the withdrawal began—as promptly as possible, McClellan felt; slowly and with unpardonable delay, Stanton and Halleck believed."[74]

Once he realized that he would at least temporarily lose his army to Pope, McClellan had a numerical change of heart. He latched on to a cavalry report that casualties and Jackson's detachment had reduced Rebel strength in his front to a mere 36,000. On August 12, he reported that number to Halleck and unsuccessfully sought rescission of the transfer order so that he could attack.[75] Fishel commented on this farcical claim: "And here was McClellan, claiming in effect that a Richmond army he numbered at 200,000 late in July had now, in a little over two weeks, lost 164,000 of those men. This was the most preposterous of all his numerical fancies. His withdrawal orders stood."[76]

Having failed to obtain a rescission, McClellan carried out his orders with at least his usual caution and dilatoriness. Unfortunately, as Nevins stated, "If McClellan, never a marvel of celerity, dragged his feet, the result would be disaster."[77] McClellan did drag his feet, and the result was disaster. A recitation of critical dates demonstrates that foot-dragging: McClellan received the orders to leave Harrison's Landing and immediately reinforce Pope on August 3, the first units did not leave there until August 14, the last troops left there on August 16, his army then marched east toward transports at Newport News at an average rate of eight miles per day, troop embarkation onto the transports started on August 19, the last entire corps to reach northern Virginia disembarked at Alexandria on August 28, and the last troops finally embarked at Fort Monroe for Washington on September 3.[78]

From August 4 to 7, McClellan did not move; instead, he oversaw some skirmishing by Hooker at Malvern Hill.[79] On August 8, he finally got around to indirectly telling Mary Ellen about the withdrawal orders by saying, "they are as bad as they can be & that I regard them as almost fatal to our cause." He told her that he was trying to induce the enemy to attack him so that he could "... beat them & follow them up to Richmond...." He explained, "My only hope now is that I can induce the enemy to attack me. I shall of course obey the orders unless the enemy gives me a very good opening—which I should at once avail myself of ...." As to the man whose order he was disobeying, McClellan told her that he suspected Halleck was a "scallawag" and that he was involved in a scheme to force McClellan to resign.[80]

Halleck, meanwhile was trying to impress upon McClellan the importance of a swift transfer of his troops. In an August 7 letter, Halleck told him it was his intention to place him in command of the reunited Union forces and pleaded, "... I must beg of you, general, to hurry along this movement...." In an urgent August 10 telegram, the general-in-chief advised, ordered, and threatened: "The enemy is crossing the Rapidan in large force.... There must be no further delay in your movements. That which has already occurred was entirely unexpected, and must be satisfactorily explained."[81]

One week after the "immediate measures" transfer order had been issued and before receiving Halleck's pleas, McClellan told Mary Ellen that "...Halleck is turning out just like the rest of the herd ... is very dull & very incompetent...." and "I am satisfied that the dolts in Washn are bent on my destruction.... The more I hear of their wickedness the more am I surprised that such a wretched set are permitted to *live* much less to occupy the positions they do." He moved on to gloat at the prospect of Pope being defeated: "*I have a strong idea that Pope will be thrashed during the coming week—& very badly whipped he will be & ought to be—such a villain as he is ought to bring defeat upon any cause that employs him....* I am inclined to believe that Pope will catch his Tartar within a couple of days & be disposed of."[82]

Then McClellan proceeded to explain his own strategy to thwart the transfer: "I hope to be ready tomorrow afternoon to move forward in the direction of Richmond—I will try to catch or thrash Longstreet & then if the chance offers follow in to Richmond while they are lamming away at Pope. It is in some respects a desperate step, but it is the best I can do for the nation just now & I would rather even be defeated than retreat without an effort to relieve Washn in the only way at all possible. If I fail—why well & good. I will fall back. If I win I shall have saved my country & will then gratefully retire to private life...." These astounding words reveal an intent to deliberately disobey his transfer orders and risk his army for self-glorification. But that was not all; he added: "*If I succeed in my coup* everything will be changed in this country so far as we are concerned & my enemies will be at my feet. It may go hard with some of them in that event, for I look upon them as the enemies of the country & of the human race...."[83] Because McClellan's perceived enemies at this time were Lincoln, Stanton, and Halleck, this statement—as well as his plan to disobey his orders—at least bordered on treason.

As McClellan completed that letter after midnight, he reported receiving Halleck's letter and telegram. Apparently realizing that Halleck actually did want the transfer ordered a week before, McClellan reluctantly concluded, "Under the circumstances I feel compelled to give up the idea of my intended attack upon Richmond & must *retrace my steps.*" But, he concluded that he would have the last laugh: "*I think the result of their machinations will be that Pope will be badly thrashed within two days & that they will be very glad to turn over the redemption of their affairs to me.*"[84] Here was McClellan gleefully anticipating a Union defeat.

In fact, the thrashing of Pope was almost three weeks in the future. But a three-week delay was certainly something at which McClellan had demonstrated considerable skill. The irony of the situation in early August is that McClellan's plan to attack toward Richmond may have succeeded in defeating Lee's army, capturing Richmond, and possibly winning the war. But it was McClellan's own insistence that he was vastly outnumbered and could not attack without massive reinforcements, as well as his considerable history of reluctance to attack, that caused the Administration to order his transfer from the Peninsula to central Virginia. There is nothing in McClellan's Civil War record to demonstrate that he had the intestinal fortitude to undertake an all-out offensive with his available troops.

Meanwhile, McClellan's inaction was creating an opportunity for Lee and Jackson. On August 8, Jackson ordered his troops to proceed to Culpeper Court House by way of Cedar Mountain. He failed to tell A.P. Hill that Hill was to lead the march and placed Hill under arrest for failing to obey the non-existent order. As a result of this confusion,

Ewell and Charles S. Winder led the way on August 9 to Cedar Mountain, where they were surprised by a flank assault from Banks' Union troops. The Battle of Cedar Mountain appeared to be a victory by Pope and Banks as the Stonewall Brigade was driven from the field and Winder was killed by an artillery shell. However, Banks had no reserves, and his forces were routed by Hill's 12,000 men arriving to support Ewell.

Realizing that he was outnumbered by Pope's army, Jackson stayed in position behind Cedar Run in hopes of being attacked. Lee sensed that the time was ripe to leave the Richmond area and moved north with Longstreet's troops. On August 15, they arrived at Gordonsville. It was at this point that Lee, Longstreet, and Jackson saw an opportunity to trap Pope between the Rapidan and Rappahannock rivers by destroying the bridges in his rear across the Rappahannock. Although a Union raiding party seized a copy of Lee's orders, along with Jeb Stuart's trademark cape and feathered hat, it was instead two Union spies and a separate Union raid on the Rebel signal station on Clark's Mountain that first alerted Pope to the danger his army faced from Lee's nearby troops. The information obtained by these intelligence efforts resulted in Pope's retreat beyond the Rappahannock and momentary escape from Lee.[85]

In response to the raid on his headquarters, an angered Stuart led a retaliatory raid on Pope's headquarters and captured a copy of Union plans for the reinforcement of Pope by McClellan. This information made Lee aware of the need to move quickly before he faced a united Union army. Continuing heavy rains precluded any river crossings, but by August 24 Lee had devised a daring plan for Jackson to sweep wide around Pope's right (west) flank and cut Pope's communications and supply line via the Orange & Alexandria Railroad. Jackson would soon be on the loose, and Pope would be desperate for immediate and numerous reinforcements from McClellan.

Meanwhile, back on the Peninsula, less than two days after feeling compelled to retrace his steps and move to Pope's support, McClellan was reconsidering whether to comply with the transfer orders. On the afternoon of August 12, he wired Halleck that less than 36,000 Rebel troops were between him and Richmond and boldly pronounced that he could push Longstreet back into Richmond or defeat and capture his force within forty-eight hours. He did admit that he lacked authority for such a movement "under existing orders," asked that they be changed, and assured, "I shall continue to forward re-enforcements and sick as rapidly as transports arrive and have given the necessary instructions to insure no delay in moving the army."[86]

McClellan's wire crossed with one coming from Halleck, who was losing his patience. Halleck said, "The Quartermaster-General informs me that nearly every available steam vessel in the country is now under your control.... Burnside moved nearly 13,000 troops to Aquia Creek in less than two days, and his transports were immediately sent back to you. All vessels in the James River and the Chesapeake Bay were placed at your disposal, and it was supposed that 8,000 or 10,000 of your men could be transported daily.... The bulk of your material on shore it was thought could be sent to Fort Monroe, covered by that part of the army which could not get water transportation...."[87]

McClellan responded that night and claimed he was doing all he could. He complained about a lack of vessels and adequate piers at Yorktown, Fort Monroe, and Aquia Creek. He added, "We are much impeded here because our wharves are used night and day to land current supplies"—a puzzling use of vessels and piers for an army that was supposed to be leaving. McClellan cited the necessity to protect his material and men while withdrawing, concluded that his army could not be moved in less than a month, and recited his current line: "If Washington is in danger now this army can scarcely arrive in time to save it. It is in much better position to do so from here than from Aquia."[88]

He made no effort to at least partially evacuate from Harrison's Landing, Yorktown, or anywhere else closer than distant Fort Monroe.

Halleck promptly and bluntly answered McClellan's foot-dragging wire: "There is no change of plans. You will send up your troops as rapidly as possible. There is no difficulty in landing them. According to your own accounts, there is now no difficulty in withdrawing your forces. Do so with all possible rapidity."[89] Once again, Halleck was cleverly throwing McClellan's "facts" back in his face. Finally, at 11 P.M. on August 14, McClellan wired Halleck, "Movement has commenced by land and water. All sick will be away to-morrow night."[90] It had taken him more than fifteen days to evacuate his sick since he was ordered to do so on July 30 and again on August 3 and more than eleven days to commence his movement. It would be another day before he had even moved his sick and wounded onto vessels.

By August 17, McClellan at long last had his army on the march toward Fort Monroe. While in the process of crossing the Chickahominy at Barrett's Ferry, the commanding general expressed his concerns that Porter had moved ahead from Williamsburg without waiting for the rest of the army. The ever-cautious McClellan explained, "My wish was to have had everything in hand until getting the wagons past Williamsburg." He forgave Porter's move and told him to embark "at once" at Fort Monroe if transports were there.[91]

That same day McClellan was visited by Burnside, who apparently was acting at Halleck's request in trying to determine the reasons for delay and to hurry McClellan along. Afterward, McClellan wrote a friendly private letter to Halleck about the visit and the current situation. He assured him that "… I had not delayed one moment in preparing to carry out your orders…," but almost let it slip that he had done so "while I availed myself of the unavoidable delay to urge upon you my own view of the case"—words that he judiciously crossed out in his draft letter. He ended by saying he hoped to have his army totally across the Chickahominy by daylight on the 18th (more than two weeks after receiving immediate transfer orders) and then would "feel justified in moving it solely with reference to its speedy embarkation."[92] Even without the missing words, Halleck could infer from this letter that McClellan had been preparing for, but not actually carrying out, execution of the transfer orders and that at long last he was prepared to execute them.

Simultaneously, McClellan wrote to his wife that the "*retreat*" was orderly and "a perfect success so far as so disgusting an operation can be." He told her that he expected to be given command of all troops in Virginia. The next day, he bragged to her that he had not left one dollar's worth of property behind and told her he would go to Yorktown on August 19, stay there for a day or two, and then go to Fort Monroe—a leisurely pace for a general under orders to immediately and rapidly move his army to the defense of the capital and another army. It was, however, a pace consistent with his feelings: "I have felt every moment that I was conducting a false movement, & which was altogether against my own judgment & that of the army."[93]

If McClellan believed that his delayed movement and the reasons for it were escaping notice, he might have thought otherwise had he consulted Private Sneden's diary. On August 18, Sneden wrote, "We [the Third Corps] made but ten miles yesterday, but our marches don't average six miles per day, though we could make fifteen if required. But McClellan is taking things easy though Pope is badly in want of reinforcements. And it [*sic*] is in a critical position with the enemy confronting him in superior numbers…."[94]

McClellan's three-week delay in moving his army off the Peninsula was unpardonable and would have disastrous consequences for Pope. Despite receiving sick troop transport orders on July 30 and immediate army transfer orders on August 3, he did not begin evacuating in earnest until August 14 or 15. Nevins concluded that "McClellan was inexcusably late and reluctant in his withdrawal." His complaints about transportation were baseless since he controlled a massive flotilla of vessels. It was two weeks, and only after Burnside's intervention, until he began marching his infantry toward Yorktown, Newport News, and Fort Monroe. Nevins added, "A capable observer, General Victor Le Duc, wrote that but for gross mismanagement, the whole army could have been transferred to Aquia within two weeks."[95] For whatever reasons, McClellan was guilty of inexcusable delays in moving off the Peninsula to Pope's assistance. He would do even worse in the coming days.[96]

On August 18, McClellan sent Halleck a rather pathetic telegram in which he asked Halleck to issue a "handsome order" praising McClellan's army for its conduct at Yorktown, Williamsburg, West Point, Hanover Court House, the Chickahominy, the Seven Days', and the current retreat. He asked that no credit be given to himself but rather just to his officers and men—as though such an order could be issued without having the effect of praising McClellan. Halleck wisely did not reply.[97]

By August 20, McClellan at long last had reached Fort Monroe, from which he wrote to Burnside. He told him that Halleck had sent telegrams "indicating that Pope was in danger, and urging that re-enforcements be sent on as rapidly as possible." McClellan said that he was doing just that even though he had learned that he probably would not be given command of all forces in Virginia.[98] The next day he had better news for Mary Ellen:

> I believe I have triumphed! Just received a telegram from Halleck stating that Pope and Burnside are very hard pressed—urging me to push forward reinforcements, & to *come myself as soon as I possibly can...!* Now they are in trouble they seem to want the "Quaker," the "procrastinator," the "coward" & the "traitor"...![99]

On August 22, he confirmed his view that opportunity for him required disaster for his fellow Union generals. He wrote, "I think they are pretty well scared in Washn & probably with good reason. I am confident that the disposition to be made of me will depend entirely upon the state of their nerves in Washn. *If they feel safe there I no doubt will be shelved....* Their sending for me to go to Washn only indicates a temporary alarm—*if they are at all reassured you will see that they will soon get rid of me.*"[100] The next afternoon, as he finally steamed north toward Aquia, McClellan wrote her more specifically of the relationship between Pope's fate and his own: "*I take it for granted that my orders will be as disagreeable as it is possible to make them—unless Pope is beaten, in which case they may want me to save Washn again.* Nothing but their fear will induce them to give me any command of importance or to treat me otherwise than with discourtesy...."[101]

Not only was McClellan slow getting off the Peninsula, but he then proceeded to delay his army's movements inland from the Potomac to Pope. McClellan and at least one of his subordinates did their best to keep reinforcements from reaching Pope. Historian Christopher R. Gabel provided some insight into the slow movement and even non-movement of McClellan's troops to Pope's relief:

> Upon arrival in Alexandria, McClellan's troops should have marched the twenty miles or so to Pope's beleaguered force, but instead they jammed into Alexandria and waited for train transport. McClellan himself sat on his hands and allowed Herman Haupt, Pope's railroad director, to sort out the mess. Haupt performed miracles in rushing troops forward and evacuating supplies threatened with capture, but not everybody appreciated his efforts. One commander bringing up reinforcements, Brigadier General Samuel D. Sturgis, stopped four trains on the main line near Alexandria and ordered them to transport

his brigade to the front immediately, even though the troops were not even ready to board. Once at the front, Sturgis' men took their time disembarking. The actions of this one irresponsible commander completely disrupted Haupt's work and blocked all other traffic for the better part of a day. When Haupt explained to him the importance of maintaining rail traffic for Pope's endangered army, Sturgis uttered the immortal words, "I don't care for John Pope one pinch of owl dung."[102]

After McClellan arrived at Aquia Creek on August 24, he reported to Mary Ellen that all his troops were under orders to disembark at Alexandria (presumably intended to be merged into Pope's army), and that he therefore would probably take a leave of absence. He told both her and Halleck that Pope apparently had retreated north from the Rappahannock, but neither he nor Halleck knew exactly where Pope was for the next few days.[103]

Likewise, Pope did not know where Jackson was. On August 26, Stonewall had started his 24,000 "foot cavalry" northwest from the Rappahannock line on a long march to Salem, Virginia, where he learned of the huge Union supply depot at Manassas. Without delay, he headed his troops east through Thoroughfare Gap in the foothills of the Blue Ridge Mountains to the Orange & Alexandria Railroad. They marched fifty-four miles in thirty-six hours.

Confederate cavalry captured Bristoe Station, southwest of Manassas on the Orange & Alexandria, by the evening of August 26. They cut all of Pope's communications with Washington and cleared the way for Jackson's infantry to conduct a destructive attack on the huge Union supply depot at Manassas. His infantry destroyed Union trains, gorged themselves on delicacies and alcohol, and burned everything they could not carry. Jackson then moved them, by early on the 28th, northwest to a hidden location (Stony Ridge) behind an unfinished railroad cut just north of the old Manassas battlefield to await the arrival of Lee with the rest of the army.

While Jackson waited for Longstreet's portion of Lee's army to join him at Manassas, Pope sensed an opportunity to catch Jackson before the Army of Northern Virginia united. He rushed his troops toward Manassas but inadequately defended Thoroughfare Gap, through which Rebel reinforcements were likely to come. In total ignorance of Jackson's whereabouts, Pope directed his scattered units to concentrate at Centreville, north of Manassas and east of Jackson and the old battlefield.

Early on the evening of August 28, Jackson's troops initiated a gambling, surprise attack on Union troops, the famed Black Hat Brigade (soon to be called the Iron Brigade), as they passed Jackson's position alongside the Warrenton Turnpike. These black-hatted Union troops from Wisconsin and Indiana constituted the only all-western brigade in the Army of the Potomac. Although surprised and inexperienced, the outnumbered Union troops under the command of Brigadier General John Gibbon, stood their ground, absorbed the loss of one-third of their number, and imposed heavy casualties on Jackson's somewhat uncoordinated soldiers. This bloody Battle of Brawner's Farm carried on into the night.[104]

The battle consisted of extremely intense, as well as deadly, rifle and musket fire. According to Confederate Brigadier General William B. Taliaferro, "In this fight there was no maneuvering and very little tactics—it was a question of endurance, and both sides endured." Although the battle was a tactical defeat for Jackson, it achieved a Rebel strategic goal by revealing Jackson's position and drawing Pope into a major battle on Lee's terms.[105]

Lee and Longstreet, meanwhile, had advanced with 30,000 troops to Thoroughfare Gap, a few miles west of Jackson's position. They arrived there late on August 28 (while fighting roared at Brawner's farm) and fought their way through the lightly defended pass on the morning of the 29th. Thus, Longstreet's larger portion of Lee's army came onto the field that morning, imperceptibly extended Jackson's line to the south, and posed a dangerous but hidden threat to Pope's gathering forces, which were focused solely on Jackson.

August 29 saw Pope's army conducting a series of costly frontal assaults on Jackson's troops, who were located in the mile-and-a-half-long cuts and fills of the unfinished railroad. This was the beginning of the two-day Battle of Second Manassas (Second Bull Run).[106] As the fighting grew fiercer during the late afternoon, Jackson's troops rebuffed attack after attack. When the soldiers in blue did manage to break through the gray lines, Rebel reinforcements from elsewhere on Jackson's line drove them back.[107] Although Lee wanted Longstreet to swoop down on Pope's vulnerable left flank that afternoon, Longstreet convinced him to wait for an even better opportunity. Thus, the scene was set for climactic events at Manassas on August 30, 1862.

In Pope's hour of need, McClellan would deliberately fail him. By August 27, McClellan had moved north to Alexandria and reported to Mary Ellen, "... Our affairs here now much tangled up & *I opine that in a day or two your old husband will be called upon to unsnarl them....*" He also told her that he had heard that a general engagement was probable that day or the next inland near Warrenton.[108] That very same morning Halleck gave him the first of six direct orders to move some of his own troops toward the scene of the expected battle. In a 10 A.M. telegram, Halleck ordered McClellan to have Franklin's corps march in the direction of Manassas "as soon as possible." By 10 A.M., McClellan responded that he had sent orders to Franklin "to prepare to march with his corps at once" and to report to McClellan about his transportation. Halleck, not perceiving McClellan's failure to order Franklin to march, put McClellan in charge of sending troops out from Alexandria.[109]

After receiving copies of dispatches from Porter to Burnside stating that a major battle was imminent, McClellan recommended to Halleck, during that same critical morning of August 27, that Sumner's corps be moved from Aquia to Alexandria "to move out with Franklin to Centreville or vicinity...." Early that afternoon Halleck approved bringing up Sumner's corps, which otherwise could have marched directly toward Manassas without coming under McClellan's direction.[110] McClellan thus would have responsibility for getting 25,000 of his troops (Franklin and Sumner's corps) promptly from Alexandria to Manassas, where a major battle was expected. His successful execution of that mission would enhance Pope's chances for victory, while his failure to execute that mission would perhaps doom Pope and open the door to an expanded command for McClellan. His priorities would become clear within hours.

Had McClellan desired to support Pope, there was an easy means to do so. His troops, in the words of railroad czar Brigadier General Henry Haupt,

> ... could have marched to Manassas in one-fourth the time required to reach that point by waiting for [rail] transportation; besides, if the troops had marched they could better have supported each other. The railroad, with frequent breaks from rebel raids, was taxed nearly to its capacity to furnish supplies. I believe that if the troops, when landed from the transports, had been marched immediately to Manassas, instead of waiting several days for rail transportation, they could have rendered efficient support to General Pope, and would, no doubt, have changed the result of the contest by giving us a decisive victory, but I do not know who was responsible for this delay...."[111]

McClellan's responsibility for those movements, and their delays, became clearer and clearer with each passing hour.

A Union disaster on the morning of the 27th set the stage for McClellan's denial of troops to Pope. After the first reports of Jackson's raid on Manassas Junction, Haupt rushed George Taylor's New Jersey brigade and two Ohio regiments by rail to that area. However, they were ambushed by Jackson's troops, and Taylor was killed. In the words of historian Ethan Rafuse, "Taylor's catastrophe was a major turning point in the campaign, for it would provide McClellan the rationale he needed to adopt a stance on the forwarding of troops that would compromise Pope's ability to fulfill the administration's desire for victory and vindicate the new political and operational approach that McClellan found so repugnant." Shortly thereafter, McClellan flatly denied Haupt's request to move troops to Bull Run to support the troops already there and open the railroad to Pope. When McClellan explained that such a move was "attended with risk," Haupt bluntly—and to no effect—replied that military options usually are attended with risk.[112]

At noon on the 27th, as Jackson was moving from Manassas to the railroad cut, Halleck advised McClellan of the whereabouts of the Army of Northern Virginia units and repeated the earlier order to get Franklin's corps moving: "Porter reports a general battle imminent. Franklin's troops should move out by forced marches, carrying three or four days' provisions, and to be supplied as far as possible by railroad." [113]

That afternoon, McClellan replied with a barrage of telegrams about why he could not or should not do as ordered. First, he suggested that Sumner be brought up from Aquia and substituted for Franklin because the latter had no horses for cavalry and only enough for four of his guns and thus could serve no useful purpose at the front—wherever that might be. He spoke of making "immediate arrangements for placing the works in front of Washington in an efficient condition of defense" and stated, "I do not see that we have force enough in hand to form a connection with Pope, whose exact position we do not know." In his second wire, McClellan described reports of Rebel activity near Manassas and then unhelpfully concluded, "I think our policy now is to make those works perfectly safe, and mobilize a couple of corps as soon as possible, but not to advance them until they can have their artillery and cavalry." McClellan's third telegram said, "... I still think that we should first provide for the immediate defense of Washington on both sides of the Potomac...." and contained a plea for him to receive authority to dispose of all available troops according to his judgment.[114]

At that point, a distracted Halleck (overseeing opposition to a Rebel invasion of Kentucky as well as Pope's crisis) gave McClellan discretion, which he chose to use to ignore the two earlier orders to advance Franklin and Sumner. Halleck told McClellan in an afternoon wire: "As you must be aware, more than three-quarters of my time is taken up with the raising of new troops and matters in the West. I have no time for details. You will therefore, as ranking general in the field, direct as you deem best...." At 6 P.M. on the 27th, McClellan reported to Halleck his receipt of a copy of Pope's 10 A.M. wire to Halleck requesting all forces to be sent to Pope's right at Gainesville (just northwest of Manassas), reported that he had 12,800 men and the First Connecticut Artillery, recommended keeping them for the defense of Washington, and then added, "If you wish me to order any part of this force to the front, it is in readiness to march at a moment's notice to any point you may indicate."[115] Halleck did not respond. He may have assumed that two orders to McClellan to advance Franklin were sufficient—particularly since McClellan had received Pope's specific request about the destination of reinforcements. He also may have erroneously assumed that McClellan was acting in good faith.

When reports were received that a Union force of 1,500 men was defending the Bull Run bridge near Manassas against enemy attackers, Brigadier General Haupt searched for McClellan among the vessels at Alexandria. After finding McClellan, Haupt recommended that reinforcements be sent to assist the apparently beleaguered Union troops. McClellan told Haupt that such an undertaking was too risky without knowing the strength of the enemy and declined to provide any troops for his use. Haupt was only able to send a basically unarmed train toward Manassas.[116]

That night (August 27–28), McClellan crossed the river to Washington and conferred with Halleck at his house from midnight to 3 A.M. As he returned by steamer to Alexandria the next morning, McClellan wrote his wife, "Pope is in a bad way—his communications with Washn cut off & I have not yet the force at hand to relieve him. He has nearly all the troops of my army that have arrived...."[117] That statement was false.

Later on the morning of the 28th, McClellan wired Halleck that he thought the enemy was between Pope and him and that "... any movement made from here must be in force, with cavalry and artillery or we shall be beaten in detail." Then he provided classic McClellanesque advice: Pope should retreat to the Washington environs. McClellan concluded, "I do not think it now worthwhile to attempt to preserve the [Orange & Alexandria] railway [to Manassas]. The great object is to collect the whole army in Washington, ready to defend the works and act upon the flank of any force crossing the Upper Potomac...."[118]

That telegram seems to have awakened Halleck to McClellan's disobedience of his earlier orders to advance. He, therefore, took matters into his own hands and wired Franklin at 12:40 P.M. on the 28th "to move with your corps to-day toward Manassas Junction, to drive the enemy from the railroad." A defiant McClellan intervened and responded twenty minutes later that "The moment Franklin can be started with a reasonable amount of artillery he shall go." At 3:30, a dissatisfied Halleck wired back to him, "Not a moment must be lost in pushing as large a force as possible toward Manassas, so as to communicate with Pope before the enemy is re-enforced."[119] In two days, General-in-Chief Halleck had issued four orders directing immediate movement of McClellan's troops toward Manassas.

McClellan still did not budge. At 4:10 that same afternoon, he telegraphed Halleck that Franklin was in no condition to move but might be in the morning. He said that Pope should cut through to Washington and expressed concern about defending the capital. Within the hour and after receiving Halleck's 3:30 "not a moment must be lost" wire, McClellan defied his commander once again:

> Your dispatch received. Neither Franklin nor Sumner's corps is now in condition to move and fight a battle. It would be a sacrifice to send them out now. I have sent aides to ascertain the condition of the Command of Cox and Tayler, but I still think that a premature movement in small force will accomplish nothing but the destruction of the troops sent out. I report [repeat?] that I will lose no time in preparing the troops now here for the field, and that whatever orders you give after hearing what I have to say will be carried out.[120]

Ignoring and defying four orders from Halleck in two days to advance troops toward Manassas and Pope, McClellan wanted to engage in a running debate about what to do. It is unlikely that such deliberate and repeated direct disobedience of orders from a commanding officer occurred anywhere else during the Civil War.

Unbelievably, while fighting flared at Brawner's Farm to the west that evening (August 28), the situation near Washington deteriorated further. At 7:40 that evening, Halleck wired McClellan, "There must be no further delay in moving Franklin's corps toward Manassas. They must go to-morrow morning, ready or not ready. If we delay too long to get ready there will be no necessity to go at all, for Pope will either be defeated or be victorious without our aid."[121] At 10 P.M., McClellan replied that Franklin's corps had been ordered to march at 6 in the morning. He also reported that Sumner's 14,000 infantry had arrived with no artillery or cavalry and would be held awaiting further orders. He specifically stated, "If you wish any of them to move toward Manassas please inform me." Just five and a half hours earlier, Halleck had ordered him to not lose a minute in forwarding as many troops as possible toward Manassas. Instead of doing so, McClellan was defiantly ignoring those orders and debating again. He also elevated his scare tactics by saying reports indicated that 120,000 enemy troops would advance on Baltimore and Washington.[122] This was a vintage McClellan fabrication.

On the next morning (August 29), while Pope was launching his uncoordinated attacks on Jackson near Manassas, McClellan reported that Franklin's corps was in motion. Then he again questioned that movement. He told Halleck: "[Thomas F.] Meagher's brigade [part of Sumner's Second Corps] is still at Aquia. If he moves in support of Franklin, it leaves us without any reliable troops in and near Washington. Yet Franklin is too weak alone. What shall be done? No more cavalry arrived; have but three squadrons. Franklin has but 40 rounds of ammunition, and no wagons to move more. I do not think Franklin is in condition to accomplish much if he meets with serious resistance. I should not have moved him but for your pressing order of last night."[123] In other words, McClellan was stating that Franklin could accomplish nothing and was vulnerable, and that he (McClellan) washed his hands of responsibility for whatever happened to him.

The disposition of Franklin's corps continued to be a troublesome issue. In the course of requesting authority to post Sumner's corps in defense of Washington, McClellan, less than three hours after his hand-washing wire, told Halleck, "I really think [Franklin] ought not under present circumstances, to advance beyond Annandale,"[124] which is less than halfway on the route from Alexandria to Manassas. Within two hours, Halleck firmly objected and spelled out his wishes: "I want Franklin's corps to go far enough to find out something about the enemy. Perhaps he may get such information at Annandale as to prevent his going farther; otherwise he will push on toward Fairfax. Try to get something from the direction of Manassas.... Our people must move more actively and find out where the enemy is. I am tired of guesses."[125]

That afternoon (August 29), while the first full day's fighting raged at Manassas, the president, who had been sending wires for two days inquiring what various generals and others knew of Pope and the front,[126] perhaps unwisely sent a telegram inquiring of McClellan, "What news from direction of Mannassas [sic] Junction? What generally?"[127] McClellan responded eagerly to this opportunity to get Lincoln to second-guess Halleck. He told Lincoln that the last, but necessarily unreliable, reports he had were that the enemy was retiring. Then he outlined the options as he saw them and requested orders:

> ... I am clear that one of two courses should be adopted: First, to concentrate all our available forces to open communication with Pope; Second, *To leave Pope to get out of his scrape* and at once use all our means to make the capital perfectly safe. No middle ground will now answer. Tell me what you wish me to do and I will do all in my power to accomplish it. I wish to know what my orders and authority are. I ask for nothing, but will obey whatever orders you give. I only ask a prompt decision, that I may at once give the necessary orders. It will not do to delay longer.[128]

What chutzpah! First, he erred by letting his feelings about Pope slip into a communication to the president. Second, he asked the president for orders when Halleck, for the last three days, had been giving him very specific orders to move toward Pope. Those orders totaled six by the time McClellan wired Lincoln. At least McClellan sent Halleck a copy of the wire.

The president then sent a doubly-wise response to McClellan. First, he told him that he thought the first alternative, pushing toward Pope, was the correct one. Second, he said, "But I wish not to control. That I now leave to Gen. Halleck, aided by your counsels."[129] Thus, the president saw things the same way as Halleck and also supported Halleck's authority to issue orders to McClellan.

In the midst of these messages, McClellan penned a note to his wife that included the statements, "Two of my Corps will either save that fool Pope or be sacrificed for the country. I do not know whether I will be permitted to save the Capital or not—I have just telegraphed very plainly to the Presdt & Halleck what I think ought to be done—I expect merely a contemptuous silence."[130] Ultimately, Franklin's corps was halted by McClellan at Annandale and "went into camp within sound of the battle" at Manassas.[131]

In late afternoon on the 29th, as Lee and Longstreet discussed when to send in Longstreet's troops at Manassas, McClellan sent Halleck a somewhat disrespectful message of his own: "Before receiving the President's message I had put Sumner's corps in motion toward Arlington and the Chain Bridge [north and northwest instead of west toward Manassas], not having received any reply from you. The movement is still under your control in either direction, though now under progress, as stated." Then he added a postscript referring to his wire to the president: "I think that one of the two alternatives should be fully carried out."[132]

While McClellan was playing word games with Halleck and Lincoln and defying Halleck's orders to expedite Franklin and Sumner's movement toward Manassas, Pope was having a bad day. He had ordered Sigel's First Corps and John Reynolds' Pennsylvania Reserves to attack Jackson's position, which they did, and Porter's Fifth Corps to get between Jackson and the oncoming Longstreet. Porter encountered Longstreet's troops, stopped, and did not advance. More Union troops arrived on the field, some attacked Jackson, Jackson's line was pierced but held, and Longstreet's troops arrived and took position on Jackson's right. Lee ordered Longstreet to attack but acquiesced in Longstreet's not doing so because of the unknown number of Union troops in the vicinity. Such an attack probably would have wreaked havoc among the disorganized Union forces. Meanwhile, Pope labored during the day of the 29th under the delusion that Jackson somehow was retreating.

Pope was angry at Porter for not advancing as ordered, but Porter correctly sensed Longstreet's presence and the folly of an attempted advance.[133] As Ethan Rafuse indicated, Pope would have been wise to have directed his anger elsewhere: "Although wrong in respect to Porter, Pope was correct to suspect there was bad faith somewhere, for farther to the east, McClellan had spent August 29 doing all he could to avoid sending reinforcements to Pope's assistance.... [In addition to quibbling with Halleck about how far Franklin's corps should proceed,] [t]o guard against the unlikely prospect of a Confederate cavalry raid or a general Confederate offensive against Washington, McClellan also spent the morning of August 29 posting Sumner's command in the Washington fortifications and corresponding with Barnard on the matter of preparing the Chain Bridge for demolition."[134]

On the evening of August 29, Halleck must have been shocked to discover that Franklin's corps was not proceeding toward Manassas but had been stopped. At 7:50 P.M., the angry general-in-chief wired McClellan, "I have just been told that Franklin's corps stopped at Annandale, and that he was this evening in Alexandria [his starting point]. This is all contrary to my orders; investigate and report the facts of this disobedience. That corps must push forward, as I directed...."[135] In his 8 P.M. response, McClellan referred to three earlier telegrams he had sent and Halleck's response to them as justification for the halt. He said he had sent Franklin's few cavalry on toward Manassas but that, "It was not safe for Franklin to move beyond Annandale, under the circumstances, until we knew what was at Vienna." He then stated that Franklin had been with him until 1 P.M. arranging for supplies—an admission that the corps commander had not moved with his troops when they supposedly marched at 6 A.M.[136]

McClellan took responsibility for all these actions, which he claimed did not violate Halleck's orders. Finally, he defiantly requested specific orders (as though he had not received several already): "Please give distinct orders in reference to Franklin's movements of to-morrow…. In regard to to-morrow's movements I desire definite instructions as it is not agreeable to me to be accused of disobeying orders when I have simply exercised the discretion you committed to me."[137] To the extent that the telegrams McClellan referred to dealt with Franklin's corps, they had been trumped by Halleck's very specific directions in his 3 P.M. message. For three days, as Pope's army faced a crisis at the old Manassas battlefield, McClellan had defied six specific orders to expeditiously send Franklin's (and even Sumner's) corps to Pope's relief.

A frustrated Halleck went on record the next morning. At 9:40 on August 30, he telegraphed McClellan, "I am by no means satisfied with General Franklin's march of yesterday. Considering the circumstances of the case, he was very wrong in stopping at Annandale. Moreover, I learned last night that the Quartermaster's Department could have given him plenty of transportation, if he had applied for it, any time since his arrival at Alexandria. He knew the importance of opening communication with General Pope's army, and should have acted more promptly."[138] McClellan responded that the quartermasters' wagons had been needed to supply the Washington area garrisons, the shortage of wagons for Franklin's extra ammunition had delayed him, and "Every effort has been made to carry out your instructions promptly."[139]

McClellan had told his wife the night before, "Pope has been in a tight place, but from the news received this evening I think the danger is pretty much over. Tomorrow will tell the story."[140] At 1:30 P.M. on the 30th, he told her, "There has been heavy firing going on all day long somewhere beyond Bull Run."[141] Indeed there was fighting near Bull Run. After deliberating all morning and astonished that Jackson was still holding on instead of retreating, Pope ordered an all-out assault on Jackson's weakened line.

Porter's corps was the primary Federal attacking force. Porter moved his troops into an open field facing Jackson's right. Lee had Longstreet's artillery enfilade Porter's corps with artillery—with devastating effect—and, as Jackson finally called for reinforcements, ordered Longstreet to launch a full-scale infantry assault. The demoralized and disorganized Union troops were swept from the field and retreated to Centreville. Only hastily organized but effective Union defensive stands at Chinn Ridge and Henry Hill prevented Longstreet's troops from cutting off Pope's route of retreat. Going on the defense, the Union troops imposed more casualties on Longstreet's troops in three hours than Jackson had suffered in three days.[142]

In response to the major fighting erupting at Manassas on the 30th, Halleck that afternoon again ordered McClellan to advance all his troops. First, he directed, "I think [Darius] Couch should land at Alexandria and be immediately pushed out to Pope. Send the troops where the fighting is."[143] Next he ordered, "Franklin's and all of Sumner's corps should be pushed forward with all possible dispatch. They must use their legs and make forced marches. Time now is everything …."[144] A day or so too late to assist Pope, McClellan responded, "Sumner's corps was fully in motion by 2:30 pm, and Franklin's was past Fairfax at 10 P.M. [A.M.?], moving forward as rapidly as possible. I have sent the last cavalryman I have to the front; also every other soldier in my command, except a small camp guard."[145]

At 10:30 that evening, perhaps sensing that the fighting was over, McClellan reported having sent all his troops ahead and belatedly requested permission to proceed to the battlefield. At 3:30 the next morning, he reported to Halleck on the disaster that had befallen Pope's army:

> My aide just in. He reports our army as badly beaten. Our losses very heavy. Troops arriving at Centreville. Have probably lost several batteries. Some of the corps entirely broken up into stragglers. Shall Couch continue his movements to the front? We have no other tried troops in Washington. Sumner between Fairfax and Centreville. Franklin now at Centreville, having fallen back from Bull Run. Enemy has probably suffered heavily.... [146]

It is telling that Sumner had marched his corps from Alexandria to an area between Fairfax and Centreville (two-thirds of the way to Manassas) in something like twelve hours. That marching time provides insight into what might have been if Franklin had marched non-stop from Alexandria to Manassas on the 27th, 28th, or 29th—as Halleck had ordered McClellan to do. Instead, nothing happened on the 27th or 28th, and Franklin's march on the 29th was halted by McClellan at Annandale, one-third of the way to Manassas.

Lincoln and many others were angered by what had happened. Nevins reported, "Ridiculing McClellan's idea that Lee had a magnificently equipped army of 200,000, the correspondents now had facts to show that all along he had really possessed fewer troops, with less artillery, arms, provisions, and transport, than the Union side." A *New York Tribune* reporter concluded at the time, "We have been whipped by an inferior force of inferior men, better handled than ours." Nevins summarized northern public opinion: "What particularly incensed Northern opinion, however, was not Pope's incompetence, but the willful limpness if not outright treachery of other officers. They would rather lose battles and sacrifice troops than abandon their jealousies." [147]

Although McClellan told Halleck on August 31 that Franklin had fallen back to Centreville from Bull Run, he told Mary Ellen later that morning, "Franklin had arrived & was in position at Centreville." [148] Did Franklin ever reach the battlefield in time to be of any use to Pope? Apparently not. On the morning after the battle, Brigadier General Samuel D. Sturgis of Franklin's corps arrived fresh on the battlefield. Sturgis, who earlier had said, "I don't care for John Pope one pinch of owl dung," was greeted by Pope with the words, "Too late, Sammy, too late." Sturgis, probably reflecting his and McClellan's views responded, "I always told you that if they gave you rope enough you would hang yourself." [149]

Sturgis was not alone among Franklin's officers and men in taunting Pope's retreating troops. One of Pope's soldiers reported that some of Franklin's men "expressed their delight at the defeat of Pope and his army." According to Brigadier General Carl Schurz, a division commander in Pope's army, some in Franklin's corps expressed "their pleasure at Pope's discomfiture without the slightest concealment, and spoke of our government in Washington with an affectation of supercilious contempt." [150] The aggressive Pope's defeat stood in contrast to McClellan's defensive escape on the Peninsula and, as a result, had an unfortunate consequence for the Army of the Potomac, historian Michael Adams asserted, "[f]or it gave credence to a belief in that army that McClellan was the best general the Union had. As their hero had fought defensively, this was tantamount to saying that outright victory over Lee was impossible. This was to be the legacy of McClellan: long after he was gone his army would fight to survive, not to win." [151]

In his August 31 letter to his wife, McClellan stated that Pope had been reporting "he was getting on splendidly, driving the enemy all day, gaining a glorious victory, etc. etc." before his defeat became known. In an early afternoon portion of that letter, he disgustedly reported that new orders gave him command of those portions of his army not sent to Pope: "... I am left in command of *nothing*—a command I feel fully competent to exercise, & to which I can do full justice. I am going to write a quiet moderate letter to Mr. [William] Aspinwall presently, explaining to him the exact state of the case, without comment, so that my friends in New York may know all...."[152]

On the evening of August 31, McClellan reported to Halleck that there were some 20,000 stragglers from Pope's army. A desperate Halleck replied, "You will retain the command of everything in this vicinity not temporarily belonging to Pope's army in the field. I beg of you to assist me in this crisis with your ability and experience. I am utterly tired out." Seeing his plans about to come to fruition, McClellan answered back, "I am ready to afford you any assistance in my power, but you will readily perceive how difficult an undefined position such as I now hold must be. At what hour in the morning can I see you alone, either at your own house or the office?"[153]

By 11:30 that night (August 31), McClellan was advising Halleck how bad conditions in the field were. He reported that Pope's left and center had been driven in and that Fairfax City was exposed on the right (north). Thus he recommended that Couch's division be halted and that all forces be drawn back to defend Washington. He summarized his thoughts: "I think these orders should be sent at once. I have no confidence in the dispositions made as I gather them. To speak frankly—and the occasion requires it—there appears to be a total absence of brains, and I fear the total destruction of the Army.... The occasion is grave and demands grave measures. The question is the salvation of the country." Two hours later, Halleck replied that he needed more definitive information before ordering a retreat and that he was "fully aware of the gravity of the crisis and [had] been for weeks."[154]

Meanwhile, battlefield struggles continued in Virginia. September 1 saw a battle at Chantilly, where Union troops, at the cost of two outstanding generals (Kearny and Isaac I. Stevens), repulsed a probing Jackson attack in a blinding rainstorm. That battle ended the immediate threat to Washington. Second Manassas, however, had cost the Union 16,054 casualties to Lee's 9,127,[155] and there was plenty of blame to spread among Union generals.

Meanwhile, Lincoln had to decide who would command the Union forces in the East. After the battle, he had told his cabinet that McClellan's behavior had been "shocking" and "atrocious." The president told his aide, John Hay, that McClellan had wanted Pope to lose and concluded, "This is unpardonable."[156]

Cabinet pressure mounted on Lincoln to terminate McClellan. On August 30, Treasury Secretary Chase drafted a letter to Lincoln, co-signed by War Secretary Stanton and Interior Secretary Caleb B. Smith, recommending McClellan's immediate removal. In cabinet members' discussions, Chase had said that McClellan ought to be shot.[157] On September 2, Attorney General Bates prepared a letter, co-signed by secretaries Stanton, Chase and Smith, declaring to Lincoln "our deliberate opinion that, at this time, it is not safe to entrust to Major General McClellan the command of any army of the United States." A contemporaneous note by Bates reported that, at a cabinet meeting, Lincoln was "in deep distress" that these cabinet members had believed it necessary to sincerely recommend McClellan's dismissal—an action Lincoln believed infeasible at that instant because of Halleck and Pope's apparent inability to take charge of the chaotic situation in the capital. Bates' note complained of the lack of offensive action and stated, "If the City fell, it would be by treachery in our leaders, & not by lack of power to defend."[158]

At a cabinet meeting on September 2, however, Stanton announced that Lincoln had placed McClellan in command of all troops in the Washington area. Because he had never been relieved of command of the Army of the Potomac, McClellan retained that command and obtained control over all of the troops Pope had commanded. Lincoln explained to his disappointed cabinet members that McClellan had been at fault in the Second Manassas disaster but was critically needed in that time of crisis and chaos because of his defensive, engineering, and organizational skills. He explained to John Hay, "McClellan has acted badly in this matter, but we must use what tools we have." Nevins credited Lincoln with "a lightning flash of magnanimity, patriotism, and courage" by rising above the anger and hate of the Radicals, Stanton, and others to take what was the correct short-term action.[159]

On the morning of September 2, Lincoln and Halleck visited McClellan and offered him command of all Pope's troops as they re-entered the Washington lines. Halleck promptly wired Pope of the situation and told him to consider troop disposition orders from McClellan as though they had come from Halleck. McClellan reiterated to Pope Halleck's order to withdraw promptly and gave him desired troop dispositions.[160]

The next day Pope communicated with Halleck about everyone's failures, except his own, that had resulted in the recent disaster.[161] Even though his performance had been flawed, he had reason to be upset. As he reported, "Sumner and Franklin arrived too late to be of service, as the army had been cut up and worried to death before they reached Centreville."[162] Pope, who believed he had been poorly served by McClellan's army, also reported to Halleck "the unsoldierly and dangerous conduct of many brigade and some division commanders of the forces sent here from the Peninsula. Every word and act and intention is discouraging, and calculated to break down the spirits of the men and produce disaster."[163]

Pope's complaint about lack of support from McClellan's army led Lincoln to pressure McClellan to send a conciliation-inducing message to Porter. McClellan told his good friend, "I ask of you for my sake, that of the country, and of the old Army of the Potomac that you and all my friends will lend the fullest and most cordial co-operation to General Pope in all the operations now going on.... Say the same thing to my friends in the Army of the Potomac, and that the last request I have to make of them is that, for their country's sake, they will extend to General Pope the same support they ever have to me." He explained that he was in charge of Washington's defense and would facilitate their retreat, if necessary.[164]

Although Pope had proven arrogant and incompetent against Lee, Jackson, and Longstreet, McClellan had done everything in his own power to ensure that Pope's mistakes would result in a resounding defeat and eliminate him as a competitor for Union military power in the East. McClellan had taken more than three weeks to move his troops off the Peninsula and into northern Virginia, where Pope needed their assistance. Then, in the critical days just before and during the Second Battle of Manassas, McClellan deliberately defied at least six direct orders from the general-in-chief to send Franklin and Sumner's corps to Pope's aid. He also stopped Franklin's corps at Annandale and delayed Sumner's corps at Alexandria until it was too late for either of them to assist Pope. Therefore, McClellan was able to prevent 25,000 Union troops from reaching the Manassas battlefield before or during that major conflict. With those additional troops, Pope probably would not have had a vulnerable and undermanned flank and likely would not have been swept off the battlefield by Longstreet's attack on the afternoon of August 30.

Pope's defeat opened the door to McClellan's resuming control over all Union troops in the Virginia theater. Lee was on Washington's doorstep, and Lincoln had to act. McClellan's conduct in undermining Pope was obvious to Lincoln, Stanton, and Halleck, but Lincoln believed he had no choice but to at least temporarily place McClellan in charge once again. Halleck was admittedly exhausted, the troops still had confidence in McClellan, and no other high-level candidate was immediately available. Thus, over the objection of most of his cabinet, Lincoln put McClellan back in charge. His rationale was, "If he can't fight himself, he excels in making others ready to fight." Thus the president provided McClellan with one more opportunity to win the war—an opportunity that he would squander.

8

Squandering Opportunities at Antietam

After being given once last chance for redemption, McClellan took Union troops into Maryland to oppose Lee's army in the Maryland Campaign, in which he failed to capitalize on the discovery of Lee's campaign order, pursued the outnumbered Rebels at his usual deliberate pace, failed to attack Lee's badly outnumbered army until it had been reinforced at Sharpsburg, and then incompetently fought a disjointed day-long battle at Antietam Creek when he could have trapped and decimated Lee's army but failed to do so.

Resuming command of all troops in a reunited Army of the Potomac, McClellan would have an opportunity given to few Civil War commanders—the chance to make amends for a prior disaster. In the ensuing Maryland (or Antietam) Campaign,[1] Lee would divide his own army, place it in a vulnerable location, and virtually invite McClellan to destroy it and perhaps end the war. In addition, McClellan would benefit from one of the greatest "gifts" in military history; a copy of Lee's strategic order would fall into his hands. This is the story of how McClellan failed to take advantage of all those opportunities and thus failed to bring the Civil War to a quicker end.

He reveled in his renewed post of power and resumed the unfortunate habit of writing directly to the president instead of Halleck.[2] Within hours of resuming command after Second Bull Run on September 2, McClellan already was anticipating the possibility that Lee would cross the Potomac and invade the North. He told the president it was essential "to be ready to attack the enemy in flank should they venture to cross the upper Potomac" and to consider the possibility that communications between Washington and Baltimore would be cut. Two days later, he reported to Halleck that he was sending troops into Maryland "to watch and check the enemy should he attempt to cross the Potomac below the Point of Rocks."[3]

After his Seven Days' experience against Lee, McClellan had good reason to believe that Lee would be aggressive and thus might leave the Confederacy to invade the North. In fact, Lee wrote to Jefferson Davis on September 3 about his plans to invade Maryland. He did so without waiting for an answer from Davis and even had the gall to suggest that Braxton Bragg's Army of Tennessee, outnumbered three-to-one in attempting to defend southeastern Tennessee, be brought east to cover Richmond while Lee moved north.[4]

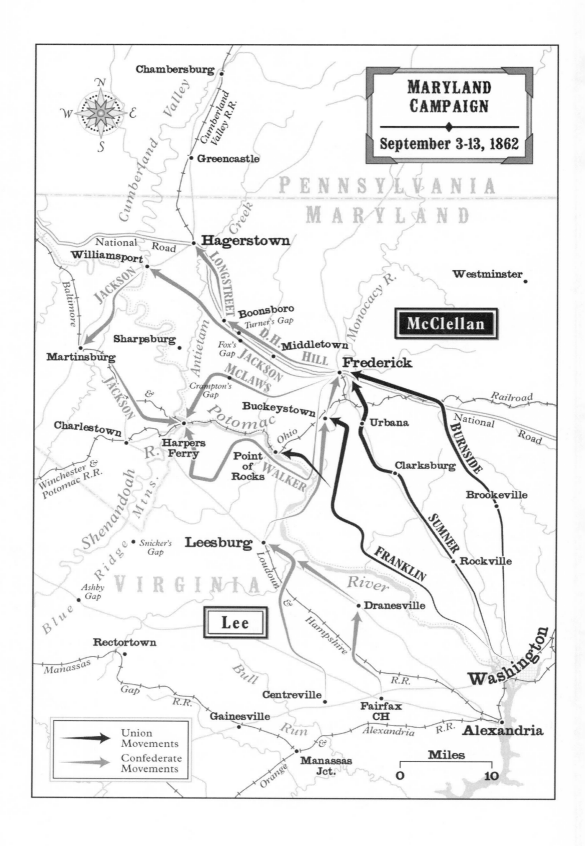

The next day Lee began carrying out his plans for what became the Maryland Campaign when he moved his 53,000 weary troops north from Manassas. On September 5, they crossed the Potomac at White's Ferry near Leesburg. Lee's purposes in invading Maryland were numerous. He told Davis he was going to take advantage of the presence of Confederate sympathizers in Maryland and might move on to Pennsylvania to destroy the critical railroad bridge crossing the Susquehanna River at Harrisburg. Lee wanted his men and horses to live off the Maryland countryside instead of the fairly exhausted Virginia lands. In addition, the remaining crops in Virginia could be harvested without Union interference if the fighting moved elsewhere. Lee also intended to keep the strategic initiative and force McClellan to fight a critical battle in a place of Lee's choosing far from McClellan's Washington base. Lee's ultimate purpose was to achieve foreign recognition of the Confederacy based on a convincing battlefield victory.[5]

Meanwhile, in Washington, a power struggle was raging about who would command the army in the field. On September 3, Lincoln ordered Halleck to "immediately commence, and proceed with all possible dispatch, to organize an army for active operations, from all the material within, and coming within his control, independent of the forces he may deem necessary for the defense of Washington, when such active army shall take the field."[6] Thus, the door was open for the appointment of someone other than McClellan to be designated commander of the army that would take the field to oppose Lee's invasion.

It appears that Lee moved so quickly that McClellan obtained that field command by default. Lincoln himself claimed that Halleck selected him for field command to respond to Lee's invasion because Burnside refused to take the position. Whatever his wishes, Lincoln named McClellan to that position on the morning of September 5. That result must have pleased Lee, whose low opinion of McClellan's "speed" and "aggressiveness" had been confirmed on the Peninsula. Lincoln agreed with that assessment; on September 12, he said of McClellan: "He can't go ahead—he can't strike a blow."[7] Regardless of how he had acquired the command, McClellan let it go to his head. In a September 5 letter, he gloated to Mary Ellen, "... Again I have been called upon to save the country—the case is desperate, but with God's help I will try unselfishly to do my best & if he wills it accomplish the salvation of the nation."[8]

During the early days of September, charges of non-support and insubordination brought by Pope against Major Generals Porter and Franklin and Brigadier General Charles Griffin caused a distraction. All three accused generals were relieved from duty on September 5 and 6 pending resolution of the charges. On September 6, however, McClellan wrote to Halleck requesting that Franklin and Porter be restored to duty, particularly since he wished to immediately move Porter's corps to the front. He separately wrote to Lincoln requesting that all three generals be restored to their commands "until I have gotten through with the present crisis." Lincoln responded succinctly, "With entire respect, I must repeat that Gen. Halleck must control these questions." In response to McClellan's request, Halleck temporarily restored the three generals to their commands. On September 8, the Commission of Inquiry investigating Pope's charges met and adjourned.[9]

That same day Banks assumed control of Washington's defenses, and McClellan was then free to pursue Lee. On the eve of his departure from Washington, McClellan was still bragging to his wife:

> ... I shall have nearly 100,000 men, old & new, & hope with God's blessing to gain a decisive victory. I think we shall win for the men are now in good spirits—confident in their general & all united in sentiment. Pope & McDowell have morally killed themselves—& are

relieved from command—a signal instance of retributive justice.... I have now the entire confidence of the Govt & the love of the army—my enemies are crushed, silent & disarmed—if I defeat the rebels I shall be master of the situation.... [10]

In McClellan's mind, there were the "enemies" and there were the "rebels"—an interesting dichotomy. Even though McClellan had almost 100,000 troops and thus outnumbered his Rebel foes by two-to-one, he would be gripped by his usual delusion that the situation was the reverse. Another of his delusions was that he had "the entire confidence" of the government.

Lee's army completed its arrival at Frederick, Maryland, on the morning of September 7, 1862, and received a disappointing reception from a populace that regarded his soldiers as rabble. Lee sent his foragers to scour the countryside, where they paid for produce and livestock with Union greenbacks and Confederate currency. At Frederick, he posed a threat to Washington, Baltimore, Harrisburg, and Philadelphia. Lee told one of his brigadiers that before McClellan was aroused, "I hope to be on the Susquehanna."[11]

By the evening of September 8, the trailing McClellan was at Rockville, Maryland, about twenty miles northwest of Washington and thirty miles southeast of Frederick, with his huge army but had little knowledge of the whereabouts of Lee. He assured Halleck, "As soon as I find out where to strike, I will be after them without an hour's delay."[12] An hour later, McClellan wrote to Pennsylvania's Governor Andrew G. Curtin about Lee's army: "My information about the enemy comes from unreliable sources, and is vague and conflicting. This army is in position to move against the Rebels whatever their plan may be. If they intend an advance towards your State, I shall act with all possible vigor. I can scarcely believe that such is their purpose...."[13] He continued to underestimate the audacity of Lee and had no idea what Lee intended.

That same day Lee issued a proclamation to the people of Maryland stating that he came to free, not harm, them; asking them to rally to the Confederate cause, and disclaiming any use of compulsion to recruit. But he would be greatly disappointed by the scarcity of Maryland volunteers. One problem Lee faced was that he had entered the generally non-slaveholding western section of the state, where there was minimal sympathy for the Confederate cause. Another problem was that those Marylanders, generally from the Eastern Shore or areas southeast of Washington, wishing to join his army had already done so. The people of Frederick, Maryland, were unimpressed and repulsed by Lee's barefoot and bedraggled men, who often were eating green apples and raw corn to survive.

Against the advice of Longstreet and Jackson, Lee issued crucial Special Orders No. 191 on September 9. That order divided his army into four (ultimately five) segments in an effort to capture Harpers Ferry before moving on toward Pennsylvania. On September 10, his army began executing the order and left Frederick. Brigadier General John Walker backtracked to Loudon Heights, Virginia, overlooking Harpers Ferry from the south. Major Generals Lafayette McLaws and Richard H. Anderson went southwest from Frederick through Crampton's Gap in South Mountain to attack Union troops guarding Maryland Heights, overlooking Harpers Ferry from the east.

The major Rebel movement involved Jackson. He led three divisions west-northwest on the National Road through Turner's Gap (farther north in South Mountain than Crampton's Gap), crossed the Potomac at Williamsport, and then moved through Martinsburg, Virginia, to close the trap on Harpers Ferry from the west. Lee, with Longstreet's corps, followed Jackson through Turner's Gap, left D.H. Hill's division at Boonsboro, and continued northwest on to Hagerstown (close to the Pennsylvania border).

While in the Rockville area with his troops slowly moving north, McClellan still had time to bemoan his herculean task and to gloat about the Bull Run disaster. To Mary Ellen, he wrote:

> You don't know what a task has been imposed upon me! I have been obliged to do the best I could with the broken & discouraged fragments of two armies defeated by no fault of mine…. I felt that under the circumstances no one else *could* save the country, & I have not shrunk from the terrible task. Pope has subsided into oblivion with the contempt of all— he has proved to be a perfect failure & all acknowledge it. McDowell has had to flee for his life—his own men would have killed him had he made his appearance among them … Pope has been foolish enough to try to throw the blame of his defeat on the Army of the Potomac—the resulting inquiry will beyond a doubt be most disastrous to him & nail him as an incompetent General.[14]

A few hours later, he continued in the same vein:

> … I hope to learn this morning something definite as to the movements of secesh to be enabled to regulate my own. I hardly expect to equal the genius of Mr. Pope but I hope to waste fewer lives & to accomplish something more than lame defeat…. It is something of a triumph that my enemies have been put down so completely, & if to that I can add the defeat of secesh I think I ought to be entitled to fall back into private life….[15]

On September 9, 10, and 11, McClellan remained at his camp near Rockville as Lee's army camped near Frederick and then left. On September 10, Lee's two corps pulled out of Frederick to carry out their assigned missions. Jackson, assigned to take charge of the Harpers Ferry operation, deliberately made to-be-overheard remarks about the best roads to Pennsylvania. Back at Rockville, McClellan received and forwarded to Halleck, on the morning of September 9, a "not fully reliable" cavalry report that 100,000 Rebels had crossed the Potomac and, later that day, a subsequent report that the enemy numbered 110,000 near Frederick.[16] That afternoon he told Mary Ellen of the 110,000-troop report and commented, "I have not so many, so I must watch them closely & try to catch them in some mistake, which I hope to do." Then, somewhat worriedly, he added, "I have just this moment learned that in addition to the force on this side of the [Potomac] the enemy have *also* a large force near Leesburg [back in Virginia]—so McC has a difficult game to play, but will do his best & try to do his duty."[17]

An anxious President Lincoln opened the door for a substantive report from McClellan by sending him a September 10 wire simply inquiring, "How does it look now?" McClellan replied at noon that day with details on his activities and the mention of disturbingly high Confederate strength estimates: "… I have scouts and spies pushed forward in every direction and shall soon be in possession of reliable and definite information. The statements I get regarding the enemy's forces that have crossed to this side range from 80,000 to 150,000…."[18] During a September 12 meeting, an unimpressed Lincoln complained to Gideon Welles about McClellan's slowness: "He got to Rockville, for instance, last Sunday night, and in four days he advanced to Middlebrook, ten miles, in pursuit of an invading enemy. This was rapid movement for him."[19]

Just before midnight on the 10th, McClellan dramatically announced to Halleck "a general advance" the next day and pleaded, "Send me up all the troops you can spare." McClellan's idea of a general advance was unique; between September 7 and 13, his troops marched a total of thirty miles.[20] On the morning of the 11th, McClellan suggested that Colonel Dixon Miles and his 9,000 troops at Harpers Ferry be ordered to join him. Halleck's immediate response was, "There is no way for Colonel Miles to join you at present. His only chance is to defend his works till you can open communication with him."[21] In other words, McClellan and his troops would have to break through to Harpers

Ferry rather than expecting that garrison, one-tenth the size of McClellan's, to make its way to him through all those Confederate troops he kept writing about.

As in his prior campaigns, McClellan became increasingly concerned about purported enemy strength and began his own campaign for reinforcements. By September 10, therefore, he was writing to Halleck, "All the evidence that has been accumulated from various sources since we left Washington goes to prove most conclusively that almost the entire rebel army in Virginia, amounting to not less than 120,000 men, is in the vicinity of Frederick City."

On the basis of this supposed Rebel numerical superiority of "at least 25 per cent" and the apparent secure condition of Washington, McClellan requested that "every available man be at once added to this army." He specifically asked for one or two of the three corps from the Washington defenses and the troops from the Harpers Ferry garrison—a total of about 25,000 reinforcements. Accompanying this request was McClellan's usual pessimistic assessment: "… the result of a general battle, with such odds as the enemy now appears to have against us, might, to say the least, be doubtful; and if we should be defeated, the consequences to the country would be disastrous in the extreme."[22]

McClellan kept pleading for reinforcements. On the afternoon of the 11th, he requested Halleck to "[p]lease send forward all the troops you can spare from Washington, particularly Porter's, Heintzelman's, Sigel's, and all other old troops." At 6 P.M., Lincoln responded positively that Porter, with 21,000 troops, "is ordered to-night to join you as quick as possible. I am for sending you all that can be spared, & hope others can follow Porter very soon."[23] McClellan's non-use of Porter's huge corps at the Battle of Antietam within the next week would nullify this addition to his army.

Until September 13, Halleck denied McClellan's request to move the garrison from Harpers Ferry and thereby doomed most of the soldiers there to ultimate capture by Jackson, Walker, and McLaws. However, by retaining the garrison at Harpers Ferry, Halleck deflected Lee from his planned invasion of Pennsylvania, caused him to divide his army in an effort to capture the garrison and remove the threat to his rear, and ultimately made Lee's divided army vulnerable to destruction. Halleck, shaken by Second Manassas and of little further use to Lincoln or Stanton, did not foresee any of this; he probably saw retention of the garrison there as the most conservative, criticism-free thing to do.[24]

While McClellan pleaded for reinforcements, Jackson began closing the noose on Harpers Ferry. On September 11, he crossed the Potomac back into Virginia at Williamsport, attacked the Union garrison at Martinsburg, and drove it back toward Harpers Ferry. His crossing of the Potomac (away from Pennsylvania) nevertheless caused Pennsylvania's Governor Andrew G. Curtin that same day to request Lincoln to send him 80,000 troops—a request that Lincoln promptly declined.[25] In fact, Lincoln reported the news of Jackson's crossing to McClellan, speculated that the "whole rebel army … is recrossing the Potomac," and pleaded, "Please do not let him get off without being hurt."[26] McClellan responded that he was afraid the Rebels would escape via Williamsport before he could catch them but assured the president, "If Harpers Ferry is still in our possession I think I can save the garrison if they fight at all."[27]

On September 12, McClellan's troops began reaching Frederick and were welcomed by the majority of its residents. Stuart's cavalry counter-attacked Union troops and captured a brigade commander before heading up the Hagerstown Road. McClellan advised Lincoln, Halleck, and his wife of his troops' entry into Frederick, his intent to pursue the enemy into Pennsylvania or cut off their retreat to Virginia, and his concern about the need to save the garrison at Harpers Ferry. To Halleck, he wrote, "I have heard no firing in that direction [Harpers Ferry], and if he [Miles] resists at all, I think I cannot only relieve him, but place the rebels who attack him in great danger of being cut off. Everything moves at daylight tomorrow."[28] Neither Miles nor McClellan would fulfill the hopes of the other.

The next day, September 13, nothing moved as promised. But good fortune fell on McClellan, and he was presented with a golden opportunity to do just what he had suggested to Halleck—cut off isolated portions of Lee's army that were planning to attack Harpers Ferry. Two of McClellan's Indiana soldiers found a copy of Lee's Special Orders No. 191 wrapped in paper with three cigars in a field near Frederick. Their find was rushed up the chain of command to the commanding general. Here was a virtually unprecedented opportunity. McClellan possessed Lee's orders showing that the Army of Northern Virginia was spread all over western Maryland and northwestern Virginia, its components separated by rivers, and vulnerable to a swift Union attack on its divided forces.

McClellan was thrilled to see Lee's order and appeared to recognize its significance. However, he did not get his troops underway in pursuit of the enemy for eighteen hours after he knew of Lee's vulnerability. The order was discovered and in his hands by midday on the 13th, but he did not order troops to move in the direction of Harpers Ferry until the morning of the 14th. McClellan waited until mid-afternoon before cautiously issuing orders to his cavalry chief, Brigadier General Alfred Pleasonton. In those 3 P.M. orders, McClellan quoted Lee's order of march from the "Lost Order," directed Pleasonton "to ascertain whether this order of march has thus far been followed," and warned him, "As the pass through the Blue Ridge may be disputed by two columns, ... approach it with great caution."

McClellan later decided to divide his army into three wings, the right wing to march northwest from Frederick on the National Road, the left wing to go southwest after McLaws on Maryland Heights above Harpers Ferry, and the center to act as a reserve. Unlike Grant or Lee, McClellan usually had troops in reserve; this practice weakened the few attacks McClellan actually ordered. It was 6:20 P.M. on the 13th before McClellan issued orders to Franklin, commanding the critical left wing, and those orders called for him to head toward Harpers Ferry through Crampton's Gap by moving "at daybreak in the morning" of the 14th.[29] Thus, although he was aware that a large contingent of Union troops likely was trapped at Harpers Ferry, McClellan was satisfied to begin movement in that direction more than eighteen hours after receiving the "Lost Order" disclosing that problem—and a full day later than previously promised.

At some time that evening, Brigadier General John Gibbon of the Iron Brigade was told by McClellan, "Here is a paper with which if I cannot whip Bobby Lee, I will be willing to go home. I will not show you the document now, but here is the signature, and it gives the movement of every division of Lee's army. Tomorrow we will pitch into his center and if you people will do two good, hard days' marching I will put Lee in a position he will find it hard to get out of."[30] Even as he spoke those words, McClellan already was fatally delaying his army's attack.

Very late on the 13th, McClellan advised Halleck of the contents of Lee's "Lost Order" and stated that he had good reason to believe Lee's army consisted of 120,000 or more troops. As to Harpers Ferry, McClellan told Halleck, "This Army marches forward early to-morrow morning and will make forced marches, to endeavor to relieve Col. Miles, but I fear unless he makes a stout resistance, we may be too late. A report came in just this moment that Miles was attacked to-day and repulsed the enemy, but I do not know what credit to attach to the statement. I shall do everything in my power to save

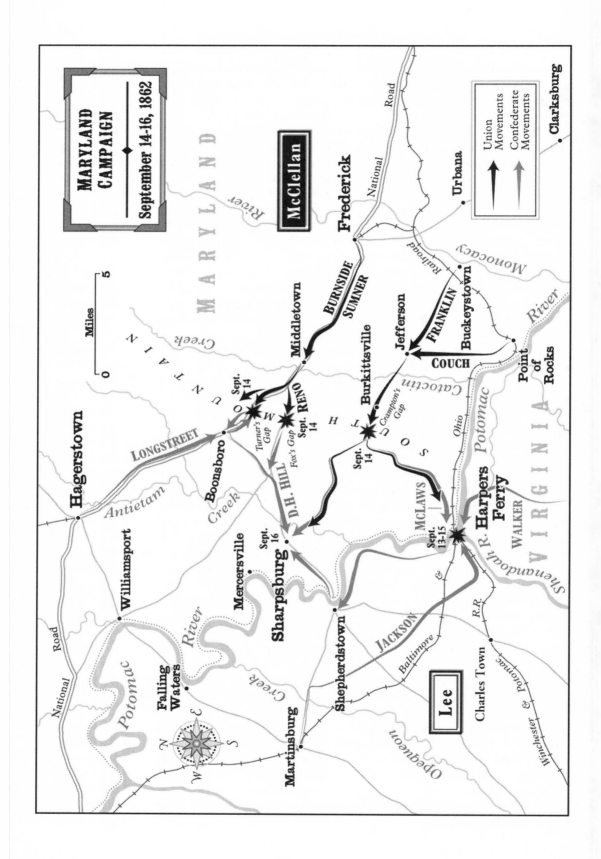

Miles if he still holds out."[31] McClellan did not allow his fears of being too late or news of an attack at Harpers Ferry to change his deliberate schedule.

At midnight on the 13th,[32] he sent a dispatch to the president bragging of the coup and appearing to promise quick action: "I have the whole rebel force in front of me, but am confident, and no time shall be lost. I have a difficult task to perform but with God's blessing will accomplish it. I think Lee has made a gross mistake, and that he will be severely punished for it. The Army is in motion as rapidly as possible. I hope for a great success if the plans of the rebels remain unchanged.... I have all the plans of the rebels, and will catch them in their own trap if my men are equal to the emergency."[33] His men were equal to the emergency, but once again he was not.

On Sunday, September 14, McClellan's troops belatedly pursued the Confederates located at three passes on South Mountain west of Catoctin Mountain and Frederick. McClellan's slow pursuit enabled Longstreet to send A.P. Hill back from Boonsboro to aid some of Jeb Stuart's cavalry in defending the main pass, Turner's Gap, and nearby Fox's Gap, about a mile to the south. During the night of the 13th, Hill had received reports of Union activity, rushed to the two gaps, and sent word to Lee of the pending Federal movement. Lee sent word for Hill to hold the passes and rushed Longstreet from Hagerstown to reinforce Hill.

Hill was badly outnumbered at the two northern gaps. His 2,300 troops most likely would have been quickly swept aside had McClellan started his army forward promptly on the 13th. Instead, Hill had a fighting, if desperate, chance to hold the gaps—at least temporarily. In typical McClellanesque fashion, several Union corps moved deliberately toward the two gaps, mounted a somewhat disjointed and unsupported assault, and then paused for reinforcements while Confederate reinforcements arrived in time to prevent a Union break-through. While Lee arrived and personally took charge of the Confederate defense, McClellan remained miles from the fighting, which he left to Generals Jesse Reno (who was killed), Burnside, Hooker, George Meade, Jacob Cox, John Gibbon, and others.[34] He apparently admired the fighting on South Mountain from a lookout back on the Catoctin Range; if so, it was the first time he had actually observed an army under his command in combat. Remarks McClellan made to Hooker may have resulted in the Iron Brigade receiving its name because of its brave attacks toward Turner's Gap.[35]

Rebel forces grimly hung on there until night, when they withdrew southwest toward the small town of Sharpsburg on Antietam Creek. Realizing that McClellan was moving faster than he had anticipated (Lee had very low expectations of him), Lee, late on the 14th, had issued an order canceling the Harpers Ferry mission and directing the consolidation of his troops at Sharpsburg. Lee was pleasantly surprised by receipt of a message from Jackson that the capture of Harpers Ferry was imminent.

Critical to the entire Maryland Campaign was the fighting at Crampton's Gap on September 14 that coincided with the Battle of South Mountain at Turner and Fox's gaps to the north. Franklin's Sixth Corps, with 13,000 troops on hand, was supposed to break through to Maryland Heights and thus foil Jackson's plans to surround Harpers Ferry. Franklin proved that he was McClellan's disciple by delaying his march in a fruitless wait for another division (a wait ordered by McClellan, according to Franklin) and then finally attacking in mid-afternoon. He probably felt no urgency when he received McClellan's routine 11:45 dispatch concluding with the words, "Continue to bear in mind the necessity of relieving Colonel [Nelson] Miles if possible."[36]

Franklin and his commanders did not realize they were being opposed by a mere 1,000 Confederates. Those well-hidden and well-positioned Rebel defenders stymied Franklin's attackers for hours until they were overwhelmed by the attackers' superior numbers. Howell Cobb's 1,300-man Georgia brigade then reinforced the defense as it was collapsing and held out until dark. The greatly outnumbered Confederates had held Crampton's Gap throughout the 14th at a cost of eight hundred casualties (to the Union's five hundred).[37]

Having reached the gap by nightfall, it was imperative for Franklin to keep the pressure on McLaws and, by the noise of their struggle, alert the Union garrison at Harpers Ferry that relief was on the way. But Franklin continued his McClellan-like reticence and failed to attack into Pleasant Valley west of South Mountain at first light on the 15th. Instead, he assumed that he was outnumbered and requested reinforcements from McClellan. By 10 P.M. the prior night, Franklin had received 7,000 additional troops and thus had 20,000 troops to attack a minuscule Confederate force between Harpers Ferry and his troops. Franklin's failure to attack early that morning led directly to the surrender of Harpers Ferry at 7:15 A.M. on the 15th.[38]

Unfortunately for the Union cause, the Federal commander of the Martinsburg and Harpers Ferry detachments huddled in Harpers Ferry, Colonel Nelson Miles, was as non-aggressive as McClellan. By the afternoon of the 13th, Jackson and his cohorts had Miles trapped. Instead of evacuating to a strong high point, such as Maryland Heights across the Potomac River railroad bridge, or breaking through to McClellan, Miles cowered in the river junction town and waited to be surrounded as the Rebels took the high ground on three sides and began shelling his position. After a brief cannonading from Maryland Heights on the east and Loudon Heights, Virginia, on the south, Miles surrendered the garrison and its 11,500 troops on the morning of September 15. He was killed by a Rebel artillery shot fired minutes after the surrender.[39]

The surrender at Harpers Ferry was a Union disaster. Although a thousand cavalrymen rode out before the surrender, Jackson captured 11,500 men, seventy-three guns, 13,000 small arms, two hundred wagons, and thousands of blue uniforms for his troops. But Allan Nevins concluded, "Nevertheless, the South would have paid too high a price if Lee had been smashed before Jackson could get back to him."[40] McClellan's usual dallying would keep that from happening.

On the morning of the 15th, McClellan boasted to Halleck of the minor victories at Turner and Crampton's Gaps against greatly outnumbered foes. He claimed a "glorious" and "complete" victory. He alleged that the routed and demoralized enemy was "in a perfect panic," Lee had admitted his army was "shockingly whipped," Lee had admitted losses of 15,000, and Lee had been wounded.[41] These statements were gross exaggerations because an uninjured Lee's army had suffered losses of about 3,400 and retreated in good order to Sharpsburg.[42] Lincoln acknowledged the wires and responded, "God bless you, and all with you. Destroy the rebel army, if possible."[43] McClellan would proceed deliberately enough to ensure that Lincoln's wish was not fulfilled.

Jackson assigned the mopping up and surrender proceedings at Harpers Ferry to A.P. Hill and force-marched the rest of his troops north to join Lee at Sharpsburg. Lee had a mere 18,000 troops there until Jackson's arrival, but McClellan hesitated and deliberated instead of attacking his greatly outnumbered foe.

About fifteen miles to the north of Harpers Ferry, McClellan arrived on the afternoon of the 15th at Sharpsburg with 70,000 troops on the east side of Antietam Creek as Lee aligned his paltry 18,000 troops in the woods and on a slight ridge on the western side of the creek. Lee's soldiers were basically trapped in a horseshoe bend of the Potomac River with only a single ford as an escape route. McClellan's army of 70,000 slowly deployed for action but took virtually no offensive action. Fearing he was outnumbered, he, in McPherson's words, "launched no probing attacks and sent no cavalry reconnaissance across the two undefended bridges or the several fords to determine Confederate strength."[44]

McClellan's temerity continued through the day of September 16. Early in the day, he had 70,000 troops to oppose Lee's reinforced but still inferior army of about 25,000. During the day, 9,000 of Jackson's weary troops arrived from Harpers Ferry to augment Lee's still outnumbered force. On either the 15th or 16th, McClellan could have reaped the benefits of the discovery of the "Missing Order" and decimated Lee's minuscule force—as he had said he would do—with his own army of 70,000 to 75,000. Instead, McClellan convinced himself that Lee had 120,000 troops and declined to attack until he was ready (and Lee was increasingly reinforced).[45]

At 7 A.M. on the 16th, McClellan wired Halleck that his troops had arrived too late on the 15th to attack Lee's force at Sharpsburg, heavy fog was preventing an attack that morning, and he would attack "as soon as the situation of the enemy is developed." At the same hour, he wrote to Mary Ellen that he had "no doubt delivered [saved] Penna & Maryland." A short while later, he wrote Franklin about the fog and blustered, "If the enemy is in force here, I shall attack him this morning."[46] The enemy was there in force (although not nearly the size of McClellan's army), but McClellan failed to attack that morning, afternoon, or evening.

The situation on the 16th was well summarized by historian Robert C. Cheeks:

> On the morning of Tuesday, September 16, McClellan had nearly 60,000 soldiers facing Lee's 15,000. His heavy 20-pound Parrott rifles were sending case shot across the creek, feeling out the enemy. As Longstreet ordered a vigorous response—more for bluff than effect—Lee realized his one chance for salvation lay with McClellan reverting to his old, timid behavior. McClellan did not disappoint him. Across the creek, the commander of the Federal Army rode about on his horse, Dan Webster, taking the salutes of his admiring infantry and superbly equipped artillery. His boys would pay dearly for their general's indecisiveness.[47]

Late that afternoon, McClellan finally sent Joe Hooker's First Corps to test Lee's left (north) flank. Hooker crossed the Antietam and positioned himself for an attack early the next morning. He was followed around midnight by Joseph K.F. Mansfield's Twelfth Corps. Lee noted that activity and shifted troops to his left.

September 17 was the bloodiest single day of the entire war. In a full day of unbelievably brave and foolish charges and counter-charges, the troops of both armies beat each other to a bloody pulp in the Battle of Antietam (Sharpsburg).[48] McClellan squandered his huge numerical superiority by attacking sequentially instead of simultaneously and never even using a quarter of his troops. From before dawn until mid-morning, Hooker's and later Mansfield's troops disjointedly attacked from the North Woods and the East Woods on the north end of the lines. Their attacks were driven back from the West Woods and the immortal "Cornfield" by Jackson's defenders, who then counterattacked. The Cornfield was the scene of about fourteen attacks and counterattacks as each side took turns massacring the other before Union troops finally seized that field. The Rebels' north flank refused to break because of reinforcements from the southern end of their line that were facilitated by the 7 A.M. arrival of more of Jackson's troops, who had marched all night to get to the battlefield. Had McClellan attacked on the 15th or 16th, those troops would not have been there to augment Lee's depleted force.[49]

As the northern portion of the battle continued to deteriorate into a bloody stalemate during the early to mid-morning hours, McClellan finally sent Sumner's huge 15,000-man Second Corps into the north and middle of the battlefield. He did so only after Sumner had come to his headquarters seeking such orders and was stalled by

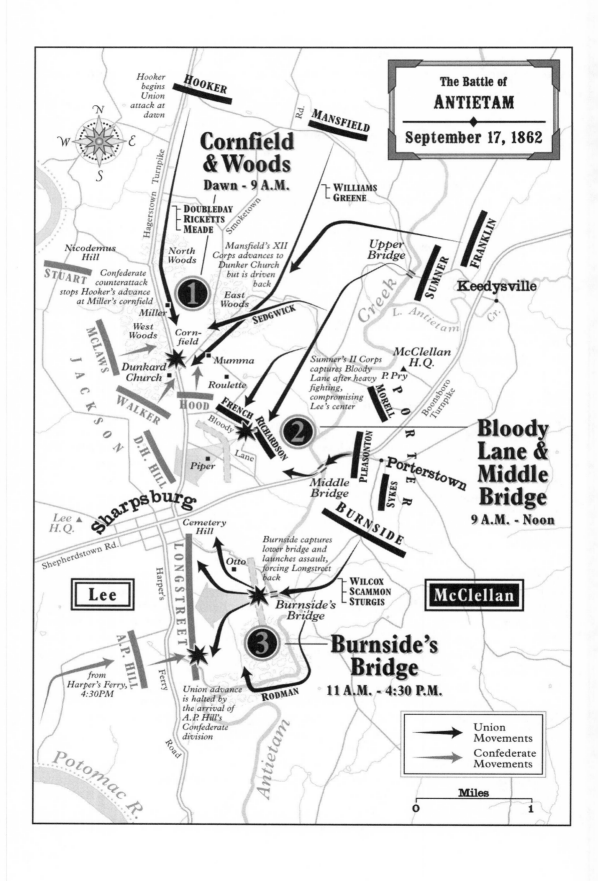

The Battle of
ANTIETAM
September 17, 1862

Hooker begins Union attack at dawn

HOOKER

MANSFIELD Rd.

Cornfield & Woods
Dawn - 9 A.M.

WILLIAMS
GREENE

DOUBLEDAY
RICKETTS
MEADE

Nicodemus Hill

Mansfield's XII Corps advances to Dunker Church but is driven back

Upper Bridge

FRANKLIN

SUMNER

Keedysville

STUART

Confederate counterattack stops Hooker's advance at Miller's cornfield

North Woods

Smoketown

East Woods

SEDGWICK

Creek

L. Antietam

Cr.

McClellan H.Q.

Miller

West Woods

MCLAWS

Cornfield

Dunkard Church

JACKSON

Mumma

Roulette

Sumner's II Corps captures Bloody Lane after heavy fighting, compromising Lee's center

P. Pry

MORELL

Boonsboro Turnpike

Bloody Lane & Middle Bridge
9 A.M. - Noon

WALKER

HOOD

FRENCH

Bloody

RICHARDSON

Piper

Lane

D.H. HILL

Middle Bridge

PLEASONTON

Porterstown

SYKES

Hagerstown Turnpike

Sharpsburg

Lee H.Q.

Cemetery Hill

Otto

BURNSIDE

Shepherdstown Rd.

LONGSTREET

Burnside captures lower bridge and launches assault, forcing Longstreet back

WILCOX
SCAMMON
STURGIS

McClellan

Harper's

A.P. HILL

Ferry

from Harper's Ferry, 4:30PM

Burnside's Bridge

Lee

RODMAN

Union advance is halted by the arrival of A.P. Hill's Confederate division

Road

Antietam

Burnside's Bridge
11 A.M. - 4:30 P.M.

Potomac R.

Union Movements

Confederate Movements

Miles

0   1

McClellan's staff, who assured him that all was going well—although trees in the East Woods precluded their viewing the early combat. Many of Sumner's disorganized and uninformed troops marched into a trap and became parties to the north-end charnel house. Sedgwick's division of Sumner's corps suffered forty-two percent casualties, the highest of any Union division on the field that day.[50]

Next, from mid- to late morning, other Union troops attacked a strong Confederate position at the Sunken Road in the center of the field. They and successive Union attackers, including Brigadier General Thomas F. Meagher's famous Irish Brigade, were mowed down by Rebels firing from the Sunken Road, which they had augmented with a breastwork of fence rails. One union division lost forty percent of its men and another lost ten percent attacking that position. Only mistaken withdrawal of Rebel troops from both ends of the Sunken Road made it vulnerable to a deadly enfilade attack by Union troops that turned the depressed road into "Bloody Lane."[51]

In that terrible center of the field, 12,000 Union soldiers had attacked 7,000 Confederates, and the result was a total of 5,500 casualties. When the attackers at last were able to enfilade the defenders trapped in Bloody Lane, the Confederates fled from that position and left the heart of the battlefield ripe for Union assault and victory. Meager Confederate reinforcements rushed to bolster the center and repelled Union progress. General Longstreet himself directed the fire from a single battery. Lee's army was spread thin, and its center had been broken and was wide open to attack.

Fortunately for Lee, Generals Sumner and Porter convinced McClellan not to send in the 20,000 potential Union reinforcements, just across the Antietam at the Middle Bridge. McClellan agreed with them that it would not be prudent to attack with those reserves of Porter and Franklin; the latter general wanted to attack. "Lee's army was ruined, and the end of the Confederacy was in sight," said Edward Porter Alexander, Longstreet's artillery chief. Longstreet himself later said that a mere 10,000 Union reserves sent in at that point could have swept the Rebels from the field.[52]

Another opportunity to break the Confederate center arose around midday. General Franklin moved up with five fresh brigades to join Sumner in a renewed assault there. But Sumner opposed the attack because his men were too disabled. When McClellan then suggested by courier that Sumner attack, Sumner replied, ".... tell General McClellan I have no command! Tell him my command, Banks' command, and Hooker's command are all cut up and demoralized. Tell him General Franklin has the only organized command on the field." McClellan naturally called off the attack that would, alone or in conjunction with Burnside's delayed efforts, have decimated Lee's army. According to Pois and Langer, "When one more assault might have routed the Confederate left flank, [McClellan] chose to believe a demoralized Maj. Gen. Edwin Sumner ... that failure could result in defeat."[53]

Late in the morning, in the same middle sector of the battlefield, Union artillerymen moved across the Middle Bridge and fired their guns from Cherry Hill west-southwest into the town of Sharpsburg. Even though some infantry and cavalry crossed the same bridge to support the artillery, they merely sought shelter behind the hill as Confederate shells flew overhead. When the infantry finally advanced in small numbers, they drove away Rebel skirmishers on the road directly into town and the center of Lee's line. But, said historian Paul Chiles, "There was no timely follow-up by McClellan, so the Confederates had time to reinforce the position ... and hold on. McClellan's failure to exploit his numerical advantage in this sector was another missed opportunity for the Union to win the battle and possibly end the war."[54]

Meanwhile, on the south end of the battlefield, nothing happened until McClellan,

Middle Bridge, where McClellan failed to reinforce successes in the center of the battle, September 1862 (Library of Congress).

at 9:10 A.M., belatedly ordered Burnside to cross the Antietam, get behind Lee's army and cut off its only retreat across the Potomac at Boteler's Ford. Burnside was tepid and angry because he had been rebuked by McClellan for non-aggressive pursuit of the enemy after South Mountain and had been effectively stripped of his wing command by McClellan's placement of Hooker's corps (part of Burnside's wing of the army) on the opposite (northern) end of the Union line.[55]

McClellan had delayed ordering Burnside to attack until Franklin's Sixth Corps arrived after having been belatedly ordered to Antietam from Pleasant Valley near Crampton's Gap. While Burnside had waited with 12,500 troops on the south end of the Antietam battlefield, Lee had shifted troops away from that quiescent front. Starting six hours after the battle had begun, Burnside tried unsuccessfully to cross Rohrbach's Bridge, which since then has been ignominiously called Burnside's Bridge.[56]

That bridge was vulnerable to descending Confederate fire from a plateau to the immediate west. Although Antietam Creek was four to five feet deep in the vicinity of the bridge, its depth in many nearby places was only three feet. Primarily because McClellan kept his cavalry back at his headquarters, Burnside's troops were slow to discover Snavely's Ford (one mile to the south). Historian John Waugh contended that the Union situation in the area of Burnside's Bridge was ridiculous: "Every resident within miles of the Antietam knew that all around the bridge, above and below, there were fords closer

Burnside's Bridge, where McClellan and Burnside delayed Federal efforts on the south side of the battlefield for many costly hours in 1862. Note in the background the high ground from which Georgia infantry fired down on Union soldiers attempting to cross the bridge (Library of Congress).

than Snavely's that could have been easily crossed out of range of the rebel guns on the heights. But nobody in the single-minded fixation with getting across that damnable bridge had seemed to consider that."[57] However, historian William Marvel argued, based on his personal soundings, that the Antietam could not have been forded between the Rohrbach Bridge and Snavely's Ford to the south.[58]

Riflemen and sharpshooters of the 2nd and 20th Georgia regiments, commanded by Colonel Henry L. Benning, easily and bloodily repelled assaults at the bridge and along a road paralleling the stream. The 11th Connecticut, 2nd Maryland, and 6th New Hampshire regiments suffered heavy casualties attempting to reach the bridge and finally retreated.

McClellan's inspector general, Colonel Delos B. Sackett, then appeared at Burnside's headquarters to order another attack. That attack was commanded by Colonel Edward Ferraro, who promised to restore the whisky ration of the 51st Pennsylvania and 51st New York regiments if they took the bridge. Their attack was preceded by a Union artillery barrage of canister on the Georgia defenders across the creek. The two 51st regiments then charged directly toward the bridge instead of exposing themselves on the creekside road. After a brief pause just east of the bridge, they successfully charged across. Thus, finally at about 1 P.M., Burnside's men took advantage of the Confederates' low ammunition and cumulative losses, and at last they were on the west bank of the Antietam—along with colleagues who had crossed at Snavely's Ford.

Burnside then unbelievably delayed his advance for two hours while he brought up ammunition and reinforcements to the men who had crossed the stream. This delay proved fatal because McClellan deferred to Burnside's delayed assault and failed to use his other resources. As historian Robert Barr Smith observed, "McClellan still had all his cavalry and a fresh infantry corps [Porter's], but as usual he dithered, his head filled with visions of hordes of imaginary Rebels. The final push to victory, then, would have to come from Burnside's men."[59]

As Burnside's troops at long last advanced up the slopes toward Sharpsburg, they faced about thirty Rebel guns and infantry rushed into place by Lee from the now-quiet northern portions of the battlefield. To Burnside's right were Union regulars, who joined in the attack until they were recalled by McClellan.[60] As Burnside's attackers were about to overwhelm Lee's south flank, they were suddenly assaulted from their left by blue-clad Rebel troops of A.P. Hill, the last of Jackson's troops to arrive from Harpers Ferry. Not only were many of Hill's troops dressed in blue uniforms they had acquired at Harpers Ferry, but some carried a captured American flag as a ruse. Burnside's men were decimated by this unexpected attack from the south, and those on his left flank fled back to and even across Burnside's Bridge. Although Burnside's right flank was still in a strong position to break Lee's line, McClellan declined to send in Porter's Fifth Corps when Porter, his protégé, told him, "Remember, General! I command the last reserve of the last Army of the Republic!" Burnside's unsupported attack faltered and ceased. Lee's army was saved.[61]

Antietam National Battlefield Historian Ted Alexander described McClellan's location during the battle: "… McClellan came onto the field only once during the battle, preferring instead to direct the action from his headquarters at the Pry House, more than two miles away. During the afternoon he rode onto the field on his favorite steed 'Daniel Webster.'"[62] McClellan thus observed the fighting—he hardly directed it—from the safety of a hillside overlooking the Antietam valley. Nevertheless, it was the second time he had actually observed an army under his command in combat. In the early afternoon, he wired his wife, "Your father with me quite safe." For all of the 17th, there are records of only three official communications from McClellan. One directed his cavalry chief, Pleasonton, not to unnecessarily expose his artillery batteries, and another requested his chief of ordnance, Brigadier General James W. Ripley, to send more ammunition to Sharpsburg.[63]

His only substantial communique that day was a short telegram to Halleck; the heart of it said:

> We are in the midst of the most terrible battle of the war—perhaps of history. Thus far it looks well, but I have great odds against me. Hurry up all the troops possible. Our loss has been terrific, but we have gained much ground. I have thrown the mass of the army on their left flank. Burnside is now attacking their right, and I hold my small reserve consisting of Porter's Fifth Corps, ready to attack the center as soon as the flank movements are developed. I hope that God will give us a glorious victory.[64]

This paragraph is classic McClellan. He did *not* have great odds against him; he greatly outnumbered his foe. He threw in his usual plea for reinforcements. His army had *not* gained much ground. His "small" reserve consisted of 20,000 troops. He apparently never believed his flank movements were sufficiently developed because he failed to use his massive, fresh reserves to attack the center. Not only did McClellan fail to use Porter's corps, he failed to use Darius Couch's division, which was near Harpers Ferry.[65]

That message reflects McClellan's ineffective leadership and command on the single bloodiest day of the war. He stayed on a safe hillside and gave minimal direction to his army. He attacked an inferior foe in piecemeal fashion, failed to use his massive superiority in a simultaneous attack all along the lines, and refused to use a quarter of his troops. That battle, which may have been McClellan's worst, resulted in a lost opportunity to decimate or trap Lee's Army of Northern Virginia.

In fact, the Maryland Campaign had offered McClellan numerous opportunities to decimate and perhaps destroy that army. First, the fortuitous discovery of Lee's campaign order informed McClellan of the divided and vulnerable state of Lee's army, but he "pursued" that opportunity and Lee's army with his usual torpidity and allowed all of Lee's troops to reunite. Second, McClellan arrived at Sharpsburg before any of the Rebel troops from Harpers Ferry had returned to Lee, but he failed to attack when he had a 70,000-to-18,000 man advantage. Third, he squandered his manpower superiority on the day of the fierce Antietam battle itself by attacking sequentially with a portion of his army on the north of the field, then a portion in the center, and finally yet another portion in the south—a process that enabled Lee to switch his defenders from one front to another during the day. Fourth, he kept more than one-fourth of his army in reserve and unused during the entire battle—even on occasions when its use would have destroyed Lee's army. Fifth, he misused his cavalry by failing to harass Lee's wings, discover fords across the Antietam, or scout for developments such as Hill's late-day arrival; instead, he kept his cavalry in reserve in the rear—apparently to protect his artillery and his headquarters.[66] Sixth, as described in the next chapter, he passed up a glorious opportunity to destroy Lee's army the next day when Lee foolishly remained at Sharpsburg.

Fortunately for McClellan, Lee matched him error-for-error during the Antietam Campaign. First, he went on the offensive into Maryland with a weakened army—an offensive from which he would have to retreat. Second, he badly divided his inferior forces. Third, he failed to reunite them quickly or to return to Virginia when he realized that his divided condition had been disclosed to McClellan—even after he had won a significant victory at Harpers Ferry. Fourth, he selected a battlefield that jeopardized his entire army by having no ready means of retreat. Fifth, instead of entrenching and remaining on the defensive at Sharpsburg, Lee counter-attacked frequently during the day, and those assaults resulted in extreme casualties to his troops. Finally, he stayed at Sharpsburg another day and defied McClellan to launch an attack that would have destroyed Lee's army.[67]

September 17 had proven to be the deadliest in American military history—never matched before or since. McClellan's army suffered 12,401 casualties (between fifteen and twenty-five percent of his force) with 2,108 dead, 9,540 wounded, and 753 missing. Lee's army incurred at least 10,318 casualties (between twenty and thirty percent of his troops): 1,546 to 2,700 dead, 7,752 to 9,024 wounded, and 1,108 missing.[68]

Neither Lee nor McClellan won at Antietam. Lee lost at Antietam. Lee's defeat and inevitable retreat to Virginia constituted a great strategic loss for the Confederacy. Not only had Lee failed to win a major battle north of the Potomac, but he terminated what had been a movement toward British and French recognition of the Confederacy and he opened the door for Lincoln to announce, on September 22, his intention to issue the Emancipation Proclamation on January 1, 1863.

Lincoln needed the cover of a claimed Union victory so that his announcement did not appear to be an act of desperation. His preliminary Emancipation Proclamation changed the nature of the war from one to restore the Union to one to both restore the Union and end slavery. That development further decreased the likelihood of European intervention to recognize the slave-holding Confederacy.

McClellan blamed the escape of Lee's army on the shameful surrender of Harpers Ferry. In his October 15 official report, which he wrote instead of pursuing Lee, McClellan claimed that he would have captured the Confederates on Maryland Heights above Harpers Ferry if the garrison there had held out one more day: "I would have had 35,000 to 40,000 less men to encounter at Antietam, and must have captured or destroyed all opposed to me. As it was, I had to engage an army fresh from a recent and to them a great victory, and to reap the disadvantages of their being freshly and plentifully supplied with ammunition and supplies."[69]

It is difficult to know where to begin in rebutting those statements. It was McClellan's own slowness and passivity that kept Harpers Ferry from being relieved in a timely manner. With Rebel cannons on Maryland Heights and Loudon Heights, the Union forces trapped in Harpers Ferry would have been decimated had they attempted to fight for another day. Even if they had been able to do so, McClellan's record does not engender confidence that relief would have arrived the next day. Jackson's victorious troops numbered perhaps 20,000—not 35,000 to 40,000—and Lee's total force at Sharpsburg was perhaps 52,000.

McClellan continued his analytical travesty by reporting that he had inflicted 30,000 casualties on the Army of Northern Virginia at Antietam—an inflation of about 20,000. Since McClellan was claiming that Lee had as many as 170,000 troops, he may have felt obliged to similarly inflate the enemy's casualties.[70] His dream-world state of mind was reflected in his September 18th letter to Mary Ellen boasting, "Those in whose judgment I rely tell me that I fought the battle splendidly & that it was a masterpiece of art."[71]

Sunset on September 18, 1862, fell on perhaps the greatest series of lost opportunities of the Civil War. Instead of destroying Lee's divided army in detail after being handed its operational order, quickly rescuing besieged Union troops at Harpers Ferry, attacking the vastly outnumbered Rebel army on September 16 at Sharpsburg, using all of his army to attack Lee's forces simultaneously and aggressively on September 17, or attacking the decimated Southerners on September 18, McClellan had settled for a tactical draw and lost an opportunity to close out the war years before it would finally end. As Brigadier General Porter Alexander reflected from a Confederate perspective, "A drawn battle, such as we did actually fight, was the best *possible* outcome one could hope for. Even that we only accomplished by the Good Lord's putting it in McClellan's heart to keep Fitz John Porter's corps entirely out of the battle, & Franklin's nearly all out."[72]

Porter later wrote, "I commanded the Reserve. At no time did I receive any order to put troops in action on the 17th—or even a suggestion." Historian John M. Priest concluded, "Both he and his commanding general feared being overrun by the numerically inferior Army of Northern Virginia."[73]

McClellan's abysmal performance was destined to play itself out for another seven frustrating weeks.

9

Earning Lincoln's Rejection

After the Battle of Antietam, McClellan squandered one opportunity after another, failed to attack Lee's battered army the next day, allowed Lee to escape with his army back to Virginia, waited six weeks before pursuing the retreating Rebels, and so irked and frustrated Lincoln that he was finally removed from command the day after the final 1862 congressional elections.

September 18, 1862, was the beginning of the end for McClellan. Lee's greatly outnumbered army had barely held on to survive at Sharpsburg on the 17th. Both armies had paid a high price for the day-long fight. McClellan's attacking 70,000 to 80,000 troops, not all of whom fought, had suffered about 12,400 casualties. But Lee's army suffered proportionally higher casualties. His 40,000 to 50,000 troops, most of whom were engaged for significant portions of the day, incurred between 10,300 and 13,700 casualties.[1] Historian Alan T. Nolan said, "In spite of McClellan's ineptitude, Lee lost 10,000 men, 31 percent of his force, at Antietam, including missing, immediately following losses in excess of 2,500 at South Mountain on September 14."[2]

In light of his army's battered condition, Lee's subordinate generals all advised him to retreat that night, but he foolishly decided to stay there for another full day. Even Gary Gallagher, a Lee admirer, said that Lee's decision to remain at Sharpsburg an additional day "seemed to pass beyond audacity to recklessness."[3] Remaining at Sharpsburg gained Lee nothing and would have cost him his army had a general other than McClellan been commanding the Union forces that day. To Lee's credit, he probably realized that McClellan did not have the fortitude to attack two days in a row.

The military force available to McClellan that day was amazing. Across the way, Lee's army was in a shambles. As related to the Joint Committee, that morning Burnside offered to attack Lee with his 9,000-plus troops if McClellan would give him 5,000 more. The commanding general declined although he had 30,000 troops available from the First, Second, Ninth, and Twelfth corps, 20,000-plus from the virtually unused Fifth and Sixth corps, 6,000 freshly recruited Pennsylvania troops who arrived early that morning, and another 6,000 Fourth Corps soldiers who arrived at midday. Similarly, McClellan rejected Franklin's recommendation to attack on the Union right. McClellan had more fresh troops than Lee had total troops. With Lee still trapped by the Potomac and his army reduced to between 25,000 and 35,000, what did McClellan do with these 62,000 able-bodied soldiers on September 18? Nothing.[4]

He failed to press Lee even though he wrote his wife that morning that "The con-

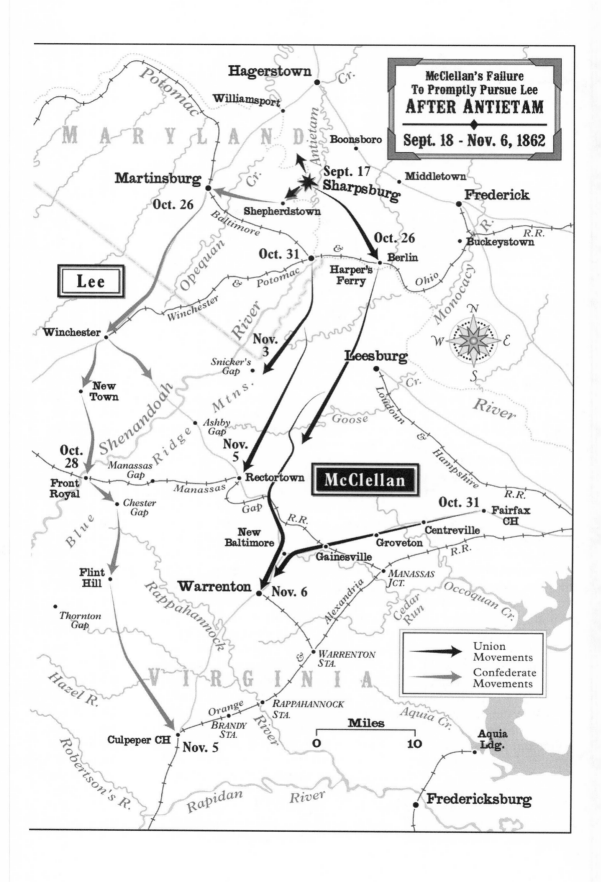

test will probably be renewed today," and "[The battle] was a success, but whether a decided victory depends upon what occurs today." After Lee retreated that night, McClellan told her, "Our victory complete."[5] In two September 19 messages to Halleck, McClellan explained that his army was fully occupied on the 18th "replenishing ammunition, taking care of wounded, &c." and claimed a "complete victory" because the Confederates had been driven across the river.[6] Unlike Lincoln, McClellan thought it was sufficient, even a great victory, to merely chase Lee out of Maryland.

In his December 1863 report on his army's operations, he wrote two small-print pages explaining why he did not attack on the 18th. The heart of his introduction reflected his perennial fear of failure: "... at this critical juncture I should have had a narrow view of the condition of the country had I been willing to hazard another battle with less than an absolute assurance of success. At that moment—Virginia lost, Washington menaced, Maryland invaded—the national cause could afford no risks of defeat. One battle lost, and almost all would have been lost. Lee's army might then have marched as it pleased on Washington, Baltimore, Philadelphia, or New York."[7]

Thus, in Alan Nolan's words, he "contented himself with a token pursuit."[8] That pursuit consisted of a half-hearted movement across Boteler's Ford from Sharpsburg to Shepherdstown on the night of September 19–20. That movement resulted in the capture of four Confederate guns and the embarrassment of Confederate Brigadier General William Nelson Pendleton, who fled the field and erroneously reported to Lee the loss of thirty guns.[9] The Union assault, however, was repelled the next morning.[10]

Even some of McClellan's own officers disagreed with his "complete victory" conclusion. A Maine captain wrote, "We should have followed them up the next day." And a Connecticut officer could "imagine no earthly reason why we did not go at them the next day with a vengeance."[11]

As historian Patrick J. Brennan has concluded, "What should have been a moment of triumph for the beleaguered president swiftly turned into a season of frustration.... Washington whispers of treasonous insubordination targeted McClellan and his 'Potomac Army Clique.'" When John J. Key of Halleck's staff (the brother of McClellan's judge advocate) boasted that an Antietam victory was "not the game" and that a battle of mutual exhaustion had been agreed upon to save the institution of slavery, Lincoln had him summarily court-martialed and dismissed from the Army.[12]

McClellan continued his victory theme when he wrote his wife on September 20 that "I feel some little pride in having with a beaten and demoralized army defeated Lee so utterly, & saved the North so completely." Riding the crest of that victory wave, he hoped to push Stanton and Halleck aside: "An opportunity has presented itself through the governors of some of the states to enable me to take my stand—I have insisted that Stanton shall be removed & that Halleck shall give way to me as Comdr in Chief." After complaining that Halleck was "an incompetent fool" and that Stanton was blaming him for the defeat at Second Manassas, McClellan concluded, "The only safety for the country & for me is to get rid of both of them—no success is possible with them." His scheme went awry when four days later all the northern governors but three voted that McClellan should be removed rather than promoted.[13]

McClellan's failure to pursue or attack Lee on September 18 was a prelude to five weeks of inactivity. From September 18 to October 26, McClellan did virtually nothing but prepare his army for a campaign and write his official Antietam Campaign report. Despite the urging of Lincoln and Halleck, McClellan dithered while Lee safely returned to the Shenandoah Valley. His feeble excuses were that his men and horses were exhausted, he needed more equipment, and he did not want to over-extend his army.[14]

Halleck wrote in his official report on the Maryland Campaign, "The long inactivity of so large an army in the face of a defeated foe, and during the most favorable season for rapid movements and a vigorous campaign, was a matter of great disappointment and regret."[15] Lincoln bided his time while McClellan dithered. The president was waiting for the congressional elections before he stirred up a hornets' nest. He also was testing McClellan. If and when Lee moved closer to Richmond than McClellan, McClellan's relief would be assured.

By September 20, Halleck already was frustrated by lack of news from, and progress by, McClellan. He wired McClellan, "We are still left entirely in the dark in regard to your own movements and those of the enemy. This should not be so." After briefly summarizing the armies' positions, McClellan complained to Halleck, "I regret that you find it necessary to couch every dispatch I have the honor to receive from you in a spirit of fault finding, and that you have not yet found leisure to say one word in commendation of the recent achievements of this army, or even to allude to them."[16]

On September 22, McClellan set forth his case for inactivity in a telegram to Halleck:

> The sanguinary battles fought by these troops at South Mountain and Antietam Creek have resulted in a loss to us of 10 general officers and many regimental and company officers, besides a large number of enlisted men. The army corps have been badly cut up and scattered by the overwhelming numbers brought against them in the battle of the 17th instant, and the entire army has been greatly exhausted by unavoidable overwork, hunger, and want of sleep and rest. When the enemy recrossed the Potomac the means of transportation at my disposal was inadequate to furnish a single day's supply of subsistence in advance. Under these circumstances I did not feel authorized to cross the river in pursuit of the retreating enemy, and thereby place that stream—which is liable at any time to rise above a fording stage—between this army and its base of supply.[17]

McClellan still was obsessed with the supposed "overwhelming numbers" of the enemy and kept seeing problems instead of opportunities. Unlike Grant, who eight months later would cross the Mississippi and live off the enemy countryside while outnumbered by his foes during his Vicksburg Campaign, McClellan feared to venture across the Potomac into northwest Virginia in the shadow of his own capital.

On September 23, McClellan warned Halleck that Lee's army was being reinforced and was likely to engage his in another battle "with all his available force." Because his own army had suffered so many casualties, he argued, "all the re-enforcements of old troops than can possibly be dispensed with around Washington and other places should be instantly pushed forward by rail to this army...." Halleck responded, "Sigel's corps is the only old one here.... On what point would you prefer it to move?"[18]

By the evening of the 24th, McClellan had a grand time-consuming scheme that would certainly justify delay. At Harpers Ferry, he proposed to build a nine hundred-foot, double-track wagon bridge across the Potomac and a four hundred-foot wagon bridge across the Shenandoah. He explained that a Colonel McCallum should come from Washington to supervise the larger construction job and should organize the gangs of workmen and procurement of all materials. McClellan concluded, "Until this or the railroad bridge is finished, it is scarcely possible to advance from Harpers Ferry, in force, as that is clearly our true line of operations." A disappointed Halleck replied on the 26th that they first needed to agree upon a plan of operations and that a crossing of the Potomac closer to Washington seemed appropriate.[19]

Meanwhile, there was a political development that McClellan detested. As a result of Lee's defeat at Sharpsburg and retreat into Virginia, Lincoln believed the time was ripe for public release of his Preliminary Emancipation Proclamation. On September 22, he announced his decision to the Cabinet and then the country. In that document, he declared free, as of January 1, 1863, all slaves in areas "in rebellion against the United States."[20]

On September 24, Lincoln issued a proclamation suspending the writ of habeas corpus for any persons detained by Union military authorities. This action precluded the detainees from seeking release through the courts. Lincoln's action was particularly aimed at persons interfering with enlistments or the draft.[21]

Also on September 24, Lincoln included an interesting remark in his brief speech to a crowd serenading him in honor of the Emancipation Proclamation. After referring to the "bravely, skillfully, and successfully fought battles" of the 14th and 17th, he cautioned, "We do not yet know the particulars. Let us be sure that in giving praise to particular individuals, we do no injustice to others."[22] This statement appears to have been cautioning against possibly undeserved praise for McClellan and his Antietam "victory."

It did not take McClellan long to react to Lincoln's actions. Because the Emancipation Proclamation contradicted his Harrison's Landing Letter to the president, McClellan seemed to sense that it spelled his own doom. Early on the 25th, he wrote to Mary Ellen, "It is very doubtful whether I shall remain in the service after the rebels have left this vicinity. The Presdt's late Proclamation, the continuation of Stanton & Halleck in office render it almost impossible for me to retain my commission & self respect at the same time. I cannot make up my mind to fight for such an accursed doctrine as that of a servile insurrection—it is too infamous. Stanton is as great a villain as ever & Halleck as great a fool—he has no brains whatever!" The next day he wrote to an elite New York City attorney, "I am very anxious to know how you and men like you regard the recent Proclamations of the Presdt inaugurating servile war, emancipating the slaves, & at one stroke of the pen changing our free institutions into a despotism—for such I regard as the natural effect of the last Proclamation suspending the Habeas Corpus throughout the land."[23]

Finally, on October 7, McClellan published an order regarding the president's Preliminary Emancipation Proclamation and sent a copy to the president. McClellan advised his officers and soldiers that, under the Constitution, the civil authorities of the Government expounded and executed the federal laws. He discouraged intemperate and disrespectful expressions of opinion about government policies as undermining discipline and efficiency. McClellan claimed that he was not questioning the army's loyalty and stated, "The remedy for political errors, if any are committed, is to be found only in the action of the people at the polls."[24] His tepid and technical support of the president's position was obvious.

Ten days before, on September 27, McClellan had demonstrated again that he just did not understand Lincoln's desire for military action. He wrote to Halleck about the condition of his army and his plans for continued inactivity. After the usual statement about the enemy being reinforced, he continued, "This Army is not now in condition to undertake another campaign nor to bring on another battle, unless great advantages are offered by some mistake of the enemy or pressing military exigencies render it necessary. We are greatly deficient in officers. Many of the old regiments are reduced to mere skeletons. The new regiments need instruction…. My present purpose is to hold the Army about as it is now, rendering Harpers Ferry secure and watching the river closely, intending to attack the enemy should he attempt to cross to this side."[25]

McClellan gave no consideration to how devastated Lee's army must have been after the Maryland Campaign and all the fighting that had preceded it. Lee was anxious to resume the offensive but hesitated because "I fear, for want of sufficient force to oppose the large army being collected by General McClellan...."[26] But McClellan was simply reiterating his position that "[i]n the last battles the enemy was undoubtedly greatly superior to us in number and it was only by very hard fighting that we gained the advantage we did...." Then he warned that if the enemy was reinforced and he was not, "it is possible that I may have too much on my hands in the next battle."[27] The next day he wrote to the Adjutant General to urge the round-up and return to duty of convalescents, stragglers, and deserters to "swell[] the ranks of the old regiments."[28] As usual, McClellan was more concerned about getting reinforced than in actively using the forces he already had.

A September 29 letter to Mary Ellen demonstrated McClellan's lackadaisical attitude at a time when Lincoln desired aggressive pursuit of the enemy. He wrote: "[If the Confederates have gone to Winchester,] I will be able to arrange my troops more with a view to comfort & if it will only rain a little so as to raise the river will feel quite satisfied in asking for a short leave." Thus, he wanted the river to rise and prevent pursuit so that he could take leave. Later in that letter, he complained that Lincoln and Stanton had failed to thank him for Antietam and that the next day he would have to walk Antietam with his aides to prepare his report of that battle.[29] He was more concerned about his Antietam report than pursuing Lee.

In an October 1 telegram to Halleck, McClellan again recommended construction of a permanent bridge across the Shenandoah River and a permanent wagon bridge across the Potomac—both at Harpers Ferry. He mentioned a three- to four-week period to build the former. Halleck quickly replied the same day and rejected the implied delay of operations: "... the Government does not contemplate the delay in your movements for the length of time required to build permanent bridges. Instead, he urged McClellan to cross downstream at once and "compel the enemy to fall back or to give you battle." McClellan's reaction was to tell his wife that Halleck "is the most stupid idiot I ever heard of—either that or he drinks hard—for he cannot even comprehend the English language."[30]

An exasperated Lincoln left Washington on October 1 to see what was happening with McClellan and his stationary army. On October 2, McClellan met him in Harpers Ferry and then wrote his wife, "[Lincoln's] ostensible purpose is to see the troops & the battle fields. I incline to think that the real purpose of his visit is to push me into a premature advance into Virginia. I may be mistaken, but think not. The real truth is that my army is not fit to advance...."[31] McClellan knew the "real" truth and continued to ignore the condition of the enemy army.

Lincoln knew that he had not gotten through to McClellan and had little hope of any significant change. During the course of his visit, the president took a walk with fellow Illinoisan Ozias M. Hatch and found a ridge with a view of the Union army. Lincoln asked Hatch, "Do you know what this is?" When Hatch responded, "It is the Army of the Potomac," Lincoln corrected him: "So it is called, but that is a mistake; it is only McClellan's bodyguard."[32] But the president decided to wait for the November elections and then replace his Democratic general—unless a miracle occurred and McClellan changed his ways.[33]

During the course of his October 2–4 visit to McClellan's headquarters and army, Lincoln obtained a breakdown of McClellan's five infantry corps, his cavalry, and other troops. They totaled 88,095.[34] Lincoln urged McClellan to make use of his troops. Immediately thereafter, visiting New York lawyer William Aspinwall told McClellan to yield to Lincoln on the issue of emancipation and to quietly carry out his military duties. The combined impact of the two visitors caused McClellan to write of his hopes for a speedy resolution to the war through another of his "victories": "I will try to find time to think over the whole affair today & tonight, & do my best to hit upon some plan of campaign that will enable me to drive the rebels entirely away from this part of the country forever."[35] He never would develop such a plan.

Following that military conference, Lincoln reaffirmed what he believed needed to be done. He directed Halleck to order McClellan to move into Virginia and engage the enemy. The result was the following firm October 6 order from Halleck to McClellan:

> I am instructed to telegraph you as follows: The President directs that you cross the Potomac and give battle to the enemy or drive him south. Your army must move now while the roads are good. If you cross the river between the enemy and Washington, and cover the latter by your operation, you can be re-enforced with 30,000 men. If you move up the Valley of the Shenandoah, not more than 12,000 or 15,000 can be sent to you. The President advises the interior line, between Washington and the enemy, but does not order it. He is very desirous that your army move as soon as possible. You will immediately report what line you adopt and when you intend to cross the river; also to what point the re-enforcements are to be sent. It is necessary that the plan of your operations be positively determined on before orders are given for building bridges and repairing railroads.
>
> I am directed to add that the Secretary of War and the General-in-chief fully concur with the President in these instructions.[36]

McClellan's immediate response was to stall by inquiring about the experience of the promised reinforcements and the condition of the railroads in northern Virginia. Halleck responded that McClellan could march more quickly than it would take to repair one of the railroads. McClellan, meanwhile, wrote to Mary Ellen about the orders to advance and complained that he could not go far because he could not carry many supplies and that the proposed campaign would last only a few days and not lead to a final result.[37]

On October 7, McClellan advised Halleck that he would operate on the line of the Shenandoah because moving closer to Washington would expose Maryland and Pennsylvania to another enemy invasion. He warned that he could not proceed more than twenty or twenty-five miles beyond Winchester or any other railroad or canal terminus. He added that three of his corps could not move for at least three days because they needed shoes, other clothing, shelter tents, and other supplies, but he "beg[ged] to assure [Halleck] that not an hour shall be lost in carrying your instructions into effect." McClellan closed with his usual plea for prompt reinforcements.[38] As late as October 11, McClellan was still complaining to Halleck about the shortage of "shoes & other indispensable articles of clothing."[39]

Meanwhile, beginning on October 10, Jeb Stuart once again rode his cavalry around a McClellan-commanded army. Stuart rode into Pennsylvania on his Chambersburg Raid, entered that town, captured 1,200 horses, inflicted $250,000 in damage, and successfully avoided McClellan's efforts to stymie his return to Virginia. On October 11, Secretary Welles wrote in his diary, "We have word that seems reliable that Stuart's Rebel cavalry have been to Chambersburg in the rear of McClellan...." Two days later he acidly wrote, "We have the mortifying intelligence that the Rebel cavalry rode entirely around our great and victorious Army of the Potomac.... It is humiliating, disgraceful.... It is not a pleasant fact to know that we are clothing, mounting, and subsisting not only our own troops but the Rebels also.... [McClellan's] opponents will triumph in this additional evidence of alleged inertness and military imbecility."[40]

In the midst of the raid, McClellan assured Halleck that he was making every disposition to cut off Stuart's retreat and he had "given every order necessary to insure the capture or destruction of these forces" and that he hoped "we may be able to teach them a

Above and opposite: **After the Battle of Antietam, President Lincoln visited McClellan near the battlefield in an unsuccessful effort to encourage him to pursue Robert E. Lee's battered army (October 1862) (Library of Congress).**

lesson they will not soon forget." McClellan blamed Stuart's escape on cavalry General Stoneman and used the occasion to complain repeatedly about the lack of sufficient horses for his army. Halleck replied that an average of 1,459 horses had been supplied to McClellan in each of the prior six weeks and that his "proportion of cavalry and of animals is much larger than that of any other of our armies." Halleck's final riposte stated, "The President has read your telegram, and directs me to suggest that, if the enemy had more occupation south of the river, his cavalry would not be so likely to make raids north of it."[41]

During October, Horace Porter, the Army of the Ohio's Chief of Ordnance, complained of "toy-soldiering" by the Union armies and was quite upset when he heard that McClellan had decided against a fall campaign. Porter had only recently escaped from McClellan's command, where he had written about the time of Antietam, "It is a shameful thing that we are exactly where we were a year ago and worse in some respects."[42] Others were more upset. The editor of the *Chicago Tribune* wrote, "What devil is it that prevents the Potomac Army from advancing? What malign influence palsies our army and wastes these glorious days for fighting? If it is McClellan, does not the president see that he is a traitor?"[43] At the end of October, Halleck wrote that he was "sick, tired, and disgusted" with McClellan's inaction: "There is an immobility here that exceeds all that any man can conceive of. It requires the lever of Archimedes to move this inert mass."[44]

Lincoln, however, was a very patient president. On October 13, he gave McClellan still another chance. He wrote McClellan a long letter explaining his reasons for wanting McClellan to move after Lee. The letter demonstrated not only Lincoln's patience but his increasing grasp of military strategy. It began: "You remember my speaking to you of what I called your over-cautiousness. Are you not over-cautious when you assume that you can not do what the enemy is constantly doing? Should you not claim to be at least his equal in prowess, and act upon the claim?"[45]

The president then contested McClellan's contention that he could not advance south to Winchester until the railroad was extended there from Harpers Ferry. Lincoln pointed out that the Confederates would be twice as far from a railhead as McClellan and that McClellan's desire for a railroad "ignores the question of *time*, which can not, and must not be ignored."[46] Lincoln thus touched on one of McClellan's major weaknesses: ignoring the importance of time.

Lincoln then quoted a standard maxim of war, "operate upon the enemy's communications as much as possible without exposing your own," and added, "You seem to act as if this applies *against* you, but cannot apply in your *favor*." He then spent the bulk of the letter explaining that if the situation were reversed Lee would cut McClellan off from Richmond, that McClellan was closer to Richmond than Lee, that McClellan had to bring on a battle, that he would be wise to do so while Lee was farther from Richmond, and that he would be well-supplied if he pressed Lee while maintaining the inside track to Richmond. The following excerpts capture the essence of the president's points:

> ... you are now nearer Richmond than the enemy is by the route that you *can*, and he *must* take. Why can you not reach there before him, unless you admit that he is more than your equal on a march. His route is the arc of a circle, while yours is the chord. The roads are as good on yours as on his.... If he should prevent our seizing his communications, and move towards Richmond, I would press closely to him, fight him if a favorable opportunity should present, and, at least, try to beat him to Richmond on the inside track. I say "try"; if we never try, we shall never succeed.... We should not so operate as to merely drive him away. As we must beat him somewhere, or fail finally, we can do it, if at all, easier near to us, than far away.... When at length running for Richmond ahead of [the enemy] enables him to move this way; if he does so, turn and attack him in rear. But I think he should be engaged long before such point is reached. It is all easy if our troops march as well as the enemy; and it is unmanly to say that they can not do it.[47]

Lincoln's "unmanly" comment demonstrated that his patience was starting to wear thin. Although McClellan apparently did not realize it, Lincoln's patience would disappear if Lee moved closer to Richmond than McClellan without a battle occurring. McClellan's only substantive response to Lincoln was, "I promise you that I will give to your views the fullest and most unprejudiced consideration, and that it is my intention to advance the moment my men are shod and my cavalry are sufficiently renovated [remounted?] to be serviceable."[48]

During this same period, McClellan learned from Major General John A. McClernand that Lincoln planned to remove McClellan from command because of his inactivity. On October 15 and 16, McClernand, through Lieutenant (and later Major General) James H. Wilson, invited McClellan to take command of a Mississippi Valley campaign he was planning, but McClellan declined the offer. Had he accepted and been allowed to assume that position, McClellan, not Ulysses S. Grant, would have been in charge of the Union efforts to capture Vicksburg and gain control of the Mississippi Valley.[49]

McClellan's time was running short, but he continued to dawdle north of the Potomac. His only "offensive" effort was a feeble October 16–17 reconnaissance-in-force he ordered after Lincoln's pressing and taunting October 13 letter. Brigadier General Andrew A. Humphreys marched 6,000 men from Boteler's Ford south of Shepherdstown to Kearneysville while Hancock led another 6,000 men from Harpers Ferry to Charles Town. Both columns advanced a few miles, skirmished with the enemy, and returned in accordance with McClellan's orders.

Five days after receiving the president's October 13 letter, McClellan wired Halleck on October 21 that his army was almost fully clothed but that the shortage of horses continued. Then, in classic McClellanesque fashion, McClellan tried to thrust responsibility back on the Lincoln: "Under the foregoing circumstances, I beg leave to ask whether the President desires me to march on the enemy at once, or to await the reception of the new horses, every possible step having been taken to insure their prompt arrival."[50]

His efforts to get the president to modify his October 6 order were rebuffed by Halleck in a responsive telegram sent that same day: "[The President] directs me to say that he has no change to make in his order of the 6th instant. If you have not been and are not now in condition to obey it, you will be able to show such want of ability. The President does not expect impossibilities, but he is very anxious that all this good weather should not be wasted in inactivity. Telegraph when you will move, and on what lines you propose to march."[51] Lincoln's patience was running out. He may have been influenced by a grossly inaccurate report from the staff of General Banks indicating that the Army of the Potomac had 231,997 men assigned, of whom 144,662 were fit for duty, while there were 21,580 Confederates in Virginia.[52] This report greatly understated the number of Confederates in Virginia.

Administration dismay with McClellan's inaction was reflected in Secretary Welles' diary entry of October 18:

> It is just five weeks since the Battle of Antietam, and the army is quiet, reposing in camp. The country groans, but nothing is done. Certainly the confidence of the people must give way under this fatuous inaction. We have sinister rumors of peace intrigues and strange management.... McClellan is not accused of corruption, but of *criminal inaction*. His inertness makes the assertions of his opponents prophetic. He is sadly afflicted with what the President calls the "slows." Many believe him to be acting on the army programme avowed by [the dismissed Major John J.] Key.[53]

On October 22, McClellan changed his plans and advised Halleck that he would move his army east of the Shenandoah, closer to Washington, along the lines originally suggested by the president on October 13. He concluded with the usual plea: "I shall need all the cavalry and other reinforcements you can send me from Washington." Although McClellan assured Halleck that he had "taken steps to execute the movement," those steps were not detectable, and McClellan's army did not advance.[54]

When the next day, October 23, Halleck promised McClellan two corps from the Washington area to reinforce his army in the Bull Run Mountains of Virginia, McClellan inquired whether he was getting two corps PLUS twenty thousand other troops. Halleck advised him that the two corps were the promised twenty thousand reinforcements.[55] As late as October 24, McClellan was explaining to Halleck that he hoped boats would be in position that day to construct a bridge for his long-delayed crossing of the Potomac.[56]

On October 25, the War Department received a cavalry report forwarded by McClellan. In it, a Massachusetts cavalry colonel reported that 128 of his 267 horses were too ill or disabled to leave camp and that "The horses, which are still sound, are absolutely broken down from fatigue and want of flesh." This report provided Lincoln with an outlet for his frustration as he wired McClellan, "I have just read your despatch about sore tongued and fatiegued [*sic*] horses. Will you pardon me for asking what the horses of your army have done since the battle of Antietam that fatigue anything?" McClellan responded with a list of cavalry activities and defiantly concluded, "If any instance can be found where overworked Cavalry has performed more labor than mine since the battle of Antietam I am not conscious of it."[57] Not surprisingly, McClellan missed the point of Lincoln's jab.[58]

On October 25, McClellan also sent Halleck a typically pompous telegram in which he pronounced, "the moment is at hand for the advance of this Army," and then posed an issue for resolution by the general-in-chief. He asked to what extent he should concern himself with guarding the Potomac River or its approaches against Confederate incursions. McClellan added his usual cautionary note about possible Rebel reinforcements from other theaters: "An important element in the solution of this problem is the fact that a great portion of Bragg's army is probably now at liberty to unite itself with Lee's command."[59] The next day Halleck responded that McClellan had orders to drive back the enemy in his front, he could determine what points to occupy and fortify, and he could worry about the approaches to the river after he had driven the enemy out of them. Finally, Halleck rejected McClellan's concerns about Bragg: "I do not think that we need have any immediate fear of Bragg's army. You are within 20 miles of Lee's, while Bragg is distant about 400 miles."[60]

At long last, on October 26, five weeks after the fighting ended at Sharpsburg, McClellan's army began crossing the Potomac on a pontoon bridge at Berlin, Maryland (between Harpers Ferry and Leesburg), as the Sixth Cavalry under Pleasonton led the way. That day Lincoln and McClellan continued their exchange of views about cavalry. Lincoln told him that Stuart's cavalry had outperformed Union cavalry during and since the Peninsula Campaign and asked whether his army's movement would not compel enemy cavalry to concentrate instead of foraging in squads. McClellan ignored the latter issue and provided an explanation of why he believed the Union cavalry was equally efficient to Stuart's. Lincoln's wire also included the overly effusive statement, "But I am so rejoiced to learn from your despatch to Gen. Halleck that you begin crossing the river this morning."[61]

The next day Lincoln concluded the discussion by apologizing if he had done an injustice to anyone but explaining: "To be told after more than five weeks total inaction of the Army, and during which period we had sent to that Army every fresh horse we possibly could, amounting in the whole to 7918 that the cavalry horses were too much fatiegued [sic] to move, presented a very cheerless, almost hopeless, prospect for the future; and it may have forced something of impatience into my despatches. If not recruited [recovered?], and rested then, when could they ever be?"[62]

Also on the 27th, McClellan recommended to Lincoln that new draftees be ordered to fill old, reduced regiments "before taking them again into action." Lincoln responded favorably about the concept but inquired, "And now I ask a distinct answer to the question, Is it your purpose not to go into action again until the men now being drafted in the states are incorporated into the old regiments?" In his response, McClellan blamed an aide for including the quoted words without his approval and concluded: "This phrase was not authorized or intended by me. It has conveyed altogether an erroneous impression as to my plans and intentions. To Your Excellency's question I answer distinctly that I have not had any idea of postponing the advance until the old regiments are filled by drafted men. I commenced crossing the army into Virginia yesterday, and shall push forward as rapidly as possible to endeavor to meet the enemy."[63] McClellan's explanation probably did not convince Lincoln, who certainly noticed that McClellan did not state that he would immediately attack the enemy but instead would merely advance as quickly "as possible" to *try* to engage the enemy.

After this exchange with the president and in the midst of another round of telegrams with Halleck about the Potomac line, McClellan exploded to his wife: "If you could know the mean & dirty character of the dispatches I receive you would boil over with anger—when it is possible to misunderstand, & when it is not possible, whenever there is a chance of a wretched innuendo—there it comes. But the good of the country requires me to submit to all this from men whom I know to be greatly my inferiors socially, intellectually & morally! There never was a truer epithet applied to a certain individual than that of the 'Gorilla.'"[64]

McClellan also complained to her about the assignment of new recruits to new, instead of the old depleted, regiments (a valid complaint) and of the detail of new cavalry regiments to Kentucky instead of to him. In addition, he told her that he hoped to succeed in the pending campaign because that would drive Stanton out of office: "... consigning the rascal to the infamous fate he deserves. If I can crush him I will—relentlessly & without remorse."[65] If only McClellan had wanted to crush the Rebels as badly!

Any doubts Lincoln may have had about McClellan's continuing reticence were erased by his army's nine-day crossing of the Potomac. On October 29, Lincoln asked McClellan to advise him when he was entirely across the river. It was November 5 when McClellan advised that the last of his troops had crossed on November 3.[66] This delayed advance at a glacial pace alerted Lee to the danger of being cut off from Richmond. He quickly responded by sending Longstreet east from the Shenandoah Valley to interpose his troops between McClellan and Richmond.[67] McClellan perplexingly explained to Mary Ellen that the enemy had moved "too fast to meet my views."[68]

It took McClellan's troops almost two weeks to cover the forty miles from Berlin on the Potomac south to Warrenton near the Rappahannock. Although actively opposed only by Rebel cavalry under Jeb Stuart, the Union troops had moved so slowly that Longstreet had moved to Culpeper Court House to get between them and Richmond while Lee was in the process of having Jackson follow Longstreet out of the Valley. Lack of forward movement and aggressive interaction with Lee's army spelled the end of McClellan's military career.[69]

McClellan's failure to execute Lincoln's October 6 order and his October 13 letter plan of operations, as well as Halleck's October 21 reaffirmation of the October 6 order, was his final mistake as commander of the Army of the Potomac. He had moved so late and so tepidly that he lost the positional advantage that he had held on Lee and that the president had tutored him about. Once Lee's army occupied Culpeper and was closer to Richmond than McClellan, it was clear McClellan had failed to understand Lincoln's not-so-veiled warning to him in early October. Lincoln now only had to await the completion of congressional elections before removing this Democratic general; he did not want to cause more Democrats to go the polls by firing "their" general.[70] Just after the northwestern elections, he had removed Buell from command of the Army of the Cumberland on October 24. McClellan's dismissal would have to await the November 4 elections in New York and New Jersey, bastions of Democratic support for him.[71]

Even the president's wife, Mary Todd Lincoln, apparently had lost all patience with McClellan. Writing from New York and reflecting some public opinion there, Mrs. Lincoln wrote to her husband on November 2: "... And McClellan & his slowness are as vehemently discussed.... Many say, they would almost worship you, if you would put a fighting General in command in place of McClellan."[72]

Lincoln, of course, was waiting for the November 4 completion of congressional elections. That very day at a cabinet meeting, Stanton complained that McClellan was writing directly to the president instead of Stanton or Halleck; the president responded that he previously had told Halleck he would remove McClellan whenever Halleck needed that done.[73] The next day, November 5, Lincoln acted to remove McClellan from command. The president had determined that McClellan lacked striking power and would never really fight. McClellan, in Sears' words, "stood for limited war, compromise peace, a return to the old order of things—all hopes that over the months of fighting had dimmed and faded and at Antietam were finally extinguished." Lincoln also was aware of widespread anti-administration disaffection in McClellan's army.[74] He issued a written directive to Halleck ordering the relief of McClellan by Ambrose Burnside as army commander and the relief of McClellan's protégé, Fitz John Porter, as Fifth Corps commander by

THE REMOVAL OF McCLELLAN.

GENERAL McCLELLAN was removed from the command of the Army of the Potomac on the 5th of November, 1862. The original of the order for his removal is herewith reproduced. It is, throughout, in the handwriting of President Lincoln. It is a paper that will be examined with interest.

Lincoln's November 5, 1862, order removing McClellan from command of the Army of the Potomac (National Archives).

Joseph Hooker.[75] Burnside had reluctantly agreed to assume the command when told that the only alternative was the appointment of his enemy, Hooker, as the army commander.

McClellan's last two telegrams to Lincoln—on November 7—complained about a snowstorm, the lack of rations, and the poor condition of the railroads upon which his army depended. That night Burnside and Brigadier General Catharinus P. Buckingham[76] came to McClellan's tent with Lincoln's order relieving him of command. McClellan read the order in their presence and then immediately wrote to his wife of the "great mistake" that had been made. He concluded, "Do not be at all worried—I am not. I have done the best I could for my country—to the last I have done my duty as I understood it. That I must have made many mistakes I cannot deny—I do not see any great blunders—but no one can judge of himself. Our consolation must be that we have tried to do what was right—if we have failed it was not our fault...."[77]

Burnside courteously provided McClellan with two days to absorb the blow of his removal and did not formally assume command until November 9. As McClellan took leave of his men, many of them apparently were quite emotional about his departure.[78] Perhaps they realized that eventually the Army of the Potomac would have a commanding general who would not be so reluctant to send them into battle.

Lee, on the other hand, was concerned when he heard the news about McClellan. According to General Longstreet, Lee said he regretted to part with McClellan because "we always understood each other so well." Actually, the understanding had been a one-way street. Lee added, "I fear they may continue to make these changes till they find some one whom I don't understand."[79]

McClellan himself claimed in his final report that, when relieved, he was on the verge of dividing the enemy and about to deliver a brilliant victory. He concluded, "I doubt whether during the whole period that I had the honor to command the Army of the Potomac it was in such excellent condition to fight a great battle." A year later he complained that "... I was confident of decisive victory, when, in the midst of the movement, while my advance guard was actually in contact with the enemy, I was removed from the command." But, as historian Patrick J. Brennan concluded, "Considering his complaints that his cavalry was crippled, that his supply lines were fatally weak, that his veteran regiments were undermanned and his officer corps woefully undertrained, it is hard to give McClellan's words much credence."[80]

McClellan's seven-week post–Antietam period of inactivity was a fitting capstone to his Civil War career. First, he failed to crush Lee's mangled and badly outnumbered army on the battlefield at Sharpsburg, where Lee remained defiantly and foolishly for a day after the war's bloodiest day of battle. Second, he failed to attack Lee aggressively as he retreated across the Potomac. Third, he failed to pursue Lee and his wounded army into Virginia with his own vastly superior force—for a period of seven weeks. Finally, he took nine days to bring his army across the Potomac when he belatedly decided to pursue. He managed to achieve the latter two failures despite the constant urgings of his commander-in-chief to promptly pursue and engage the enemy.

Having twice been given command of an immense army with an offensive mission, McClellan had twice failed to effectively use that resource and to move the Union anywhere close to a decisive offensive victory. As in his entire Civil War experience, McClellan's inflated ego and contempt for the president consistently accompanied, and perhaps justified in his mind, his inactivity and failure.

10

McClellan's Motivations

McClellan craved authority and disdained his superiors; his fear of failure caused him to inflate enemy strength estimates and avoid the very battles the Union needed for victory; he fought timidly and sometimes in a cowardly manner; and, worst of all, he deliberately undercut Pope before and during Second Manassas in a course of conduct that can only be described as treasonous.

What were the motivations of George McClellan that led to his numerous failures during the first two years of the Civil War? Even a McClellan supporter had to concede that "he missed many important opportunities in his conduct of operations. He probably should have been willing to accept the casualties that a quick push through the weakly manned works at Yorktown would have entailed and should have made more of the opportunities presented to him during the 1862 Maryland Campaign."[1]

The possibility of McClellan being a coward or a traitor was raised as early as 1863 by Columbia University Professor Francis Lieber. He wrote, "McClellan may be a coward.... Or he may be one of those people who possess everything except the faculty of resolving.... Or he may have a good deal of copper in his head, and shrink from decisive action against the wayward sisters. Or he may be a downright traitor.... Whatever he may be I think there is a large portion of the bona fide fool in his composition." Similarly, a 1903 history concluded that he "did not wish to fight" and must have been "either a coward or disloyal."[2]

What were the motivations that underlaid this timidity? These motivations require examination at each stage of his generalship before they can be summarized.

Western Virginia

Beginning with his first communications with Ohio's Governor, McClellan demonstrated an overriding concern about not losing a battle. He said, "there is only one safe rule in war—i.e., to decide what is the very worst thing that can happen to you & prepare to meet it." In addition, he was motivated by a desire to make a name for himself and to obtain promotion to the highest level of Union command.

At Rich Mountain, the only significant battle that occurred under his command in Western Virginia, he left the fighting to Rosecrans and failed to carry out his own self-

156

assigned role in the battle. After sending Rosecrans off on a dangerous mission and promising to come to his aid when fighting started, McClellan failed to respond to the sounds of fighting and left "Rosy" to fend for himself. Timothy Johnson blamed this lapse on McClellan's caution, indecision, and lack of the moral courage necessary "to bend events to his will."[3]

Pois and Langer ascribed McClellan's failure to support Rosecrans in this moderate-risk situation to his fear of failure and blame:

> McClellan did not send his remaining forces forward at the critical moment because he could not be absolutely certain that Rosecrans's movement was coming off as planned. On the other hand, he could not be absolutely certain Rosecrans *had not* attacked as ordered. His fear was that by engaging in a move that might lead to a repulse if Rosecrans had misfired, he would be liable for all the blame. Still, Rosecrans was out there somewhere on the Confederate flank—and on McClellan's orders. Torn between fears of Rosecrans's possible failure and the promise to support him, he hesitated and wound up doing nothing. Fortunately for McClellan, Rosecrans, being a less tormented soul, had turned the flank by himself.[4]

Their intriguing assessment was that McClellan desired low-risk situations where victory was assured or high-risk situations in which he could escape blame for defeat. What he feared, they asserted, was medium-risk situations where victory was not assured and blame could fall on him.

Martin K. Fleming described four negative traits that McClellan demonstrated in western Virginia and that would be repeated in future campaigns: "(1) The ability and desire to shape bold strategy, then being painfully cautious in executing it; (2) Grossly overestimating enemy strength, and the tendency to almost always interpret the sights and sounds in front of him as unfavorable to his operations; (3) Hesitancy to commit his whole force when circumstances demanded bold action; and (4) The keen ability to keep the press on his side and to maintain favorable public relations (often through bold proclamations) when he had failed or was failing in his endeavors."[5]

A sympathetic Joseph Harsh pointed to this campaign as an example of his "vigor, efficiency and speed unrivalled [*sic*] by any commander on either side during the same period." Harsh cited this campaign to rebut charges that McClellan was too slow,[6] but as early as 1901 Brevet Brigadier General Peter Michie criticized McClellan's speed in western Virginia: "His movements were slow, for his cautiousness grew as he approached the field of battle."[7] This negative trait was one McClellan had not yet fully developed.

Despite his weaknesses (much more obvious later), McClellan rode his seniority and publicity to a promotion in Washington at a time when any perceived success by a Union general was unusual. Pois and Langer commented that it is a pity that no one debriefed Ohio Colonel Beatty, who closely observed McClellan and described him as "indecisive" at the critical moment when he was supposed to launch an attack supporting Rosecrans.[8]

The most significant military and character traits McClellan had demonstrated in western Virginia were desire for promotion, fear of failure or defeat, a propensity to overestimate enemy strength, hesitancy to use his full force, aversion to closeness to the battlefield, and timidity bordering on cowardice.[9]

Washington

While in Washington, McClellan's most obvious initial motive was to unseat and replace Winfield Scott as the general-in-chief. By going outside the chain of command to Lincoln, Stanton, senators, and congressmen, he created an intolerable situation for Scott, who duly retired.

At Lincoln's request, McClellan submitted a strategic plan for fighting the war. His plan rested on two principles: (1) limited war aims reflected in the phrase, "the Union as it was and the Constitution as it is," and (2) a short period of fighting to avoid exacerbating emotions that would tear the nation further apart.[10]

Once he had achieved his goal of general-in-chief, McClellan did not know what to do with it. He sat back and watched as Grant took Forts Henry and Donelson, Burnside captured Roanoke Island and the Outer Banks of North Carolina, and Farragut moved toward the capture of New Orleans. He instigated the ill-conceived Potomac crossing that resulted in disaster at Ball's Bluff and let General Stone take the blame and be imprisoned for that fiasco.

Meanwhile, McClellan focused on building a mammoth army under his direct command. The Army of the Potomac became a powerful fighting force—a force that McClellan refused to use. In response to pressure from Lincoln and Stanton to initiate an offensive campaign, McClellan did nothing but make excuses for why he could not move on the Confederates at Manassas/Centreville and why he could not even break the Rebel blockade of the lower Potomac River. As Stephen Sears has opined, "The Army of the Potomac was McClellanized at birth, and it never quite outgrew that crippling disease of 'bad blood and paralysis.'" [11]

Major General Winfield Scott, 1861 (Library of Congress).

His favorite reason for inaction was that he was greatly outnumbered by the enemy. Fear of defeat seems to have been his primary motivator during this period. That fear seems to have been so strong that it led him to grossly inflate the enemy's strength. So long as he did not attack, he believed he could not lose. That motive would appear again and again.

John Waugh concluded that paranoia set in almost immediately after McClellan arrived in Washington. His paranoia was not totally irrational. Senior generals were jealous of his quick rise to power, and English journalist William Howard Russell called him "'the little corporal' of unfought fields." Reality, however, was insufficient to explain the level of his paranoia about being vastly outnumbered by the Confederates and being undercut within his own government. McClellan estimated Rebel strength in his front at 100,000 on August 8, 1861, and 150,000 by August 19. By the time the estimates reached 170,000, the true Rebel strength in his front was all of 45,000. As to the rest of the Federal Government, McClellan expanded his distrust from Scott to Lincoln to Stanton to the whole cabinet and then to all the Republican Radicals in Congress. In summary, McClellan in Washington convinced himself the Rebels were so strong and he was being so weakened by Federal Government "enemies" that any offensive action was out of the question.[12]

McClellan's months in Washington were increasingly marked by a refusal to share his plans with the president—although he shared them with others when doing so suited his purposes. His motives for excluding Lincoln apparently included fear of information disclosure, a disinclination to share power, and a dread of being second-guessed by Lincoln. McClellan's disrespect, reticence to share information, and typhoid fever provided an opening for Lincoln to become involved in military planning during the first two weeks of 1862. The result was a decline in McClellan's power. Ethan Rafuse summarized the change:

> In calling these meetings, Lincoln had abandoned his passive role in the management of the war effort. He had taken his first faltering steps as commander in chief. For the first time, he had taken a role in planning the movements of the nation's most important army. And for the first time he had solicited advice from someone other than McClellan on what was to be done with that army. Never again would Lincoln defer completely to McClellan, or leave the authority over strategic planning in his hands.... [13]

McClellan, however, allowed his "streak of willful, self-destructive obstinacy" to control events when he had the opportunity to discuss his Urbana Plan with Lincoln, four cabinet members, and three generals at a crucial Executive Mansion meeting.

Although he told General Meigs that the president could not keep a secret, McClellan himself held a three-hour briefing for a *New York Herald* reporter the very next day. It was only when the president ordered implementation of a different plan that McClellan scrambled to reveal all to his commander-in-chief.[14]

Lincoln's action forced McClellan's hand. "It caused McClellan to take the administration into his confidence and explain thoroughly his assumptions about the tactical and strategic nature of the war," according to Herman Hattaway and Archer Jones. McClellan, however, failed to understand Lincoln's political need for a victory in the East, and he failed to take the time to explain to the president how his threatening Richmond would safeguard Washington.[15] To the extent, however, that anyone gave credence to McClellan's overestimation of Rebel strength, Washington would seem to have required greater protection than McClellan provided

President Abraham Lincoln. Photograph undated, ca. 1862–64 (Library of Congress).

when he initiated his Peninsula Campaign. Further, he had not demonstrated sufficient aggressiveness to make anyone believe he would pressure Richmond sufficiently to prevent the Confederates from moving on Washington.[16]

In summary, during his dual reign as army commander and general-in-chief in Washington, McClellan demonstrated a more fully developed version of the same traits he had shown in western Virginia: desire for promotion to the highest level, fear of failure or defeat, a tendency to grossly overestimate his enemy's numbers, hesitancy to use his army at all, and an extreme reticence to fight. To these he added: refusal to accept responsibility for failure, belief in a war strictly for limited goals, and extreme disrespect and contempt for anyone in authority who questioned his actions or judgment or who appeared to stand in his way—up to and including the president.

The Peninsula

McClellan's slowness in moving up the Peninsula, particularly his one-month delay at Yorktown and the Warwick River, have been the subject of considerable criticism.[17] Although Joseph Harsh has attempted to defend McClellan against the charges of slowness on the Peninsula,[18] it is difficult to overlook his failure to press the enemy and his loss of initiative to Magruder, Johnston, and Lee when the burden was on McClellan to produce offensive results. Before the Seven Days', Confederate General D.H. Hill concluded, "I do not feel sure that McClellan will venture to attack at all. His movements have been characterized by great prudence, not to say great timidity."[19]

Military historian John Keegan saw the Union campaign as crippled by "McClellan's capacity for procrastination" and his constitutional incapability of accepting the objective evidence of his numerical superiority. He criticized McClellan's hanging back because of "dangers visible only to himself," his allowing the enemy to strengthen its position, and his taking eight weeks to move from Fort Monroe to the Richmond environs without inflicting any significant damage on the Rebels.[20] William J. Miller explained that the delay at Yorktown severely weakened McClellan's army because of the swamp-related illnesses that afflicted thousands of his troops, resulted in subsequent battles (Williamsburg, Seven Pines, and Seven Days') that would have been unnecessary if McClellan's troops had quickly moved on Richmond, and resulted from McClellan's desire for bloodless victories.[21]

Even if Lincoln was overly cautious in securing Washington and thus depriving McClellan of some of the troops he desired, his approach did not justify McClellan's inaction on the Peninsula when he had overwhelming superiority against the Confederates in the early stages of that campaign. McClellan's inactivity beforehand while in Washington and later at Antietam demonstrated that he was unlikely to have taken the offensive on the Peninsula until absolutely compelled to do so—regardless of how many troops he had.

There have been several explanations for McClellan's failure on the Peninsula. Some early critics contended he was simply incompetent. Thus, Governor William Sprague of Rhode Island, who had observed McClellan's performance while serving in a volunteer staff position, testified that there were many reasons for the Peninsula failure and "The first, of course, was, in my opinion, the incompetency of the commanding general." Similarly, Major General Hooker explained the campaign's failure to the Joint Committee: "I do not hesitate to say that it is to be attributed to the want of generalship on the part of our commander."[22]

Joseph Waugh entitled his first chapter on the Peninsula Campaign "High Hopes and Paranoia." He argued that McClellan suffered from two paranoias. Just before the Seven Days' Battle, Waugh wrote, "McClellan's twin paranoias quickened. He continued to see folly in his rear and overwhelming numbers in his front."[23] Pinkerton, understanding his role to boost the enemy's purported numbers, estimated Confederate strength at Yorktown as 120,000 and at Richmond as more than 180,000. McClellan was convinced he was outnumbered.

According to Peter Michie, "This constitutional defect of McClellan's judgment in overestimating the strength of the enemy was ever in evidence…; it seriously detracted from his efficiency as a commander, compelling him to adopt a cautious and inactive course when he should have been bold and aggressive." Later Bruce Catton, writing about the Peninsula Campaign, similarly explained the serious impact this misconception had on the general:

> It was just tragic that this had to happen to McClellan, of all generals; for this man must always listen, at the last, to the voice of caution, the subconscious warning that action may bring unlooked-for perils, the lurking fear that maybe some contingency has not been calculated. Before he can act, everything must be ready, every preparation must be made, every possible mischance must be provided for. Now, with his own career and the nation's fate balanced on a knife's edge, with Lincoln quietly warning him that he must at all costs *do* something, there is this final deterrent: conducting an offensive campaign deep in enemy territory, he finds himself to be dreadfully outnumbered—so much so that only a very great daring would make an offensive possible at all. Almost everything he did and failed to do in this campaign can be explained by that one fact.[24]

The challenge was too much for the general who had written to Governor Dennison at the outset of the war about preparing for the very worst thing that can happen to you.

Even H.J. Eckenrode and Bryan Conrad, admirers of McClellan, noted that after Gaines' Mill he lacked the capacity to rebound as Lee had done after Mechanicsville:

> McClellan had ability, courage, a nature singularly noble and high-minded (all in all, he was one of the noblest figures in American history), but he did not alas! have the lion's heart. In the night … after Mechanicsville, it had been Lee's turn to agonize in the hours following a humiliating defeat—a far worse defeat than McClellan's—but Lee's proud nature had not known despair or dreamed of retreat.[25]

Another McClellan admirer, Ethan S. Rafuse, praised McClellan's planning and general execution of the Peninsula Campaign but faulted his "obstinate rationality" for not indulging the administration's "irrational fear of an attack on Washington" and concluded that his successes were "more than offset by the impact the move to the James had on the Lincoln administration and Northern public opinion."[26] Another pro-McClellan writer, William Starr Myers, concluded that McClellan likely would have taken Richmond had he been fully supported by Lincoln and Washington officials but admitted, "… one must wonder whether or not an experienced soldier, cognizant of all the risks, might not have taken the city anyway and in spite of the adverse influences at home, and that by risking everything and going ahead. McClellan never was a gambler, and possibly only a gambler against fate could have won in the summer of 1862."[27]

Throughout the battles of Williamsburg, Seven Pines, and Seven Days', McClellan was notably absent from the battlefields. Bruce Catton noted that during Gaines' Mill, as in all the great fights under his command, McClellan stayed close to his headquarters. Catton explained, "His physical courage was high enough … but there seems to have been in him a deep, instinctive shrinking from the sight of bloodshed and suffering, an emotional reaction to the horrors of the front lines that was more than he could stand."[28]

Extremely difficult to justify is the commanding general's total absence from the battlefields during the Glendale and Malvern Hill struggles. As early as 1901, Peter S. Michie described his absence at Glendale as "astounding" and concluded that "every explanation ... put forward by [McClellan's] defenders [for his Malvern Hill absence] must ever be in the nature of an unsatisfactory apology."[29] Stephen Sears directed attention to McClellan's apparent cowardice during the height of the Seven Days' fighting: "McClellan's well-documented desertion (there is no gentler word for it) of his army at Glendale, assigning no one to command in his stead during that pivotal battle of the Seven Days, ought by itself to guarantee his infamy. At Malvern Hill the next day he again boarded the gunboat *Galena* for a wholly unnecessary excursion, then squatted in a distant corner of the battlefield, like the lowliest coffee-boiler, during the fighting."[30] Sears opined that, due to demoralization, "McClellan had lost the courage to command" by the sixth day of the Seven Days' Battle.[31]

Steven Norton described the Peninsula Campaign as "an exercise in how to ruin a good strategy with second-rate, over-cautious leadership."[32] Similarly, Timothy Johnson concluded that McClellan failed on the Peninsula because he lacked moral courage, was indecisive, and "lacked [Winfield] Scott's steadiness and his calm disposition, which contributed to the younger commander's inaccurate interpretation of intelligence and his overestimation of enemy strength."[33]

McClellan's poisoned relationship with Washington officials impaired his campaign. One of the major problems was that McClellan "overestimated Lincoln's willingness and ability to provide the time and resources needed to implement his strategy."[34] According to Stephen Sears, McClellan had solidified his "them versus us" thinking by the Peninsula Campaign and blamed his defeat there on the radicals in Washington, who allegedly failed to reinforce him in order to extend the war and advance abolition.[35]

Pois and Langer, in their recent psychological analysis of command failures, concluded that "McClellan ... was himself an almost textbook case of someone who, while outwardly concerned with success, was in reality a hollow shell more concerned with avoiding any personal responsibility for failure." They described him as "paralyzed by fears of failure" and applied their analysis to his Peninsula Campaign:

> ... [O]nce the campaign was under way, he hesitated at every critical moment. To justify his fears, he clung to a set of self-justifying beliefs that included wildly inflated estimates regarding the strength of Lee's heavily outnumbered forces. That being the case, he had to proceed with caution. On occasion, however, this otherwise most cautious of generals placed his army in tactically dangerous situations. *At such times it appeared he was inviting a military disaster for which he could blame the distant and increasingly unsympathetic civilian leaders in Washington.* He seemed to revel equally in the roles of martyr and general.[36]

Their analysis finds support in the much earlier synopsis of the Peninsula Campaign provided by Major General George Meade: "McClellan was always waiting to have everything just as he wanted before he would attack, and before he could get things arranged as he wanted them, the enemy pounced on him and thwarted all his plans.... Such a general will never command success, though he may avoid disaster."[37]

He capped his Peninsula Campaign with another failure to attack a vulnerable opponent—Lee's battered army at Malvern Hill. As Geoffrey Perret observed, "... with the Confederates on the ropes—with thousands dead, thousands more wounded and Confederate regiments in disarray—McClellan did not order a counterattack. Had he done so, he might well have routed Lee's army and walked into Richmond."[38] Once again his timidity cost the Union a chance for decisive victory early in the war.

In executing his Peninsula Campaign, therefore, McClellan demonstrated full-blown versions of his by-then familiar fear of defeat, illusions of overwhelming enemy strength, paranoia about (and loathing of) his perceived political enemies in Washington, evasion of battle (contrary to the whole purpose of his "offensive" campaign), avoidance of responsibility for failure by placing blame on others even before events unfolded, cowardice reflected in constant absence from the battlefields, and incompetence as an army commander.

Second Manassas

When Lincoln, Stanton and Halleck decided that McClellan's reinforcement demands had become ridiculous, that his army was useless at Harrison's Landing, and that Pope's army needed support in central Virginia, they ordered McClellan to quickly get his army off the Peninsula and into a position to support Pope. As historian McPherson said, "The efficiency of this Union movement was not helped by McClellan's bitter protests against it or by his subordinates' distaste for coming under Pope's command."[39] McClellan waited two weeks before starting to move troops to Fort Monroe to get them off the Peninsula,

took over three weeks to get them to northern Virginia, and then held 25,000 in or near Alexandria instead of rushing them to aid Pope. But McClellan testified to the Joint Committee, "I think that every effort was made to hurry forward the troops, and to give cordial assistance to General Pope."[40]

According to Bruce Catton, Halleck passed on an immediate opportunity to condemn McClellan:

> In the midst of all the Bull Run confusion Secretary Stanton sent in a demand for the full record regarding McClellan's withdrawal from the peninsula: when was he ordered to leave, when did he leave, was the whole operation handled with such slackness as to endanger the country? Recognizing this as Stanton's search for ammunition to destroy McClellan, but bearing in mind also that McClellan might yet ride out the storm and be the hero of the nation, Halleck sent a facing-both-ways reply. He gave all the dates, stated that the withdrawal was not made with the speed the national safety required, but added that once McClellan did begin to move he moved fast and that McClellan at the time reported the delay as unavoidable.[41]

Major General Henry W. Halleck. Photograph undated, ca. 1862–64 (Library of Congress).

At the same time, however, Michigan Senator Zachariah Chandler wrote that the recent disasters were the result of *"treason, rank treason,* call it by what name you will" and that Lincoln was being "bullied by those *traitor Generals."*[42] A week after Second Manassas, Secretary Welles wrote of McClellan: "He has military acquirements and capacity, dash, but has not audacity, lacks decision, delays, hesitates, vacillates; will, I fear, persist in delays and inaction and do nothing affirmative. *His conduct during late events* aggravates his indecision and *is wholly unjustifiable and inexcusable."*[43]

The following year the Joint Committee and Halleck agreed with Welles. The crucial issue was stated in a March 11, 1863 question put to Halleck by Benjamin F. Wade, Chairman of the Joint Committee: "Had the army of the Peninsula been brought to cooperate with the army of Virginia with the utmost energy that circumstances would have permitted, in your judgment as a military man, would it not have resulted in our victory instead of our defeat?" Halleck's answer: "I thought so at the time, and still think so."[44]

Although some have blamed Halleck for not forcing his views on McClellan,[45] the latter's direct disobedience of Halleck's six orders to send troops immediately toward Manassas came just before and during the fighting at Second Manassas—when Halleck was at his mercy. McClellan's disobedience resulted in two of the Union's finest corps not taking part in Second Bull Run although they were within marching distance of the battlefield.[46] Before Halleck could respond to McClellan's delays, the battle was lost, Washington was in chaos, and Lincoln believed he had no choice but to restore McClellan to command for at least an interim period.

Historian James Murfin focused on McClellan's defiance of Halleck:

> Throughout ... three days, McClellan delivered to his superiors one of the most flagrant examples of insubordination that the Civil War produced. He deliberately refused direct orders from his general-in-chief, orders that were written with good cause, validity, and sincerity. He attempted on almost every occasion to counteract the orders with open defiance, manufactured and unjustified excuses, and suggestions to help Pope's Army of Virginia.[47]

Contemporaries judged McClellan equally harshly. Immediately after Second Manassas, Secretary Welles stated that he disagreed with Chase and others who said McClellan was an "imbecile, a coward, a traitor." However, Welles concluded, "He was wanting, in my opinion, in several of the essential requisites of a general in chief command; in short, he was not a fighting general. These are my present convictions." He hinted at worse, "Some statements of Stanton and some recent acts indicate failings, delinquencies of a more serious character."[48]

Alan Nevins analyzed McClellan's failure ("willful limpness if not outright treachery") to provide reinforcements to Pope that Halleck had ordered: "McClellan knew well that if Pope won a dramatic victory, then Pope would be given command of the combined armies in Virginia. The idea was intolerable to him.... If he did not consciously wish Pope to fail so that he might emerge as the rescuer of the nation, subconsciously that was his desire, and he acted throughout on the callous principle of letting Pope, as he put it, get out of his scrape as best he could."[49]

Over the objections of his cabinet, Lincoln placed McClellan in command of all Union forces in the Washington area after the Union defeat at Second Manassas. Even the president, however, described McClellan's conduct during that campaign as "unpardonable."[50]

The crux of the issue is whether McClellan was willing and eager to see Pope lose at Second Manassas so that McClellan could regain command of all Union troops in the Eastern Theater. The evidence indicates that he was and that he acted accordingly. As

John Waugh said, "The young general had dragged his feet shamefully before sending help to Pope, and had ungraciously suggested letting him shift for himself."[51] The consequences of such traitorous behavior could have been the collapse of the Union's eastern armies, the capture of Washington, and loss of the Civil War.

Relying on 1864 and post-war statements by McClellan, however, Sears concluded, "Whether at headquarters or on the battlefield or in the political arena, in defeat and disappointment, George McClellan never wavered in his determination to put down the rebellion."[52] His actions in preventing reinforcements from promptly reaching Pope, however, indicated that defeating the Rebels was not at the very top of his list of priorities.

There are a variety of views on the reasons for McClellan's failure to support Pope. Peter Michie contended that transportation problems were the reason that McClellan was slow getting off the Peninsula. He excused McClellan's failure to carry out Halleck's orders because of McClellan's greater concern for the safety of Washington than that of Pope's army and his usual overestimation of enemy strength and activity. Michie also asserted that Halleck was too distracted by matters in the West and recruiting issues and neglected to "give that controlling and directing attention to the crisis which was then involving the safety of Pope's army."[53] Michie apparently believed that a field commander with his own views of a complex situation was free to disobey six specific orders from a general-in-chief (who was sufficiently focused to have issued those orders and might reasonably have expected compliance with them).

Secretary Stanton, immediately after McClellan's anti-Pope actions, prepared a letter to Lincoln urging removal of McClellan from any command and said that "... by recent disobedience of superior orders and inactivity he has twice imperiled the fate of the army commanded by General Pope, and while he continues in command will daily hazard the fate of our armies and our national existence...."[54] And Secretary Welles quoted Lincoln as saying, "There has been a design, a purpose, in breaking down Pope, without regard to the consequences to the country, and that is atrocious."[55]

A generous appraisal by Sears also concluded that McClellan did not deliberately cause Pope's defeat:

> It is too much to say (as detractors later said) that George McClellan was deliberately conspiring to have the Army of Virginia beaten at Bull Run, if for no other reason than his strong feeling for the men of his own army fighting on that field. What can be said, however, is that his bruised sensibilities and his unreasoning contempt for Pope convinced him that general would be—and deserved to be— defeated. Nor can it be doubted

Secretary of War Edwin Stanton. Photograph undated, ca. 1862–64 (Library of Congress).

that he would have acted far more vigorously at Alexandria had one of his favorites, such as Fitz John Porter, commanded the Army of Virginia. Instead, the captive of his delusions, he put his own interests and his messianic vision ahead of doing everything possible to push reinforcements to the battlefield.[56]

Sears' conclusion, based on McClellan's feeling for his men, is surprising and doubtful. This was, after all, the same general who virtually abandoned those troops to their own fate during the last two days of fighting on the peninsula. Also, the men of Franklin and Sumner's corps were not in danger so long as McClellan kept them away from the Manassas battlefield.

Eckenrode and Conrad asserted that McClellan failed to send troops far away from Alexandria in order to protect Washington from Lee and Jackson.[57] Jeffry Wert similarly concluded that McClellan's actions at Alexandria seemed reasonable to him at the time, that he was affected by a report that Jackson was between Pope and Washington, and that he "should not be blamed for the consequences of Pope's woeful generalship at Second Bull Run."[58] Eckenrode, Conrad, and Wert did not explain how McClellan was justified in disobeying six direct orders from the general-in-chief—especially after the commander-in-chief had told McClellan to do whatever Halleck decided. Wert, like some others, was willing to excuse McClellan because he was being his usual tepid self and was willing to allow him to decide what orders he wanted to obey.

Russell F. Weigley condemned McClellan's failure to support Pope but similarly concluded that McClellan was not a traitor:

> Not only did McClellan withhold two army corps from the battle. Again and again since the creation of Pope's Army of Virginia he had made it clear to all his friends that he hoped Pope would fail. He was completely indiscreet and completely petty. It is no wonder that consequently the belief spread among Pope and his partisans, to linger forever after, that McClellan deliberately sabotaged the Army of Virginia. There is no good reason to think that. Looking west and south from Alexandria in the last days of August 1862, the Federals could see only chaos and therefore much that was unknown. Facing the unknown, McClellan always conjured up vast enemy armies to fill it. McClellan did not behave traitorously during the second battle of Bull Run, but only like McClellan.[59]

In reaching that conclusion, Weigley overlooked or forgave McClellan's disobedience of six direct orders from Halleck to move those corps to Manassas. That disobedience distinguishes this situation from those in which McClellan was the senior officer making final decisions. Was McClellan only being McClellan? At Second Manassas, there was an element of malevolence added to the usual concoction of obsession and timidity.

Concurring with this view was military intelligence historian Edwin C. Fishel, who concluded:

> But Pope's mistakes, numerous and ruinous though they were, were not the only cause of his defeat. Equally damaging was McClellan's slowness in getting his divisions to his beleaguered fellow general. Only Porter's and Heintzelman's corps and Reynolds' small division got into the fight, although the corps of Sumner and Franklin, which might well have saved the day if they had arrived a little sooner, did participate in the retreat. McClellan suffered no regrets over this failure. His letters show him taking pleasure in Pope's difficulties that seems almost treasonous. On August 21 he wrote his wife, "I believe I have triumphed!! Just received a telegram from Halleck stating that Pope and Burnside are very hard pressed." On the 29th he suggested to Lincoln that as an alternative to opening communication with the embattled army, Pope should be left "to get out of his own scrape" while Washington was being made "perfectly safe." He had written to his wife that upon Pope's defeat "they will be very glad to turn over the redemption of their affairs to me."[60]

Even the pro-McClellan Ethan Rafuse concluded that McClellan acted in bad faith. He said, "... McClellan clearly, in Lincoln's words, 'acted badly' after his arrival in Alexandria ... it is also clear that McClellan took full advantage of the discretion Halleck irresponsibly granted at critical moments regarding the movements of Franklin's corps in a way that he clearly understood could compromise, perhaps fatally, Pope's efforts—and serve his own self-interest." Rafuse described McClellan's hatred of Pope and of the new non-conciliatory approach to the war that he represented. Rafuse concluded, "[That approach] was a development the general believed fatal to the hopes of enlightened statesmen and military professionals for a true reconciliation of the warring sections and one that had to be reversed at almost any cost. In August 1862 that cost turned out to be a second Union defeat on the plains of Manassas."[61]

A strong argument, therefore, can be made that McClellan's delay in moving his army from the Peninsula to support Pope's pressed forces in central Virginia and particularly his defiant disobedience of six direct orders from Halleck to immediately move Franklin and Sumner's corps to the battlefield at Manassas reflected something other than a determination to put down the rebellion. It appears that McClellan put his self-interest and lust for return to power above the fate of Pope's army, the battle result at Second Manassas, the safety of Washington, and the possible outcome of the war. His conduct at that time appears to have been traitorous. For this, he deserves more condemnation than history thus far has bestowed upon him.

Maryland Campaign

On the eve of the Maryland Campaign, Secretary Welles wrote this evaluation of McClellan and his loyalties:

> McClellan is an intelligent engineer and officer, but not a commander to head a great army in the field. To attack or advance with energy and power is not in him; to fight is not his forte. I sometimes fear his heart is not earnest in the cause, yet I do not entertain the thought that he is unfaithful....Wishes to outgeneral the Rebels, but not to kill and destroy them. In a conversation which I had with him in May last..., he said he desired of all things to capture Charleston; he would demolish and annihilate the city. He detested, he said, both South Carolina and Massachusetts, and should rejoice to see both States extinguished. Both were and always had been ultra and mischievous, and he could not tell which he hated most. These were the remarks of the General-in-chief at the head of our armies then in the field, and when as large a proportion of his troops were from Massachusetts as from any State in the Union, while as large a proportion of those opposed, who were fighting the Union, were from South Carolina as from any State. He was leading the men of Massachusetts against the men of South Carolina, yet he, the General, detests them alike.[62]

Only a few days later, on September 7, Welles expressed his concerns about McClellan's motives and behavior: "While McClellan may have had some cause to be offended with Pope, he has no right to permit his personal resentments to inflict injury upon the country. I may do him injustice, but I think his management has been generally unfortunate, to say the least, and culpably wrong since his return from the Peninsula."[63] The next day, Welles recorded a New York political report, indirectly from Democratic leader Barlow, that McClellan was not interested in the presidency but that: "All with him was military, and he had no particular desire to close this war immediately, but would pursue a line of policy of his own, regardless of the Administration, its wishes and objects."[64]

On the contrary, historian Steven Newton sympathetically commented, "We have to credit [McClellan] with moving quickly enough in Maryland (after his men found those three cigars) to trap Lee's outnumbered army on the banks of the Potomac; if the result at Antietam was disappointing, if bloody, very few generals did any better in their first major offensive battle."[65] Similarly, Joseph Harsh praised McClellan for quickly taking charge of "disorganized, dispirited and chaotically intermingled fragments of five separate armies," marching into Maryland within a week, "bringing Lee to bay at Antietam Creek" within the next week, and inflicting on him "the severest casualty rate ever suffered by the Army of Northern Virginia in the bloodiest day's battle of the entire war."[66]

Timothy J. Reese credited McClellan with analyzing the Lost Order, devising a counter-stroke, and convincing Franklin and himself that it would work. He continued, "McClellan critics may be justified in arguing that he took too long to react, but in counter-point McClellan may be praised for skillfully devising a strategically sound plan, *crafted to negate his perceived numerical inferiority when confronting a united Confederate army.*"[67] Reese's praise of McClellan assumes he was justified in acting as though Lee's army was twice its actual size—a grievous miscalculation that typified McClellan's entire wartime experience and prevented his achieving offensive success that the Union needed to win the war.

Pois and Langer pointed to four distinct missed opportunities by McClellan during the Maryland Campaign: (1) his initial hesitation after receiving Lee's Lost Order, (2) his piecemeal attacks at Sharpsburg, (3) his failure to launch a follow-up assault at "Bloody Lane," and (4) his failure to use his massive reserves for a crushing blow after the initial break-through at that same mid-field location.[68] They attributed all of these to his avoidance of any failure for which he could be blamed.

Rare indeed was the opportunity presented to McClellan by the discovery of the Lost Order. Instead of taking immediate advantage of that discovery, McClellan focused on telling a number of people, including Lincoln, that he now had Bobby Lee where he wanted him and could not fail to whip him. James M. McPherson described the general's inaction:

> But McClellan was determined to be careful. No rashness. After all, in McClellan's mind the rebels outnumbered him by 40,000 men (in reality, the disparity was almost the opposite). Thus he must move cautiously. *Six hours passed* before McClellan issued the first orders to the commanders who were to march to the South Mountain gaps and attack the divided enemy. And when were they to march? Immediately? No, *tomorrow morning would do.* One can readily imagine what would have happened if the situation had been reversed and Lee had discovered that McClellan's army was split into four parts too distant from each other for mutual support. He would have had Jackson on the march within the hour, with Longstreet right behind. The first Union troops did not move until *eighteen hours* after McClellan had seen Lee's orders. And that was all the margin Lee needed to avert disaster.[69]

On September 16, McClellan had about 70,000 troops at Sharpsburg while Lee, with the first reinforcements just starting to arrive from Harpers Ferry, had only 25,000. But McClellan thought he faced at least 120,000 Rebels. Catton said, "McClellan was facing an imaginary army rather than the real one which was spread so thin on the Sharpsburg ridge: an army that drew upon fabulous numbers and transcended all of the limitations which poor transportation and insufficient supplies always imposed on Confederate commanders. Whether the fault lay with the Pinkerton reports, with McClellan himself, or somewhere else, the incredible fact remains that McClellan was preparing to fight an army that simply did not exist."[70] Intelligence expert Edwin C. Fishel contended that McClellan was obsessed with, and believed his own exaggerations of, Rebel strength.[71]

On September 17, the single bloodiest day of the war, McClellan deployed his army incompetently. He attacked piecemeal ("various attacks occurred seriatim, division by division, instead of going forward in coordinated fashion"), never had more than 20,000 of his approximately 75,000 troops in action at a single time, allowed Lee to switch his defenders from sector to sector, kept his cavalry in reserve and unused (even for scouting the flanks), failed to follow up on battlefield successes, and allowed 20,000 troops to remain out of the action all day.[72] Stephen Sears concluded that "… McClellan imagined three Rebel soldiers for every one he faced on the Antietam battlefield. Every decision he made that September 17 was dominated by his fear of counterattack by phantom Confederate battalions."[73]

Paul Chiles, Artillery Specialist and Ranger Historian at Antietam National Battlefield Park, provided this summary of the battle:

> McClellan actually made five major attacks. Had any two of these gone in at the same time, Lee's lines likely would have been stretched too thin and unable to hold against 'Mac's' superior strength. But by shrewd and desperate maneuvers, the Southerners hung on. Lee can be criticized for fighting the Battle of Antietam at all, but once the battle was joined, the Confederates did almost everything right. Tactically, this was one of Lee's best fought battles of the war.[74]

In other words, Lee had jeopardized his army by slowly gathering them in the vulnerable position at Sharpsburg, but McClellan had squandered the opportunity to destroy that army by launching ineffective piecemeal attacks throughout the day of the crucial battle. Gary Gallagher agreed: "Had McClellan managed to coordinate his attacks or used the thousands of Federal soldiers who remained idle during the day, he probably would have shattered Lee's army."[75]

According to Ethan Rafuse, however, McClellan passed up opportunities to destroy Lee's army because "such an outcome, although desirable, was not critical to McClellan's strategic vision in September 1862." He added, "Victory north of the Potomac was not in McClellan's mind an end in itself but merely one step in a logical, clearly reasoned program for returning the Union war effort to the path of enlightened statesmanship from which he believed it had foolishly departed in the summer of 1862. To McClellan it was enough that he had saved the North from the consequences of political folly…."[76]

Catton pointed to a major irony resulting from such an approach to Antietam. He said that McClellan's partial victory opened the door for Lincoln to take his next planned step, issuance of the Preliminary Emancipation Proclamation, and to change the very nature of the war to an anti-slavery crusade. Had McClellan instead, said Catton, won the complete victory that Lee had almost invited on several occasions during the campaign, the Union could have won the war on McClellan's preferred non-abolitionist terms.[77]

In summary, McClellan's Maryland Campaign performance represented the culmination and the epitome of his major flaws as a Union general. He grossly overestimated enemy strength, failed to aggressively pursue the divided and vulnerable Rebels, failed to attack them at Sharpsburg until Lee had reassembled most of his forces, and finally attacked in an uncoordinated, disjointed, and timid manner with far less than the full complement of forces available to him. His perennial fear of defeat resulted in a lack of moral fortitude and precluded his performing in the manner required for Union success.

Failure to Pursue Lee

McClellan's final military failure involved staying at Sharpsburg and its environs north of the Potomac for five weeks after the battle there instead of aggressively pursuing Lee's battered army. That failure began on September 18, when Lee foolishly stayed on the Antietam battlefield and challenged McClellan to resume the attack. McClellan's decision not to do so raised suspicions about his motives. Ninth Corps Brigade Commander Thomas Welsh wrote that he was "thoroughly disgusted with the management of this army.... The whole Rebel Army could have been captured or destroyed easily before it could have crossed the Potomac—but indeed it seems to me that McClellan let them escape purposely."[78]

Despite Lincoln's visit with him at Sharpsburg and numerous prodding communications from the president, McClellan failed to advance until late October and finally proceeded to do so at his usual leisurely pace. When Longstreet moved between McClellan and Richmond, Lincoln had had enough. Lincoln explained his doubts about McClellan to his private secretary, John Hay: "I peremptorily ordered him to advance," but McClellan kept "delaying on little pretexts of wanting this and that. *I began to fear that he was playing false—that he did not want to hurt the enemy.* I saw how he could intercept the enemy on the way to Richmond. I determined to make that the test. If he let them get away I would remove him. He did so & I relieved him."[79]

In the seven post-Antietam weeks, beginning with the day after the Sharpsburg bloodbath, McClellan passed up the opportunity to attack Lee's decimated forces and move the North toward victory. He appears to have been motivated by a lack of desire for fighting at all, a continuing fear of failure aggravated by his usual misreading of enemy strength, and an anathema for Lincoln and his emancipation policies.

Weigley summed up the termination of McClellan: "In the light of the Emancipation Proclamation, the departure of McClellan signified the failure not only of a glamorous but grievously flawed general, but also of a whole manner of waging war."[80] Actually, his departure was the beginning of the end of **not** waging war. McClellan's successors increasingly attempted to carry the fight to the Rebels, something he seemed incapable of doing.

Overview

Intriguingly, Robert E. Lee is supposed to have considered McClellan to be the best Union general he encountered.[81] Perhaps this opinion was the result of Lee's continued success against McClellan, whom Lee may have viewed as a gentleman fighter of the old school, and his unwillingness to give credit to his most successful foe, Ulysses S. Grant.[82] As Pois and Langer commented, "... McClellan probably contributed as much or more to Lee's career and subsequent legendary status than any other Union general...."[83]

An example of Lee's sympathetic approach to McClellan is his contemporaneous description of the Seven Days' Battle: "Under ordinary circumstances, the Federal army should have been destroyed. Its escape was due to causes already stated. Prominent among these was the want of correct and timely information. This fact, attributable chiefly to the character of the country, enabled Gen. McClellan skillfully to conceal his retreat, and to add much to the obstructions with which nature had beset the way of our pursuing columns." This language was quoted by Edward A. Pollard to support his own contention that "McClellan had managed his retreat with skill." In his 1866 pro-Confederate version of the war, *Daily Richmond Examiner* editor Pollard unsurprisingly expressed his admiration for McClellan's views set forth in his Harrison's Landing Letter.[84]

Some commentators have been willing to "cut McClellan some slack" because he commanded so early in the war. Even Ulysses S. Grant, fourteen years after the war, said, "If McClellan had gone into the war as Sherman, George Thomas, or Meade, had fought his way along and up, I have no reason to suppose that he would not have won as high a distinction as any of us."[85] Grant, however, admitted that he had not studied McClellan's campaigns "enough to make up my mind" about his military skills.[86]

The reality was that McClellan rose very high very quickly, failed to fight his army aggressively, failed to capture Richmond in the Peninsula Campaign, deliberately sabotaged Union efforts at Second Manassas, failed to destroy Lee's inferior and vulnerable army in the Maryland Campaign, and continued to demonstrate timidity and defy orders after that. One possible cause of these wartime failures is that he may have been too successful as a wealthy youth and upper-class young man, military officer, and railroad official. McPherson noted, "He had never known, as Grant had, the despair of defeat or the humiliation of failure. He had never learned the lessons of adversity and humility."[87] McClellan's aristocratic background may also have contributed to a perspective that the aristocratic South had a more disciplined and effective army than the democratic North.[88]

Whatever the reasons, timidity and lack of aggressiveness became the hallmark of McClellan's campaigns—or the absence of them. Peter Michie pointed to his "timidity and extreme prudence as a commander."[89] Thomas Rowland commented, "McClellan has been verbally pilloried by historians for his excessive caution and timidity. In the main, this criticism has been justified."[90] Thomas J. Goss concluded,

> ... McClellan's immense army was never quite prepared enough to act aggressively, and the resulting caution proved the source of Lincoln's greatest frustration during the war.... In order to maintain support for the war, Lincoln had to keep up the impression of forward progress and military success, and the fierce resistance of the Confederate field armies convinced him they were the main obstacles to winning the war. As McClellan appeared not to share these views, he had to go.[91]

Beginning with his first letter to Governor Dennison, a recurring theme in McClellan's correspondence was that avoiding defeat must be the primary concern of a commanding general. This theme was a reflection of McClellan's fear of failure. Jeffry Wert observed that McClellan "waged his campaigns not to lose, rather than to win."[92]

McClellanism, the reluctance to fight, has been blamed for the Army of the Potomac's lack of consistent success prior to the 1864 arrival of Ulysses Grant. Grant's 1861–62 aggressive successes in the Mississippi Valley Theater (Paducah, Smithfield, Belmont, Forts Henry and Donelson, Shiloh, Iuka and Corinth) provided models of what could be done by maximum use of a commander's resources. They stand as a rebuttal to those who claimed McClellan fought too early in the war to be expected to be aggressive and successful.[93] In contrast to McClellan's army, Grant's Army of the Tennessee in the Mississippi Valley Theater was gaining confidence in itself—even after, perhaps partially because of, the bloody two-day Battle of Shiloh in April 1862. Steven E. Woodworth commented, "Perhaps in part at least it was not so much that Grant infused confidence into his army as that he refrained from destroying—by timid campaigning—the confidence of men who knew they had survived the worst the enemy had to throw at them."[94] "Timid campaigning" is an apt description for McClellan's approach.

Michael Adams saw a connection between McClellan's overestimating enemy strength (relative to his own) and his debilitating effect on the Army of the Potomac: "But in understating the strength of his army, McClellan gave it an unworthy definition of success: avoiding outright defeat became an accomplishment." Perhaps the shrewdest comment on McClellan's moral failure as a leader was made by General Cox, who wrote of him, "the general who indoctrinates his army with the belief that it is required by its government to do the impossible, may preserve his popularity with the troops and be received with cheers as he rides down the line, but he has put any great military success far beyond his reach."[95]

McClellan consistently demonstrated a self-defeating disrespect for those in authority over him. As Sears concluded,

> Yet surely what historian would not find it significant that from West Point onward, McClellan had never gotten on with *anyone* in authority. He disputed those who assigned class rankings at the Academy. He scorned his superiors in the Mexican War. Back at West Point, he endlessly debated the superintendent on the pettiest of issues. During his antebellum army assignments he battled authority on the Pacific railroad survey, and suffered his fellow observers sent to the Crimea as fools. In civilian life, he repeatedly tangled with fellow executives of the railroads that employed him. McClellan the major general would have been changing his spots had he not regarded Generals Scott and Halleck, Secretary of War Stanton, and President Lincoln as fools, and worse.[96]

McClellan's most significant hostility was toward Lincoln, his commander-in-chief. As historian Alexander McClurg wrote to Mrs. McClellan in 1892, "The General's single mistake, that was the source of all his misfortunes, was his distrust of Lincoln. Had he understood and treated Lincoln as his friend, as I knew Lincoln was, he could have mastered all his combined enemies."[97] Ulysses S. Grant came to a similar conclusion: "McClellan's main blunder was in allowing himself political sympathies, and in permitting himself to become the critic of the President, and in time his rival."[98]

McClellan's religiosity may have acerbated his weaknesses. Although he often wrote that God was on his side, he used divine intervention as an excuse when adverse results occurred. Sears said, "Under the fierce pressures of the battlefield, however, [McClellan's] messianic vision became his crutch, his ultimate escape from responsibility—it was beyond his power to shape an outcome that God had ordained." He provided as an example McClellan's explanation of his Seven Days' defeat: "I think I begin to see [God's] wise purpose in all this & that events of the last few days will prove it. If I had succeeded in taking Richmond now the fanatics of the North might have been too powerful & reunion impossible. However that may be I am sure that it is all for the best."[99]

A primary debilitating flaw of McClellan's was his consistent exaggeration of enemy strength. He did so in western Virginia, in Washington, at Yorktown and outside Richmond on the Peninsula, and before, during, and after the fighting at Antietam.[100] Michie concluded that these exaggerations exacerbated his apprehension of failure.[101] Sears said that "no other general exaggerated in such monumental proportions or for so long a period.... More important, no other general was in a comparable position for his delusion to so profoundly influence his strategy—and, on the field of battle, his tactics." Sears also concluded that the exaggerations were the responsibility of McClellan, not Allan Pinkerton, his hand-picked intelligence chief: "Nor, as was long believed, was [McClellan] victimized by the blunders of his intelligence chief Allan Pinkerton. Exhaustive research into the operations of detective Pinkerton and his intelligence-gatherers reveals that it was the general commanding, not the detective, who initiated the wildly inflated counting of Confederate forces."[102]

Edwin Fishel's analysis of the McClellan-Pinkerton relationship provided the basis for Sears' conclusion. It revealed that Pinkerton kept changing his methodology for estimating enemy strength in order to produce ever-larger numbers for McClellan, that McClellan was aware of the flaws in Pinkerton's methodology, and that McClellan regularly exceeded Pinkerton's estimates in his own reports to his superiors. McClellan's inflation of the numbers was so great that he never dared to submit Pinkerton's reports to support his own numbers.

Cox, one of Burnside's division commanders, wrote, "The fiction as to the strength of Lee's forces is the most remarkable in the history of modern wars. Whether McClellan was the victim or the accomplice of the inventions of his 'secret service,' we cannot tell. It is almost incredible that he should be deceived, except willingly." Fishel, who concluded that McClellan actually had convinced himself of the accuracy of the inflated numbers, rendered this verdict: "Among Civil War generals McClellan had many companions in believing himself outnumbered. With no other army commander, however, did this belief so firmly condemn his campaigns to failure, as on the Peninsula, or deny him a decisive victory, as on the Antietam."[103]

Fishel's conclusions are significant:

> McClellan did not just *believe* he was badly outnumbered; he *knew* it. It was an obsession, a fixation.... With Pinkerton the controlling character trait is not obsessiveness but a personal loyalty of a kind for which there is no other name but sycophancy.... The necessity that mothered Pinkerton's inventions was McClellan's conviction of being outnumbered.... A neurotic general and a sycophantic intelligence officer—that is a dangerous combination.... Someone did deceive General McClellan about enemy numbers; it was McClellan himself.

Most importantly, concludes Fishel, McClellan's obsession with enemy numbers prevented him from aggressively using his army, capturing Richmond, defeating Lee in Maryland, and going down in history as the general who won the war.[104]

Early commentator Peter Michie concluded that there was an "unaccountable weakness in McClellan's mental equipment" that explained his combat failures.[105] In his 1994 psychological study of Civil War leaders, Joseph Glatthaar concluded that McClellan had a paranoid personality disorder with narcissistic tendencies. His specific conclusion was:

> McClellan's psychological baggage impeded his ability to function as army commander and general in chief. Mistrustful by nature, he discovered deliberately threatening or demeaning remarks in innocuous comments. His excessive secrecy, need to dominate, and hypersensitivity to rank and power inhibited his capacity to labor under Lincoln or anyone else.... McClellan formed initial or preconceived expectations and clung to them rigidly, obscuring all information that contradicted the original assessments. He grossly exaggerated the strength of obstacles, took extreme precautions, and in failure blamed everyone except himself. Severely critical of others, he reacted bitterly to criticism and justified himself at every turn. These qualities, all characteristic of paranoid personality disorder with narcissistic tendencies, prevented McClellan from performing his duties as commanding general and general in chief satisfactorily.[106]

Sears expressed concern that such mental disorder characterization of McClellan would leave the door open for mockery by McClellan apologists. He cited Thomas J. Rowland's conclusion that McClellan was not "plagued by crippling mental instability" and his mocking deduction that the purported psychological faults of the general led inevitably to a picture of him as "a lurking, brooding, out-of-control manic waiting to uncork on the Virginia Peninsula."[107] In fact, Rowland, in his later book on McClellan, summarized his view of this issue: "The injudicious characterization of McClellan as an individual who suffered from crippling neuroses, wild hallucinations, manic depression, paralyzing persecutory and grandiose delusions, and, most improbably, demonic possession violates basic tenets of medical diagnosis.... I am contending that [McClellan's] correspondence, while full of frank opinion and personal invective, even conniving and braggadocio, does not reflect in any substantive way the serious psychological disorders attributed to McClellan."[108]

Sears summarized McClellan's long-term impact on the Army of the Potomac: "McClellanism was a corrosive legacy, producing divided loyalties and undue caution among Potomac army generals, causing them to look back over their shoulder even as they advanced."[109]

As indicated, Sears' criticisms of McClellan were attacked by Rowland, who argued against the assignment of modern diagnostic classifications to a Civil War general.[110] Pois and Langer, in turn, responded, "Yet, if one were to eschew the assignment of such modern clinical classifications as manic-depressive, delusional, paranoidal, and so on, the fact remains that McClellan did have some crippling psychological problems that precluded battlefield success, especially where he was solely responsible. The historical evidence is there: Despite all his advantages, McClellan failed in both the Seven Days' and Antietam campaigns, where success in either instance could have ended the war much earlier."[111]

They concluded that McClellan's fear of failure caused him to avoid moderate-risk situations—those in which he might lose and be unable to blame someone else. Instead, they asserted, he opted for low-risk options that were certain to bring him victory or high-risk options that would allow him to blame others if he were defeated.[112] Here is their pithy synopsis:

> Although caution is not necessarily considered a defect in combat, at some point it becomes a pathological indecisiveness, an unwillingness to do something. After all, he did move to Rich Mountain in the western Virginia campaign, he did land on the Yorktown Peninsula in his efforts to take Richmond, and he eventually did attack at Antietam. In each instance, however, there arose at a critical point that moment of truth when McClellan's fragile ego betrayed him. It was not military caution in any normal sense of the word, but an overwhelming fear of failure that could be directly attributed to him, without any mitigating circumstances."[113]

Joseph Waugh put it succinctly: "... the Young Napoleon had been a victim of his own paranoia. He had failed to understand the rebel commanders in his front, who were his enemies. Perhaps worse, he had failed to understand Lincoln in his rear, who had been ready to be his friend."[114]

One reason for his failure to understand Lincoln was that he did not even try to do so. He was so convinced of the correctness of his own grand strategy to preserve both the Union and slavery that he disregarded and disrespected Lincoln and the Radical Republicans who controlled Congress. According to Thomas Goss, "McClellan did not seek to wage military campaigns completely divorced from the politics of the war, but instead sought a ... relationship between himself as military commander and the national government that would allow him to fight the strategy he envisioned would lead to the return of the Union without impacting the issue of slavery." His lack of military success, however, destroyed any political leverage he hoped he would have.[115]

The conclusions are not pretty. McClellan was a privileged, egotistic and pompous man who craved authority and disdained his superiors. His fear of failure or defeat led him to avoid combat—an avoidance that was antithetical to the North's need to affirmatively win the war. In order to avoid battle and blame for any defeat (or lack of success), he arranged for inflated estimates of enemy strength and then boosted the numbers further himself. When circumstances compelled him to fight, he behaved in a timid and sometimes cowardly manner. Worst of all, his craving for power led him to deliberately undercut Pope before and during Second Manassas—actions which could have resulted in the destruction of Pope's army and the loss of the Civil War. Whether or not he was conscious of it, McClellan was a traitor to the cause he served in the days leading up to and during the Battle of Second Manassas. McClellan was not the commander-in-chief, he often was not even the general-in-chief, and thus his political or philosophical views cannot excuse his conduct.

Appendix:
Historians' Treatment
of George B. McClellan

Biographies of McClellan began appearing in 1864, when he was the Democratic candidate opposing the reelection of Lincoln. McClellan cooperated with the author of one, G.S. Hillard, who wrote *Life and Campaigns of George B. McClellan, Major-General U.S. Army*. Many campaign biographies and commentaries relied upon McClellan's own *Report on the Organization of the Army of the Potomac, and of Its Campaigns in Virginia and Maryland*. In the *North American Review*, James Russell Lowell commented that McClellan "makes affidavit in one volume octavo that he is a great military genius, after all."[1]

An anonymous campaign biography, *The Life, Campaigns, and Public Services of General McClellan...*, commented on the diversity of opinion concerning McClellan: "By some persons he is considered the greatest strategist of the age. By others he is regarded as unfit to command even a hundred men."[2] As T. Harry Williams has stated, historians have continued this dispute. He called McClellan "the problem child of the Civil War. People reacted to him in violent extremes.... His contemporaries revered or reviled him, and historians have defended or attacked him."[3]

After the war, McClellan decided to create a definitive defense of his generalship. Relying upon all of his headquarters archives, which he took with him upon his final relief of command, McClellan constructed his military memoir. The only copy was destroyed in an 1881 fire, and he started over. His unexpected death occurred when he not even half finished. His friend and literary executor, William C. Prime, stepped in to complete the task. He cobbled together a book containing McClellan's draft, his earlier writings, and excerpts from McClellan's letters to his wife. He published this concoction as *McClellan's Own Story* in 1887. The result was a rabid, pro–McClellan book that unintentionally exposed many of the general's imperfections. Decades later, Allan Nevins commented, "Students of history must always be grateful that McClellan so frankly exposed his own weaknesses in this posthumous book."[4] In reality, however, Prime was the major mover behind that volume and published many documentary excerpts that McClellan would not have revealed.[5]

Peter S. Michie, a Civil War engineer, published a critical biography of McClellan in 1901. His *General McClellan* was part of Appleton's "Great Commanders" series. Although Michie stated that McClellan was a patriot and gentleman, he seriously criti-

cized the general's timidity, slowness, reluctance to initiate battle, and constant overestimation of enemy strength. He was brutally critical of McClellan's absence from the field
at Glendale and Malvern Hill but forgiving of his failure to support Pope at Second Manassas (on the questionable grounds that McClellan and Halleck had an honest disagree-
ment and Halleck was not forceful enough).[6] Just two years later, Guy Carleton Lee
concluded that McClellan's reluctance to fight indicated that he was "either a coward or
disloyal."[7]

A legal brief supporting McClellan was produced by attorney James Havelock Campbell in his *McClellan: A Vindication of the Military Career of General George B. McClellan*
(1916). Sears pointed out that Campbell's credibility was reflected in his judgment about
McClellan's performance at Glendale and Malvern Hill as "wise, prudent, brave, skilful
[*sic*], with a mind which grasped everything down to the minutest detail and with an
energy which governed all."[8]

Two mundane biographies were those of William Starr Myers (*General George Brinton McClellan* [1934]) and Clarence W. Macartney (*Mac* [1940]).[9] Myers concluded that
both McClellan and Lincoln were guileless men who unfortunately did not understand
each other and that Stanton was the villain who drove them apart.[10] These two books
were shortly followed by another adulatory volume: *George B. McClellan: The Man Who
Saved the Union* (1941) by H.J. Eckenrode and Bryan Conrad. As demonstrated by their
title, these two Virginia Conservation Commission historians set out to prove that he was
a great Union general and downplayed his alleged faults. Their forward stated:

> Since there seemed to be no military reasons for the animadversions cast on McClellan,
> the historians of the commission were persuaded that the hostile feeling toward him is polit-
> ical, springing mainly from his candidacy against Lincoln in the election of 1864. Believ-
> ing that politics should not be permitted to influence military judgments, they have written
> this book, partly for the purpose of doing justice to a great man who has suffered at the
> hands of history.

The general theme of this work is that Lee and Jackson were great generals whom McClellan had no chance of defeating but that McClellan did a commendable job of saving the
Union's eastern army after First and Second Manassas.[11]

As late as 1957, Warren W. Hassler, Jr. persistently praised McClellan in *General
George B. McClellan: Shield of the Union*.[12] In a manner reminiscent of Douglas Southall
Freeman's *Lee's Lieutenants*,[13] Hassler blamed McClellan's problems on everyone else: his
subordinates, Pinkerton's faulty intelligence, and the Radical Republicans in Washington. Although Hassler took McClellan's side on all disputed issues, even he admitted that
"McClellan would have done better to have used more tact and to have treated his civilian superiors in a somewhat less cavalier fashion."[14]

Joseph L. Harsh described those and several other biographies of McClellan as por-
traying him as a patriot, a master strategist, and great administrator whose war efforts
were undermined by a clique of Radical Republicans and Secretary of War Stanton, who
turned a weak Lincoln against McClellan. Harsh concluded that these works were undermined by their eulogistic treatment of the general, their failure to paint a complete portrait, and their omission of the impact of his political views. Harsh also found sympathy
for McClellan in the memoirs and other histories written by Civil War veterans, who wrote
that he was a victim of his "earliness"—the fact that he fought the Confederates when
they were at full strength.[15]

In his masterful eight-volume *Ordeal of the Union*[16] (1947–71), Alan Nevins treated
McClellan fairly, honestly, and critically. He sympathized with McClellan's disappointment when Lincoln deprived him of expected reinforcements on the Peninsula. How-

ever, he explained the general's slowness, temerity, and caution on the Peninsula, during the Maryland Campaign, and after Antietam. McClellan's record, Nevins concluded, left the patient Lincoln with no choice but to remove him from command.

Contemporaries of Nevins, such as Bruce Catton, T. Harry Williams, and Kenneth P. Williams, were equally critical of McClellan's performance. In his *Lincoln Finds a General*, Kenneth P. Williams acidly concluded that "McClellan was merely an attractive but vain and unstable man, with considerable military knowledge, who sat a horse well and wanted to be President."[17]

In 1973, Joseph Harsh wrote a famous article entitled "On the McClellan-Go-Round." In it, he summarized the historiography of McClellan, concluded that a Unionist school of Civil War historians had denigrated him, found him psychologically unfit for senior command, determined he failed to grasp the basics of modern warfare, and compared him unfavorably with his nemesis, Abraham Lincoln, "easily the strongest figure in United States history." Harsh closed with a plea for reconsideration of McClellan—a "more honest, more human, and more historical ... view [of] McClellan as a man with at least some control over his own conduct and some commitment to ideas beyond his own selfishness and ambition."[18] Harsh continued his sympathetic treatment of McClellan in a series of books about the war during 1861 and 1862.[19]

A similarly sympathetic approach to McClellan was taken by Rowena Reed in *Combined Operations in the Civil War* (1978). She glowingly described his grand strategic plans to capture Confederate ports and to move inland and disrupt their railroad connections. She also praised his Peninsula Campaign and stated that it was undermined by "a complex of accidents unparalleled in the Civil War"—"poor maps, unreliable allies [in Washington and the Navy], public pressure, government interference, professional jealousy, and an alert, intelligent enemy...."[20] She specifically blamed Lincoln's vacillation on the disposition of McDowell's corps and the Navy's lack of support for McClellan on the York and James rivers for the campaign's failure, which "...signalled [*sic*] both the demise of [McClellan's] Federal grand strategy and the breakdown of combined operations planning."[21] Stephen Sears commented acidly on her work: "So warm are Reed's feelings toward the general that she invents explanations and excuses for his failures that even he never thought of."[22]

Sears himself hit McClellan's reputation with a devastating one-two punch in 1988 and 1989. First he published his critical *George B. McClellan: The Young Napoleon*,[23] and then he backed his findings up with publication of *The Civil War Papers of George B. McClellan*.[24] The latter volume contains previously unpublished portions of McClellan's acerbic letters to his wife, which, when read in conjunction with his simultaneous military correspondence and letters to Democratic friends, constitute damning evidence of McClellan's less-than-noble motives. In his *McClellan*, Sears exposed the general's egotistical, haughty, anti-civilian authority attitudes; his overestimation of enemy strength, and his cowardly conduct. He did, however, contend that McClellan did not deliberately conspire to cause Pope's defeat at Second Manassas.

Primarily in response to Sears, Thomas J. Rowland came to the partial defense of McClellan in his 1998 book, *George B. McClellan and Civil War History in the Shadow of Grant and Sherman*. Interestingly, Rowland admitted that, in light of McClellan's lack of success, he was not "claiming he was a great commander" but contending that he was not "an abject failure" and "was essentially a competent commander." He contended that McClellan did not suffer from "crippling mental instability," that he had the disadvantage of commanding the Union's most prominent army early in the war, that he did not have to work his way to the top, and that his flaws were no worse than those of some other Union generals. The best Rowland could do for McClellan, however, was to con-clude, "McClellan can scarcely be elevated to the ranks of the great captains of war, but he was hardly the worst that the conflict dragged onto center stage."[25]

More recently, Timothy J. Reese attempted to mitigate McClellan's responsibility for the lost opportunities during the Antietam Campaign. In his *High-Water Mark: The 1862 Maryland Campaign in Strategic Perspective* (2004), Reese contended that McClel-lan developed an effective battle plan within hours of receiving the Lost Order, that his plan was reasonable given his assumption that Lee had 120,000 (not 40,000) men with him, and that Franklin's lack of aggressiveness at and after Crampton's Gap was the real reason Lee's army was not destroyed.[26]

A contrary view was set forth by Pois and Langer in their 2004 study of *Command Failure in War: Psychology and Leadership*. In a chapter on "McClellan's Failed Cam-paign: The Wounded Ego," they found that, during the Peninsula Campaign, McClel-lan was driven by a need to avoid failure. The result, they said, was that "he always contributed much less to gaining a victory than he did to avoiding defeat." Their final comment on him was: "Yet, one can only wonder how the course of American history, and most certainly presidential politics, would have changed if McClellan had struck directly and swiftly at Richmond or ordered up his reserves at Antietam through the gap formed at Bloody Lane."[27]

In his 2005 *McClellan's War*, Ethan S. Rafuse stressed that McClellan's conserva-tive political beliefs greatly influenced his military actions (and inactions). Rafuse con-tended that McClellan's belief in a limited Federal role and strong states' rights put him at odds with Lincoln's emancipation and confiscation policies. He explained but did not, however, excuse McClellan's military failures because there was some intellectual or philosophical basis for them.[28] After being ordered to vacate the Peninsula, in Rafuse's words, McClellan's first step [to steer the Union back to the "proper path"] ... was the destruction of the man who symbolized the change in union policy, which McClellan contributed to during the Second Manassas Campaign by holding back much needed reinforcements from Pope's army."[29]

Notes

Introduction

1. Symonds, Craig L.; Simon, John Y.; Poulter, Keith; Newton, Steven H.; Sears, Stephen W., and Woodworth, Steven E., "Who Were the Worst Ten Generals?," *North & South*, Vol. 7, No. 3 (May 2004) [hereafter Symonds *et al.*, "Who Were the Worst?"], pp. 12–25. Appropriately, Mc-Clellan did not appear in any of six historians' votes for the top ten Civil War generals. Woodworth, Steven E.; Mitchell, Reid; Rhea, Gordon C.; Simon, John Y.; Newton, Steven H., and Poulter, Keith, "Who Were the Top Ten Generals?," *North & South*, Vol. 6, No. 4 (May 2003), pp. 12–22. Current examples of a current pro–McClellan analysis are Rafuse, Ethan S. *McClellan's War* (Bloomington: Indiana University Press, 2005) [hereafter Rafuse, *McClellan's War*] and Rafuse, Ethan S., "Fighting for Defeat? George B. Mc-Clellan's Peninsula Campaign and the Change of Base to the James River" in Woodworth, Steven E. (ed.), *Civil War Generals in Defeat* (Lawrence: University of Kansas Press, 1999), pp. 71–94 [hereafter Rafuse, "Fighting"].

2. Rowland, Thomas J., *George B. McClellan and Civil War History in the Shadow of Grant and Sherman* (Kent, Ohio, and London: Kent State University Press, 1998) [hereafter Rowland, *McClellan and History*], p. ix.

3. Jones, Archer, *Civil War Command & Strategy: The Process of Victory and Defeat* (New York: The Free Press, 1992) [hereafter Jones, *Command & Strategy*], p. 19.

4. Johnston later commented that "no one but McClellan would have hesitated to attack." *Ibid.*, p. 62.

5. Joseph Stalin said that General Georgi "Zhukov is my George B. McClellan. Like McClellan he always wants more men, more cannon, more guns. He never has enough...." Barnett, Glenn, "Russo-Japanese Clash at Nomonhan," *WWII History*, Vol. 4, No. 3 (May 2005), pp. 68–75 at pp. 73–74. Barnett added, "General Zhukov's overestimation of the enemy forces in front of him certainly bears out the comparison to McClellan." *Ibid.*, p. 74.

6. Sears, Stephen W., "McClellan at Antietam," *Hallowed Ground*, Vol. 6, No. 1 (Spring 2005), pp. 30–33 [hereafter Sears, "McClellan at Antietam"], p. 30.

7. Symonds *et al.*, "Who Were the Worst?," pp. 17, 18.

8. U.S. House of Representatives, 37th Congress, 3rd session, *Report of the Joint Committee on the Conduct of the War* (3 vols.) (Washington: Government Printing Office, 1863) [hereafter *Joint Committee Report*], Part I, p. 62.

Chapter 1

1. Waugh, John C., *The Class of 1846: From West Point to Appomattox: Stonewall Jackson, George McClellan and*

Their Brothers (New York: Warner Books, Inc., 1994) [hereafter Waugh, *Class of 1846*], pp. 8–9; McPherson, James M., *Battle Cry of Freedom: The Civil War Era* (New York: Ballantine Books, 1988) [hereafter McPherson, *Battle Cry*], p. 359; Jones, R. Steven, *The Right Hand of Command: Use & Disuse of Personal Staffs in the Civil War* (Mechanicsburg, Pennsylvania: Stackpole Books, 2000) [hereafter Jones, *Right Hand*], pp. 12–13; Michie, Peter S., *General McClellan* (New York: D. Appleton and Company, 1901) [hereafter Michie, *McClellan*], p. 8.

2. Beatie, Russel H., *Army of the Potomac* (2 vols.) (Cambridge: Da Capo Press, 2002, 2004) [hereafter Beatie, *Army of Potomac*], I, p. 389; Sears, Stephen W., *George B. McClellan: The Young Napoleon* (New York: Ticknor & Fields, 1988) [hereafter, Sears, *McClellan*], pp. 5–10.

3. Waugh, *Class of 1846*, pp. 36, 41, 54, 66–67.

4. *Ibid.*, pp. 73–76.

5. *Ibid.*, pp. 107–08, 123–24.

6. Johnson, Timothy D., "McClellan and His Mentor," *Military History Quarterly: The Quarterly Journal of Military History*, Vol. 13, No. 2 (Winter 2001), pp. 88–95 [hereafter Johnson, "McClellan and Mentor"] at pp. 92–93.

7. Sears, *McClellan*, pp. 28–30; Beatie, *Army of Potomac*, I, p. 391.

8. Sears, *McClellan*, pp. 36–41. McClellan's erroneous conclusion that the Yakima, Stampede, and Snoqualmie passes through the Cascades were unsuitable for rail transportation put him in the good graces of Secretary of War Jefferson Davis, who favored a southern transcontinental route. Beatie, *Army of Potomac*, pp. 393–94.

9. Waugh, *Class of 1846*, pp. 161–72. Hill's youthful indiscretion resulted in prostatitis, which caused him to slip from the class of 1846 (McClellan's) to the class of 1847 and caused him physical pain for the rest of his life. *Ibid.*, pp. 166–67. When Hill complained to Marcy that his wife had spread the vicious tales about Hill, Marcy wrote to his wife that "a just reparation" would be for Mary Ellen to marry Hill if Mrs. Marcy had done such a thing. Mrs. Marcy apparently convinced him of her innocence. *Ibid.*, p. 172.

10. The fact that McClellan was a protegé of Jefferson Davis, later the President of the Confederacy, created doubts about his loyalty to the Union during the Civil War. Sears, Stephen W., *To the Gates of Richmond: The Peninsula Campaign* (New York: Ticknor & Fields, 1992) [hereafter Sears, *To the Gates*], p. 4.

11. Nosworthy, Brent, *The Bloody Crucible of Courage: Fighting Methods and Combat Experience of the Civil War* (New York: Carroll & Graf Publishers, 2003) [hereafter Nosworthy, *Bloody Crucible*, p. 81; Jones, *Right Hand*, p. 14.

12. McClellan to John H. B. McClellan, Sept. 9, 1855, Sears, *McClellan*, p. 45.

13. *Ibid.*, pp. 81–83.

14. Waugh, *Class of 1846*, pp. 174–79.

15. McClellan to Samuel L.M. Barlow, Dec. 27, 1860, Sears, Stephen W., *The Civil War Papers of George B. McClellan: Selected Correspondence, 1860–1865* (New York: Ticknor & Fields, 1989) [hereafter Sears, *Papers of McClellan*, where Sears provides comments or information beyond McClellan's own writings, or simply *Papers of McClellan*], p. 3.

16. McClellan to Thomas C. English, *Papers of McClellan*, Feb. 7, 1861, p. 4.

Chapter 2

1. McClellan to Fitz John Porter, *Ibid.*, April 18, 1861, pp. 4–5 at p. 5.

2. *Ibid.*, p. 1; McClellan to Major General Robert Patterson of Pennsylvania, April 18, 1861, *Ibid.*, p. 5; McClellan to Pennsylvania Governor Andrew G. Curtin, April 24, 1861, *Ibid.*, p. 10; Waugh, *Class of 1846*, pp. 246–47; Jones, *Right Hand*, p. 15; Goss, Thomas J., *The War Within the Union High Command: Politics and Generalship During the Civil War* (Lawrence: University Press of Kansas, 2003) [hereafter Goss, *High Command*], pp. 55–56.

3. McClellan to Governor William Dennison, April 18, 1861, *Papers of McClellan*, pp. 6–7 at p. 7 (emphasis added).

4. McClellan to [Brevet] Lieutenant General Winfield Scott, April 23, 1861, *Official Records of the War of Rebellion* [hereafter OR], Ser. I, LI, Part I, pp. 333–34; Sears, *Papers of McClellan*, p. 10n.

5. McClellan to Allan Pinkerton, April 24, 1861, *Papers of McClellan*, p. 11.

6. Ohio Volunteer Militia General Order No. 1, April 25, 1861, *Ibid.*

7. McClellan to Scott, April 27, 1861, OR, Ser. I, LI, Part I, pp. 338–39; Sears, *Ibid.*, p. 13n.

8. McClellan to Scott, May 7, 1861, *Ibid.*, p. 16.

9. McClellan to Scott, May 9, 1861, OR, Ser. I, LI, Part I, pp. 373–74 at p. 373.

10. McClellan to Dennison, May 13, 1861, *Papers of McClellan*, pp. 18–19 at p. 19; McClellan to Secretary of War Simon Cameron, May 20, 1861, OR, Ser. I, II, p. 642; Scott to McClellan, May 21, 1861, OR, Ser. I, LI, Part I, pp. 386–87.

11. McClellan to Dennison, May 25, 1861, OR, Ser. I, LII, Part I, pp. 146–47.

12. McClellan to the Troops of the Department of Ohio, May 26, 1861, OR, Ser. I, II, p. 49.

13. McClellan to the Union Men of Western Virginia, May 26, 1861, *Ibid.*, pp. 48–49.

14. *Ibid.*, pp. 44–48; McClellan to Lt. Col. E.D. Townsend, May 30, 1861, *Ibid.*, pp. 49–50 at p. 50; Waugh, *Class of 1846*, pp. 248–49.

15. Mallinson, David, "Confused First Fight," *America's Civil War*, Vol. 4, No. 5 (Jan. 1992), pp. 46–52; Waugh, *Class of 1846*, pp. 251–55.

16. McClellan to President Abraham Lincoln, May 30, 1861, *Papers of McClellan*, pp. 28–9.

17. McClellan to Lincoln, June 1, 1861, *Ibid.*, pp. 29–30.

18. McClellan to Col. E.D. Townsend, June 11, 1861, OR, Ser. I, II, p. 674.

19. McClellan to Scott, June 26, 1861 (telegram and letter), OR, Ser. I, LII, Part I, pp. 182–83; *Ibid.*, pp. 183–84.

20. McClellan to Mary Ellen McClellan, June 21, 1861, *Papers of McClellan*, pp. 32–3.

21. Nosworthy, *Bloody Crucible*, p. 283.

22. McClellan to Mary Ellen McClellan, June 29 and 30, July 2, 1861, *Papers of McClellan*, pp. 40–1.

23. McClellan to Salmon P. Chase, June 26, 1861, *Ibid.*, pp. 36–7.

24. McClellan to Brigadier General T.A. Morris, July 3, 1861, OR, Ser. I, II, pp. 208–9.

25. McClellan to Mary Ellen McClellan, July 3, 1861, *Papers of McClellan*, pp. 43–4.

26. Castel, Albert, "West Virginia 1861: A Tale of a Goose, A Dog, and a Fox," *North & South*, Vol. 7, No. 7 (Nov. 2004), pp. 44–55 [hereafter Castel, "West Virginia"] at p. 46.

27. *Ibid.*, pp. 46, 48.

28. Castel, "West Virginia," p. 48; Waugh, *Class of 1846*, pp. 255–57; Cox, Jacob D., "McClellan in West Virginia," *Battles and Leaders*, I, p. 131.

29. McClellan to Col. E.D. Townsend, July 5, 1861, OR, Ser. I, II, pp. 198–9 at p. 199.

30. Castel, "West Virginia," p. 48.

31. Rosecrans, William Starke, "King of the Hill, Part I," *New Tribune*, Feb. 22, 1883; reprinted in *Civil War Times*, XL, No. 3 (June 2001), pp. 24–6, 68–70 and No. 4 (Aug. 2001), pp. 22–9. For a good description of the Battle of Rich Mountain, see Newell, Clayton R., *Lee vs. McClellan: The First Campaign* (Washington, D.C.: Regnery Publishing, Inc., 1996), pp. 124–34.

32. Castel, "West Virginia," pp. 48–49.

33. *Ibid.*, p. 49.

34. Overall, McClellan had 8,000 troops against a mere 1,300 Confederates. Nevertheless, he hesitated to attack. This was a general who only recently had berated a slightly outnumbered subordinate for asking for reinforcements and told him he wanted only men of action who would fight and die with their troops. Adams, Michael CC. *Fighting for Defeat: Union Military Failure in the East, 1861–1865* (Lincoln and London: University of Nebraska Press, 1978, 1992) [hereafter Adams, *Fighting for Defeat*], pp. 88–89.

35. Castel, "West Virginia," p. 49, quoting Beatty, John, *The Citizen-Soldier; or, Memoirs of a Volunteer* (Cincinnati, 1879), p. 26; Pois and Langer, *Command Failure*, p. 55; Fleming, Martin K., "The Northwestern Virginia Campaign of 1861: McClellan's Rising Star—Lee's Dismal Debut," *Blue & Gray Magazine*, VIII, Issue 1 (October 1990), pp. 8–22, 44–53 [hereafter Fleming, "Northwestern Virginia"] at p. 54.

36. Castel, "West Virginia," pp. 49–50; Fleming, "Northwestern Virginia," p. 54.

37. *Ibid.*, No. 4, pp. 27–29.

38. Johnson, "McClellan and Mentor," p. 93.

39. Sears, *Young Napoleon*, pp. 90–91.

40. Cox, *Reminiscences*, I, p. 58.

41. McClellan had seen the telegraph used for military purposes in Crimea. He made the first use of it by an American army going into battle. Waugh, *Class of 1846*, p. 263.

42. Heidler & Heidler, *Encyclopedia*, p. 1636; McClellan to Col. E.D. Townsend, July 12, 1861, *Papers of McClellan*, pp. 51–2.

43. Sears, *Papers of McClellan*, p. 52 note.

44. McClellan to Mary Ellen McClellan, July 13, 1861, *Papers of McClellan*, p. 53.

45. McClellan to Mary Ellen McClellan, July 14–5, 1861, *Ibid.*, pp. 54–5 at p. 54.

46. McClellan to Mary Ellen McClellan, July 14–5, 1861, *Ibid.*, pp. 54–5 at p. 55.

47. Michie, *McClellan*, pp. 91–92.

48. McClellan to Mary Ellen McClellan, July 15, 1861, *Papers of McClellan*, p. 58; McClellan to Brigadier General Charles W. Hill, July 16, 1861, *Ibid.*; *Ibid.*, note.

49. McClellan to Col. E.D. Townsend, July 19, 1861, OR, Ser. I, II, p. 288.

50. McClellan to Brigadier General J.D. Cox, July 19, 1861, *Papers of McClellan*, p. 62; OR, Ser. I, II, p. 288 note.

51. McClellan to Soldiers of the Army of the West, July 16, 1861, OR, Ser. I, II, p. 236.

52. Sears, *Papers of McClellan*, pp. 60–1 note.

53. McClellan to Major General Winfield Scott, July 18, 1861, *Ibid.*, p. 60.

54. McClellan to Randolph B. Marcy, July 21, 1861, *Ibid.*, p. 64; McClellan to Mary Ellen McClellan, July 21, 1861, *Ibid.*, p. 65.

55. Fleming, "Northwestern Virginia," pp. 60–61.

56. Scott to McClellan, July 21, 1861, OR, Ser. 1, II, p. 749.

57. McClellan to Scott, July 21, 1861, *Ibid.*, p. 752.

58. Adams, *Fighting for Defeat*, pp. 88–89.

59. Adjutant General Lorenzo Thomas to McClellan, July 22, 1861, OR, Ser. 1, II, p. 753; McClellan to Thomas, July 22, 1861, *Papers of McClellan*, p. 66; Scott to McClellan, July 22, 1861, OR, Ser. 1, II, p. 755.

60. McClellan to Brigadier General Jacob D. Cox, July 22, 1861, *Papers of McClellan*, p. 67.

61. Waugh, *Class of 1846*, p. 265.

Chapter 3

1. McClellan to Mary Ellen McClellan, July 27, 1861, *Papers of McClellan*, p. 70.

2. Johnson, "McClellan and Mentor," pp. 93–94.

3. McClellan to Mary Ellen McClellan, July 30, 1861, *Papers of McClellan*, p. 71.

4. McClellan to E. J. Allen (Allan Pinkerton), July 30, 1861, *Ibid.*, p. 70.

5. Fishel, Edwin C., "Pinkerton and McClellan: Who Deceived Whom?," *Civil War History*, XXXIV, No. 2 (June 1988), pp. 115–142 [hereafter Fishel, "Pinkerton"] at p. 141. Among the many historians who blamed Pinkerton for misleading McClellan were H.J. Eckenrode and Bryan Conrad, idolizers of McClellan. Eckenrode, H.J. and Conrad, Bryan, *George B. McClellan: The Man Who Saved the Union* (Chapel Hill: University of North Carolina Press, 1941), pp. 74, 80. For an interesting discussion of this issue, see the chapter entitled "Too Many Bayonets" in Horan, James D., *The Pinkertons: The Detective Dynasty That Made History* (New York: Crown Publishers, Inc., 1967), pp. 115–22. Horan blamed both Pinkerton and McClellan for the gross overestimation of Rebel strength.

6. McClellan to Abraham Lincoln, Aug. 2, 1861, OR, Ser. I, V, pp. 6–8.

7. Rafuse, Ethan S., "McClellan, von Clausewitz, and the Politics of War, *Columbiad: A Quarterly Review of the War Between the States*, Vol. I, No. 3 (Fall 1997), pp. 23–37 [hereafter Rafuse, "McClellan"].

8. In fact, Secretary of the Navy Welles complained that McClellan "appeared indifferent and had little confidence in our success" in the New Orleans Expedition. Welles, *Diary*, I, p. 61.

9. McClellan to Mary Ellen McClellan, Aug. 2, 1861, *Papers of McClellan*, pp. 75–76.

10. McClellan to Mary Ellen McClellan, Aug. 4, 1861, *Ibid.*, pp. 78–79.

11. McClellan's Instructions to General Officers, Division of the Potomac, c. Aug. 4, 1861, *Ibid.*, pp. 76–78.

12. Nosworthy, *Bloody Crucible*, p. 207.

13. Catton, Bruce, *Grant Takes Command* (New York: Book-of-the-Month Club, 1994) (originally Little, Brown & Co., Inc., 1968, 1969), pp. 159–60.

14. Sherman, William Tecumseh, *Memoirs of General W.T. Sherman* (2 vols.) (New York: D. Appleton and Company, 1889), I, p. 219.

15. McClellan to Major General Nathaniel P. Banks and others, Aug. 4 and 6, 1861, Sears, *Papers of McClellan*, p. 79 and note.

16. McClellan to Scott, Aug. 8, 1861, OR, Ser. I, XI, Part III, pp. 3–4.

17. Catton, Bruce, *The Army of the Potomac: Mr. Lincoln's Army* (Garden City, New York: Doubleday & Company, Inc., 1951, 1962) [hereafter, Catton, *Mr. Lincoln's Army*], pp. 66–67. Another author states that in mid–August, McClellan thought that Beauregard had 150,000 troops while in reality he had no more than 45,000. Peskin, Allan, *Winfield Scott and the Profession of Arms* (Kent and London: Kent State University Press, 2003), pp. 259–60.

18. Fishel, "Pinkerton," pp. 116–17.

19. Catton, *Mr. Lincoln's Army*, pp. 66–67.

20. Fishel, "Pinkerton," p. 117; Sears, Stephen, "Lincoln and McClellan," [hereafter Sears, "Lincoln and McClellan"] in Boritt, Gabor S. (ed.), *Lincoln's Generals* (New York and Oxford: Oxford University Press, 1994) [hereafter Boritt, *Lincoln's Generals*], pp. 1–50 at pp. 15–17.

21. McClellan to Mary Ellen McClellan, Aug. 9, 1861, *Papers of McClellan*, p. 81.

22. McClellan to Mary Ellen McClellan, Aug. 9, 1861, *Ibid.*, pp. 81–2. McClellan's 1864 presidential candidacy is beyond the scope of this book. See Appendix III, "The Critical Election of 1864: How Close Was It?," in Bonekemper, Edward H., III, *A Victor, Not a Butcher: Ulysses S. Grant's Overlooked Military Genius* (Washington: Regnery Publishing, Inc., 2004), pp. 325–332.

23. Scott to Secretary of War Simon Cameron, Aug. 9, 1861, OR, Ser. I, XI, Part III, p. 4.

24. McClellan to Lincoln, Aug. 10, 1861, OR, Ser. I, XI, Part III, pp. 4–5; Sears, *Papers of McClellan*, p. 83n. Only a month later the same General McClellan who had gone outside the chain of command to write to the president would comment unfavorably to one his generals who had the temerity to write directly to the secretary of state and advise him to "fully communicate your wants direct to me through the proper military channel." McClellan to Nathaniel P. Banks, Sept. 16, 1861, *Papers of McClellan*, pp. 101–2.

25. McClellan to Gideon Welles, Aug. 12, 1861, OR, Ser. I, V, p. 47.

26. McClellan to Mary Ellen McClellan, Aug. 14–15, 1861, *Papers of McClellan*, pp. 84–5.

27. McClellan to Mary Ellen McClellan, Aug. 16, 1861, *Ibid.*, pp. 85–6.

28. McClellan to Brigadier General Charles P. Stone, Aug. 18, 1861, OR, Ser. I, V, pp. 567–8.

29. McClellan to Mary Ellen McClellan, Aug. 19, 1861, *Papers of McClellan*, p. 87.

30. Waugh, *Class of 1846*, pp. 344–47; Sears, Stephen W., *Landscape Turned Red: The Battle of Antietam* (New York: Book-of-the-Month Club, Inc., 1994) [hereafter Sears, *Landscape*], pp. 24–25 at p. 25.

31. Headquarters Army of the Potomac, General Orders No. 1, August 20, 1861, OR, Ser. I, V, p. 575.

32. McClellan to Lincoln, Aug. 20, 1861, Sears, *Papers of McClellan*, p. 88 and note.

33. McClellan to Cameron, Sept. 6, 1861, OR, Ser. I, V, pp. 586–87.

34. McClellan to Mary Ellen McClellan, Sept. 7, 1861, *Papers of McClellan*, p. 95.

35. Simon Cameron to McClellan, Sept. 7, 1861, Sears, *Ibid.*, p. 97 note.

36. McClellan to Cameron, Sept. 8, 1861, OR, Ser. I, V, pp. 587–89 at pp. 588–89..

37. Sears, *Papers of McClellan*, pp. 97–8 note.

38. McClellan to Cameron, Sept. 8, 1861, OR, Ser. I, V, pp. 587–89 at p. 589.

39. McClellan to Nathaniel P. Banks, Sept. 12, 1861, Sears, *Papers of McClellan*, p. 99 and note; McClellan to Samuel S. Cox, Feb. 12, 1864, *Ibid.*, p. 565.

40. McClellan to Mary Ellen McClellan, Sept. 18, 1861, *Ibid.*, p. 102.

41. McClellan to Cameron, Sept. 13, 1861, *Ibid.*, p. 100.

42. *Ibid.*

43. Wert, Jeffrey D., *The Sword of Lincoln: The Army of the Potomac* (New York: Simon & Schuster, 2005) [hereafter Wert, *Sword*], p. 43.

44. McClellan to Mary Ellen McClellan, Sept. 27, 1861, *Papers of McClellan*, pp. 103–4.

45. Welles, Gideon, *Diary of Gideon Welles* (Boston and New York: Houghton Mifflin Company, 1911), 3 vols. [hereafter Welles, *Diary*], I, pp. 241–2.

46. McClellan to Mary Ellen McClellan, Oct. 2, 1861, *Papers of McClellan*, p. 105.

47. McClellan to Mary Ellen McClellan, Oct. 6, 1861, *Ibid.*, pp. 105–6.

48. McClellan to Mary Ellen McClellan, Oct. 11, 1861, *Ibid.*, pp. 106–7.

49. McClellan to Mary Ellen McClellan, Oct. 13, 1861, *Ibid.*, p. 107.

50. McClellan to Mary Ellen McClellan, Oct. 19, 1861, *Ibid.*, p. 109.

51. McClellan to Cameron, Sept. 30, 1861, *Ibid.*, pp. 104–5.

52. McClellan to Brigadier General Charles P. Stone [two telegrams], Oct. 21, 1861, OR, Ser. I, LI, Part I, pp. 499 and 500; OR, Ser. I, V, p. 32; Testimony of Edward P. Stone, *Report of the Joint Committee on the Conduct of the War*, Part II (1863), pp. 488–89.

53. McClellan to Stone, Oct. 21, 1861 [10 P.M.], OR, Ser. I, LI, Part I, p. 500; McClellan to Stone, Oct. 21, 1861 [after 11 P.M.], *ibid.*; McClellan to Major General Nathaniel P. Banks, Oct. 21, 1861 [10:45 P.M.], *Papers of McClellan*, p. 110.

54. Hattaway, Herman, and Jones, Archer, *How the North Won: A Military History of the Civil War* (Urbana and Chicago: University of Illinois Press, 1991) (Reprint of 1983 edition) [hereafter Hattaway and Jones, *How the North Won*], pp. 81–82. For details of the Battle of Ball's Bluff, see Morgan, James A., III, "Ball's Bluff: 'A Very Nice Little Military Chance," *America's Civil War*, Vol. 18, No. 5 (Nov. 2005), pp. 30–38, 56.

55. McClellan to Army of the Potomac Division Commanders, Oct. 24, 1861, OR, Ser. I, V, p. 626.

56. McClellan to Mary Ellen McClellan, Oct. 25, 1861, *Papers of McClellan*, p. 111.

57. McClellan to Brigadier General Andrew Porter, Provost Marshall, Feb. 8, 1862; McClellan to Commanding Officer, Fort Lafayette, Feb. 8, 1862, OR, Ser. I, V, pp. 341–42; Sears, *Papers of McClellan*, p. 173 and note; Weigley, Russell F., *A Great Civil War: A Military and Political History, 1861–1865* (Bloomington and Indianapolis: Indiana University Press, 2000) [hereafter Weigley, *Great Civil War*], pp. 82–85. Michael Adams commented that "this Union defeat reflected no credit on McClellan, whose vague orders were partly responsible for the debacle and who was quick to shift the whole blame onto the luckless commander of the expedition, Brigadier General Charles P. Stone." Adams, *Fighting for Defeat*, p. 89. Actually, McClellan blamed both Stone and Baker for the disaster.

58. McClellan to Brigadier General Charles P. Stone, Dec. 5, 1862, OR, Ser. I, V, p. 345; Sears, *McClellan*, pp. 144–46. At the beginning of the Antietam Campaign, McClellan (possibly with a guilty conscience) did recommend to Stanton that Stone, who had been released from prison on August 16, 1862, be allowed to serve with his army. McClellan to Stanton, Sept. 7, 1862, OR, Ser. I, V, p. 342.

59. McClellan to Mary Ellen McClellan, Oct. 26, 1861, *Papers of McClellan*, p. 112.

60. McClellan to Mary Ellen McClellan, Oct. 30, 1861, *Ibid.*, pp. 112–3.

61. Johnson, "McClellan and Mentor," p. 94.

62. McClellan to Mary Ellen McClellan, Oct. 31, 1861, *Papers of McClellan*, pp. 113–4.

63. McClellan to Cameron, Oct. 31, 1861, Sears, OR, Ser. I, V, pp. 9–11; *Papers of McClellan*, pp. 114–9 and notes.

64. Fishel, "Pinkerton," pp. 119–20, citing Pinkerton to McClellan, Nov. 15, 1861.

65. *Ibid.*, pp. 118–23.

66. In a paper prepared for use—but not used—in his report on the Army of the Potomac under his command, McClellan attempted to justify his inflation of Pinkerton's already inflated numbers: "The certainty that the enemy had ... at ascertained places, other troops than those known in detail, in considerable numbers necessarily caused in my estimates additions to be made for the sake of safety, to the known quantities: which may have created the impression that the force of the enemy in front of Washington was exaggerated." *Ibid.*, p. 120.

67. McClellan to Cameron, Oct. 31, 1861, Sears, OR, Ser. I, V, pp. 9–11; *Papers of McClellan*, pp. 114–9 and notes.

Chapter 4

1. McClellan to Mary Ellen McClellan, Oct. 31/Nov. 1, 1861, *Papers of McClellan*, pp. 113–4.

2. Army of the United States General Orders No. 19, Nov. 1, 1861, OR, Ser. III, I, pp. 613–14.

3. McClellan to Mary Ellen McClellan, Nov. 7, 1861, *Papers of McClellan*, p. 126.

4. McClellan to Mary Ellen McClellan, Nov. 2, 1861, *Papers of McClellan*, pp. 123–4.

5. Sears, *McClellan*, p. 125, citing Hay, John, *Letters and Diaries*, pp. 32–33.

6. McClellan to Brigadier General Don Carlos Buell, Nov. 7, 1861, OR, Ser. I, IV, p. 342. Although this letter may not have been issued or reached Buell, it may have been the basis for discussions between the two generals. Sears, *Papers of McClellan*, p. 126 note. There is no reason to doubt that it reflects the views of McClellan at that time.

7. McClellan to Samuel L.M. Barlow, Nov. 8, 1861, *Papers of McClellan*, pp. 127–8.

8. McClellan to Samuel L.M. Barlow, Nov. 8, 1861, *Papers of McClellan*, pp. 127–8.

9. McClellan to Cameron, Nov. 15, 1861, *Papers of McClellan*, pp. 133–4 at p. 134.

10. McPherson, James M., *Crossroads of Freedom: Antietam, the Battle That Changed the Course of the Civil War* (Oxford: Oxford University Press, 2002) [hereafter McPherson, *Crossroads*], p. 14.

11. McClellan to Major General Henry W. Halleck, Nov. 11, 1861, OR, Ser. I, III, pp. 568–69 at p. 568.

12. McClellan to Buell, Nov. 12, 1861, OR, Ser. I, IV, pp. 355–56 at p. 355..

13. McClellan to Mary Ellen McClellan, Nov. 8, 1861, *Papers of McClellan*, pp. 132–3 at p. 132.

14. McPherson, *Crossroads*, p. 14.

15. *Ibid.*, citing Montgomery Blair to Francis P. Blair, Oct. 1, 1861.

16. McClellan to Mary Ellen McClellan, Nov. 17, 1861, *Papers of McClellan*, pp. 135–6.

17. McClellan, George B., *McClellan's Own Story: The War for the Union, The Soldiers Who Fought It, The Civilians Who Directed It, and His Relations to It and to Them* (New York: Charles L. Webster & Company, 1887) (Scituate, Mass.: Digital Scanning, Inc., 1998) [hereafter *McClellan's Own Story*], p. 152.

18. Nicolay and Hay, *Abraham Lincoln*, IV, p. 469n. Nicolay and Hay's work must be used with caution concerning McClellan because of Hay's August 10, 1885 letter to Nicolay in which Hay said, "I think I have left the impression of [McClellan's] mutinous imbecility, and I have done it in a perfectly courteous manner.... It is of the utmost moment that we should *seem* fair to him, while we are destroying him." Thayer, W. R., *Life and Letters of John Hay* (Boston: Houghton Mifflin Company, 1914), Vol. II, p. 31.

19. Hay, *Lincoln and the Civil War*, pp. 34–35.

20. McClellan to Buell, Dec. 2, 3 and 5, 1861, OR, Ser. I, VII, pp. 457–58 (misdated); *Ibid.*, p. 468; *Ibid.*, pp. 473–74; Sears, *Papers of McClellan*, pp. 138–41 and notes.

21. 174. Sears, *McClellan*, p. 134; Waugh, *Class of 1846*, p. 350.

22. Pois, Robert and Langer, Philip, *Command Failure in War: Psychology and Leadership* (Bloomington: Indiana University Press, 2004) [hereafter Pois and Langer, *Command Failure*], p. 50.

23. U.S. House of Representatives, 37th Congress, 3rd session, *Report of the Joint Committee on the Conduct of the War* (3 vols.) (Washington, D.C.: Government Printing Office, 1863) [hereafter *Joint Committee Report*], Part I, p. 7.

24. Lincoln to McClellan, c. Dec. 1, 1861, Basler, *Works of Lincoln*, V, pp. 34–5; McClellan to Lincoln, Dec. 10, 1861, OR, Ser. I, XI, Part 3, p. 6.

25. McClellan to Halleck, Dec. 10, 1861, OR, Ser. I, VIII, p. 419.

26. Welles, *Diary*, I, September 1, 1862, pp. 102–103.

27. *Ibid.*, September 1, 1862, p. 103.

28. *Joint Committee Report*, Part I, pp. 7–8; testimony of Captain Gustavus V. Fox, Assistant Secretary of the Navy, Feb. 10, 1862, *Ibid.*, pp. 239–42.

29. McClellan to Halleck, Jan. 3, 1862, OR, Ser. I, VII, pp. 527–28.

30. McClellan to Buell, Jan. 6, 1862, *Ibid.*, p. 531.

31. McClellan to Buell, Jan. 13, 1862, *Ibid..*, p. 547.

32. McClellan to Ambrose E. Burnside, Jan. 7, 1862, OR, Ser. I, IX, pp. 352–53.

33. McClellan to Major General Nathaniel P. Banks, Jan. 7, 1862, Sears, *Papers of McClellan*, p. 150 and note; Warner, *Generals in Blue*, p. 274.

34. Rafuse, Ethan S., "Lincoln Takes Charge," *Civil War Times Illustrated*, XXXIX, No. 7 (Feb. 2001), pp. 26–32, 62–63 [hereafter Rafuse, "Lincoln"] at pp. 27–28.

35. Rafuse, "Lincoln," pp. 28–29.

36. *Ibid.*, "Lincoln," pp. 29–31.

37. *Ibid.*, "Lincoln," pp. 31–32.

38. *Ibid.*, "Lincoln," p. 32.

39. *Ibid.*, "Lincoln," pp. 32, 62.

40. *Ibid.*, "Lincoln," p. 62; Waugh, *Class of 1846*, p. 352.

41. Sears, *McClellan*, pp. 142–43.

42. Rafuse, "Lincoln," pp. 62–63; Sears, *Papers of McClellan*, p. 153 note.

43. McClellan to Lincoln, Jan. 15, 1862, *Ibid.*, p. 154 and note.

44. Welles, *Diary*, I, pp. 60–61.

45. Bonekemper, *A Victor, Not a Butcher*, p. 26.

46. McClellan to Stanton, Jan. 26, 1862, Sears, *Papers of McClellan*, p. 158; McClellan to Halleck, Jan. 29, 1862, OR, Ser. I, VII, pp. 930–31; Sears, *Papers of McClellan*, p. 159 and note; McClellan to Halleck and Buell, Jan. 29, 1862, OR, Ser. I, VII, p. 571.

47. Sears, "Lincoln and McClellan," pp. 26–28; McClellan to Stanton, Feb. 3, 1862, OR, Ser. I, V, pp. 42–45; Sears, *Papers of McClellan*, pp. 162–70 and notes.

48. OR, Ser. I, V, p. 44.

49. *Ibid.*, p. 45. The last sentence did not appear in the OR version, but Sears stated that it was in the original and deleted in a later copying process. Sears, *Papers of McClellan*, pp. 170–71n.

50. McClellan to Halleck, Feb. 6, 1862, OR, Ser. I, VII, p. 937; McClellan to Buell, Feb. 6, 1862, *ibid.*, p. 587; Buell to McClellan, Feb. 6, 1862, *ibid.*, pp. 587–88.

51. Halleck to McClellan, Feb. 7, 1862, *Ibid.*, p. 590; Halleck to McClellan, Feb. 7, 1862, *ibid.*, pp. 590–91; McClellan to Halleck, *ibid.*, p. 591.

52. McClellan to Burnside, Feb. 12, 1862, OR, Ser. I, IX, pp. 362–63 at p. 363.

53. McClellan to Brigadier General Thomas W. Sherman, Feb. 14, 1862, OR, Ser. I, VI, p. 225.

54. Halleck to McClellan, Feb. 8, 1862, OR, Ser. I, VII, p. 595; McClellan to Halleck, Feb. 14, 1862, *Ibid.*, p. 614.

55. McClellan to Brigadier General Ulysses S. Grant, Feb. 15, 1862, OR, Ser. I, LII, Part 1, p. 212; Sears, *Papers of McClellan*, p. 181 and note.

56. Halleck to McClellan, Feb. 15, 1862, OR, Ser. I, VII, p. 617.

57. McClellan to Halleck, Feb. 15, 1862, *Ibid.*, pp. 617–18 at p. 617; McClellan to Buell, Feb. 15 or 16, 1862, *Ibid.*, p. 626.

58. McClellan to Stanton, Feb. 15, 1862, *Papers of McClellan*, p. 182.

59. Assistant Secretary of War Thomas A. Scott to McClellan, Feb. 19, 1862, OR, Ser. I, VII, p. 635; Halleck to McClellan, Feb. 19, 1862, *Ibid.*, pp. 636–7.

60. Halleck to McClellan, Feb. 20, 1862, *Ibid.*, p. 641; McClellan to Halleck, Feb. 21, 1862, *Ibid.*, p. 645.

61. Draft and unissued General Order from McClellan to the Army of the Potomac, Feb. 17, 1862, Sears, *Papers of McClellan*, pp. 183–4 and note.

62. McClellan to Thomas A. Scott, Feb. 20, 1862, OR, Ser. I, VII, p. 641.

63. McClellan to Lincoln, Feb. 22, 1862, *Papers of McClellan*, p. 187.

64. McClellan to Buell, Feb. 20, 1862, OR, Ser. I, VII, p. 640.

65. McClellan to Stanton, Jan. 25, 1862, OR, Ser. I, VI, pp. 677–78 at p. 678; McClellan to Major General Benjamin F. Butler, Feb. 23, 1862, *Ibid.*, pp. 694–95.

66. McClellan to Halleck, Feb. 24, 1862, *Papers of McClellan*, p. 190.

67. McClellan to Stanton, Feb. 26, 1862, OR, Ser. I, V, p. 727.

68. McClellan to Mary Ellen McClellan, Feb. 27, 1862, *Papers of McClellan*, pp. 191–2.

69. McClellan to Stanton, Feb. 27, 1862, OR, Ser. I, V, p. 728.

70. McClellan to Lincoln, Feb. 28, 1862, *Ibid.*, p. 730.

71. McClellan to the War Department, March 1, 1862, *Ibid.*, pp. 48–49.

72. Jones, *Right Hand*, p. 22.

73. McClellan to Brigadier General Randolph B. Marcy, Feb. 27, 1862, OR, Ser. I, V, p. 728.

74. McClellan Memorandum on Potomac Batteries, March 1, 1862, Sears, *Papers of McClellan*, p. 195 and note.

75. McClellan to Halleck, March 3, 1862, OR, Ser. I, XI, Part 3, pp. 7–8 at p. 7.

76. Halleck to McClellan, March 2, 1862, OR, Ser. I, VII, pp. 679–80.

77. McClellan to Halleck, March 3, 1862, *Ibid.*, p. 680.

78. Marszalek, John F., "Henry W. Halleck: The Early Seeds of Failure," *North & South*, Vol. 8, No. 1 (Jan. 2005), pp. 78–86 [hereafter Marszalek, "Halleck"] at pp. 82–83.

79. Sears, *McClellan*, p. 154.

80. Goss, *High Command*, p. 112.

81. McClellan to Lincoln and Stanton, March 9, 1862, *Papers of McClellan*, p. 200.

82. Pois and Langer, *Command Failure*, p. 56.

83. Fishel, "Pinkerton," pp. 115–24.

84. Fishel, Edwin C., *The Secret War for the Union: The Untold Story of Military Intelligence in the Civil War* (Boston and New York: Houghton Mifflin, 1996), pp. 127–29; Fishel, "Pinkerton," pp. 124–26. To justify his abandoning unit counts as the basis for his new estimate, Pinkerton wrote this confusing and circular justification in his report: "It may ... safely be assumed that in so large an army as our information shows them to possess very much of its composition and very many of its forces have not been specifically ascertained, which, added to those already known, would largely increase their numbers and considerably swell its proportions."

85. McClellan to Major General John A. Dix, March 9, 1862, OR, Ser. I, LI, Part I, p. 549; McClellan to Major General John E. Wool, March 9, 1862, OR, Ser. I, IX, p. 23; McClellan to Stanton, March 9, 1862, *Papers of McClellan*, p. 199.

86. McClellan to Wool, March 9, 1862, OR, Ser. I, IX, p. 23.

87. McClellan to Stanton, March 9, 1862, *Papers of Mc-Clellan*, p. 199.
88. McClellan to Stanton and Stanton to McClellan, March 9, 1862, OR, Ser. I, V, pp. 18, 739.
89. McClellan to Stanton, March 10, 1862, *Ibid.*, pp. 740–41.
90. Stanton to McClellan, *Ibid.*, p. 741.
91. Sears, *To the Gates* , p. 17.
92. McClellan to Stanton, March 11, 1862, OR, Ser. I, V, p. 742.
93. *Ibid.*
94. McClellan to Marcy, March 11, 1862, OR, Ser. I, LI, Part I, p. 550, *Papers of McClellan*, pp. 201–2.
95. Marcy to McClellan, March 11, 1862, Sears, *Papers of McClellan*, p. 202 note.
96. McClellan to Mary Ellen McClellan, March 11, 1862, *Ibid.*, pp. 202–3.
97. Marcy to McClellan, March 12, 1862, Sears, *Ibid.*, p. 206 note.
98. McClellan to Lincoln, March 12, 1862, *Ibid.*, p. 207.
99. Sears, *Ibid.*, p. 69.

Chapter 5

1. Johnson, "McClellan and Mentor," pp. 94–5.
2. McClellan to Gustavus V. Fox, March 12, 1862, OR, Ser. I, IX, p. 27; Fox to McClellan, March 13, 1862, *Ibid.*
3. McClellan to Fox, March 12, 1862, Sears, *Papers of McClellan*, p. 206.; Wool to Stanton, March 13, 1862, OR, Ser. I, IX, p. 30.
4. Stanton to McClellan, March 13, 1862, OR, Ser. I, V, 55–56, 750; McClellan to Stanton, March 13, 1862, *Papers of McClellan*, p. 207; Stanton to McClellan, March 13, 1862, OR, Ser. I, V, p. 56.
5. McClellan to Lorenzo Thomas, March 13, 1862, OR, Ser. I, V, p. 751.
6. McClellan to Stanton, March 13, 1862, *Ibid.*
7. McClellan to Gustavus Fox, March 14, 1862, *Papers of McClellan*, p. 209.
8. McClellan to Stanton, March 14, 1862, *Ibid.*, pp. 209–10.
9. McClellan to Banks, March 16, 1862, OR, Ser. I, V, p. 56.
10. McClellan to Stanton, March 14, 1862, and McClellan to Barlow, March 16, 1862, *Papers of McClellan*, pp. 209–10, 213.
11. McClellan to Soldiers of the Army of the Potomac, March 14, 1862, *Ibid.*, p. 211 (emphasis added).
12. McClellan to Barlow, March 16, 1862, *Ibid.*, p. 213.
13. McClellan to Edmund C. Stedman, March 17, 1862, *Ibid.*, p. 214.
14. McClellan to Stanton, March 18, 1862, *Ibid.*, pp. 15–16.
15. McClellan to Stanton, March 19, 1862, OR, Ser I, V, pp. 57–58 at p. 58.
16. *Ibid.*
17. McClellan to Marcy, March 22, 1862, Sears, *Papers of McClellan*, pp. 216–7 and note.
18. McClellan to Banks, March 24, 1862, OR, Ser. I, XII, Part III, p. 16; Banks to McClellan, March 24, 1862, *Ibid.*
19. McClellan to Brigadier General (brevet) Joseph G. Totten, March 28, 1862, *Papers of McClellan*, p. 218.
20. McClellan to Brigadier General Samuel P. Heintzelman, March 28, 1862, OR, Ser. I, XI, Part III, p. 43, responding to Heintzelman to McClellan, March 27, 1862, *Ibid.*, p. 42.
21. Lincoln to McClellan, *Works of Lincoln*, V, pp. 175–76.
22. McClellan to Lincoln, March 31, 1862, *Papers of McClellan*, pp. 219–20.

23. O'Neill, Robert F., "Cavalry on the Peninsula: Fort Monroe to the Gates of Richmond, March to May, 1862, " *Blue & Gray Magazine*, XIX, Issue 5 (Campaign 2002), pp. 6–24, 38–51 [hereafter O'Neill, "Cavalry on Peninsula"] at p. 12.
24. McClellan to Banks, April 1, 1862, Or, Ser. I, XI, pp. 59–60.
25. McClellan to Thomas, April 1, 1862, OR, Ser. I, V, pp. 60–61.
26. Catton, *Mr. Lincoln's Army*, p. 106.
27. Thomas and Hitchcock to Stanton, April 2, 1862, *Joint Committee Report*, Part I, pp. 15–17.
28. Tanner, Robert G., *Stonewall in the Valley: Thomas J. "Stonewall" Jackson's Shenandoah Valley Campaign Spring 1862* (Mechanicsburg, Pennsylvania: Stackpole Books, 1996), p. 139.
29. McClellan to Mary Ellen McClellan, April 1, 1862, *Papers of McClellan*, p. 223.
30. McClellan to Mary Ellen McClellan, April 2, 1862, *Papers of McClellan*, p. 225.
31. McClellan to Mary Ellen McClellan, April 3, 1862, *Papers of McClellan*, p. 225.
32. McClellan to Flag Officer Louis M. Goldsborough, April 3, 1862, *Official Records of the Union and Confederate Navies in the War of the Rebellion* (Harrisburg: The National Historical Society, 1987) (reprint of Washington, D.C.: Government Printing Office, 1921) (31 vols.) [hereafter NOR], Ser. I, VII, pp. 195–96.
33. This lack of naval support is well described in Reed, Rowena, *Combined Operations in the Civil War* (Lincoln and London: University of Nebraska Press, 1978, 1993) [hereafter Reed, *Combined Operations*], pp. 125–55.
34. McClellan to Stanton, April 3, 1862, OR, Ser. I, XI, Part III, p. 64.
35. McClellan to McDowell, April 4, 1862, OR, Ser. I, XI, Part III, p. 68.
36. Foote, *Civil War*, I, p 405.
37. Thomas to McClellan, April 4, 1862, OR, Ser. 1, XI, Part I, p. 10, Part III, p. 66.
38. Foote, *Civil War*, I, p. 408.
39. Sears, *Papers of McClellan*, p. 205.
40. Miller, William J., "No American Sevastopol," *America's Civil War*, Vol. 13, No. 2 (May 2000), pp. 30–36, 74 [hereafter Miller, "No American Sevastopol"] at pp. 33–34.
41. McClellan to Flag Officer Louis M. Goldsborough, April 5, 1862, 10:30 P.M., NOR, Ser. 1, VII, pp. 205–206.
42. Waugh, *Class of 1846*, p. 358; Sears, *To the Gates*, p. 45; Johnson, Clint, *Civil War Blunders* (Winston-Salem: John F. Blair, 1997) p. 92.
43. McClellan to Lincoln, April 5, 1862, OR, Ser. I, XI, Part III, p. 71. McClellan wrote the bracketed words, but they were omitted in the copy delivered to Lincoln. Sears, *Papers of McClellan*, p. 229n..
44. McClellan to Goldsborough, April 5, 1862, NOR, Ser. I, VII, pp. 205–02; Goldsborough to McClellan, April 6, 1862, OR, Ser. I, XI, Part III, p. 80.
45. McClellan to Mary Ellen McClellan, April 6, 1862, *Papers of McClellan*, p. 230.
46. Pois and Langer, *Command Failure*, p. 59; Sears, *McClellan*, p. 175.
47. Adams, *Fighting for Defeat*, p. 90.
48. Nicolay and Hay, *Abraham Lincoln*, V, p. 366.
49. McClellan to Lincoln, April 6, 1862, OR, Ser. I, XI, Part III, pp. 73–74; Lorenzo Thomas to McClellan, April 4, 1862, OR, Ser. I, XI, Part III, pp. 67–8; Lincoln to McClellan, April 6, 1862, *Works of Lincoln*, V, p. 182.
50. McClellan to Brigadier General William B. Franklin, April 6, 1862, Sears, *Papers of McClellan*, p. 231; Franklin to McClellan, April 7, 1862, *Ibid.*, p. 231n.
51. Stanton to McClellan, April 6, 1862, OR, Ser. I, XI, Part III, p. 73.
52. McClellan to Stanton, April 7, 1862, OR, Ser. I, XI, Part I, pp. 11–12 at p. 12.

53. *Ibid.* at pp. 11–12.

54. O'Neill, "Cavalry on Peninsula," p. 15.

55. Lincoln to McClellan, April 6, 1862, *Works of Lincoln*, V, p. 182.

56. McClellan to Lincoln, April 7, 1862, OR, Ser. I, XI, Part I, p. 11.

57. Lincoln to McClellan, April 9, 1862, *Works of Lincoln*, V, pp. 184–5 at p. 184.

58. *Ibid.*, pp. 184–5. On the same day that Lincoln wrote to McClellan, conservative ex–Democrat Montgomery Blair, Lincoln's postmaster general, provided a similar warning to McClellan: "I hope for your sake & that of the country that you now feel that it is both necessary & proper to fight at once." Montgomery Blair to McClellan, April 9, 1862, Sears, *Papers of McClellan*, p. 238 note.

59. McClellan to Mary Ellen McClellan, April 8, 1862, *Papers of McClellan*, p. 234.

60. McClellan to Stanton, April 11, 1862, OR, Ser. I, XI, Part III, p. 86.

61. McClellan to Mary Ellen McClellan, April 11, 1862, *Papers of McClellan*, p. 235.

62. McClellan to Scott, April 11, 1862, *Ibid.*, pp. 236–7.

63. Stanton to McClellan, April 11, 1862, OR, Ser. I, XI, Part III, p. 90.

64. McClellan to Lincoln, April 14, 1862, OR, Ser. I, XI, Part III, p. 98; Statement of Major General Irvin McDowell, Feb. 9, 1863, OR, Ser. 1, XII, Part I, pp. 275–322 at p. 277.

65. McClellan to Mary Ellen McClellan, April 14, 1862, Sears, *Papers of McClellan*, p. 239 and note.

66. Reed, *Combined Operations*, p. 147.

67. McClellan to Mary Ellen McClellan, April 18, 1862, *Papers of McClellan*, pp. 240–1.

68. Perret, Geoffrey, *Lincoln's War: The Untold Story of America's Greatest President as Commander in Chief* (New York: Random House, 2004) [hereafter Perret, *Lincoln's War*], p. 172; Miller, "No American Sevastopol," pp. 34–35; Report of Brigadier General William F. Smith to Brigadier General R. B. Marcy, April 18, 1862, OR, Ser. I, XI, Part I, pp. 365–66 at p. 366.

69. Waugh, *Class of 1846*, p. 358; Sears, *Papers of McClellan*, pp. 204–5.

70. Miller, "No American Sevastopol," p. 30. At Sevastopol, tens of thousands of British, French, and Turkish troops had died in assaults on the strong Russian fortifications, but their siege guns had killed as many as 1,000 Russians a day. *Ibid.*

71. *Ibid.*, pp. 35–36.

72. McClellan to Lincoln, April 18, 1862, OR, Ser. I, LI, Part I, p. 578.

73. McClellan to Mary Ellen McClellan, April 19, 1862, *Papers of McClellan*, pp. 243–4 (emphasis added).

74. Robertson, James I., Jr., *Stonewall Jackson: the Man, the Soldier, the Legend* (New York: Macmillan Publishing USA, 1997), p. 366.

75. McClellan to Lincoln, April 20, 1862, *Papers of McClellan*, pp. 244–5.

76. McClellan to Lincoln, April 23, 1862, *Ibid.*, pp. 246–7.

77. McClellan to Stanton, April 27, 1862, *Ibid.*, pp. 247–9.

78. McClellan to Mary Ellen McClellan, April 27, 1862, *Ibid.*, pp. 249–50

79. McClellan to Mary Ellen McClellan, April 30, 1862, *Ibid.*, pp. 250–1.

80. Lincoln to McClellan, May 1, 1862, *Works of Lincoln*, V, p. 203.

81. McClellan to Lincoln, May 1, 1862, *Papers of McClellan*, p. 251.

82. Sneden, Robert Knox, *Eye of the Storm: A Civil War Odyssey* (New York: The Free Press: 2000) [hereafter Sneden, *Eye of Storm*], May 2, 1862, pp. 56–57. Sneden, in addition to being a topographer, was a skilled artist, and this book is filled with beautiful color drawings as well as his diary/memoir.

83. McClellan to Goldsborough, May 2, 1862, OR, Ser. I, LI, Part I, p. 589.

84. McClellan to Mary Ellen McClellan, May 3, 1862, *Papers of McClellan*, p. 252.

85. McClellan to Stanton, May 4, 1862, 9 A.M., OR, Ser. I, Vol. XI, Part III, p. 133.

86. Sears, *To the Gates*, p. 62.

87. McClellan to Stanton, May 4, 1862, OR, Ser. I, Vol. XI, Part III, p. 134.

88. O'Neill, "Cavalry on Peninsula," p. 19, citing U.S. Congress, *Report of the Joint Committee on the Conduct of the War*, Part I (Washington D.C., 1863), p. 568.

89. McClellan to Stanton, May 5, 1862, OR, Ser. I, XI, Part III, pp. 134–35 at p. 135; Sneden, *Eye of Storm*, May 4, 1862, pp. 59–60; Wright, Mike, "The Infernal Machine: How a Confederate officer invented the land mine and changed the face of warfare," *Invention and Technology*, Summer 1999, pp. 44–50. The inventor of the land mine was Confederate Brigadier General Gabriel J. Rains, who had been angered by the Union shelling of his home town of New Bern, North Carolina. *Ibid.*

90. McClellan to Mary Ellen McClellan, May 4, 1862, *Papers of McClellan*, p. 255.

91. McClellan to Mary Ellen McClellan, May 8, 1862, *Ibid.*, p. 260.

92. Sneden, *Eye of Storm*, May 4, 1862, p. 58.

93. McClellan to Scott, May 4, 1862, *Papers of McClellan*, pp. 253–4.

94. Fishel, "Pinkerton," p. 127.

95. Pois and Langer, *Command Failure*, pp. 58–59.

96. Sears, *To the Gates*, pp. 67–68.

97. McClellan to Stanton, May 4, 1862, 9 A.M., OR, Ser. I, XI, Part III, p. 134.

98. McClellan to Stanton, May 4, 1862, 7 P.M., *Ibid.*, pp. 134–35.

99. Sears, *Papers of McClellan*, p. 205; Reed, *Combined Operations*, p. 158. Sears questioned why McClellan waited to be called to Williamsburg when he had been hearing sounds of the fighting throughout the entire day. Sears, *McClellan*, p. 183.

100. Foote, *Civil War*, I, p. 412.

101. *Report of the Joint Committee*, Part I, p. 429; McClellan, *McClellan's Own Story*, p. 324; O'Neill, "Cavalry on Peninsula," p. 39.

102. McClellan to Mary Ellen McClellan, May 6, 1862, *Papers of McClellan*, pp. 257–8.

103. Sears, *To the Gates*, p. 81, quoting Francis W. Palfrey.

104. Reed, *Combined Operations*, pp. 158–9; McClellan to Franklin, OR, Ser. I, XI, Part III, p. 143.

105. McClellan to Stanton, May 5, 1862, 10 P.M., OR, Ser. I, XI, Part I, pp. 448–49.

106. McClellan to Mary Ellen McClellan, May 6, 1862, *Papers of McClellan*, pp. 256–7.

107. Reed, *Combined Operations*, pp. 159–60.

108. Foote, *Civil War*, I, p. 414.

109. McClellan to Stanton, May 7, 1862, OR, Ser. I, XI, Part III, p. 146.

110. *Ibid.*

111. Lincoln to Goldsborough, May 7, 1862, *Works of Lincoln*, V, p. 207.

112. McClellan to Stanton, May 11, 1862, OR, Ser. I, XI, Part III, p. 164.

113. McClellan to Stanton, May 8, 1862, *Ibid.*, pp. 153–54.

114. McClellan to Stanton, May 8, 1862, 12:30 P.M., *Ibid.*, pp. 150–51.

115. Lincoln to McClellan, May 9, 1962, *Works of Lincoln*, V, pp. 207–8.

116. Lincoln to McClellan, May 9, 1862, *Ibid.*, V, pp. 208–9.

117. McClellan to Stanton, May 10, 1862, 5 A.M., OR, Ser. I, XI, Part I, p. 26.

118. McClellan to Stanton, May 10, 1862, 5 P.M., OR, Ser. I, XI, Part III, pp. 160–61.

119. Reed, *Combined Operations*, p. 161.

120. His May 9 House of Representatives Resolution thanked McClellan "for the display of those high military qualities which secure important results with but little sacrifice of human life." Sears, *Papers of McClellan*, p. 263 note.

121. McClellan to Mary Ellen McClellan, May 10–12, 1862, *Papers of McClellan*, pp. 262–3.

122. McClellan to Mary Ellen McClellan, May 15, 1862, *Papers of McClellan*, pp. 267–8 at p. 267.

123. Sears, *Papers of McClellan*, p. 205.

124. McClellan to Lincoln, May 14, 1862, OR, Ser. I, XI, Part I, pp. 26–27.

125. Lincoln to McClellan, May 15, 1862, *Works of Lincoln*, V, p. 216.

126. Sears, *To the Gates*, p. 99.

127. Lincoln to McDowell, May 16, 1862, *Works of Lincoln*, V, p. 218; McDowell to Lincoln, May 16, 1862, OR, Ser. I, XII, Part III, p. 195.

128. Lincoln to McDowell, May 16, 1862, *Works of Lincoln*, V, p. 218 and note; Stanton to McDowell, May 17, 1862, *Ibid.*, pp. 219–20 and note at p. 220; Lincoln to McDowell, May 17, 1862, *Ibid.*, p. 219; Stanton to McClellan, May 18, 1862, *Ibid.*, p. 220 note.

129. McClellan to Mary Ellen McClellan, May 18, 1862, *Papers of McClellan*, pp. 268–9 at p. 269.

130. McClellan to Lincoln, May 21, 1862, OR, Ser. I, XI, Part I, pp. 28–29 at p. 29.

131. Lincoln to McClellan, May 21, 1862, *Works of Lincoln*, V, p. 226. There is some dispute about the date of Lincoln's response. *Ibid.*, p. 226 note.

132. Nevins, *Ordeal of the Union*, VI, pp. 118–121.

133. Nevins, *Ibid.*, p. 121.

134. Pois and Langer, *Command Failure*, pp. 62–63.

135. Lincoln to Fremont, May 24, 1862, *Works of Lincoln*, p. 231; Lincoln to McDowell, May 24, 1862, *Ibid.*, pp. 232–3.

136. McClellan to Mary Ellen McClellan, May 22, 1862, *Papers of McClellan*, pp. 273–4.

137. Lincoln to McClellan, May 24, 1862, *Works of Lincoln*, p. 232.

138. McClellan to Lincoln, May 24, 1862, *Papers of McClellan*, p. 275.

139. Lincoln to McClellan, May 25, 1862, *Works of Lincoln*, V, pp. 235–6.

140. McClellan to Mary Ellen McClellan, May 25, 1862, *Papers of McClellan*, pp. 275–6 at p. 275.

141. McClellan to Lincoln, May 25, 1862, OR, Ser. I, XI, Part I, p. 32.

142. McClellan to Mary Ellen McClellan, May 25, 1862, *Papers of McClellan*, pp. 275–6 at p. 275.

143. Lincoln to McClellan, May 25, 1862, 8:30 P.M., *Works of Lincoln*, V, pp. 236–7.

144. McClellan to Mary Ellen McClellan, May 26, 1862, *Papers of McClellan*, pp. 277–8 at p. 278.

145. Lincoln to McClellan, May 26, 1862, *Works of Lincoln*, V, p. 239 (including the words, "Can you not cut the Acquia Creek Railroad also?"); McClellan to Mary Ellen McClellan, May 26, 1862, *Papers of McClellan*, pp. 277–8; McClellan to Stanton, May 28, 1862, OR, Ser. I, XI, Part I, p. 35. In his later general report, McClellan played down Lincoln's role, "It was thus imperative to dislodge or defeat this force [at Hanover Court House], independently even of the wishes of the President, as expressed in his telegram of the 26th."). *Ibid.*, p. 33.

146. Lincoln to McClellan, May 28, 1862, *Works of Lincoln*, V, p. 279.

147. McClellan to Stanton, May 30, 1862, OR, Ser. I, XI, Part III, p. 201.

148. McClellan to Stanton, May 27, 1862, *Ibid.*, p. 193.

149. Sears, *Papers of McClellan*, p. 205.

150. Piston, William Garrett, *Lee's Tarnished Lieuten-*

ant: James Longstreet and His Place in Southern History (Athens and London: The University of Georgia Press, 1987), p. 19.

151. Hubbell, John T., "The Seven Days of George Brinton McClellan," [hereafter, Hubbell, "Seven Days"] in Gallagher, Gary W. (ed.), *The Richmond Campaign of 1862: The Peninsula & the Seven Days* (Chapel Hill and London: The University of North Carolina Press, 2000) [hereafter Gallagher, *Richmond Campaign*], pp. 28–43 at p. 32.

152. Marcy to Sumner, May 31, 1862, OR, Ser. I, XI, Part III, p. 203; Nevins, *Ordeal of the Union*, VI, pp. 122–3.

153. McClellan to Samuel P. Heintzelman, May 31, 1862, OR, Ser. I, XI, Part III, p. 203.

154. McClellan to Marcy, May 31, 1862, *Papers of McClellan*, OR, Ser. I, LI, Part I, p. 647.

155. McClellan to Stanton, June 1, 1862, 12 midnight, OR, Ser. I, XI, Part I, p. 749.

156. Miller, William J., "The Disaster of Casey," *Columbiad: A Quarterly Review of the War Between the States*, Vol. 3, No. 4 (Winter 2000), pp. 21–44 [hereafter, Miller, "Disaster"], at pp. 21–9.

157. Miller, "Disaster," pp. 21, 29–41.

158. Nevins, *Ordeal of the Union*, VI, p. 123.

159. O'Neill, "Cavalry on Peninsula," pp. 49–50.

160. McClellan to Stanton, June 2, 1862, OR, Ser. I, XI, Part I, pp. 749–50.

Chapter 6

1. McClellan to Soldiers of the Army of the Potomac, June 2, 1862, OR, Ser. I, XI, Part III, p. 210.

2. McClellan to Mary Ellen McClellan, June 2, 1862, *Papers of McClellan*, p. 287.

3. McClellan to Mary Ellen McClellan, June 2, 1862, *Ibid.*, pp. 287–8 at p. 288.

4. McClellan to Lincoln, June 4, 1862, OR, Ser. I, XI, Part I, p. 45.

5. McClellan to Lincoln, June 5, 1862, *Ibid.*, p. 215.

6. Lincoln to McClellan. June 7, 1862, *Works of Lincoln*, V, p. 263 and note.

7. McClellan to Mary Ellen McClellan, June 6, 1862, *Papers of McClellan*, pp. 289–90 at p. 290.

8. Stanton to McClellan, OR, Ser. I, XI, Part III, p. 219.

9. McClellan to Stanton, June 7, 1862, OR, Ser. I, XI, Part I, p. 46.

10. McDowell to McClellan, June 8, 1862, OR, Ser. 1, XI, Part III, pp. 220–1.

11. McClellan to Mary Ellen McClellan, June 9, 1862, *Papers of McClellan*, p. 293.

12. Smith had been named the Confederate commander when Johnston was injured on May 31. Within hours he had a nervous breakdown and was superseded by Lee.

13. McClellan to Mary Ellen McClellan, June 10, 1862, *Papers of McClellan*, pp. 294–5 at p. 295.

14. McClellan to Stanton, June 10, 1862, OR, Ser. I, XI, Part I, pp. 46–47.

15. McClellan to Mary Ellen McClellan, June 11, 1862, *Papers of McClellan*, p. 296.

16. Stanton to McClellan, June 11, 1862, OR, Ser. I, XI, Part I, p. 47.

17. Mewborn, Horace, "A Wonderful Exploit: Jeb Stuart's Ride Around the Army of the Potomac, June 12–15, 1862," *Blue & Gray Magazine*, XV, Issue 6 (Aug. 1998), pp. 6–21, 46–54 [hereafter Mewborn, "Wonderful Exploit"]; Longacre, Edward G., "All the Way Around," *Civil War Times*, XLI, No. 3 (June 2002), pp. 22–29, 59; McClellan to Stanton, June 14, 1862, OR, Ser. I, XI, Part I, p. 1005.

18. Mewborn, "Wonderful Exploit," pp. 49–50. During the Peninsula Campaign, McClellan destroyed the potential effectiveness of his own cavalry by dispersing his troopers among his infantry commanders. Schiller, Laurence D., rebuttal to a letter to the editor, *North & South*, Vol. 2, No. 4 (April 1999), p. 67.

19. McClellan to Stanton, June 14, 1862, OR, Ser. I, XI, Part I, pp. 47–48.

20. McClellan to Stanton, June 15, 1862, OR, Ser. I, XI, Part III, pp. 229–30.

21. McClellan to Mary Ellen McClellan, June 15, 1862, *Papers of McClellan*, pp. 300–302 at p. 301.

22. McClellan to Lincoln, June 18, 1862, OR, Ser. I, XI, Part III, p. 233.

23. Lincoln to McClellan, June 15, 1862, *Works of Lincoln*, V, pp. 272–3.

24. McClellan to Lincoln, June 18, 1862, 10:30 A.M., *Ibid.*, p. 276 note.

25. Lincoln to McClellan, June 18, 1862, *Ibid.*, p. 276.

26. McClellan to Lincoln, June 18, 1862, OR, Ser. I, XI, Part III, p. 233.

27. Lincoln to McClellan, June 19, 1862, *Works of Lincoln*, V, p. 277.

28. Lincoln to McClellan, June 20, 1862, *Ibid.*, pp. 277–8.

29. McClellan to Burnside, June 20, 1862, OR, Ser. I, XI, Part III, p. 237.

30. McClellan to Lincoln, June 20, 1862, 2 P.M., OR, Ser. I, XI, Part I, p. 48.

31. Lincoln to McClellan, June 21, 1862, 6 P.M., *Works of Lincoln*, V, p. 279.

32. Nevins, *Ordeal of the Union*, VI, 131–3. Sears contended that on June 20 McClellan had 127,327 troops present for duty plus 7,000 more under Burnside available to him.

33. Memorandum of Winfield Scott, Lincoln Papers, *Works of Lincoln*, V, p. 284 note.

34. McClellan to Mary Ellen McClellan, June 22, 1862, *Papers of McClellan*, pp. 304–5 at p. 305.

35. McClellan to Stanton, June 24, 1862, OR, Ser. I, XI, Part I, p. 49.

36. Pois and Langer describe this message as McClellan "announcing his anticipated crucifixion." Pois and Langer, *Command Failure*, p. 65.

37. McClellan to Stanton, June 25, 1862, 6:15 P.M., OR, Ser. I, XI, Part I, p. 51.

38. Lincoln to McClellan, June 26, 1962, *Works of Lincoln*, V, p. 286.

39. For details of the Seven Days' Battle, see Freeman, Douglas Southall, *R.E. Lee* (4 vols.) (New York and London: Charles Scribner's Sons, 1934–5) [hereafter Freeman, *Lee*], II, pp. 108–249; Robertson, *Stonewall Jackson*, pp. 471–512; Sears, *To the Gates*, pp. 179–356.

40. Sears, *Papers of McClellan*, p. 282.

41. Fishel, "Pinkerton," pp. 127–28.

42. McClellan to Stanton, June 25, 1862, 10:40 P.M., OR, Ser. I, XI, Part III, p. 254.

43. Foote, *Civil War*, I, p. 470.

44. Nevins, *Ordeal of the Union*, VI, p. 133.

45. A.P. Hill was a frequent adversary of McClellan during 1862. Some believed that he was particularly aggressive at that time because of his earlier loss of Mary Ellen Marcy to McClellan. One of the latter's soldiers, goes an apocryphal tale, once complained when Hill aggressively attacked, "God's sake, Nelly—Why didn't you marry him?" Smith, "Killing Zone," p. 40.

46. McClellan to Goldsborough, June 26, 1862, NOR, Ser. I, VII, p. 510.

47. McClellan to Porter, June 26, 1862, 3:15 P.M., *Papers of McClellan*, pp. 314–5.

48. McClellan to Stanton, June 26, 1862, 7:40 P.M., OR, Ser. I. XI, Part III, p. 259; McClellan to Stanton, June 26, 1862, 8 P.M., *Ibid.*, p. 260; McClellan to Stanton, June 26, 1862, 9 P.M., *Ibid.*

49. Sears, *McClellan*, p. 211.

50. McClellan to Brigadier General William B. Franklin, June 27, 1862, Sears, *Papers of McClellan*, p. 319 and note; McClellan to Porter, June 27, 1862, 3:25 P.M., OR, Ser. I, XI, Part I, p. 58; McClellan to Porter, June 27, 1862, OR, Ser. I, XI, Part III, p. 265, *Papers of McClellan*, p. 320; McClellan to Porter, June 27, 1862, 5:30 P.M., *Ibid.*, p. 321; Hubbell, "Seven Days," pp. 34–35; Michie, *McClellan*, pp. 346–48. Michie was horrified by McClellan's poor intelligence on enemy strength: "Language is scarcely strong enough to condemn in appropriate terms the inefficient administration of the service of information whereby so gross a miscalculation should have been evolved, and especially since the two armies, with the exception of Jackson's corps, had been in close contact for more than a month." *Ibid.*, p. 347.

51. McClellan to Stanton, June 27, 1862, 10 A.M., OR, Ser. I, XI, Part III, p. 264.

52. Sears, *McClellan*, p. 211; Pois and Langer, *Command Failure*, p. 68.

53. Hubbell, "Seven Days," p. 35; McClellan to Stanton, June 27, 1862, 8 P.M., OR, Ser. I, XI, Part III, p. 266, *Papers of McClellan*, p. 321.

54. Catton, *Mr. Lincoln's Army*, pp. 135–36; Foote, *Civil War*, I, pp. 514–15.

55. McClellan to Stanton, June 28, 1862, 12:20 A.M., OR, Ser. I, XI, Part I, p. 61.

56. Pois and Langer said, "... [McClellan] engaged in behavior that was dangerously close to treason." Pois and Langer, *Command Failure*, p. 68. Eckenrode and Conrad concluded that McClellan should not have written those final words because they changed Stanton's dislike for him to enmity for an implacable enemy. ("He was insane enough to pour out his tortured soul to the cold-blooded, unhuman Stanton, who valued nothing but efficiency.... Is there any wonder that Stanton, disliking him before, became his implacable enemy?") Eckenrode and Conrad, *McClellan*, pp. 98–99. But Stanton did not see those words until years later.

57. Catton, *Mr. Lincoln's Army*, pp. 142, 149.

58. Lincoln to McClellan, June 28, 1862, *Works of Lincoln*, V, pp. 289–90.

59. Stanton to Halleck, June 28, 1862, OR, Ser. I, XVI, Part II, pp. 69–70.

60. Halleck to Stanton, June 30, 1862, OR, Ser. I, XI, Part III, pp. 279–80; Lincoln to Halleck, June 30, 1862, *Works of Lincoln*, V, p. 295. Halleck, however, had assigned the Chattanooga mission to the reticent General Don Carlos Buell, instead of the aggressive Ulysses S. Grant, and Buell failed.

61. Stanton addendum to Lincoln to Seward, June 29, 1862, 6 P.M., *Works of Lincoln*, V, pp. 292–3 at p. 293.

62. Pois and Langer, *Command Failure*, p. 68.

63. McClellan to Major General John A. Dix, June 29, 1862, 2 P.M., *Papers of McClellan*, pp. 324–5.

64. Sneden, *Eye of Storm*, June 29, 1862, pp. 68–83. Unfortunately, Sneden's diary entries between May 4 and June 29, 1862, are missing.

65. *Ibid.*, June 30, 1862, p. 86. Over 140 years later, William J. Miller commented, "...surprisingly, McClellan himself did not remain to conduct the all-important defense. He rode southward to locate a safe haven for the army on the James." Miller, "The Seven Days Battles: Robert E. Lee Makes a Spectacular Entrance Upon the Main Stage and in Less than a Week the Federal War Effort is Set Back Almost a Year," *Hallowed Ground*, Vol. 4, No. 4 (Winter 2003), pp. 18–23 at p. 23.

66. McClellan to Marcy, June 26, 1862, *Papers of McClellan*, pp. 325–6.

67. Michie, *McClellan*, pp. 354–55.

68. Testimony of Major General Samuel P. Heintzelman, Feb. 17, 1863, *Joint Committee Report*, Part I, pp. 346–59 at pp. 358–59; Sears, *McClellan*, pp. 218–19.

69. For details of the battle of Frayser's Farm (Glen-

dale), see Sears, Stephen W., "Glendale: Opportunity Squandered," *North & South*, Vol. 5, No. 1 (Dec. 2001), pp. 12–24.

70. Sneden, *Eye of Storm*, June 30, 1862, p. 86.

71. Pois and Langer, *Command Failure*, p. 69.

72. McClellan to Stanton, June 30, 1862, 7 P.M., OR, Ser. I, XI, Part III, p. 280.

73. McClellan to Lorenzo Thomas, July 1, 1862, 2:40 A.M., *Ibid.*, p. 281.

74. Lincoln to McClellan, July 1, 1862, *Works of Lincoln*, V, p. 298; Lincoln to McClellan, July 2, 1862, *Ibid.*, p. 301.

75. William H. Seward's Draft Call for Troops, June 30, 1862 [not issued by President Lincoln], *Ibid.*, pp. 293–4 at p. 293.

76. McClellan to Thomas, July 1, 1862, OR, Ser. I, XI, Part III, p. 282.

77. McClellan to Dix, July 1, 1862, *Papers of McClellan*, pp. 328–9.

78. "On June 30 and July 1, 1862, the commanding general literally fled these two Peninsula battlefields, boarding the gunboat *Galena* for useless excursions on the James and both days leaving his army to get out of its scrape (to use a favorite phrase of his) as best it could." Sears, "Mac," p. 63. "Indeed, when he deserted his army on the Glendale and Malvern Hill battlefields during the Seven Days, he was guilty of dereliction of duty. Had the Army of the Potomac been wrecked on either of those fields (at Glendale the possibility was real), that charge under the Articles of War would likely have been brought against him." *Ibid.*, p. 68. See also Hubbell, "Seven Days," p. 38.

79. Sneden, *Eye of Storm*, July 1, 1862, pp. 96–97. According to Sears, "Nothing so publicly damaged George McClellan's military reputation as this expedition aboard the *Galena*. The canal boats at Harper's Ferry and the Quaker guns at Manassas were simply embarrassments, but this incident cast doubt not only on his competence but his courage as well." Sears, *McClellan*, p. 221. Interestingly, he failed in his supposed mission of ascertaining the suitability of Harrison's Landing for a farther retreat by his army; he overlooked its vulnerability to artillery assault from nearby high ground unless that high ground was secured by Union troops. Jeb Stuart later discovered that error and then foolishly disclosed it with preliminary shellfire.

80. Nosworthy, *Bloody Crucible*, pp. 463–4.

81. Matloff, Maurice (ed.), *American Military History* (Washington, D.C.: U.S. Army Center of Military History, 1985) [hereafter Matloff, *American Military History*], p. 224.

82. *Joint Committee Report*, Part I, p. 26.

83. Nevins, *Ordeal of the Union*, VI, p. 137.

84. Hubbell, "Seven Days," p. 39.

85. Pois and Langer, *Command Failure*, p. 50.

86. Matloff, *American Military History*, p. 224.

Chapter 7

1. Testimony of Brigadier General Silas Casey, March 5, 1863, *Joint Committee Report*, Part I, pp. 441–47 at p. 446.

2. McClellan to Lincoln, July 2, 1862, 5:30 P.M., OR, Ser. I, XI, Part III, pp. 287–88.

3. Lincoln to McClellan, July 3, 1862, *Works of Lincoln*, V, p. 303.

4. McClellan to Stanton, July 3, 1862, OR, Ser. I, XI, Part III, pp. 291–92.

5. Lincoln to McClellan, July 4, 1862, *Works of Lincoln*, V, pp. 305–6.

6. Nevins, *Ordeal of the Union*, VI, p. 144.

7. McClellan to Marcy, July 4, 1862, *Papers of McClellan*, p. 334; McClellan to Mary Ellen McClellan, July 4, 1862, *Ibid.*, pp. 334–5; McClellan to Dix, July 4, 1862, *Ibid.*, p. 336.

8. McClellan to Lincoln, July 4, 1862, noon, OR, Ser. I, XI, Part 1, pp. 71–72; McClellan to Lincoln, July 4, 1862, 1 P.M., *Ibid.*, Part III, p. 294.

9. McClellan's proclamation was met with ridicule in Richmond. General D.H. Hill began referring to McClellan as "the great Mover of his Base." Sears, *To the Gates*, p. 348.

10. McClellan to Soldiers of the Army of the Potomac!, July 4, 1862, OR, Ser. I, XI, Part III, p. 299.

11. Rhodes, Robert Hunt (ed.), *All for the Union: The Civil War Diary and Letters of Elisha Hunt Rhodes* (New York: Orion Books, 1991), p. 74.

12. McClellan to Mary Ellen McClellan, July 6, 1862, 2:15 A.M., *Papers of McClellan*, p. 340; McClellan to Mary Ellen McClellan, July 7, 1862, 7:30 A.M., *Ibid.*, pp. 340–1 at p. 341; McClellan to Stanton, July 7, 1862, OR, Ser. I, XII, Part 2 supplement, p. 1111. For his battlefield service at Seven Days,' Porter was promoted to major general of volunteers and brevet brigadier in the regular army. Warner, *Generals in Blue*, p. 379.

13. Order Constituting the Army of Virginia, June 26, 1862, *Works of Lincoln*, V, p. 287.

14. McClellan to Major General John Pope, July 7, 1862, OR, Ser. I, XI, Part III, p. 306.

15. Nevins, *Ordeal of the Union*, VI, p. 159.

16. Catton, *Mr. Lincoln's Army*, p. 151.

17. McClellan to Lincoln, July 7, 1862, OR, Ser. I, XI, Part I, pp. 73–74. On July 9, McClellan sent a copy of this letter to his wife for her to "preserve carefully as a very important record." McClellan to Mary Ellen McClellan, July 9, 9:30 P.M., *Papers of McClellan*, p. 348.

18. McPherson, *Battle Cry*, pp. 502–03.

19. Guelzo, Allen C., "'Not One Word ... Will I Ever Recall': Abraham Lincoln and the Emancipation Proclamation," *North & South*, Vol. 7, No. 2 (March 2004) [hereafter Guelzo, "'Not One Word'"], pp. 74–82 at p. 79.

20. Catton, *Mr. Lincoln's Army*, p. 150.

21. Gallagher, Gary W., "A Civil War Watershed: The 1862 Richmond Campaign in Perspective," in Gallagher, Gary W. (ed.), *The Richmond Campaign of 1862: The Peninsula & the Seven Days* (Chapel Hill and London: The University of North Carolina Press, 2000) [hereafter Gallagher, *Richmond Campaign*], pp. 3–27 at pp. 14–15.

22. Catton, *Mr. Lincoln's Army*, pp. 154–55.

23. *Ibid.*

24. Lincoln's Appeal to Border State Representatives To Favor Compensated Emancipation, July 12, 1862, *Works of Lincoln*, V, pp. 317–9.

25. Lincoln's First Draft of an Emancipation Proclamation, July 22, 1862, *Works of Lincoln*, V, pp. 336–7.

26. Lincoln's Memorandum of Interviews Between Lincoln and Officers of the Army of the Potomac, July 8–9, 1862, *Ibid.*, pp. 309–12.

27. *Ibid.*

28. Interestingly, General Keyes, who believed that Lee was heading to Washington and that McClellan's army could be moved, wrote to Lincoln on August 25 that he only recently had learned that his views on leaving Harrison's Landing differed from those of McClellan and most of his corps commanders, that he had been left behind on the Peninsula and stripped of two brigades, and that he should be maintained in a command commensurate with his rank. *Ibid.*, p. 405 note.

29. McClellan to Mary Ellen McClellan, July 9, 1862, *Papers of McClellan*, p. 348.

30. McClellan to Stanton, July 8, 1862, *Ibid.*, pp. 346–7 at p. 347.

31. McClellan to Mary Ellen McClellan, July 10, 1862, *Ibid.*, pp. 348–9.

32. McClellan to Mary Ellen McClellan, July 11, 1862, *Ibid.*, p. 351.

33. McClellan to Hill Carter, July 11, 1862, OR, Ser. I, XI, Part III, p. 316. The next day McClellan wrote to Senator Ira Harris of New York that all Negroes seeking protection in his camps had been suitably employed. McClellan to Senator Ira Harris, July 12, 1862, *Papers of McClellan*, p. 353.

34. McClellan to Lincoln, July 11, 1862, 8 A.M., OR, Ser. I, XI, Part III, p. 315.

35. McClellan to Lincoln, July 12, 1862, OR, Ser. I, XI, Part I, pp. 74–75 at p. 75.

36. Lincoln to McClellan, July 13, 1862, *Works of Lincoln*, V, p. 322.

37. McClellan to Lincoln, July 14, 1862, OR, Ser. I, XI, Part III, pp. 321–22.

38. McClellan to Mary Ellen McClellan, July 13, 1862, 7:45 A.M., *Papers of McClellan*, pp. 354–5 at p. 354; McClellan to Mary Ellen McClellan, July 15, 1862, *Ibid.*, pp. 358–9 at p. 358.

39. Marcy to McClellan, July 13, 1862, Sears, *Ibid.*, p. 359n; McClellan to Marcy, July 15, 1862, 8 A.M., *Ibid.*, p. 359.

40. McClellan to Mary Ellen McClellan, July 13, 1862, 7:45 A.M., *Ibid.*, pp. 354–5 at p. 354.

41. McClellan to Samuel L.M. Barlow, July 15, 1862, *Ibid.*, pp. 360–1 at p. 361.

42. McClellan to Lincoln, July 17, 1862, 8 A.M., OR, Ser. I, XI, Part I, p. 75; Burnside to McClellan, July 15, 1862, Sears, *Papers of McClellan*, p. 362n.

43. Lincoln's Order Designating Henry W. Halleck as General-in-chief, July 11, 1862, *Works of Lincoln*, pp. 312–3.

44. For a discussion of how the willful McClellan bullied and outmaneuvered the indecisive Halleck before and during Second Manassas, see Marszalek, John F., *Commander of All Lincoln's Armies: A Life of General Henry W. Halleck* (Cambridge and London: Belknap Press of Harvard University Press, 2004), pp. 134–47.

45. McClellan to Mary Ellen McClellan, July 17, 1862, A.M., *Papers of McClellan*, pp. 362–3 at p. 362; McClellan to Mary Ellen McClellan, July 18, 1862, 9 P.M., *Ibid.*, p. 364 (emphasis added); McClellan to William H. Aspinwall, July 19, 1862, *Ibid.*, pp. 355–6 at p. 365; McClellan to Mary Ellen McClellan, July 20, 1862, P.M., *Ibid.*, pp. 367–8.

46. 547. McClellan to Mary Ellen McClellan, July 17, 1862, A.M., *Ibid.*, pp. 362–3.

47. McClellan to Mary Ellen McClellan, July 18, 1862, 9 P.M., *Ibid.*, p. 364 (emphasis added); McClellan to Mary Ellen McClellan, July 20, 1862, P.M.., *Ibid.*, pp. 367–8 at p. 367.

48. McClellan to Lincoln, July 17, 1862, 8 A.M., OR, Ser. I, XI, Part I, p. 75; McClellan to Lincoln, July 18, 1862, 8 A.M., *Ibid.*; McClellan to Mary Ellen McClellan, July 18, 1862, 9 P.M., *Ibid.*, p. 364; McClellan to Marcy, July 19, 1862, 8 A.M.., *Papers of McClellan*, pp. 364–5; McClellan to William H. Aspinwall, July 19, 1862, *Ibid.*, pp. 365–6 at p. 365; McClellan to Lincoln, July 20, 1862, 1:30 P.M., OR, Ser. I, XI, Part III, pp. 328–29. In the letter to Aspinwall, McClellan asked him to try to locate possible employment for him in New York City.

49. Pope's Address to the Army of Virginia, July 14, 1862, OR, Ser. I, XII, Part III, pp. 473–4 at p. 474.

50. McClellan to Mary Ellen McClellan, July 22, 1862, 7:30 A.M., *Papers of McClellan*, pp. 368–9 at p. 368.

51. General Orders, Headquarters of the Army of Virginia, July 18, 1862, OR, Ser. I, XII, Part II, pp. 50–52; Hennessy, John, "The Miscreant Suppressed: Lee vs. Pope at Second Manassas," *Hallowed Ground*, Vol. 5, No. 2 (Summer 2004), pp. 20–27 [hereafter Hennessy, "Miscreant"] at p. 20. Hennessy described the saga of Second Manassas in that article and in an earlier one. Hennessy, John, "The Second Battle of Manassas: Lee Suppresses the 'Miscreant' Pope," *Blue & Gray Magazine*, IX, Issue 6 (Aug. 1992), pp. 10–34, 46–58.

52. McClellan to Mary Ellen McClellan, July 22, 1862,

7:30 A.M., *Papers of McClellan*, pp. 368–9; McClellan to Barlow, July 23, 1862, *Ibid.*, pp. 369–70.

53. McClellan to Mary Ellen McClellan, July 24, 1862, *Ibid.*, pp. 370–1 at p. 371.

54. "Lee was believed to have lost 40,000 in casualties and another 40,000 sent toward the Valley under Jackson; yet the enemy's total strength was claimed to be the same 200,000 McClellan had estimated as Lee's offensive began. To credit the enemy with 80,000 reinforcements received in that short time bordered on fantasy." Fishel, "Pinkerton," p. 128. Also, Fishel, *Secret War*, p. 162.

55. In testimony before the Joint Committee, McClellan said, "I have no recollection of having asked at a subsequent period [after agreeing with Halleck on 20,000 reinforcements] for a greater number than 20,000 as a necessary preliminary to a movement." *Joint Committee Report*, Part I, p. 28; testimony of McClellan, *Ibid.*, Feb. 28 [incorrectly described as 1862] and March 2, 1863, pp. 419–441 at p. 437.

56. McClellan to Major General Henry W. Halleck, July 26, 1862, OR, Ser. I, XI, Part III, pp. 333–34.

57. McClellan may have seen an opportunity in Halleck's plea for his cooperation. On July 30, Halleck wrote to him, "In whatever has occurred heretofore, you have had my full approbation and cordial support. There was no one in the army under whom I could serve with greater pleasure. And now I ask you that same support and cooperation and that same free interchange of opinion as in former days." Halleck to McClellan, July 30, 1862, OR, Ser. I, XI, Part III, p. 343.

58. McClellan to Mary Ellen McClellan, July 27, 1862, *Papers of McClellan*, pp. 373–4 at p. 374; McClellan to Halleck, July 28, 1862, OR, Ser. I, XI, Part I, p. 75.

59. McClellan to Halleck, July 30, 1862, OR, Ser. I, XI, Part III, p. 342; McClellan to Barlow, July 30, 1862, *Papers of McClellan*, pp. 376–7.

60. McClellan to Mary Ellen McClellan, July 30, 1862, 10:15 P.M., *Papers of McClellan*, pp. 377–8.

61. Lincoln's Proclamation of the Act To Suppress Insurrection, July 25, 1862, *Works of Lincoln*, p. 341.

62. Army of the Potomac General Orders No. 154, Aug. 9, 1862, OR, Ser. I, XI, Part III, pp. 363–4.

63. McClellan to Mary Ellen McClellan, July 31, 1862, *Papers of McClellan*, pp. 378–80 at p. 379.

64. McClellan to Mary Ellen McClellan, Aug. 2, 1862, *Ibid.*, pp. 382–3 (emphasis added).

65. McClellan to Halleck, Aug. 1, 1862, OR, Ser. I, XI, Part III, pp. 345–46 at p. 346.

66. *Ibid.*

67. Lincoln to Agenor-Etienne de Gasparin, August 4, 1862, *Works of Lincoln*, V, pp. 355–6 at p. 355.

68. Lincoln's Address to Union Meeting at Washington, August 6, 1862, *Ibid.*, pp. 358–60.

69. Halleck to Burnside, Aug. 1, 1862, OR, Ser. I, XII, Part III, p. 524; Report of Halleck, Nov. 25, 1862, OR, Ser. I, XII, Part II, pp. 4–8 at p. 5; Nevins, *Ordeal of the Union*, VI, pp. 161–2.

70. Burnside to Halleck, Aug. 2, 1862, OR, Ser. I, XII, Part III, p. 524. In sharp contrast, McClellan soon would use the absence of a corps' artillery or cavalry as a reason to disobey orders to send a corps into battle.

71. Halleck to McClellan, Aug. 3, 1862, OR, Ser. I, XI, Part I, pp. 80–81 (emphasis added).

72. McClellan to Halleck, Aug. 4, 1862, noon, *Ibid.*, pp. 81–82.

73. Halleck to McClellan, Aug. 5, 1862, *Ibid.*, p. 82; Halleck to McClellan, Aug. 6, 3 A.M., *Ibid.*, p. 78; Halleck to McClellan, Aug. 6, 1862, *Ibid.*, Ser. I, XII, Part II, pp. 9–11.

74. Catton, *Mr. Lincoln's Army*, p. 156.

75. McClellan to Halleck, Aug. 12, 1862, OR, Ser. I, XI, Part III, pp. 372–73.

76. Fishel, "Pinkerton," p. 129.

77. Nevins, *Ordeal of the Union*, VI, p. 162.

78. McPherson, *Crossroads*, p. 79; Weigley, *Great Civil War*, pp. 136–37. On August 14, Private Sneden wrote, "Marching orders were sent all the corps commanders this morning to be in readiness to move tomorrow on Yorktown via Williamsburg. There was much surprise manifested among officers who thought we would move on Malvern Hill and Richmond.... The corps of Fitz John Porter (V) marched this morning.... These are the first troops to march." Sneden, *Eye of Storm*, pp. 111–12.

79. McClellan to Mary Ellen McClellan, Aug. 4–5, 1862, *Papers of McClellan*, pp. 385–6; McClellan to Marcy, Aug. 5, 1862, 1 P.M., *Ibid.*, p. 386; McClellan to Hooker, Aug. 6, 1862, 10 P.M., OR, Ser. I, XI, Part I, p. 79.

80. McClellan to Mary Ellen McClellan, Aug. 8, 1862, *Papers of McClellan*, pp. 387–8.

81. Halleck to McClellan, Aug. 7, 1862, OR, Ser. I, XI, Part III, pp. 359–60; Halleck to McClellan, Aug. 10, 1862, OR, Ser. I, XI, Part I, p. 86.

82. McClellan to Mary Ellen McClellan, Aug. 10–11, 1862, *Papers of McClellan*, pp. 389–90 (emphasis added).

83. *Ibid.* (emphasis added).

84. *Ibid.*, p. 390 (emphasis added).

85. Lamb, John W., "Pope's Narrow Escape from Clark's Mountain," *America's Civil War*, Vol. 11, No. 3 (July 1998), pp. 38–45.

86. McClellan to Halleck, Aug. 12, 1862, 4 P.M., OR, Ser. I, XI, Part III, pp. 372–73.

87. Halleck to McClellan, Aug. 12, 1862, noon, OR, Ser. I, XI, Part I, p. 87.

88. McClellan to Halleck, Aug. 12, 1862, 11 P.M., *Ibid.*, pp. 87–88. Peter Michie agreed with McClellan that the transportation system was to blame for his delay in moving from the Peninsula to northern Virginia. Michie, *McClellan*, pp. 381–82.

89. Halleck to McClellan, Aug. 14, 1862, 1:40 P.M., OR, Ser. I, XI, Part I, p. 89.

90. McClellan to Halleck, Aug. 14, 1862, 11 P.M., *Ibid.*

91. McClellan to Porter, Aug. 17, 1862, 12:30 P.M., *Papers of McClellan*, pp. 393–4.

92. McClellan to Halleck, Aug. 17, 1862, 2:30 P.M., OR, Ser. I, XI, Part III, p. 378, *Papers of McClellan*, p. 394.

93. McClellan to Mary Ellen McClellan, Aug. 17, 1862, 3 P.M., *Papers of McClellan*, p. 395; McClellan to Mary Ellen McClellan, Aug. 18, 1862, P.M., *Ibid.*, pp. 395–6.

94. Sneden, *Eye of Storm*, August 18, 1862, pp. 113–14.

95. Nevins, *Ordeal of the Union*, VI, p. 171.

96. The facts contradict McClellan's late 1863 assertion, "I proceeded to obey this [August 3, 1862] order with all possible rapidity, firmly impressed, however, with the conviction that the withdrawal of the army of the Potomac from Harrison's Landing ... would, at that time, have the most disastrous effect upon our cause." McClellan, George B., *Report of Major General George B. McClellan upon the organization of the Army of the Potomac, and its campaigns in Virginia and Maryland, from July 26, 1861, to November 7, 1862*, House of Representatives, 38th Congress, 1st Session, Ex. Doc. No. 15, Dec. 22, 1863 (Washington, Government Printing Office, 1864) [hereafter McClellan, *Report on Army of the Potomac*], p. 153. It is hard to believe he was interested in quickly executing an order that he still disagreed with more than a year later.

97. McClellan to Halleck, Aug. 18, 1862, 11 P.M., OR, Ser. I, XI, Part I, pp. 91–92; Sears, *Papers of McClellan*, p. 396n.

98. McClellan to Burnside, Aug. 20, 1862, OR, Ser. I, XII, Part III, p. 605.

99. McClellan to Mary Ellen McClellan, Aug. 21, 1862, 8 P.M., *Papers of McClellan*, pp. 397.

100. McClellan to Mary Ellen McClellan, Aug. 22, 1862, 10 A.M., *Ibid.*, pp. 398–9 at p. 399 (emphasis added).

101. McClellan to Mary Ellen McClellan, Aug. 23, 1862, 3 P.M., *Ibid.*, pp. 399–400 (emphasis added).

102. Gabel, Christopher R., *Railroad Generalship: Foun-dations of Civil War Strategy* (Fort Leavenworth, Kansas: Combat Studies Institute, U.S. Army Command and General Staff College, 1997), pp. 16–17.

103. McClellan to Mary Ellen McClellan, Aug. 24, 1862, *Papers of McClellan*, p. 404; McClellan to Halleck, Aug. 24, 1862, 2 P.M., OR, Ser. I, XI, Part I, pp. 93–94; Halleck to McClellan, Aug. 24, 1862, 12:30 P.M., OR, Ser. I, XII, Part III, p. 645; Halleck to McClellan, Aug. 24, 1862, P.M., OR, Ser. I, XI, Part I, p. 94.; McClellan to Halleck, Aug. 25, 1862, 12:45 A.M., OR, Ser. I, XII, Part III, p. 659. In his letter to his wife, McClellan said of Pope's retreat (allegedly without notice to adjoining Union forces): "It was most infamous conduct & he deserves hanging for it." *Ibid.*, p. 404.

104. Nolan, Alan T. And Storch, Marc, "The Iron Brigade Earns Its Name: John Gibbon's Brigade in the Maryland Campaign, 1862," *Blue & Gray Magazine*, Vol. XXI, Issue 6 (Holiday 2004), pp. 6–20, 47–63.

105. Hennessy, "Miscreant," pp. 21–22.

106. For details of Second Manassas, see Sears, Stephen W., *Landscape Turned Red: The Battle of Antietam* (New York: Book-of-the-Month Club, Inc., 1994); Hennessy, John, "The Miscreant Suppressed: Lee vs. Pope at Second Manassas," *Hallowed Ground*, Vol. 5, No. 2 (Summer 2004), pp. 20–27; and Hennessy, John, "The Second Battle of Manassas: Lee Suppresses the 'Miscreant' Pope," *Blue & Gray Magazine*, IX, Issue 6 (Aug. 1992), pp. 10–34, 46–58 [hereafter Hennessy, "Miscreant"].

107. Hennessy, "Miscreant," pp. 22–24.

108. McClellan to Mary Ellen McClellan, Aug. 27, 1862, A.M., *Papers of McClellan*, p. 406 (emphasis added).

109. Halleck to McClellan, Aug. 27, 1862, 10 A.M., OR, Ser. I, XI, Part I, p. 95; McClellan to Halleck, Aug. 27, 1862, 10:20 A.M., OR, Ser. I, XI, Part I, p. 95; Halleck to McClellan, Aug. 27, 1862, *Ibid.*

110. Burnside to Halleck, Aug. 27, 1862, OR, Ser. I, XII, Part III, p. 701; McClellan to Halleck, Aug. 27, 1862, 11:20 A.M., OR, Ser. I, XII, Part III, p. 689; Halleck to McClellan, Aug. 27, 1862, 1:50 P.M., Ser. I, XII, Part III, p. 691.

111. Testimony of Brigadier General Henry Haupt, Feb. 1863, *Joint Committee Report*, Part I, pp. 370–86 at p. 384.

112. Rafuse, *McClellan's War*, pp. 258–60.

113. Halleck to McClellan, Aug. 27, 1862, noon, OR, Ser. I, XI, Part I, p. 94

114. McClellan to Halleck, Aug. 27, 1862, 1:15 P.M., OR, Ser. I, XI, Part I, p. 96; McClellan to Halleck, Aug. 27, 1862, 1:35 P.M., *Ibid.*, XII, Part III, p. 690; McClellan to Halleck, Aug. 27, 1862, 2:30 P.M., *Ibid.*, XI, Part I, pp. 96–97.

115. Halleck to McClellan, Aug. 27, 1862, P.M., OR, Ser. I, XII, Part III, p. 691; McClellan to Halleck, Aug. 27, 1862, 6 P.M., *Ibid.*, XI, Part I, p. 97.

116. Testimony of Brigadier General Henry Haupt, Feb. 1863, *Joint Committee Report*, pp. 370–86 at pp 379–80.

117. McClellan to Mary Ellen McClellan, Aug. 28, 1862, 9:30 A.M., *Papers of McClellan*, p. 411.

118. McClellan to Halleck, Aug. 28, 1862, A.M., OR, Ser. I, XII, Part III, p. 708.

119. Halleck to Franklin, Aug. 27, 1862, 12:40 P.M., OR, Ser. I, XII, Part III, p. 707; McClellan to Halleck, Aug. 27, 1862, 1 P.M., *Ibid.*, p. 708; Halleck to McClellan, Aug. 27, 1862, 3:30 P.M., *Ibid.*, p. 709.

120. McClellan to Halleck, Aug. 28, 1862, 4:10 P.M., OR, Ser. I, XI, Part I, p. 97; McClellan to Halleck, Aug. 28, 1862, 4:45 P.M., *Ibid.*, XII, Part III, p. 709.

121. Halleck to McClellan, Aug. 28, 1862, 7:40 P.M., OR, Ser. I, XII, Part III, p. 710.

122. McClellan to Halleck, Aug. 28, 1862, 10 P.M., *Ibid.*

123. McClellan to Halleck, Aug. 29, 1862, 10:30 A.M., OR, Ser. I, XI, Part I, pp. 97–98.

124. McClellan to Halleck, Aug. 29, 1862, 1 P.M., *Ibid.*, p. 99.

125. Halleck to McClellan, Aug. 29, 1862, 3 P.M., OR, Ser. I, XII, Part III, p. 722.

126. *Works of Lincoln*, V, pp. 395–9.

127. Lincoln to McClellan, Aug. 29, 1862, *Ibid.*, p. 399.

128. McClellan to Lincoln, Aug. 29, 1862, 2:45 P.M., OR, Ser. I, XI, Part I, p. 98 (emphasis added).

129. Lincoln to McClellan, Aug. 29, 1862, *Works of Lincoln*, V, p. 339.

130. McClellan to Mary Ellen McClellan, Aug. 29, 1862, 3 P.M., *Papers of McClellan*, p. 417.

131. McPherson, *Crossroads*, p. 84.

132. McClellan to Halleck, Aug. 29, 1862, 5:25 P.M., OR, Ser. I, XII, Part III, p. 723.

133. Porter's disobedience led to his court-martial and dismissal from the army. About sixteen years later, a review board exonerated him and recommended his reinstatement.

134. Rafuse, *McClellan's War*, p. 263.

135. Halleck to McClellan, Aug. 29, 1862, 7:50 P.M., *Ibid.*

136. McClellan to Halleck, Aug. 29, 1862, 8 P.M., OR, Ser. I, XI, Part I, pp. 99–100 at p. 99.

137. *Ibid.* at pp. 99–100.

138. Halleck to McClellan, Aug. 30, 1862, 9:40 A.M., OR, Ser. I, XII, Part III, p. 744.

139. McClellan to Halleck, Aug. 30, 1862, 11:30 A.M., *Ibid.*, pp. 744–45.

140. McClellan to Mary Ellen McClellan, Aug. 29, 1862, 9:30 P.M., *Papers of McClellan*, pp. 418–9.

141. McClellan to Mary Ellen McClellan, Aug. 30, 1862, *Ibid.*, p. 419.

142. Hennessy, "Miscreant," pp. 26–27.

143. Halleck to McClellan, Aug. 30, 1862, 12:20 P.M., OR, Ser. I, XII, Part III, pp. 746–47 at p. 746.

144. Halleck to McClellan, Aug. 30, 1862, 2:10 P.M., *Ibid.*, p. 747.

145. McClellan to Halleck, Aug. 30, 1862, P.M., *Ibid.*, pp. 747–48.

146. McClellan to Halleck, Aug. 31, 1862, 3:30 A.M., *Ibid.*, pp. 771–72.

147. Nevins, *Ordeal of the Union*, VI, p. 182.

148. McClellan to Mary Ellen McClellan, Aug. 31, 1862, 9:30 A.M. and later, *Papers of McClellan*, pp. 423–4 at p. 423.

149. Nevins, *Ordeal of the Union*, VI, p. 184.

150. McPherson, *Crossroads*, p. 84.

151. Adams, *Fighting for Defeat*, p. 101.

152. *Ibid.*, p. 423.

153. McClellan to Halleck, Aug. 31, 1862, 7:30 P.M., OR, Ser. I, XII, Part III, p. 773; Halleck to McClellan, Aug. 31, 1862, OR, Ser. I, XI, Part I, pp. 102–3; McClellan to Halleck, Aug. 31, 1862, 10:25 P.M., OR, Ser. I, XII, Part III, p. 773.

154. McClellan to Halleck, Aug. 31, 1862, 11:30 P.M., OR, Ser. I, XI, Part I, p. 103; Halleck to McClellan, Sept. 1, 1862, 1:30 A.M., OR, Ser. I, XII, Part III, p. 786.

155. The Union had 1,724 killed, 8,372 wounded, and 5,958 missing, while the Confederates had 1,481 killed, 7,627 wounded, and a mere 89 missing. Heidler & Heidler, *Encyclopedia*, p. 321.

156. Nevins, *Ordeal of the Union*, VI, p. 185.

157. Welles, *Diary*, I, September 1, 1862, p. 102. Although he agreed with the thrust of the document, Welles declined to sign the protest against McClellan because he thought it was disrespectful to the president. *Ibid.*, pp. 101–02.

158. *Works of Lincoln*, V, p. 486 note.

159. Nevins, *Ordeal of the Union*, VI, pp. 184–8.

160. McClellan to Mary Ellen McClellan, Sept. 2, 1862, 12:30 P.M., *Papers of McClellan*, p. 428; Halleck to Pope, Sept. 2, 1862, OR, Ser. I, XII, Part III, p. 797; McClellan to Pope, Sept. 2, 1862, OR, Ser. I, XIX, Part I, p. 38.

161. Pope to Halleck, Sept. 3, 1862, OR, Ser. I, XII, Part II, pp. 19–20.

162. *Ibid.*, p. 19.

163. McClellan to Mary Ellen McClellan, Sept. 1, 1862, 2 P.M., *Papers of McClellan*, p. 427; McClellan to Mary Ellen McClellan, Sept. 2, 1862, 1 A.M., *Ibid.*, p. 428; Pope to Halleck, Sept. 1, 1862, OR, Ser. I, XII, Part II, pp. 82–3.

164. McClellan to Porter, Sept. 1, 1862, 5:30 P.M., OR, Ser. I, XII, Part III, pp. 787–88. Porter's response: "You may rest assured that all your friends, as well as every lover of his country, will ever give, as they have given, to General Pope their cordial co-operation and constant support in the execution of all orders and plans..." Porter to McClellan, Sept. 2, 1862, 10 A.M., *ibid.*, p. 798.

Chapter 8

1. For details of the Antietam (or Maryland) Campaign, see Freeman, *Lee*, II, pp. 350–414; Reese, Timothy J., *High-Water Mark: The 1862 Maryland Campaign in Strategic Perspective* (Baltimore: Butternut and Blue Press, 2004) [hereafter, Reese, *High-Water Mark*]; McPherson, James M., *Crossroads of Freedom: Antietam* (Oxford: Oxford University Press, 2002); Sears, Stephen W., *Landscape Turned Red: The Battle of Antietam* (New York: Book-of-the-Month Club, Inc., 1994) [hereafter Sears, *Landscape*]; Luvaas, Jay, and Nelson, Harold W., *The U.S. Army War College Guide to the Battle of Antietam: The Military Campaign of 1862* (Carlisle, Pennsylvania: South Mountain Press, Inc., 1987) [hereafter Luvaas and Nelson, *Army War College Guide*]; and Priest, John M., *Antietam: The Soldiers' Battle* (Shippensburg, Pennsylvania: White Mane Publishing Company, Inc., 1989) [hereafter Priest, *Antietam*].

2. McClellan to Lincoln, Sept. 2, 1862, 12:30 P.M., *Papers of McClellan*, pp. 428–29; McClellan to Lincoln, Sept. 2, 1862, 3 P.M., *Ibid.*, pp. 430–1.

3. McClellan to Lincoln, Sept. 2, 1862, 3 P.M., *Ibid.*, pp. 430–1; McClellan to Halleck, Sept. 4, 1862, 12:30 P.M., OR, Ser. I, XIX, Part II, pp. 174–75.

4. Lee to Jefferson Davis, Sept. 3, 1862, Dowdey and Manarin, *Papers of Lee*, pp. 292–3. At this time, Braxton Bragg's Army of Tennessee was outnumbered 124,000 to 35,000 and the Union Army of the Ohio was within twenty miles of Chattanooga. Connelly, "Lee and the Western Confederacy," p. 124.

5. Lee to Davis, Sept. 3, 1862, Dowdey and Manarin, *Papers of Lee*, pp. 292–3; Bonekemper, *How Lee Lost*, p. 65; Sears, *Papers of McClellan*, p. 433.

6. Lincoln to Halleck, Sept. 3, 1862, *Works of Lincoln*, V, p. 404.

7. Welles, *Diary*, I, Sept. 12, 1862, p. 124.

8. McClellan to Mary Ellen McClellan, Sept. 5, 1862, 11 A.M., *Papers of McClellan*, p. 435.

9. Army Hd. Qtrs. Special Orders No. 223 (Sept. 5, 1862) and No. 224 (Sept. 6, 1862), OR, Ser. I, XIX, Part II, pp. 188, 197; McClellan to Halleck, Sept. 6, 1862, OR, Ser. I, XIX, Part II, pp. 189–90; McClellan to Lincoln, Sept. 6, 1862, *Papers of McClellan*, pp. 436–7; Lincoln to McClellan, September 6, 1862, *Works of Lincoln*, V, p. 407.

10. McClellan to Mary Ellen McClellan, Sept. 7, 1862, 2:30 P.M., *Papers of McClellan*, pp. 437–8.

11. Nevins, *Ordeal of the Union*, VI, pp. 215–218.

12. McClellan to Halleck, Sept. 8, 1862, 8 P.M., OR, Ser. I, XIX, Part II, p. 211.

13. McClellan to Governor Andrew G. Curtin, Sept. 8, 1862, 9 P.M., *Ibid.*, p. 216.

14. McClellan to Mary Ellen McClellan, Sept. 8–9, 1862, *Papers of McClellan*, pp. 439–40.

15. McClellan to Mary Ellen McClellan, Sept. 9, 1862, 8:30 A.M., *Ibid.*, p. 441.

16. McClellan to Halleck, Sept. 9, 1862, 7:30 P.M.,

OR, Ser. I, XIX, Part II, pp. 218–19; McClellan to Halleck, 6 P.M., *Ibid.*, p. 219.

17. McClellan to Mary Ellen McClellan, Sept. 9, 1862, 5 P.M., *Papers of McClellan*, p. 442.

18. Lincoln to McClellan, Sept. 10, 1862, 10:15 A.M., *Works of Lincoln*, V, p. 412; McClellan to Lincoln, Sept. 10, 1862, OR, Ser. I, XIX, Part II, p. 233. On September 8, Lincoln had sent an identical query, to which McClellan had provided a mundane response.

19. Welles, *Diary*, I, Sept. 12, 1862, p. 124.

20. McClellan to Halleck, Sept. 10, 1862, 11:55 P.M., OR, Ser. I, XIX, Part II, p. 234; Adams, *Fighting for Defeat*, p. 91.

21. McClellan to Halleck, Sept. 11, 1862, *ibid.*, Part I, p. 758; Halleck to McClellan, Sept. 11, 1862, *ibid.* The night before McClellan had written to Pennsylvania's governor Andrew Curtin that he concurred with an assessment that the Confederates had no less than 120,000 troops at Frederick. Curtin to McClellan, Sept. 10, 1862, 10 A.M., OR, Ser. I, XIX, Part II, p. 248; McClellan to Curtin, Sept. 10, 1862, 10:30 P.M., OR, Ser. I, XIX, Part II, pp. 248–49.

22. McClellan to Halleck, Sept. 10, 1862, OR, Ser. I, XIX, Part II, pp. 254–55.

23. McClellan to Halleck, Sept. 11, 1862, 3:45 P.M., *Ibid.*, p. 253; Lincoln to McClellan, Sept. 11, 1862, 6 P.M., *Works of Lincoln*, V, p. 415.

24. Catton, *Mr. Lincoln's Army*, pp. 195–96.

25. Andrew G. Curtin to Lincoln, Sept. 11, 1862, 8 P.M., *Works of Lincoln*, V, p. 417 note; Lincoln to Curtin, Sept. 12, 1862, 10:35 A.M., *Ibid.*, p. 417.

26. Lincoln to McClellan, Sept. 12, 1865, 5:45 P.M., *Ibid.*, p. 418.

27. McClellan to Lincoln, Sept. 12, 1862, 9 P.M., *Ibid.*, p. 418 note.

28. McClellan to Lincoln, Sept. 12, 1862, 9 P.M., OR, Ser. I, XIX, Part II, 272; McClellan to Halleck, Sept. 12, 1862, 6 P.M., *Ibid.*, pp. 271–2; McClellan to Mary Ellen McClellan, Sept. 12, 1862, 3 P.M., *Papers of McClellan*, pp. 449–50.

29. McClellan to Franklin, Sept. 13, 1862, 6:20 P.M., OR, Ser. I, XIX, Part I, pp. 45–46 at p. 45; Vol. LI, Part I, pp. 826–27.

30. Gibbon, John, *Personal Recollections of the Civil War*, quoted in Reese, Timothy J., "A typographical shortcut distorts George B. McClellan's reactions to the September 1862 'Lost Order,'" *America's Civil War*, Vol. 17, No. 5 (Nov. 2004), pp. 18–20, 72 [hereafter Reese, "typographical shortcut"] at p. 72.

31. McClellan to Halleck, Sept. 13, 1862, 11 P.M., OR, Ser. I, XIX, Part II, pp. 281–2.

32. Although the time on this message appears as "12 M" in the OR, the original is dated "Sept. 13, 12 Midnight." Stephen Sears mistakenly stated that the message was sent at noon in his *Landscape Turned Red*, *Young Napoleon*, and *Papers of McClellan*. Reese, "typographical shortcut." Reese asserted that "...the mistaken belief that the Lincoln telegram was sent at noon has allowed unfair criticism of the general and skewed the historiography of the critical 1862 campaign." *Ibid.*, p. 72. Even when the telegram is placed in its proper chronological order, however, the timeliness of McClellan's response to the discovery of the Lost Order remains a viable issue.

33. McClellan to Lincoln, OR, Ser. I, XIX, Part II, p. 281.

34. Heidler & Heidler, *Encyclopedia*, pp. 1831–2.

35. Nolan and Storch, "Iron Brigade," p. 16.

36. Testimony of William B. Franklin, March 30, 1863, *Joint Committee Report*, Part I, pp. 625–28 at pp. 625–26; McClellan to Franklin, Sept. 14, 1862, OR, Ser. I, LI, Part I, p. 833.

37. Heidler & Heidler, *Encyclopedia*, pp. 513–5, 1831–2.

38. *Ibid.*, pp. 514–5.

39. Nevins, *Ordeal of the Union*, VI, p. 219. Jackson's successful mini-campaign against Harper's Ferry is described in Frye, Dennis E., "'Through God's Blessing,'" *North & South*, Vol. 5, No. 7 (Oct. 2002), pp. 66–74. Five hundred African-American "contrabands" were captured at Harper's Ferry and returned to slavery. McPherson, *Crossroads*, p. 114.

40. Nevins, *Ordeal of the Union*, VI, p. 219.

41. McClellan to Halleck, Sept. 14, 1862, 9:40 P.M., OR, Ser. I, XIX, Part II, p. 289; Sept.15, 1862, 8, 8 (again), and 10 A.M., *Ibid.*, pp. 294–5.

42. Nevins, *Ordeal of the Union*, VI, p. 221.

43. Lincoln to McClellan, September 15, 1862, 2:45 P.M., *Works of Lincoln*, V, p. 426.

44. McPherson, *Crossroads*, p. 114.

45. *Ibid.*, p. 115.

46. McClellan to Halleck, Sept. 16, 1862, 7 A.M., OR, Ser. I, XIX, Part II, pp 307–8; McClellan to Mary Ellen McClellan, Sept. 16, 1862, 7 A.M., *Papers of McClellan*, p. 466; McClellan to Franklin, Sept. 16, 1862, 7:45 A.M., OR, Ser. I, LI, Part I, p. 839.

47. Cheeks, Robert C., "Carnage in a Cornfield," *America's Civil War*, Vol. 5, No. 2 (July 2002), pp. 30–37 [hereafter Cheeks, "Carnage"] at p. 30.

48. For details of the Battle of Antietam, see Priest, *Antietam*; Luvaas and Nelson, *Army War College Guide*; and Alexander, Ted, "Antietam: The Bloodiest Day," *North & South*, Vol. 5, No. 7 (Oct. 2002), pp. 76–89.

49. Cheeks, "Carnage," pp. 30–37; Heidler & Heidler, *Encyclopedia*, p. 60.

50. Wert, Jeffrey D., "Disaster in the West Woods," *Civil War Times*, LXI, No. 5 (Oct. 2002), pp. 32–39 [hereafter Wert, "Disaster"].

51. Hattaway, Herman, "The Changing Face of Battle," *North & South*, Vol. 4, No. 6 (August 2001), pp. 34–43 at p. 38.

52. Chiles, Paul, "Artillery Hell! The Guns of Antietam," *Blue & Gray Magazine*, XVI, Issue 2 (Dec. 1998), pp. 6–16, 24–25, 41–59 [hereafter Chiles, "Artillery Hell!"] at p. 49; McPherson, *Crossroads*, pp. 123–24; Alexander, *Military Memoirs*, p. 262; Catton, *Mr. Lincoln's Army*, p. 304.

53. Pois and Langer, *Command Failure*, p. 55.

54. Chiles, "Artillery Hell!," pp. 51–52.

55. Sears, "McClellan at Antietam," p. 30.

56. For details on the fighting at Burnside's Bridge, see Smith, Robert Barr, "Killing Zone at Burnside's Bridge," Vol. 21, No. 2 (June 2004) [hereafter Barr, "Killing Zone"], pp. 34–40.

57. Waugh, *Class of 1846*, p. 385.

58. Marvel, William, "More Than Water Under Burnside's bridge," *America's Civil War*, Vol. 18, No. 6 (January 2006), pp. 46–52.

59. Barr, "Killing Zone," p. 39.

60. *Ibid.* Barr wrote, "Although the Young Napoleon had promised to support Burnside, he failed to issue the necessary orders, and just as the regulars were on the verge of punching a hole in the thin Rebel line before them, he recalled them." *Ibid.*

61. McPherson, *Crossroads*, pp. 128–29. Although not excusing Burnside's abysmal performance, Sears catalogued McClellan's failures related to Burnside's wing: "...McClellan's catalog of failures is lengthy and manifest. The Ninth Corps made its battle under an unwieldy command structure he imposed on it and without clearly stated objectives. Reconnaissance of the Antietam fords was ineptly performed, and by McClellan's staff rather than by cavalry. No use was made of the potential reinforcement of Couch's [just-arrived] division. The decision to open the attack was taken not only inexplicably late but without coordination with the rest of the army. The elementary precaution of guarding the army's left flank with cavalry was ignored, granting Powell Hill the decisive advantages of surprise and position. Finally, the Ninth Corps was denied any support from the more than ample reserve, either

to exploit victory or to salvage defeat." Sears, *Landscape*, pp. 356–57.

62. Alexander, Ted, "Antietam Stories of Human Interest and Sites off the Beaten Path," *Blue & Gray Magazine*, XX, No. 1 (Fall 2002), pp. 6–19, 48–62 [hereafter Alexander, "Antietam Stories,"] at p. 7.

63. McClellan to Mary Ellen McClellan, Sept. 17, 1862, 1:45 P.M., *Papers of McClellan*, p. 468; McClellan to Alfred Pleasonton, Sept. 17, 1862, 11:45 A.M., *Ibid.*, p. 467; McClellan to Brigadier General James W. Ripley, Sept. 17, 1862, OR, Ser. I, XIX, Part II, p. 312.

64. McClellan to Halleck, Sept. 17, 1862, 1:25 P.M., OR, Ser. I, XIX, Part II, p. 312.

65. Waugh, *Class of 1846*, p. 391.

66. Schiller, Laurence D., rebuttal to letter to editor, *North & South*, Vol. 2, No. 4 (April 1999), p. 67.

67. Bonekemper, *How Lee Lost*, p. 75; Jones, *Command & Strategy*, p. 96.

68. Heidler & Heidler, *Encyclopedia*, p. 66; McPherson, *Crossroads*, p. 129 and fn 56.

69. Heidler & Heidler, *Encyclopedia*, p. 67.

70. *Ibid.*

71. McClellan to Mary Ellen McClellan, Sept. 18, 1862, *Papers of McClellan*, p. 469.

72. Alexander, *Fighting for the Confederacy*, pp. 105–6.

73. Priest, John M., *Antietam: The Soldiers' Battle* (Shippensburg, Pennsylvania: White Mane Publishing Co., Inc., 1989), p. 290, quoting Porter to Lafayette McLaws, June 16, 1886.

Chapter 9

1. See "Challenging the Numbers" and rebuttal by Antietam National Battlefield Historian Ted Alexander in *North & South*, Vol. 6, No. 2 (Feb. 2003), pp. 4–5.

2. Nolan, Alan T., *Lee Considered: General Robert E. Lee and Civil War History* (Chapel Hill and London: University of North Carolina Press, 1991), p. 81.

3. Gallagher, "Great General," p. 16.

4. *Joint Committee Report*, Part I, pp. 41–43; Testimony of Ambrose E. Burnside, *Ibid.*, pp. 637–42 at p. 642; Testimony of William B. Franklin, March 30, 1863, *Ibid.*, pp. 625–28 at p. 627; Heidler & Heidler, *Encyclopedia*, pp. 66–7; McPherson, *Crossroads*, p. 129. "At the end of the fighting on the seventeenth, Lee no longer had the strength for anything but defensive action. McClellan did; he had not used his reserve and, according to his own estimate, 15,000 fresh troops had joined him during the battle. They were not used." Adams, *Fighting for Defeat*, p. 91. Edward J. Stackpole contrasted McClellan's statement that his new fresh divisions were tired and "needed rest and refreshment" with Lee's use of A.P. Hill's exhausted troops the prior afternoon. Stackpole, Edward J., "Showdown at Sharpsburg—Story of the Battle," *Civil War Times Illustrated* (August 1962), pp. 4–8, 28–32 at p. 32.

5. McClellan to Mary Ellen McClellan, Sept. 18, 1862, 8 A.M. (telegram), *Papers of McClellan*, p. 469; 8 A.M. (letter), *Ibid.*; Sept. 19, 1862, 8 A.M., *Ibid.*

6. McClellan to Halleck, September 19, 1862, 8:30 A.M., OR, Ser. I, XIX, Part II, p. 330; 10:30 A.M., *Ibid.*; 1:30 P.M., OR, Ser. I, XIX, Part I, p. 68.

7. McClellan, *Report on Army of the Potomac*, p. 211.

8. Nolan, Alan T., *The Iron Brigade: A Military History* (Bloomington and Indianapolis: Indiana University Press, 1961, 1994), p. 144.

9. Carmichael, Peter S., "We Don't Know What on Earth To Do with Him: William Nelson Pendleton and the Affair at Shepherdstown, September 19, 1862," pp. 259–88 in Gallagher, *Antietam Campaign* at pp. 269–77. The incompetent Pendleton, along with Major General Jubal Early, later created the Myth of the Lost Cause,

deified Lee, and forever distorted Civil War historiography.

10. For details on the fighting at Boteler's Ford, see Norris, David A., "Bloody Day at Boteler's Ford," *America's Civil War*, Vol. 18, No. 4 (Sept. 2005), pp. 38–44, 72.

11. McPherson, *Crossroads*, p. 130.

12. Brennan, Patrick J., "Mac's Last Stand: Autumn 1862 in Loudon Valley, Virginia," *Blue & Gray Magazine*, XVII, Issue No. 2 (Dec. 1999), pp. 6–20, 48–57 [hereafter Brennan, "Mac's Last Stand"] at p. 7. Secretary Welles reported on the Key incident: "The President informed us of his interview with Key, one of Halleck's staff, who said it was not the game of the army to capture the rebels at Antietam, for that would give the North advantage and end slavery; it was the policy of the army officers to exhaust both sides and then enforce a compromise which would save slavery." Welles, *Diary*, I, Sept. 29, 1862, p. 156.

13. McClellan to Mary Ellen McClellan, Sept. 20, 1862, *Papers of McClellan*, pp. 473, 474 note.

14. Heidler & Heidler, *Encyclopedia*, p. 67.

15. *Ibid.*

16. Halleck to McClellan, Sept. 20, 1862, 2 P.M., OR, Ser. I, XIX, Part I, p. 68; McClellan to Halleck, Sept. 20, 1862, 8 P.M., *Ibid.*, pp. 68–69 at p. 68.

17. McClellan to Halleck, Sept. 22, 1862, OR, Ser. I, XIX, Part II, pp. 342–3 at p. 342.

18. McClellan to Halleck, Sept. 23, 1862, 9:30 A.M., OR, Ser. I, XIX, Part I, p. 70; Halleck to McClellan, Sept. 24, 1862, 2 P.M., OR, Ser. I, XIX, Part II, p. 353.

19. McClellan to Halleck, Sept. 24, 1862, 10 P.M., OR, Ser. I, XIX, Part II, pp. 354–5; Halleck to McClellan, Sept. 26, 1862, *ibid.*, p. 360.

20. Lincoln's Preliminary Emancipation Proclamation, September 22, 1862, *Works of Lincoln*, V, pp. 433–6.

21. Lincoln's Proclamation Suspending the Writ of Habeas Corpus, Sept. 24, 1862, *Ibid.*, pp. 436–7.

22. Lincoln's Reply to Serenade in Honor of Emancipation Proclamation, Sept. 24, 1862, *Ibid.*, pp. 438–9.

23. McClellan to Mary Ellen McClellan, Sept. 25, 1862, 7:30 A.M., *Papers of McClellan*, pp. 481–2 at p. 482; McClellan to William H. Aspinwall, Sept. 26, 1862, *Ibid.*, p. 482.

24. McClellan to Lincoln, Oct. 7, 1862, 11:35 P.M., OR, Ser. I, XIX, Part II, p. 395.

25. McClellan to Halleck, Sept. 27, 1862, 10 A.M., OR, Ser. I, XIX, Part I, pp. 70–71. Contrary to Lincoln's desires, Halleck had expressed some concern about a McClellan movement up the Shenandoah leaving Washington unprotected. Halleck to McClellan, Sept. 26, 1862, OR, Ser. I, XIX, Part II, pp. 359–60.

26. Lee to Gustavus W. Smith, Sept. 24, 1862, OR, Ser. I, XIX, Part II, pp. 624–25 at p. 624.

27. McClellan to Halleck, Sept. 27, 1862, OR, Ser. I, XIX, Part I, pp. 70–71 at p. 71.

28. McClellan to Brigadier General Lorenzo Thomas, Sept. 28, 1862, OR, Ser. I, XIX, Part II, . 365.

29. McClellan to Mary Ellen McClellan, Sept. 29, 1862, *Papers of McClellan*, pp. 485–6.

30. McClellan to Halleck, Oct. 1, 1862, 11 A.M., OR, Ser. I, XIX, Part I, p. 10; Halleck to McClellan, Oct. 1, 1862, OR, *ibid.*; McClellan to Mary Ellen McClellan, Oct. 2, 1862, *Papers of McClellan*, p. 488.

31. McClellan to Mary Ellen McClellan, Oct. 2, 1862, *Papers of McClellan*, p. 488.

32. Nicolay and Hay, *Abraham Lincoln*, VI, p. 175.

33. Brooks D. Simpson contended that many in the Army of the Potomac shared McClellan's hesitancy to pursue Lee. After admitting that McClellan may have contributed to shaping those attitudes, Simpson said, "Considerable evidence suggests that in the seven weeks between Antietam and McClellan's removal from command the qualities of hesitation, intrigue, and wariness to-

ward civil superiors epitomizing the general were characteristic of his army as a whole." Simpson, Brooks D., "General McClellan's Bodyguard: The Army of the Potomac after Antietam" pp. 44–73 in Gallagher, Gary W. (ed.), *The Antietam Campaign* (Chapel Hill and London: University of North Carolina Press, 1999), p. 45.

34. Lincoln's Memorandum on Troops at Antietam, Oct. 1–3, 1862, *Works of Lincoln*, V, p. 448.

35. McClellan to Mary Ellen McClellan, Oct. 5, 1862, *Papers of McClellan*, pp. 489–90 at p. 490.

36. Halleck to McClellan, Oct. 6, 1862, OR, Series I, Vol. XIX, Part I, p. 72.

37. McClellan to Halleck, Oct. 6, 1862, 4:30 P.M., OR, Ser. I, XIX, Part II, p. 387; Halleck to McClellan, Oct. 7, 1862, *ibid.*, p. 393; McClellan to Mary Ellen McClellan, Oct. 7, 1862, *Papers of McClellan*, p. 492.

38. McClellan to Halleck, Oct. 7, 1862, 1 P.M., OR, Ser. I, XIX, Part I, pp. 11–12.

39. McClellan to Halleck, Oct. 11, 1862, 3:30 P.M., *Ibid.*, p. 12.

40. Welles, *Diary*, I, Oct. 11 and 13, 1862, p. 169. Two days later Welles reported the publication of a letter written by the late and revered General Philip Kearny in which Kearny had said McClellan "positively has no talents." *Ibid.*, Oct. 15, 1862, p. 174.

41. Brennan, "Mac's Last Stand," p. 8; McClellan to Halleck, Oct. 10, 1862, 10 P.M., OR, Ser. I, XIX, Part II, p. 59; Oct. 11, 1862, 9 A.M., *Ibid.*, p. 66; Oct. 12, 1862, 12:45 P.M., *Ibid.*, Part I, p. 13; Oct. 12, 1862, 6 P.M., *Ibid.*, Part II, p. 30; Oct. 13, 1862, 7:30 P.M., *Ibid.*, p. 417; Halleck to McClellan, Oct.14, 1862, *Ibid.*, Part I, p. 15; Halleck to McClellan, Oct. 14, 1862, *Ibid.*, Part II, p. 421. On October 18, McClellan complained to Halleck that his army had received only 1,964 horses since September 8. McClellan to Halleck, Oct. 18, 1862, OR, Ser. I, XIX, Part I, pp. 16–17. In response, Quartermaster General Montgomery Meigs wrote that ten thousand horses had been distributed in that period either to the Washington area or to McClellan's army in the field; he concluded, "Had you so ordered, not less than 10,000 so distributed to troops under your command would have been sent to Harper's Ferry or Frederick." Meigs to McClellan, Oct. 22, 1862, OR, Ser. I, XIX, Part II, pp. 464–5. See also Meigs to Halleck, Oct. 21, 1862, OR, Ser. I, XIX, Part I, pp. 17–20.

42. Owens, Richard H., "An Astonishing Career," *Military Heritage*, Vol. 3, No. 2 (Oct. 2001), pp. 64–73 at p. 67.

43. Joseph Medill to O.M. Hatch, Oct. 13, 1862, quoted in Murfin, James V., *The Gleam of Bayonets: The Battle of Antietam and the Maryland Campaign of 1862* (Baton Rouge and London: Louisiana State University Press, 1965, 1990) [hereafter Murfin, *Gleam of Bayonets*], p. 300.

44. Halleck to Hamilton O. Gamble, Oct. 30, 1862, OR, Ser. III, II, pp. 703–4.

45. Lincoln to McClellan, October 13, 1862, *Works of Lincoln*, V, pp. 460–1 at p. 460.

46. *Ibid.*

47. *Ibid.*, pp. 460–1.

48. McClellan to Lincoln, Oct. 17, 1862, OR, Series I, Vol. XIX, Part I, p. 16, *Papers of McClellan*, p. 499.

49. Meyers, Christopher C., "'Two Generals Cannot Command This Army': John A. McClernand and the Politics of Command in Grant's Army of the Tennessee," *Columbiad: A Quarterly Review of the War Between the States*, Vol. 2, No. 1 (Spring 1998), pp. 27–41 at pp. 32–3, citing James H. Wilson Diary, Delaware Historical Society and Wilson, James H., *Under the Old Flag* (New York: D. Appleton and Company, 1912), Vol. 1, pp. 119–23.

50. McClellan to Halleck, Oct. 21, 1862, OR, Ser. I, XIX, Part I, p. 81.

51. Halleck to McClellan, Oct. 21, 1862, *ibid.*, p. 81.

52. Lincoln's memorandum on the Army of the Potomac, October 20, 1862, *Works of Lincoln*, V, pp. 468–9 and note. Unlike the reports McClellan expected and purportedly relied on, the Confederate estimates in the report Lincoln received were inaccurately low.

53. Welles, *Diary*, I, Oct. 18, 1862, pp. 176, 177.

54. McClellan to Halleck, Oct. 22, 1862, 2:30 P.M., OR, Ser. I, XIX, Part II, p. 464.

55. Halleck to McClellan, Oct. 23, 1862, OR, Ser. I, XIX, Part II, p. 470; McClellan to Halleck, Oct. 24, 1862, 3:30 P.M., *ibid.*, p. 476; Halleck to McClellan, Oct. 25, 1862, *ibid.*, p. 483.

56. McClellan to Halleck, Oct. 24, 1862, *Papers of McClellan*, p. 506.

57. McClellan to Halleck, Oct. 25, 1862, OR, Ser. I, XIX, Part II, pp. 484–85; Lincoln to Halleck, Oct. 25, 1862, *Works of Lincoln*, V, p. 474; McClellan to Lincoln, Oct. 25, 1862, 6 P.M., OR, Ser. I, XIX, Part II, p. 485.

58. McClellan did, however, complain to his wife about Lincoln's jab as "one of those dirty little flings that I can't get used to when they are not merited." McClellan to Mary Ellen McClellan, Oct. 26, 1862, *Papers of McClellan*, p. 511.

59. Bragg's army had ended its invasion of Kentucky and retreated from that state after the indecisive October 8 Battle of Perryville.

60. McClellan to Halleck, Oct. 25, 1862, 10:45 P.M., OR, Ser. 1, XIX, Part I, p. 84; Halleck to McClellan, Oct. 26, 1862, OR, Ser. I, XIX, Part I, pp. 84–85.

61. Brennan, "McClellan's Last Stand," p. 10; Lincoln to Halleck, Oct. 26, 1862, 11:30 A.M., *Works of Lincoln*, V, p. 477; McClellan to Lincoln, Oct. 26, 1862, 9 P.M., OR, Ser. I, XIX, Part II, pp. 490–91.

62. Lincoln to McClellan, Oct. 27, 1862, *Works of Lincoln*, V, p. 479.

63. McClellan to Lincoln, October 27, 1862, 3 P.M., OR, Ser. I, XIX, Part II, p. 496; Lincoln to McClellan, October 27, 1862, 3:25 P.M., *Works of Lincoln*, V, p. 479; McClellan to Lincoln, October 27, 1862, 7:15 P.M., OR, Ser. I, XIX, Part II, pp. 497–98 at p. 497.

64. McClellan to Halleck, Oct. 29, 1862, 1:15 P.M., OR, Ser. I, XIX, Part I, p. 85; Halleck to McClellan, Oct. 30, 1862, OR, Ser. I, XIX, Part I, p. 85; McClellan to Mary Ellen McClellan, Oct. 29, 1862, *Papers of McClellan*, pp. 514–5 at p. 515.

65. McClellan to Mary Ellen McClellan, Oct. 30, 1862, *Papers of McClellan*, p. 515; Oct. 31, 1862, *Ibid.*, p. 516.

66. Lincoln to McClellan, October 29, 1982, *Works of Lincoln*, V, p. 481; McClellan to Lincoln, November 5, 1862, 11:20 P.M., *ibid.*

67. Glatthaar, *Partners*, p. 90.

68. McClellan to Mary Ellen McClellan, November 4, 1862, *Papers of McClellan*, p. 518.

69. For details of this torpid movement and desultory campaign, see Brennan, "McClellan's Last Stand."

70. Catton, *Mr. Lincoln's Army*, p. 327.

71. Goss, *High Command*, p. 117.

72. Mary Todd Lincoln to Abraham Lincoln, Nov. 2, 1862, Abraham Lincoln Papers, Library of Congress.

73. Welles, *Diary*, I, November 4, 1862, p. 179.

74. Sears, *Landscape*, p. 339; Stoddard, William O., *New York Citizen* (Sept. 22, 1866), reprinted in Stoddard, William O., *Inside the White House in War Times: Memoirs and Reports of Lincoln's Secretary* (edited by Michael Burlingame) (Lincoln and London: University of Nebraska Press, 2000), p. 167. Stoddard was Lincoln's "third secretary" from 1861 to 1864.

75. Lincoln to Halleck, Nov. 5, 1862, *Works of Lincoln*, V, p. 485. A month later, Welles (who had stopped his diary entries between November 4 and December 3) wrote that he had expected McClellan's removal in October, "...when McClellan seemed testing the forbearance of the Government, and not one good word was said for him...," but was shocked by his removal after he had started to move after Lee.

76. According to Sears, "...General Buckingham was told [by Stanton] he had been chosen for his task because

of fears that McClellan might not surrender control of the army. 'The Secretary [of War] had not only no confidence in McClellan's military skill,' Buckingham wrote, 'but he very much doubted his patriotism and even his loyalty....'" Sears, *Landscape*, p. 340.

77. McClellan to Mary Ellen McClellan, Nov. 7–8, 1862, *Papers of McClellan*, pp. 519–20 at p. 520.

78. McClellan to Mary Ellen McClellan, Nov. 10, 1862, *Ibid.*, p. 522.

79. Longstreet, James, "The Battle of Fredericksburg," *Battles & Leaders*, III, pp. 70–85 at p. 70.

80. OR, Ser. I, XIX, Part I, p. 89; McClellan, *Report on Army of the Potomac*, p. 242; Brennan, "McClellan's Last Stand," p. 56.

Chapter 10

1. Rafuse, Ethan S., "McClellan, von Clausewitz, and the Politics of War," *Columbiad: A Quarterly Review of the War Between the States*, Vol. 1, No. 3 (Fall 1977), pp. 23–37 [hereafter Rafuse, "McClellan"] at p. 25.

2. Harsh, "McClellan-Go-Round," p. 101, quoting Francis Lieber to Charles Sumner, April 28, 1863, Lieber Collection, Huntington Library, and Lee, Guy Carleton, *The True History of the Civil War* (Philadelphia, 1903), p. 296.

3. Johnson, "McClellan and Mentor," p. 93. Pro-McClellan historians, like William Starr Myers, described Rich Mountain as a brilliant victory but failed to mention or downplayed the role of Rosecrans, whom McClellan had left to his own fate without the assistance he had promised. Myers, *McClellan*, p. 188. Similarly, Thomas Rowland complained that "Rosecrans," the subordinate, is given most of the praise resulting from the success there." Rowland, *McClellan and History*, p. 67.

4. Pois and Langer, *Command Failure*, p. 55.

5. Fleming, "Northwestern Virginia," p. 61.

6. Harsh, "McClellan-Go-Round," p. 114.

7. Michie, *McClellan*, p. 90.

8. Pois and Langer, *Command Failure*, p. 55.

9. Michie said that "his constitutional timidity was in full possession of his mind" in western Virginia. Michie, *McClellan*, p. 91.

10. Rafuse, "McClellan," p. 33.

11. Rhea, Gordon; Rollins, Richard; Sears, Stephen; and Simon, John Y., "What Was Wrong with the Army of the Potomac?," *North & South*, Vol. 4, No. 3 (March 2001), pp. 12–19 [hereafter Rhea *et al.*, "What Was Wrong?"] at p. 12.

12. Waugh, *Class of 1846*, pp. 341–53.

13. Rafuse, "Lincoln," p. 63.

14. Sears, "Lincoln and McClellan," pp. 23–27.

15. Hattaway and Jones, *How the North Won*, pp. 95–96.

16. *Ibid.*, p. 96.

17. For a contrary view, see Rafuse, "Fighting." He concluded, "When viewed from a purely rational perspective—which McClellan maintained throughout the campaign—the merits of his generalship during the peninsula campaign are difficult to dispute." *Ibid.*, p. 92.

18. Harsh wrote, "Later, on the peninsula, McClellan was roundly criticized for his slowness. Yet that campaign lasted scarcely four months from its start to its abortive finish. [Lee aborted it for him.] And on three separate occasions, he moved his army with what in fairness one must call alacrity: the two week amphibious operation carrying the army to Fort Monroe [after months of inactivity]; the fighting change of base during the last week of June [in which his army fled for its life]; and the removal of the army from the James at the close of the campaign [slowly enough to deprive Pope of critical reinforcements]. True, these were not movements directly against the enemy...." Harsh, "McClellan-Go-Round," p. 114.

19. Sears, *To the Gates*, p. 103.

20. Keegan, John, *Intelligence in War: Knowledge of the Enemy from Napolean to Al-Qaeda* (New York: Alfred A. Knopf, 2003), p. 72.

21. Miller, "No American Sevastopol," pp. 36, 74.

22. Testimony of William Sprague and Joseph Hooker, March 6, 10 and 11, 1863, *Joint Committee Report*, Part I, pp. 565–70 at p. 566 and pp. 575–82 at p. 575.

23. Waugh, *Class of 1846*, p. 360.

24. Michie, *McClellan*, pp. 320–21; Catton, *Mr. Lincoln's Army*, p. 123.

25. Eckenrode and Conrad, *McClellan*, p. 98.

26. Rafuse, *McClellan's War*, pp. 230–31.

27. Myers, William Starr, *General George Brinton McClellan: A Study in Personality* (New York and London: D. Appleton-Century Company, 1934) [hereafter Starr, *McClellan*], pp. 325–26.

28. Catton, *Mr. Lincoln's Army*, p. 135.

29. Michie, *McClellan*, pp. 354, 362. As to the Malvern Hill absence, Michie also said, "No argument has ever been considered strong enough to justify this separation of General McClellan from his army, then manifestly on the eve of battle. Not only the security but the salvation of the army was in jeopardy.... The continued presence of General McClellan with his troops, seeing to their best tactical disposition and giving them the inspiration of his undoubted personal magnetism, was a duty of first importance, in comparison with which everything else was relatively of no military value whatever...." *Ibid.*, pp. 361–62. Thomas Rowland admitted that McClellan should have remained near the battlefields and let a subordinate choose a post-retreat campsite. But he argued that he properly avoided being at the front and cited Grant as an example. Rowland, *McClellan and History*, p. 71. Rowland, however, failed to discuss Grant's being in the thick of the fighting at Belmont, Fort Donelson, Shiloh, and Champion's Hill—something that McClellan never did.

30. Stephen Sears in Symonds *et al.*, "Who Were the Worst?," p. 24. Elsewhere Sears similarly said, "At Glendale McClellan ran away and hid on a gunboat. At Malvern Hill the next day he hid in a corner of the battlefield until the fighting was over." Rhea *et al.*, "What Was Wrong?," p. 17.

31. Sears, *To the Gates*, p. 281.

32. Symonds *et al.*, "Who Were the Worst?," p. 21.

33. Johnson, "McClellan and Mentor," p. 95.

34. Rafuse, "McClellan," p. 33.

35. Rhea *et al.*, "What Was Wrong?," p. 13.

36. Pois and Langer, *Command Failure*, p. 221 (emphasis added).

37. Meade, George Gordon, *The Life and Letters of George Gordon Meade* (New York: Scribner's, 1913) (2 vols.), I, p. 345.

38. Perret, *Lincoln's War*, p. 180.

39. McPherson, *Battle Cry*, p. 525.

40. Testimony of McClellan, *Joint Committee Report*, Part I, March 2, 1863, pp. 431–41 at p. 438.

41. Catton, *Mr. Lincoln's Army*, p. 198.

42. *Ibid.*, p. 199 (emphasis added).

43. Welles, *Diary*, Sept. 8, 1862, I, p. 118 (emphasis added).

44. *Joint Committee Report*, Part I, p. 454.

45. John Y. Simon in Symonds *et al.*, "Who Were the Worst?, pp. 23–4.

46. McPherson, *Battle Cry*, p. 528.

47. Murfin, *Gleam of Bayonets*, p. 61.

48. Welles, *Diary*, I, September 2, 1862, p. 103.

49. Nevins, *Ordeal of the Union*, VI, pp. 182, 184.

50. Wert, "Disaster," p. 34.

51. Waugh, *Class of 1846*, p. 364.

52. Sears, "Mac," p. 70.

53. Michie, *McClellan*, pp. 381–82, 390–91.

54. *Ibid.*, pp. 393–94.

55. *Ibid.*, p. 396.

56. Sears, *McClellan*, p. 254.
57. Eckenrode and Conrad, *McClellan*, p. 144.
58. Wert, *Sword*, p. 136.
59. Weigley, *Great Civil War*, p. 142.
60. Fishel, *Secret War*, pp. 206–7.
61. Rafuse, *McClellan's War*, pp. 271–72.
62. Welles, *Diary*, I, September 3, 1862, p. 107.
63. *Ibid.*, September 7, 1862, p. 115.
64. *Ibid.*, Sept. 8, 1862, pp. 116–17 at 117.
65. Symonds *et al.*, "Who Were the Worst?," p. 21.
66. Harsh, "McClellan-Go-Round," p. 114.
67. Reese, "typographical shortcut," p. 72 (emphasis added).
68. Pois and Langer, *Command Failure*, pp. 55, 221, 240fn74.
69. McPherson, *Crossroads*, p. 109 (emphasis supplied).
70. Catton, *Mr. Lincoln's Army*, p. 252.
71. Fishel, Edwin C., *The Secret War for the Union: The Untold Story of Military Intelligence in the Civil War* (Boston and New York: Houghton Mifflin, 1996), p. 587.
72. McPherson, *Crossroads*, p. 116.
73. Sears, "McClellan at Antietam," p. 30.
74. Chiles, Paul, "Artillery Hell!," p. 12.
75. Gallagher, Gary W., "'A Great General Is So Rare': Robert E. Lee and the Confederacy," pp. 1–41 [hereafter Gallagher, "Great General"] in Gallagher, Gary W. and Glatthaar, Joseph T. (eds.) *Leaders of the Lost Cause: New Perspectives on the Confederate High Command* (Mechanicsburg, Pennsylvania: Stackpole Books, 2004), p. 16.
76. Rafuse, *McClellan's War*, p. 332.
77. Catton, *Mr. Lincoln's Army*, p. 324. Similarly, had McClellan been successful in capturing Richmond during the Peninsula Campaign, the war might have ended without emancipation. Gallagher, "Civil War Watershed," p. 8.
78. McPherson, *Crossroads*, p. 130.
79. Burlingame, Michael and Ettlinger, John R. Turner (eds.), *Inside Lincoln's White House: The Complete Civil War Diary of John Hay* (Carbondale: Southern Illinois University, 1997), p. 232 (emphasis added), quoted in McPherson, *Crossroads*, p. 152.
80. Weigley, *Great Civil War*, p. 161.
81. Pois and Langer, *Command Failure*, p. 51, citing Lee, Captain Robert, *Recollections and Letters of General Robert E. Lee*, p. 416.
82. "McClellan had been the best thing to ever happen to Lee." Reese, *High-Water Mark*, p. 63. Reese praised the gentlemen's approach to war of Lee and McClellan, and he contrasted them favorably with Lincoln, Grant, Sherman, and Sheridan (who, of course, won the war). *Ibid.*, pp. 61–63.
83. Pois and Langer, *Command Failure*, p. 51.
84. Pollard, Edward A., *The Lost Cause. A New Southern History of the War of the Confederates* (New York: Gramercy Books, 1994) (Reprint of New York: E.B. Treat & Company, 1866), pp. 293–99.
85. Rhodes, James Ford, *History of the Civil War, 1861–1865* (New York: Macmillan & Co., 1917), p. 182, quoting Schurz, Carl, *Speeches, Correspondence and Political Papers, selected and edited by Frederic Bancroft* (New York: G.P. Putnam's Sons, 1913) (8 vols.), I, p. 220.
86. Simon, John in Symonds *et al.*, "Who Were the Worst," p. 21. Stephen Sears retorted, "I'll wager Grant didn't know about [McClellan's desertion at] Glendale and Malvern Hill when he remarked on McClellan." *Ibid.*, p. 24.
87. McPherson, *Battle Cry*, p. 359.
88. Adams, *Fighting for Defeat*, p. 96. For example, in an August 4, 1861 memorandum to the president, McClellan wrote, "...in this contest it has become necessary to crush a population sufficiently numerous, intelligent and warlike to constitute a nation. We have not only to defeat their armed and organized forces in the field, but to display such an overwhelming strength as will convince all our antagonists, especially those of the governing, aristocratic class,

of the utter impossibility of resistance." McClellan, *Report on Army of the Potomac*, p. 3.
89. Michie, *McClellan*, p. 469.
90. Rowland, *McClellan and History*, p. 129. Concerning the Peninsula Campaign, however, Rowland contended that Lincoln and Stanton were more timid than McClellan with respect to taking "acceptable risks concerning the safety of the capital." *Ibid.* Of course, once McClellan left it, the capital's safety was someone else's concern and responsibility.
91. Goss, *High Command*, pp. 118, 121.
92. Wert, *Sword*, p. 414.
93. See Joseph Harsh's description of McClellan's military contemporaries' sympathy for him as a casualty of his "earliness." Harsh, "McClellan-Go-Round," p. 105. This "earliness" theme runs through Thomas J. Rowland's *George B. McClellan & Civil War History: In the Shadow of Grant and Sherman*, in which he states, "...it seems like a much more valid question to ask why anyone would have expected a Northern triumph in 1862, rather than why McClellan and others failed to deliver it." p. 235. The primary issue is why McClellan failed to use effectively and aggressively the resources that he had rather than why he did not win the war.
94. Woodworth, Steve E., "The Army of the Tennessee and the Elements of Military Success," *North & South*, Vol. 6, No. 4 (May 2003), pp. 44–55 at p. 52.
95. Adams, *Fighting for Defeat*, p. 103.
96. Sears, "Mac," p. 66.
97. Sears, "Lincoln and McClellan," p. 50, citing McClure to Mary Ellen McClellan, Jan. 13, 1892.
98. Simon, John Y., "Grant, Lincoln, and Unconditional Surrender," in Boritt, *Lincoln's Generals*, pp. 161–98 at p. 170, quoting Young, John Russell, *Around the World with General Grant* (2 vols.) (New York: American News Company, 1879), p. 463.
99. Sears, "Mac," p. 67; McClellan to Mary Ellen McClellan, July 10, 1862, *Papers of McClellan*, pp. 348–9 at p. 349.
100. Joseph Harsh acknowledged the allegations of numerical exaggerations at all these places except western Virginia but then argued that McClellan may have been simply cautious in counting all the Confederates who might possibly be brought against him. He concluded, "This is certainly a conservative, cautious way to plan a campaign, but it is not hallucinatory." Harsh, "McClellan-Go-Round," pp. 115–16. Such a cautious approach, however, was not going to win battles or the war for the Union, which had the strategic burden of actually defeating the Confederacy; only the South could and should have played for a tie. Furthermore, the numbers McClellan cited as Rebel strengths were sometimes beyond the realm of reason.
101. Michie, *McClellan*, p. 469. Michie marveled that McClellan could think it possible for the weaker Confederacy to assemble the numbers he cited. He described the impact of this fallacy: "This unaccountable weakness in McClellan's mental equipment is always so conspicuously in evidence that its influence in the formation of his plans of campaign or in his dispositions for battle can never be ignored. Reacting against the dictates of sound reason, the emotional and imaginative side of his nature unduly affected his judgments with vacillating indecision, accentuated his constitutional timidity as a commander, weakened his determination by strengthening his prudence, and eventually robbed him of the fruits of victory at the supreme moment." *Ibid.*
102. Sears, "Mac," p. 67. In blaming McClellan instead of Pinkerton for the exaggerated Rebel numbers, Sears and Fishel (see below) rejected the traditional (and probably incorrect) view expressed by many that McClellan had been misled by Pinkerton. See, e.g., Johnson, *Civil War Blunders*, pp. 88–95; Murfin, *Gleam of Bayonets*, pp. 40–41.

103. Fishel, "Pinkerton," pp. 115–42; Cox, *Military Reminiscences*, I, p. 250; Fishel, *Secret War*, p. 239. See also "Mr. Pinkerton's Unique Arithmetic," pp. 102–129, and "Appendix 6: The McClellan-Pinkerton Estimates of Confederate Numbers," pp. 581–87, in Fishel, *Secret War*.

104. Fishel, "Pinkerton," pp. 140–42. McClellan's over-estimates of Rebel strength also backfired on him: "Later, when he made desperate pleas for additional troops, the administration was able to point to his inflated estimates as proof that additional reinforcement requests were fruitless against such imposing odds." Rowland, *McClellan and History*, p. 120.

105. Michie, *McClellan*, p. 469.

106. Glathaar, Joseph T., *Partners in Command: The Relationships Between Leaders in the Civil War* (New York: Free Press, 1994), p. 242.

107. Sears, "McClellan," p. 66, citing Rowland, Thomas J., "In the Shadows of Grant and Sherman: George B. McClellan Revisited," *Civil War History* (Sept. 1994), p. 210.

108. Rowland, *McClellan and History*, p. 22, 23–24 n12.

109. Rhea *et al.*, "What Was Wrong?," p. 14.

110. Rowland, *McClellan and History*, pp. 21–24.

111. Pois and Langer, *Command Failure*, p. 53.

112. *Ibid,*, pp. 54–55. They stated that "...people motivated to avoid failure will select tasks at the extremes of risk because they tend to reduce the possibility of personal loss either by practically guaranteeing success or assigning the cause of failure elsewhere." *Ibid.*, p. 54.

113. Pois and Langer, *Command Failure*, p. 55.

114. Waugh, *Class of 1846*, p. 403.

115. Goss, *High Command*, p. 168.

Appendix

1. Sears, "Mac," p. 62, citing Lowell, James Russell, "General McClellan's Report," *North American Review* (April 1864), p. 552; *Letter of the Secretary of War Transmitting Report on the Organization of the Army of the Potomac, and of Its Campaigns in Virginia and Maryland, Under the Command of Maj. Gen. George B. McClellan from July 26, 1861, to November 7, 1862.* House of Representatives, 35th Cong., 1st Sess., Exec. Doc. No. 15. Washington: Government Printing Office, 1864.

2. Harsh, "McClellan-Go-Round, " p. 101, quoting *The Life, Campaigns, and Public Services of General McClellan* (Philadelphia: T.B. Peterson & Brothers, c. 1864), p. 19.

3. Williams, T. Harry, *Lincoln and His Generals* (New York: Knopf, 1952), p. 25.

4. Sears, "Mac," pp. 62–63; Nevins, *Ordeal of the Union*, V, pp. 294–95n.

5. Sears, *McClellan*, pp. 403–6. The title *McClellan's Own Story* has played a role in misleading many historians to conclude that McClellan himself released the damning excerpts from the letters to his wife. For example, William C. Davis wrote, "Years after the Civil War, when almost everyone on the planet recognized that Abraham Lincoln had become America's first true household god, McClellan in his memoirs still somehow thought he could vindicate himself by publishing his own blatantly conceited wartime correspondence in which he called the martyred president a 'gorilla' and worse." Davis, William C., "A Revealing Look at How the Union General's Conservative Views Shaped His Leadership," History Book Club brochure (July 2005).

6. Michie, *McClellan*, pp. 354–55, 361–62, 381–82, 386–91, 460–75.

7. Harsh, "McClellan-Go-Round," p. 101, citing Lee, Guy Carleton, *The True History of the Civil War* (Philadelphia, 1903), p. 296.

8. Sears, "Mac," pp. 63–64, citing Campbell, James Havelock, *McClellan: A Vindication of the Military Career of General George B. McClellan* (New York: Neale, 1916), p. 228.

9. *Ibid.*, p. 64.

10. Myers, *McClellan*, p. 403.

11. Eckenrode and Conrad, *McClellan*.

12. Hassler, Warren W., Jr., *General George B. McClellan: Shield of the Union* (Baton Rouge: Louisiana State University Press, 1957) [hereafter Hassler, *McClellan*].

13. Freeman, Douglas Southall, *Lee's Lieutenants: A Study in Command* (3 vols.) (New York: Charles Scribner's Sons, 1942–44 [1972 reprint]).

14. Hassler, *McClellan*, p. 81.

15. Harsh, "McClellan-Go-Round," pp. 102–105.

16. Nevins, *Ordeal of the Union*, VI (Volume II of *The War for the Union*).

17. Williams, Kenneth Powers, *Lincoln Finds a General: A Military Study of the Civil War* (2 vols.) (New York: Macmillan, 1949–59), II, p. 479.

18. Harsh, "McClellan-Go-Round," pp. 106–118.

19. Harsh, *Confederate Tide Rising, Sounding the Shallows*, and *Taken at the Flood*.

20. Reed, *Combined Operations*, p. 147.

21. *Ibid.*, p. 189.

22. Sears, "Mac," p. 65.

23. Sears, *McClellan*.

24. Sears, *Papers of McClellan*.

25. Rowland, *McClellan and History*, p. ix, 18–36, 71–75, 237.

26. Reese, *High-Water Mark*. See also, Reese, "typographical shortcut."

27. Pois and Langer, *Command Failure*, pp. 72, 221.

28. Rafuse, *McClellan's War*.

29. *Ibid.*, p. 394.

Bibliography

Memoirs, Letters, Papers and Other Primary Documents

Alexander, Edward Porter. *Fighting for the Confederacy: The Personal Recollections of General Edward Porter Alexander*, ed. by Gary W. Gallagher. Chapel Hill: University of North Carolina Press, 1989.

_____. *The Military Memoirs of a Confederate.* New York: Charles Scribner's Sons, 1907.

Basler, Roy P. (ed.). *The Collected Works of Abraham Lincoln.* 8 vols. New Brunswick: Rutgers University Press, 1953.

Blackford, William Willis. *War Years with Jeb Stuart.* Baton Rouge and London: Louisiana State University Press, 1945. 1993 Reprint.

Chesnut, Mary. *Mary Chesnut's Civil War*, ed. by C. Vann Woodward. New Haven and London: Yale University Press, 1981.

Cox, Jacob Dolson. *Military Reminiscences of the Civil War.* 2 vols. New York: Charles Scribner's Sons, 1900.

Dana, Charles A. *Recollections of the Civil War.* New York: Collier Books, 1893, 1963.

Davis, Jefferson. *The Rise and Fall of the Confederate Government.* 2 vols. New York: Da Capo Press, Inc., 1990. Reprint of 1881 edition.

Dowdey, Clifford, and Manarin, Louis H. (eds.). *The Wartime Papers of R.E. Lee.* New York: Bramhall House, 1961.

Freeman, Douglas Southall, and McWhiney, Grady. (eds.) *Lee's Dispatches: Unpublished Letters of General Robert E. Lee, C.S.A., to Jefferson Davis and the War Department of the Confederate States of America 1862–65.* Baton Rouge and London: Louisiana State University Press, 1957, 1994. Update of Freeman's original 1914 edition.

Gaff, Alan D. *On Many a Bloody Field: Four Years in the Iron Brigade.* Bloomington and Indianapolis: Indiana University Press, 1996.

Gibbon, John. *Personal Recollections of the Civil War.* New York and London: G. P. Putnam's Sons, 1928.

Gordon, John B. *Reminiscences of the Civil War.* Baton Rouge and London: Louisiana State University Press, 1993. Reprint of New York: Charles Scribner's Sons, 1903.

Gorgas, Josiah. *The Civil War Diary of General Josiah Gorgas*, ed. by Frank E. Vandiver. Birmingham: University of Alabama Press, 1947.

_____. *The Journals of Josiah Gorgas 1857–1878*, ed. by Sarah Woolfolk Wiggins. Tuscaloosa and London: The University of Alabama Press, 1995.

Grant, Ulysses S. *Personal Memoirs of U.S. Grant.* 2 vols. New York: Charles L. Webster & Company, 1886.

Hay, John. *Lincoln and the Civil War in the Diaries and Letters of John Hay*, ed. by Tyler Bennett. New York: Dodd, Mead & Company, 1939.

Johnson, Robert Underwood, and Buel, Clarence Clough (eds.). *Battles and Leaders of the Civil War.* 4 vols. New York: Thomas Yoseloff, Inc., 1956. Reprint of Secaucus, New Jersey: Castle, 1887–8.

Jones, J.B. *A Rebel War Clerk's Diary at the Confederate States Capital.* 2 vols. Philadelphia: J.B. Lippincott & Co., 1866. 1982 reprint.

Jones, J. William. *Personal Reminiscences of General Robert E. Lee.* Richmond: United States Historical Society Press, 1989. Reprint.

Longstreet, James. *From Manassas to Appomattox: Memoirs of the Civil War in America.* New York: Smithmark Publishers, Inc., 1994.

McClellan, George B. *McClellan's Own Story: The War for the Union, The Soldiers Who Fought It, The Civilians Who Directed It and His Relations to It and to Them.* Scituate, Mass.: Digital Scanning, Inc., 1998. Reprint of New York: Charles L. Webster & Company, 1887.

_____. *Report of Major General George B. McClellan upon the Organization of the Army of the Potomac, and its campaigns in Virginia and Maryland, from July 26, 1861, to November 7, 1862.* House of Representatives, 38th Congress, 1st Session, Ex. Doc. No. 15. Washington, D.C.: Government Printing Office, 1864.

Nicolay, John G. *The Outbreak of Rebellion.* Harrisburg: The Archive Society, 1992. Reprint of New York: Charles Scribner's Sons, 1881.

_____, and Hay, John. *Abraham Lincoln: A History.* 10 vols. New York: Century Co., 1886.

Official Records of the Union and Confederate Navies in the War of the Rebellion. 31 vols. Harrisburg: The National Historical Society, 1987. Reprint of Washington: Government Printing Office, 1921.

Pope, John. *Report of Major General John Pope to the Hon. Committee on the Conduct of the War.* Extracted from U.S. Congress, Joint Committee on the Conduct of the War, 1863–1866. 2 vols. Millwood, N.Y.: Kraus Reprint Co., 1977.

Rhodes, Robert Hunt (ed.). *All for the Union: The Civil War Diary and Letters of Elisha Hunt Rhodes.* New York: Orion Books, 1991. Originally published by Andrew Mowbray Incorporated in 1985.

Rosecrans, William Starke. "King of the Hill," *New Tribune*, Feb. 22, 1883; reprinted in *Civil War Times*, XL, No. 3 (June 2001), pp. 24–6, 68–70 and No. 4 (Aug. 2001), pp. 22–9.

Sears, Stephen W. *The Civil War Papers of George B. McClellan: Selected Correspondence, 1860–1865.* New York: Ticknor & Fields, 1989.

Sherman, William Tecumseh. *Memoirs of General W. T. Sherman.* 2 vols. New York: D. Appleton and Company, 1889.

Simon, John Y. (ed.). *The Papers of Ulysses Grant.* 24 vols. Carbondale and Edwardsville: Southern Illinois University Press, 1967–2000.

Sneden, Robert Knox. *Eye of the Storm: A Civil War Odyssey.* New York: The Free Press, 2000.

Stoddard, William O. *Inside the White House in War Times: Memoirs and reports of Lincoln's Secretary*, ed. by Michael Burlingame. Lincoln and London: University of Nebraska Press, 2000.

Taylor, Walter H. *General Lee: His Campaigns in Virginia 1861–1865 with Personal Reminiscences.* Lincoln and London: University of Nebraska Press, 1994. Reprint of Norfolk: Nusbaum Books, 1906.

Tower, R. Lockwood (ed.). *Lee's Adjutant: The Wartime Letters of Colonel Walter Herron Taylor, 1862–1865.* Columbia: University of South Carolina Press, 1995.

U.S. Congress. *Report of the Joint Committeee on the Conduct of the War.* House of Representatives, 37th Cong., 3rd Sess. 3 vols. Washington, D.C.: Government Printing Office, 1863.

The War of Rebellion: A Compilation of the Official Records of the Union and Confederate Armies. 128 vols. Washington, D.C.: Government Printing Office, 1880–1901.

Welles, Gideon. *Diary of Gideon Welles.* 3 vols. Boston and New York: Houghton Mifflin Company, 1911.

Statistical Analyses

Fox, William F. *Regimental Losses in the American Civil War, 1861–1865: A Treatise on the Extent and Nature of the Mortuary Losses in the Union Regiments, with Full and Exhaustive Statistics Compiled from the Official Records on File in the State Military Bureaus and at Washington.* Dayton: Morningside House, Inc., 1985. Reprint of Albany: Brandow Printing Company, 1898.

Livermore, Thomas L. *Numbers & Losses in the Civil War in America: 1861–1865.* Millwood, New York: Kraus Reprint Co., 1977. Reprint of Bloomington: Indiana University Press, 1957.

Phisterer, Frederick. *Statistical Record of the Armies of the United States.* Edison, New Jersey: Castle Books, 2002. Reprint of 1883 book, a supplementary volume to Scribner's Campaigns of the Civil War series.

Atlases

Cobb, Hubbard. *American Battlefields: A Complete Guide to the Historic Conflicts in Words, Maps, and Photos.* New York: Macmillan, 1995.

Davis, George B., Perry, Leslie J., and Kirkley, Joseph W. *Atlas To Accompany the Official Records of the Union and Confederate Armies.* Washington, D.C.: Government Printing Office, 1891–95.

Esposito, Vincent J. (ed.) *The West Point Atlas of American Wars.* 2 vols. New York, Washington and London: Frederick A. Praeger, Inc., 1959.

Greene, A. Wilson, and Gallagher, Gary W. *National Geographic Guide to the Civil War Battlefield Parks.* Washington, D.C.: The National Geographic Society, 1992.

McPherson, James M. (ed.). *The Atlas of the Civil War.* New York: Macmillan, Inc., 1994.

Nelson, Christopher. *Mapping the Civil War: Featuring Rare Maps from the Library of Congress.* Golden, Colorado: Fulcrum Publishing, 1992.

Chronologies

Bishop, Chris, and Drury, Ian. *1400 Days: The Civil War Day by Day.* New York: Gallery Books, 1990.

Bowman, John S. (ed.). *The Civil War Almanac.* New York: World Almanac Publications, 1983.

Mosocco, Ronald A. *The Chronological Tracking of the American Civil War Per the Official Records of the War of the Rebellion.* Williamsburg: James River Publications, 1994.

Encyclopedias

Chambers, John Whiteclay, II. *The Oxford Companion to American Military History.* Oxford: Oxford University Press, 1999.

Current, Richard N. (ed.). *Encyclopedia of the Confederacy.* 4 vols. New York: Simon & Schuster, 1993.

Faust, Patricia L. (ed.). *Historical Times Illustrated Encyclopedia of the Civil War.* New York: HarperPerennial, 1991.

Heidler, David S., and Heidler, Jeanne T. (ed.). *Encyclopedia of the American Civil War: A Political, Social, and Military History.* New York and London: W.W. Norton & Company, 2002.

Wagner, Margaret E., Gallagher, Gary W., and Finkelman, Paul (ed.). *The Library of Congress Civil War Desk Reference.* New York: Simon & Schuster, 2002.

Other Books and Papers

Adams, Michael C.C. *Fighting for Defeat: Union Military Failure in the East, 1861–1865.* Lincoln and London: University of Nebraska Press, 1978, 1992.

Alexander, Bevin. *How Great Generals Win.* New York and London: W. W. Norton & Co., 1993.

Ambrose, Stephen E. *Halleck: Lincoln's Chief of Staff.* Baton Rouge and London: Louisiana State University Press, 1962, 1990.

Beatie, Russel H. *Army of the Potomac.* 2 vols. Cambridge: Da Capo Press, 2002, 2004.

Beringer, Richard E., Hattaway, Herman, Jones, Archer, and Still, William N., Jr. *Why the South Lost the Civil War.* Athens: University of Georgia Press, 1986.

Black, Robert C., III. *The Railroads of the Confederacy.*

Chapel Hill and London: University of North Carolina Press, 1998.

Bonekemper, Edward H., III. *How Robert E. Lee Lost the Civil War*. Fredericksburg, Virginia: Sergeant Kirkland's Press, 1998.

_____. *A Victor, Not a Butcher: Ulysses S. Grant's Overlooked Military Genius*. Washington, D.C.: Regnery Press, 2004.

Boritt, Gabor S. (ed.). *Lincoln, the War President*. New York and Oxford: Oxford University Press, 1992.

_____. *Lincoln's Generals*. New York and Oxford: Oxford University Press, 1994.

_____ (ed.). *Why the Confederacy Lost*. New York and Oxford: Oxford University Press, 1992.

Botkin, B.A. (ed.). *A Civil War Treasury of Tales, Legends and Folklore*. New York: Promontory Press, 1960.

Bowers, John. *Stonewall Jackson: Portrait of a Soldier*. New York: William Morrow and Company, Inc., 1989.

Bridges, Hal. *Lee's Maverick General: Daniel Harvey Hill*. Lincoln and London: University of Nebraska Press, 1991. Reprint of New York: McGraw-Hill, c1961.

Buell, Thomas B. *The Warrior Generals: Combat Leadership in the Civil War*. New York: Crown Publishers, Inc., 1997.

Bushong, Millard Kessler. *Old Jube: A Biography of General Jubal A. Early*. Shippensburg, Pennsylvania: White Mane Publishing Company, Inc., 1955, 1990.

Casdorph, Paul D. *Lee and Jackson: Confederate Chieftains*. New York: Paragon House, 1992.

Catton, Bruce. *The American Heritage New History of the Civil War*. New York: Penguin Books USA Inc., 1996.

_____. *The Army of the Potomac: Glory Road*. Garden City, New York: Doubleday & Company, Inc., 1952.

_____. *The Army of the Potomac: Mr. Lincoln's Army*. Garden City, New York: Doubleday & Company, Inc., 1951, 1962.

_____. *The Army of the Potomac: A Stillness at Appomattox*. Garden City, New York: Doubleday & Company, Inc., 1953.

_____. *Grant Moves South*. Boston: Little, Brown and Company, 1960.

_____. *Grant Takes Command*. Boston: Little, Brown and Company, 1969.

_____. *Terrible Swift Sword*. Garden City, New York: Doubleday & Company, Inc., 1963.

_____. *This Hallowed Ground: The Story of the Union Side of the Civil War*. Garden City, New York: Doubleday & Company, Inc., 1956, 1962.

_____. *U.S. Grant and the American Military Tradition*. Boston: Little, Brown and Company, 1954.

Civil War Times Illustrated. The Battle of Antietam! Harrisburg: Historical Times Inc., 1962.

_____. *Great Battles of the Civil War*. New York: W. H. Smith, Inc., 1984.

Clark, John E., Jr. *Railroads in the Civil War: The Impact of Management on Victory and Defeat*. Baton Rouge: Louisiana State University Press, 2001.

Commager, Henry Steele (ed.). *The Blue and the Gray. Two Volumes in One. The Story of the Civil War as Told by Participants*. New York: The Fairfax Press, 1982. Reprint of Indianapolis: Bobbs-Merrill, c. 1950.

Connelly, Thomas Lawrence. *Army of the Heartland: The Army of Tennessee, 1861–1862*. Baton Rouge and London: Louisiana State University Press, 1967.

_____. *Autumn of Glory: The Army of Tennessee, 1862–1865*. Baton Rouge and London: Louisiana State University Press, 1971, 1991.

_____. *The Marble Man: Robert E. Lee and His Image in American Society*. New York: Alfred A. Knopf, 1977.

_____, and Bellows, Barbara R. *God and General Longstreet: The Lost Cause and the Southern Mind*. Baton Rouge: Louisiana State University Press, 1982.

_____, and Jones, Archer. *The Politics of Command: Factions and Ideas in Confederate Strategy*. Baton Rouge: Louisiana State University Press, 1973.

Davis, William C. *The Cause Lost: Myths and Realities of the Confederacy*. Lawrence: University Press of Kansas, 1996.

_____. *Jefferson Davis: The Man and His Hour*. Baton Rouge: Louisiana State University Press, 1991.

Dew, Charles B. *Apostles of Disunion: Southern Secession Commissioners and the Causes of the Civil War*. Charlottesville: University Press of Virginia, 2001.

Donald, David Herbert. *Lincoln*. New York: Simon & Schuster, 1995.

_____ (ed.). *Why the North Won the Civil War*. New York: Macmillan Publishing Co., 1962.

_____, Baker, Jean Harvey, and Holt, Michael F. *The Civil War and Reconstruction*. New York and London: W.W. Norton & Company, 2001.

Dowdey, Clifford. *Lee*. Gettysburg: Stan Clark Military Books, 1991. Reprint of 1965 edition.

Eckenrode, H.J., and Conrad, Bryan. *George B. McClellan: The Man Who Saved the Union*. Chapel Hill: University of North Carolina Press, 1941.

Eckert, Ralph Lowell. *John Brown Gordon: Soldier o Southerner o American*. Baton Rouge and London: Louisiana State University Press, 1989.

Eicher, David J. *The Civil War in Books: An Analytical Bibliography*. Urbana and Chicago: University of Illinois Press, 1997.

Feis, William B. *Grant's Secret Service: The Intelligence War from Belmont to Appomattox*. Lincoln and London: University of Nebraska Press, 2002.

Fishel, Edwin C. *The Secret War for the Union: The Untold Story of Military Intelligence in the Civil War*. Boston and New York: Houghton Mifflin, 1996.

Foote, Shelby (ed.). *The Civil War: A Narrative*. 3 vols. New York: Random House, 1958–1974.

Freeman, Douglas Southall. *Lee's Lieutenants: A Study in Command*. 3 vols. New York: Charles Scribner's Sons, 1942–4 (1972 reprint).

_____. *R.E. Lee*. 4 vols. New York and London: Charles Scribner's Sons, 1934–5.

Fuller, J.F.C. *The Generalship of Ulysses S. Grant*. Bloomington: Indiana University Press, 1958. Reprint of 1929 edition.

_____. *Grant and Lee: A Study in Personality and Generalship*. Bloomington: Indiana University Press, 1957. Reprint of 1933 edition.

Furgurson, Ernest B. *Ashes of Glory: Richmond at War*. New York: Alfred A. Knopf, 1996.

Gabel, Christopher R. *Railroad Generalship: Foundations of Civil War Strategy*. Fort Leavenworth, Kansas: Combat Studies Institute, U.S. Army Command and General Staff College, 1997.

Gallagher, Gary W. (ed.). *The Antietam Campaign*. Chapel Hill and London: University of North Carolina Press, 1999.

_____ (ed.). *Antietam: Essays on the 1862 Maryland Campaign*. Kent and London: The Kent State University Press, 1989.

_____. *Lee and His Generals in War and Memory*. Baton Rouge: Louisiana State University, 1998.

_____ (ed.). *Lee the Soldier*. Lincoln and London: University of Nebraska Press, 1996.

_____ (ed.). *The Richmond Campaign of 1862: The Peninsula & the Seven Days*. Chapel Hill and London: The University of North Carolina Press, 2000.

_____, and Glatthaar, Joseph T. (eds.) *Leaders of the Lost Cause: New Perspectives on the Confederate High Command*. Mechanicsburg, Pennsylvania: Stackpole Books, 2004.

Gienapp, William E. (ed.). *The Civil War and Reconstruction: A Documentary Collection*. New York and London: W.W. Norton & Company, 2001.

Glatthaar, Joseph T. *Partners in Command: The Relationships Between Leaders in the Civil War*. New York: Macmillan, Inc., 1994.

Goss, Thomas J. *The War Within the Union High Command: Politics and Generalship During the Civil War*. Lawrence: University Press of Kansas, 2003.

Grant, Susan-Mary and Parish, Peter J. (eds.). *Legacy of Disunion: The Enduring Significance of the American Civil War*. Baton Rouge: Louisiana State University Press, 2003.

Griffith, Paddy. *Battle Tactics of the Civil War*. New Haven and London: Yale University Press, 1996.

Guernsey, Alfred H., and Alden, Henry M. (eds.). *Harper's Pictorial History of the Civil War*. New York: The Fairfax Press, 1977. Reprint of *Harper's Pictorial History of the Great Rebellion in the United States*. New York: Harper & Brothers, 1866.

Hagerman, Edward. *The American Civil War and the Origins of Modern Warfare: Ideas, Organization, and Field Command*. Bloomington and Indianapolis: Indiana University Press, 1992.

Harsh, Joseph L. *Confederate Tide Rising: Robert E. Lee and the Making of Southern Strategy, 1861–1862*. Kent, Ohio, and London: The Kent State University Press, 1998.

Hassler, Warren W., Jr. *Commanders of the Army of the Potomac*. Baton Rouge: Louisiana State University Press, 1962.

_____. *General George B. McClellan: Shield of the Union*. Baton Rouge: Louisiana State University Press, 1957.

Hattaway, Herman, and Jones, Archer. *How the North Won: A Military History of the Civil War*. Urbana and Chicago: University of Illinois Press, 1991. Reprint of 1983 edition.

Henderson, G.F.R. *Stonewall Jackson and the American Civil War*. New York: DaCapo Press, Inc., 1988. Reprint of New York: Grossett & Dunlap, 1943.

Hennessy, John J. *Return to Bull Run: The Campaign and Battle of Second Manassas*. New York: Simon & Schuster, 1993.

Horan, James D. *The Pinkertons: The Detective Dynasty That Made History*. New York: Crown Publishers, Inc., 1967.

Johnson, Clint. *Civil War Blunders*. Winston-Salem: John F. Blair, 1997.

Jones, Archer. *Civil War Command & Strategy: The Process of Victory and Defeat*. New York: The Free Press, 1992.

Jones, R. Steven. *The Right Hand of Command: Use & Disuse of Personal Staffs in the Civil War*. Mechanicsburg, Pennsylvania: Stackpole Books, 2000.

Jones, Terry L. *Lee's Tigers: The Louisiana Infantry in the Army of Northern Virginia*. Baton Rouge and London: Louisiana State University Press, 1987.

Jordan, David M. *Winfield Scott Hancock: A Soldier's Life*. Bloomington and Indianapolis: Indiana University Press, 1996.

Katcher, Philip. *The Army of Robert E. Lee*. London: Arms and Armour Press, 1994.

Keegan, John. *Intelligence in War: Knowledge of the Enemy from Napoleon to Al-Qaeda*. New York: Alfred A. Knopf, 2003.

_____. *The Mask of Command*. New York: Viking, 1987.

Ketchum, Richard M. *The American Heritage Picture History of the Civil War*. 2 vols. New York: American Heritage Publishing Co., Inc., 1960.

Konstam, Angus. *Seven Days Battles 1862: Lee's Defense of Richmond*. Westport, Connecticut, and London: Praeger Publishers, 2004.

Lamers, William M. *The Edge of Glory: A Biography of General William S. Rosecrans, U.S.A.* Baton Rouge: Louisiana State University Press, 1999. Reprint and expansion of New York: Harcourt, Brace & World, 1961.

Langellier, John. *Second Manassas 1862: Robert E. Lee's Greatest Victory*. Westport, Connecticut, and London: Praeger Publishers, 2004.

Lawson, Melinda. *Patriot Fires: Forging a New American Nationalism in the Civil War North*. Lawrence: University Press of Kansas, 2002.

Lee, Fitzhugh. *General Lee: A Biography of Robert E. Lee*. New York: Da Capo Press, 1994. Reprint of Wilmington, North Carolina: Broadfoot Publishing Company, 1989, and New York: D. Appleton and Company, 1894.

Lossing, Benson. *A History of the Civil War, 1861–65, and the Causes That Led up to the Great Conflict*. New York: The War Memorial Association, 1912.

Luvaas, Jay, and Nelson, Harold W. (ed.). *The U.S. Army War College Guide to the Battle of Antietam: The Maryland Campaign of 1862*. Carlisle, Pennsylvania: South Mountain Press, Inc., 1987.

Marszalek, John F. *Commander of All Lincoln's Armies: A Life of General Henry W. Halleck*. Cambridge and London: Belknap Press of Harvard University Press, 2004.

Matloff, Maurice (ed.). *American Military History*. Washington, D.C.: U.S. Army Center of Military History, 1985.

McFeely, William. *Grant: A Biography*. New York and London: W.W. Norton & Company, 1981.

McKenzie, John D. *Uncertain Glory: Lee's Generalship Re-Examined*. New York: Hippocrene Books, 1997.

McMurry, Richard M. *Two Great Rebel Armies: An Essay in Confederate Military History*. Chapel Hill and London: The University of North Carolina Press, 1989.

McPherson, James M. *Battle Cry of Freedom: The Civil War Era*. New York: Ballantine Books, 1988.

_____. *Crossroads of Freedom: Antietam, the Battle That Changed the Course of the Civil War*. Oxford: Oxford University Press, 2002.

McWhiney, Grady, and Jamieson, Perry D. *Attack and Die: Civil War Military Tactics and the Southern Heritage*. Tuscaloosa: The University of Alabama Press, 1982.

Meade, Robert Douthat. *Judah P. Benjamin: Confederate Statesman*. Baton Rouge: Louisiana State University Press, 1943, 2001.

Michie, Peter S. *General McClellan*. New York: D. Appleton and Company, 1901.

Miller, William J. *Mapping for Stonewall: The Civil War*

Service of Jed Hotchkiss. Washington, D.C.: Elliott & Clark Publishing, 1993.

Mitchell, Joseph B. *Decisive Battles of the Civil War*. New York: Ballantine Books, 1955.

Murfin, James V. *The Gleam of Bayonets: The Battle of Antietam and the Maryland Campaign of 1862*. Baton Rouge and London: Louisiana State University Press, 1965, 1990.

Myers, William Starr. *General George Brinton McClellan: A Study in Personality*. New York and London: D. Appleton-Century Company, 1934.

Neely, Mark E., Jr., Holzer, Harold, and Boritt, Gabor S. *The Confederate Image: Prints of the Lost Cause*. Chapel Hill and London: The University of North Carolina Press, 1987.

Nevins, Alan. *Ordeal of the Union*. 8 vols. New York and London: Charles Scribner's Sons, 1947–71. [Although the entire eight-volume set was called *Ordeal of the Union*, several volumes had alternative names and their own different volume numbers. Volumes I and II are entitled *Ordeal of the Union*; Volumes III and IV are *The Emergence of Lincoln* (Volumes I and II), and Volumes V through VIII are *The War for the Union* (Volumes I through IV).]

Newell, Clayton R. *Lee vs. McClellan: The First Campaign*. Washington, D.C.: Regnery Publishing, Inc., 1996.

Nolan, Alan T. *The Iron Brigade: A Military History*. Bloomington and Indianapolis: Indiana University Press, 1961, 1994.

_____. *Lee Considered: General Robert E. Lee and Civil War History*. Chapel Hill and London: University of North Carolina Press, 1991.

Nosworthy, Brent. *The Bloody Crucible of Courage: Fighting Methods and Combat Experience of the Civil War*. New York: Carroll & Graf Publishers, 2003.

Osborne, Charles C. *Jubal: The Life and Times of General Jubal A. Early, CSA, Defender of the Lost Cause*. Baton Rouge and London: Louisiana State University Press, 1992.

Perret, Geoffrey. *A Country Made by War: From the Revolution to Vietnam—the Story of America's Rise to Power*. New York: Random House, 1989.

_____. *Lincoln's War: The Untold Story of America's Greatest President as Commander in Chief*. New York: Random House, 2004.

_____. *Ulysses S. Grant: Soldier & President*. New York: Random House, 1997.

Peskin, Allan. *Winfield Scott and the Profession of Arms*. Kent, Ohio, and London: The Kent State University Press, 2003.

Pfanz, Donald C. *Richard S. Ewell: A Soldier's Life*. Chapel Hill and London: University of North Carolina Press, 1998.

Piston, William Garrett. *Lee's Tarnished Lieutenant: James Longstreet and His Place in Southern History*. Athens and London: The University of Georgia Press, 1987.

Pois, Robert, and Langer, Philip. *Command Failure in War: Psychology and Leadership*. Bloomington: Indiana University Press, 2004.

Pollard, Edward A. *The Lost Cause. A New Southern History of the War of the Confederates*. New York: Gramercy Books, 1994. Reprint of New York: E.B. Treat & Company, 1866.

Priest, John M. *Antietam: The Soldiers' Battle*. Shippensburg, Pennsylvania: White Mane Publishing Co., Inc., 1989.

Rafuse, Ethan S. *McClellan's War*. Bloomington: Indiana University Press, 2005.

Reed, Rowena. *Combined Operations in the Civil War*. Lincoln and London: University of Nebraska Press, 1993. Reprint of Annapolis: United States Naval Institute, 1978.

Reese, Timothy J. *High-Water Mark: The 1862 Maryland Campaign in Strategic Perspective*. Baltimore: Butternut and Blue Press, 2004.

Robertson, James I., Jr. *General A.P. Hill: The Story of a Confederate Warrior*. New York: Random House, 1987.

_____. *The Stonewall Brigade*. Baton Rouge and London: Louisiana State University Press, 1991. Reprint of 1963 edition.

_____. *Stonewall Jackson: The Man, the Soldier, the Legend*. New York: Macmillan Publishing USA, 1997.

Rowland, Thomas J. *George B. McClellan and Civil War History in the Shadow of Grant and Sherman*. Kent, Ohio, and London: The Kent State University Press, 1998.

Royster, Charles. *The Destructive War: William Tecumseh Sherman, Stonewall Jackson, and the Americans*. New York: Vintage Books, 1993.

Sears, Stephen W. *The Civil War: The Best of American Heritage*. New York: American Heritage Press, 1991.

_____. *Controversies & Commanders: Dispatches from the Army of the Potomac*. Boston and New York: Houghton Mifflin Company, 1999.

_____. *George B. McClellan: The Young Napoleon*. New York: Ticknor & Fields, 1988.

_____. *Landscape Turned Red: The Battle of Antietam*. New York: Book-of-the-Month Club, Inc., 1994.

_____. *To the Gates of Richmond: The Peninsula Campaign*. New York: Ticknor & Fields, 1992.

Simpson, Brooks D. *Ulysses S. Grant: Triumph Over Adversity, 1822–1865*. Boston and New York: Houghton Mifflin Company, 2000.

Simpson, Harold B. *Hood's Texas Brigade: Lee's Grenadier Guard*. Fort Worth: Landmark Publishing, Inc., 1970. Vol. 2 of four-volume set on Hood's Texas Brigade.

Smith, Gene. *Lee and Grant: A Dual Biography*. New York: Promontory Press, 1984.

Smith, Jean Edward. *Grant*. New York: Simon & Schuster, 2001.

Stern, Philip Van Doren. *Robert E. Lee: The Man and the Soldier*. New York: Bonanza Books, 1963.

Stoddard, William O., Jr. *William O. Stoddard: Lincoln's Third Secretary*. New York: Exposition Press, 1955.

Swinton, William. *Campaigns of the Army of the Potomac*. New York: Richardson, 1866.

Tanner, Robert G. *Stonewall in the Valley: Thomas J. "Stonewall" Jackson's Shenandoah Valley Campaign Spring 1862*. Mechanicsburg, Pennsylvania: Stackpole Books, 1996.

Thomas, Emory M. *Robert E. Lee: A Biography*. New York and London: W.W. Norton & Company, 1995.

Vandiver, Frank E. *Mighty Stonewall*. College Station: Texas A&M University Press, 1989. Reprint of 1957 edition.

Ward, Geoffrey C., Burns, Ric, and Burns, Ken. *The Civil War: An Illustrated History*. New York: Alfred A. Knopf, Inc., 1990.

Warner, Ezra J. *Generals in Blue: Lives of the Union Commanders*. Baton Rouge and London: Louisiana State University Press, 1964.

_____. *Generals in Gray: Lives of the Confederate Commanders*. Baton Rouge and London: Louisiana State University Press, 1959.

Waugh, John C. *The Class of 1846: From West Point to Appomattox: Stonewall Jackson, George McClellan and Their Brothers*. New York: Warner Books, Inc., 1994.

Weber, Thomas. *The Northern Railroads in the Civil War, 1861–1865*. Bloomington and Indianapolis: Indiana University Press, 1999. Reprint of 1952 edition.

Weigley, Russell F. *The American Way of War: A History of United States Military Strategy and Policy*. New York: Macmillan Publishing Co., Inc., 1973.

_____. *A Great Civil War: A Military and Political History, 1861–1865*. Bloomington and Indianapolis: Indiana University Press, 2000.

Weir, William. *Fatal Victories*. Hamden, Connecticut: Archon Books, 1993.

Werstein, Irving. *Abraham Lincoln Versus Jefferson Davis*. New York: Thomas Y. Crowell Company, 1959.

Wert, Jeffrey D. *A Brotherhood of Valor: The Common Soldiers of the Stonewall Brigade, C.S.A., and the Iron Brigade, U.S.A.* New York: Simon & Schuster, 1999.

_____. *General James Longstreet: The Confederacy's Most Controversial Soldier—A Biography*. New York: Simon & Schuster, 1993.

_____. *The Sword of Lincoln: The Army of the Potomac*. New York: Simon & Schuster, 2005.

Wiley, Bell Irvin. *The Life of Billy Yank: The Common Soldier of the Union*. Baton Rouge and London: Louisiana State University Press, 1952, 1991.

_____. *The Life of Johnny Reb: The Common Soldier of the Confederacy*. Baton Rouge and London: Louisiana State University Press, 1943, 1991.

_____. *The Road to Appomattox*. Baton Rouge and London: Louisiana State University Press, 1994. Reprint of Memphis: Memphis State College Press, 1956.

Williams, Kenneth P. *Grant Rises in the West*. 2 vols. Lincoln: University of Nebraska Press, 1997. Originally vols. 3 and 4 of *Lincoln Finds a General: A Military Study of the Civil War*, New York: Macmillan, 1952.

_____. *Lincoln Finds a General: A Military Study of the Civil War*. Vol. 1. Bloomington: Indiana University Press, 1985. Reprint of 1949 edition.

_____. *Lincoln Finds a General: A Military Study of the Civil War*. Vols. 2 and 5 (Prelude to Chattanooga). New York: The Macmillan Company, 1959. Reprint of 1949 edition.

Williams, T. Harry. *Lincoln and His Generals*. New York: Alfred A. Knopf, Inc., 1952.

_____. *McClellan, Sherman and Grant*. New Brunswick: Rutgers University Press, 1962.

Wilson, Harold S. *Confederate Industry: Manufacturers and Quartermasters in the Civil War*. Jackson: University of Mississippi Press, 2002.

Winders, Richard Bruce. *Polk's Army: The American Military Experience in the Mexican War*. College Station: Texas A&M University Press, 1997.

Woodworth, Steven E. (ed.). *Civil War Generals in Defeat*. Lawrence: University of Kansas Press, 1999.

_____ (ed.). *Davis and Lee at War*. Lawrence: University of Kansas Press, 1995.

Periodical Articles

Alexander, Ted. "Antietam: The Bloodiest Day," *North & South*, Vol. 5, No. 7 (Oct. 2002), pp. 76–89.

_____. "Antietam Stories of Human Interest and Sites off the Beaten Path," *Blue & Gray Magazine*, XX, Issue 1 (Fall 2002), pp. 6–19, 48–62.

Brennan, Patrick J. "Mac's Last Stand: Autumn 1862 in Loudon Valley, Virginia," *Blue & Gray Magazine*, XVII, Issue 2 (Dec. 1999), pp. 6–20, 48–57.

Carmichael, Peter S. "The Manly Art of Staying Put: When Instinct and Reason Screamed 'Run Away!' What Kept Civil War Soldiers on the Firing Line?," *Civil War Times*, XLII, No. 5 (Dec. 2003), pp. 32–39.

Castel, Albert. "West Virginia 1861: A Tale of a Goose, a Dog, and a Fox," *North & South*, Vol. 7, No. 7 (Nov. 2004), pp. 44–55.

Cheeks, Robert C. "Carnage in a Cornfield," *America's Civil War*, Vol. 5, No. 2 (July 1992), pp. 30–37.

Chiles, Paul. "Artillery Hell! The Guns of Antietam," *Blue & Gray Magazine*, XVI, Issue 2 (Dec. 1998), pp. 6–16, 24–25, 41–59.

Connelly, Thomas Lawrence. "Robert E. Lee and the Western Confederacy: A Criticism of Lee's Strategic Ability," *Civil War History*, 15 (June 1969), pp. 116–32.

Fishel, Edwin C., "Pinkerton and McClellan: Who Deceived Whom?," *Civil War History*, XXXIV, No. 2 (June 1988), pp. 115–142.

Fleming, Martin K. "The Northwestern Virginia Campaign of 1861: McClellan's Rising Star—Lee's Dismal Debut," *Blue & Gray Magazine*, VIII, Issue 1 (October 1990), pp. 8–22, 44–53.

Frye, Dennis E. "'Through God's Blessing,'" *North & South*, Vol. 5, No. 7 (Oct. 2002), pp. 66–74.

Guelzo, Allen C. "'Not One Word ... Will I Ever Recall': Abraham Lincoln and the Emancipation Proclamation," *North & South*, Vol. 7, No. 2 (March 2004), pp. 74–82.

Harsh, Joseph L. "On the McClellan-Go-Round," *Civil War History*, Vol. 19, No. 2 (June 1973), pp. 101–18.

Hartwig, D. Scott, "'It Looked Like a Task To Storm': The Pennsylvania Reserves Assault South Mountain, September 14, 1862," *North & South*, Vol. 5, No. 7 (Oct. 2002), pp. 36–49.

Hattaway, Herman. "The Changing Face of Battle," *North & South*, Vol. 4, No. 6 (Aug. 2001), pp. 34–43.

Hennessy, John. "The Miscreant Suppressed: Lee vs. Pope at Second Manassas," *Hallowed Ground*, Vol. 5, No. 2 (Summer 2004), pp. 20–27.

_____. "The Second Battle of Manassas: Lee Suppresses the 'Miscreant' Pope," *Blue & Gray Magazine*, IX, Issue 6 (Aug. 1992), pp. 10–34, 46–58.

Johnson, Timothy D. "McClellan and His Mentor," *Military History Quarterly: The Quarterly Journal of Military History*, Vol. 13, No. 2 (Winter 2001), pp. 88–95.

Lamb, John W. "Pope's Narrow Escape from Clark's Mountain," *America's Civil War*, Vol. 11, No. 3 (July 1998), pp. 38–45.

Longacre, Edward G. "All the Way Around," *Civil War Times*, XLI, No. 3 (June 2002), pp. 22–29, 59.

Mallinson, David. "Confused First Fight," *America's Civil War*, Vol. 4, No. 5 (Jan. 1992), pp. 46–52.

Marszalek, John F. "Henry W. Halleck: The Early Seeds of Failure," *North & South*, Vol. 8, No. 1 (Jan. 2005), pp. 78–86.

Marvel, William. "More Than Water Under Burnside's Bridge," *America's Civil War*, Vol. 18, No. 6 (January 2006), pp. 46–52.

McPherson, James M. "Antietam: The Decisive Event

of the War," *North & South*, Vol. 5, No. 7 (Oct. 2002), pp. 12–21.

Mewborn, Horace. "A Wonderful Exploit: Jeb Stuart's Ride Around the Army of the Potomac, June 12–15, 1862," *Blue & Gray Magazine*, XV, Issue 6 (Aug. 1998), pp. 6–21, 46–54.

Miller, William J. "No American Sevastopol," *America's Civil War*, Vol. 13, No. 2 (May 2000), pp. 30–36, 74.

_____. "The Seven Days Battles: Robert E. Lee Makes a Spectacular Entrance Upon the Main Stage and in Less than a Week the Federal War Effort is Set Back Almost a Year," *Hallowed Ground*, Vol. 4, No. 4 (Winter 2003), pp. 18–23.

Morgan, James A., III. "Ball's Bluff: 'A Very Nice Little Military Chance," *America's Civil War*, Vol. 18, No. 5 (Nov. 2005), pp. 30–38, 56.

Nolan, Alan T. And Storch, Marc. "The Iron Brigade Earns Its Name: John Gibbon's Brigade in the Maryland Campaign, 1862," *Blue & Gray Magazine*, Vol. XXI, Issue 6 (Holiday 2004), pp. 6–20, 47–63.

Norris, David A. "Bloody Day at Boteler's Ford," *America's Civil War*, Vol. 18, No. 4 (Sept. 2005), pp. 38–44, 72.

O'Neill, Robert F. "Cavalry on the Peninsula: Fort Monroe to the Gates of Richmond, March to May, 1862," *Blue & Gray Magazine*, XIX, Issue 5 (Campaign 2002), pp. 6–24, 38–51.

Owens, Richard H. "An Astonishing Career," *Military Heritage*, Vol. 3, No. 2 (Oct. 2001), pp. 64–73.

Rafuse, Ethan S. "Lincoln Takes Charge," *Civil War Times Illustrated*, XXXIX, No. 7 (Feb. 2001), pp. 26–32, 62–63.

_____. "McClellan, von Clausewitz, and the Politics of War," *Columbiad: A Quarterly Review of the War Between the States*, Vol. 1, No. 3 (Fall 1997), pp. 23–37.

Reese, Timothy J. "A typographical shortcut distorts George B. McClellan's reactions to the September 1862 'Lost Order,'" *America's Civil War*, Vol. 17, No. 5 (Nov. 2004), pp. 18–20, 72.

Rhea, Gordon, Rollins, Richard, Sears, Stephen, and Simon, John Y. "What Was Wrong with the Army of the Potomac?," *North & South*, Vol. 4, No. 3 (March 2001), pp. 12–18.

Sears, Stephen W. "Glendale: Opportunity Squandered," *North & South*, Vol. 5, No. 1 (Dec. 2001), pp. 12–24.

_____. "Mac and the Historians," *North & South*, Vol. 2, No. 3 (March 1999), pp. 61–71.

_____. "McClellan at Antietam," *Hallowed Ground*, Vol. 6, No. 1 (Spring 2005), pp. 30–33.

_____. "The Twisted Tale of the Lost Order," *North & South*, Vol. 5, No. 7 (Oct. 2002), pp. 54–65.

Smith, Robert Barr. "Killing Zone at Burnside's Bridge," *Military History*, Vol. 21, No. 2 (June 2004), pp. 34–40.

Symonds, Craig L., Simon, John Y., Poulter, Keith, Newton, Steven H., Sears, Stephen W., and Woodworth, Steven E. "Who Were the Worst Ten Generals?," *North & South*, Vol. 7, No. 3 (May 2004), pp. 12–25.

Wert, Jeffrey D. "Disaster in the West Woods," *Civil War Times*, XLI, No. 5 (Oct. 2002), pp. 32–39.

Woodworth, Steven E. "The Army of the Tennessee and the Elements of Military Success," *North & South*, Vol. 6, No. 4 (May 2003), pp. 44–55.

_____, Mitchell, Reid, Rhea, Gordon C., Simon, John Y., Newton, Steven H., and Poulter, Keith. "Who Were the Top Ten Generals?," *North & South*, Vol. 6, No. 4 (May 2003), pp. 12–22.

Wright, Mike. "The Infernal Machine: How a Confederate officer invented the land mine and changed the face of warfare," *Invention and Technology*, Summer 1999, pp. 44–50.

Index